Simon Sarris

HTML5

UNLEASHED

SAMS | 800 East 96th Street, Indianapolis, Indiana 46240 USA

HTML5 Unleashed

ISBN-13: 978-0-672-33627-0

ISBN-10: 0-672-33627-8

Library of Congress Control Number: 2013938300

Printed in the United States of America

First Printing July 2013

Trademarks

Warning and Disclaimer

Bulk Sales

Sams Publishing offers excellent discounts on this book when ordered in quantity for bulk purchases or special sales. For more information, please contact

U.S. Corporate and Government Sales
1-800-382-3419
corpsales@pearsontechgroup.com

For sales outside of the U.S., please contact

International Sales
international@pearsoned.com

Editor-in-Chief
Greg Wiegand

Executive Editor
Neil Rowe

Development Editor
Mark Renfrow

Managing Editor
Kristy Hart

Senior Project Editor
Betsy Gratner

Copy Editor
Karen Annett

Indexer
Heather McNeill

Proofreader
Debbie Williams

Technical Editor
Spike Xavier

Editorial Assistant
Cindy Teeters

Cover Designer
Mark Shirar

Compositor
Nonie Ratcliff

Contents at a Glance

Table of Contents

About the Author

Simon Sarris is a web developer focusing primarily on the HTML5 Canvas. Simon has earned a reputation as a go-to source for HTML5 answers. He contributes to the question-and-answer website StackOverflow and has provided the most answers for both the Canvas and HTML5 tags. Simon blogs about Canvas and JavaScript topics, and you can find him online at www.simonsarris.com.

Dedication

To my parents

Acknowledgments

If you look at the hours involved, writing at length is decidedly a solitary act, but it would have been impossible for me to finish this book without the support of several friends.

Book writing is not just time consuming, but life consuming, and I'd like to thank my girlfriend, Betsy Green, for enduring with patience and support over nearly a year of research and writing.

I'd like to express my deepest thanks to Aaron Friel, the greatest friend and colleague I have ever known, for his encouragement and advice for my entire conscious life and for his suggestions and reviews of draft material. I also owe huge thanks to Walter van Roggen, for being the most important mentor of my programming career and for reviewing large portions of this book.

I would like to sincerely thank the people at Sams, especially Neil Rowe and Betsy Gratner, for guiding me through the book-writing process. I owe extra thanks to Spike Xavier for his technical editing and his excellent, thoughtful suggestions.

Many thanks are due to the StackOverflow JavaScript chat room crowd for their encouragement, friendship, and expertise during my research and writing. Among many others I'd like to thank are Jason Brown, Robert Lemon, Abhishek Hingnikar, Amaan Cheval, and Florian Margaine.

My parents are not technology people, but I owe them the biggest thanks. They have supported me from cradle through college with love and resources, allowing me to freely learn and explore in this wonderful world.

We Want to Hear from You!

As the reader of this book, *you* are our most important critic and commentator. We value your opinion and want to know what we're doing right, what we could do better, what areas you'd like to see us publish in, and any other words of wisdom you're willing to pass our way.

We welcome your comments. You can email or write to let us know what you did or didn't like about this book—as well as what we can do to make our books better.

Please note that we cannot help you with technical problems related to the topic of this book.

When you write, please be sure to include this book's title and author as well as your name and email address. We will carefully review your comments and share them with the author and editors who worked on the book.

Email: consumer@samspublishing.com

Mail: Sams Publishing
           ATTN: Reader Feedback
           800 East 96th Street
           Indianapolis, IN 46240 USA

Reader Services

Visit our website and register this book at informit.com/register for convenient access to any updates, downloads, or errata that might be available for this book.

Introduction

This is a book about the future of the Web.

For most of human history, it has proven difficult to speculate about the future. Only since the Industrial Revolution have we gotten a grasp of what it might mean to predict things years in advance. Aside from the promise of flying cars that occurred every decade in the 1900s, the future of technological change was often about predictable refinement.

We can imagine that few people considered ambitious futures in the Middle Ages, and only in the 1900s did people begin to see an optimistic nearness: The future was a time just 10 years away. New televisions that were more accurate, better waste treatment, maybe even a man on the moon.

By 1980, the future was clearly a computer-centric world, albeit one still a few years out. By 2010, one third of the world carried in their pockets what would have been billed as a supercomputer in 1980.

Today, the future is near instant. New gadgets and impressive technologies are released almost daily. One set of new technologies is called HTML5, a series of refinements to the Web that has seen rapid adoption since 2010.

This is a book about the future of the Web, and, fortunately for us, it's already here.

HTML5 is an umbrella term for a series of new features, standards, and application programming interfaces (APIs) that collectively change the way web pages are created and used. With HTML5, applications that were once only possible on desktops or via browser plug-ins are now natively possible in modern browsers. The adoption of HTML5 aims to take us to an age where the Web is more interoperable, consistent, and easier to author.

Who Should Read This Book?

Web developers and web designers exist in a Yin-Yang of roles, sometimes filled by the same person and sometimes by very large teams. This book is intended for both roles, and not only the ones that deal with pure HTML and JavaScript but also the developers and designers who have up until now exclusively worked in Flash and Silverlight. HTML5 offers several replacement opportunities for these rich media plug-ins. The goal of HTML5 is not to obsolete plug-ins, but the new functionality does intend to herald a web where plug-ins, especially ones that provide now-common functionality, are much less necessary.

HTML5 has been around in some agreed-upon form since 2006 and starting in 2009 has had the force of all major browser vendors behind its implementation. In recent years, it has graduated from being a novelty to a set of standards in use by some of the world's largest websites. If you concern yourself with modern web development, then concerning yourself with HTML5 is essential, and you should read this book.

HTML5 is not strictly HTML; it also encompasses a good deal of new JavaScript APIs. Almost all the contents of HTML5 are relevant to both developers and designers, and even if you do not plan on using many of the parts of HTML5, it is a good idea to get a reading of what is now possible to achieve natively within the browser.

This book assumes basic prior knowledge of JavaScript and HTML. This book assumes no knowledge of JavaScript libraries, no matter how popular they may be, and this book's code examples do not reference or introduce any libraries except where it is necessary for a component to reasonably function.

HTML5 and Related Technologies

HTML5 typically refers to two concepts:

▶ Technologies and changes contained within the new HTML specifications put forth by the World Wide Web Consortium (W3C) and Web Hypertext Application Technology Working Group (WHATWG).

▶ The new HTML specifications plus a larger set of new web technologies. This is sometimes called *HTML5 and friends*, or *HTML5 and related technologies*, but is often shortened to just *HTML5*.

There are several common misconceptions about what precisely is contained within HTML5. Mozilla used to host a page titled, *"Technologies Often Called Part of HTML5 That Aren't."* They have since removed that page, and instead focus on covering HTML5 and related technologies like everybody else.

For those of us busy building the Web, any distinction does not matter. If a new technology is supported by enough browsers and suits your needs, then you should use it.

Therefore, like most of the HTML5 resources available today, this book encompasses *HTML5 and related technologies*, and we casually call this *HTML5*.

Software Requirements

The code in this book is intended for use in development on modern browsers. When the term *modern browser* is referenced in this book, it refers to the versions of any popular desktop browser commonly available, except for Internet Explorer, where it refers to only Internet Explorer 9 and above. Although there are less-modern fallback options for many areas of HTML5, it is expected that you will be using a modern browser during development.

If there is a discrepancy in browser support, topics typically note which desktop and mobile browsers are supported. However, no mention of browser support in this book will be as up to date as online compatibility guides, and several websites provide compatibility tables for HTML5 features.

Many JavaScript-centric examples make use of the browser developer console to output data. This console is a common feature of any desktop browser and is accessible through the browser's developer tools. Developer tools are different for every browser, but are typically enabled via a Tools menu, or with a hotkey such as Ctrl+Shift+I, or F12.

If you are a JavaScript developer or web designer and have never used the browser's developer tools, I *highly* recommend seeking out a tutorial. There are several online guides on using the developer console, such as the one for Chrome at https://developers.google.com/chrome-developer-tools/docs/console.

Code Examples

The numbered source code listings in this book can be downloaded via the online repository at http://github.com/simonsarris/HTML5Unleashed or http://simonsarris.com/HTML5Unleashed.

Occasionally, when a line of code is too long to fit on one line in the printed book, a code-continuation arrow (➡) is used to mark the continuation.

How This Book Is Organized

This book is arranged into four parts. The first provides a briefing on the history and terminology of HTML5, and the other three represent the main areas of HTML5.

HTML5 contains a very broad set of features, and it's unlikely that a developer would find all of them relevant for any given project. If you are totally new to HTML5 development, it would do you well to begin with Part I. After Part I, every chapter in this book is written to stand on its own, so that you may discover each topic as you please.

Part I: Background

Part I contains a short history and overview of HTML5, as well as explanations of common conventions used in many HTML5 resources, including this book.

▶ Chapter 1, "Why HTML5?"

▶ Chapter 2, "Important Concepts for HTML5"

Part II: New HTML Elements

Part II covers most of the new (and visual) HTML elements in HTML5. It begins with semantic tags, new HTML element attributes, and functionality. It then covers the new rich media tags, which enable native audio and video in the browser.

This part introduces two important concepts seen throughout HTML5: the semantic web (also visited in Chapter 13) and ways to achieve common functionality with less code and fewer plug-ins.

▶ Chapter 3, "Getting Started with HTML5: Semantic Tags, Forms, and Drag and Drop"

▶ Chapter 4, "Rich Media Tags: Video and Audio"

Part III: Canvas

Part III contains four chapters concerning HTML5 canvas. Those both new to and experienced with canvas will benefit from reading the first chapter, which gives a rundown of the API with many detailed notes about canvas context functionality. Canvas has a low-level API compared with Flash, and Chapter 6 covers basic interactivity and state management with the element. Chapter 7 covers canvas performance, but also contains a discussion on tips and peculiarities for canvas newcomers. Finally, Chapter 8 discusses the newer additions to the canvas API and briefly considers the 3D canvas (WebGL) API.

▶ Chapter 5, "2D Canvas"

▶ Chapter 6, "Making Canvas Interactive and Stateful"

▶ Chapter 7, "Canvas Performance, Tips, and Peculiarities"

▶ Chapter 8, "The Future of Canvas and 3D Canvas"

Part IV: HTML5's JavaScript APIs

Part IV is composed of *mostly* JavaScript APIs, and is more relevant to developers than artists or designers. The topics in these chapters cover the new native solutions to needs that have arisen over the years as the Web has progressed. The book ends with the small-but-powerful API for adding truly semantic markup to HTML pages, and a brief look at the future.

► Chapter 9, "Geolocation API"

► Chapter 10, "HTML5 Storage Options"

► Chapter 11, "Messaging and Web Workers"

► Chapter 12, "Network Communication: WebSockets and XMLHttpRequest Level 2"

► Chapter 13, "Microdata, Other Small Things, and Beyond HTML5"

Links and Real-World Examples

This book contains many links and real-world examples from existing websites. Links and project mentions do not constitute endorsement, and typically only the most popular projects and libraries are mentioned.

This book does not endorse any particular browser, but most examples try to use Chrome or Firefox because they are the most popular cross-platform browsers and widely support nearly every feature covered in the book.

CHAPTER 1

Why HTML5?

This chapter begins with a brief history of HTML and the World Wide Web. The chapter then covers the rise of HTML5 and some practical reasons to care about using HTML5.

How Did We End Up Here?

Technology moves quickly in the computing world.

People have envisioned interconnected computers since there have been computers. Like with most technologies, "networks" of computers began as military and academic tools, but as time passes most nonlethal novelties trickle into public use, and so it was with what we now call the Internet.

When the Internet was more of an academic fancy than a public one, a man named Tim Berners-Lee working at the European nuclear research organization CERN wanted to propose a standard that everybody could use to share (mostly research) documents.

Berners-Lee chose hypertext as the focal point of his standard. Hypertext is text displayed on computers that contains many references to other hypertext documents that the user can access, which was an important feature to the work of Berners-Lee and his colleagues. It had a lot of uses, according to his personal notes, such as easing the creation of encyclopedias, documentation, personal note-books, and any endeavors requiring "linked" documents.

The hypertext that became the backbone of the Hypertext Markup Language (HTML) standard only accomplished half of Berners-Lee's goal. The other half was to share this information, so Berners-Lee wanted to devise a way to marry HTML with the Internet. With the aid of Robert Cailliau, he set out to build a project that deployed HTML easily over the Internet, calling the project WorldWideWeb (written back then as one word). This was to be a "web" of hypertext documents that would be readable and discoverable by anyone with a "browser" program. The hypertext documents would be accessible via a client/server relationship, and would use standardized addresses to locate and refer to documents.

Berners-Lee expected this WorldWideWeb to be a read-only project in the first few months, and hoped within half a year the browsing users would be capable of authorship, so much so that authorship would be a universal concept of the Web. It took a little longer than half a year for the second part of this vision to take hold, but the rise of blogs, wikis, and social networking has certainly let it ring true.

By 1990, Berners-Lee had HTML, a web server, and a web browser ready for his organization. On August 6, 1991, he publicly posted his work on an Internet newsgroup and the World Wide Web got its start.

The Internet had existed in many shapes for some time, but the World Wide Web, which can be thought of as a layer running atop the Internet, was what brought it to the public's eye, and with such a force that as far as the public is concerned they have always been one and the same.

For the World Wide Web to be useful to the public, it needed more accessible tools. In 1993, the Mosaic web browser was introduced (see Figure 1.1), heralding an age where both text and images were to be commonplace. The interface and usability of Mosaic were considered impressive at the time, and the program enabled common folk to browse the Web in a meaningful and intuitive way. In other words, Mosaic allowed the Web to catch on.

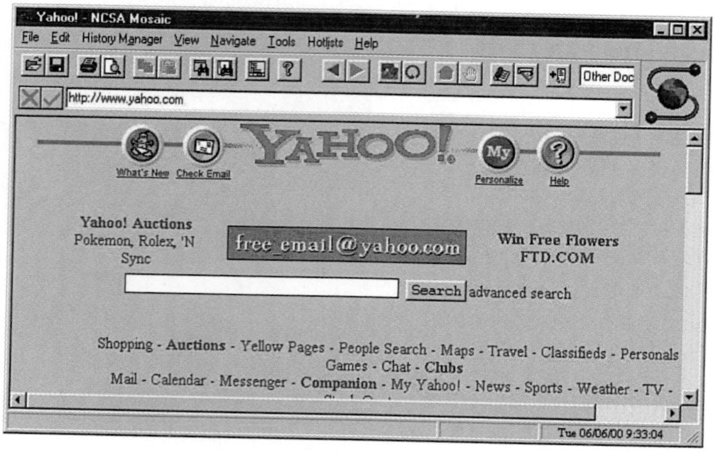

FIGURE 1.1   Screen capture from original Mosaic browser. Image courtesy of Computer History Museum.

> **NOTE**
>
> Mozilla was the code name for a product that came to be called Netscape Navigator. The name Mozilla was created as a portmanteau of "Mosaic killer," hinting that it was intended to replace Mosaic. The modern Firefox browser has its roots in Netscape Navigator, and the Mozilla foundation that develops Firefox today borrowed its name from Netscape's old code name.

In 1994, the World Wide Web Consortium (W3C) was founded by Berners-Lee at MIT. Over the next several years, the World Wide Web, guided by the W3C, took on enormous life and purpose as it sought to bring the Internet into the public eye through the Web.

The Web Takes Off

The Web has since become a playground of commerce and communication, but it took a long time to get where it is today. Browsers and the W3C attempted to enhance the utility of HTML alongside the growth of the Web.

The W3C published several new versions of the HTML specification. Over the years, HTML elements were added, removed, deprecated, forbidden, or in the case of `<blink>` and `<marquee>`, sometimes unofficial, and perhaps regretted, but still occasionally implemented.

Forms with file upload were introduced in 1995 in HTML 2.0. Tables were introduced in 1996 with HTML 3.0. HTML 4.0 was introduced in 1997 and adopted many browser-specific elements and emphasized style sheets. If you remember the `<font>` tag, this was the revision that deprecated it. The very familiar `<span>`, `<iframe>`, and `<button>` were added.

Finally in 1999, HTML 4.0.1 was introduced with minor adjustments. So minor that the third change listed in this version was merely the update to the copyright!

From the W3C's point of view, HTML at the turn of the millennium seemed to be reaching an end of development. The W3C looked toward the future with Extensible Markup Language (XML) and Extensible Hypertext Markup Language (XHTML), which were a kind of strictly structured HTML. XHTML was more concerned with obsessing over details than it was with adding functionality, and the lack of meaningful new utility stunted its adoption. Nonetheless, many organizations backed the W3C's goals, convinced they were the future. HTML was more or less considered frozen.

Websites and their developers were not satiated by this direction in web standards, and where developers craved new functionality and innovation, there were people and organizations willing to fill in the gap.

The Rise of the Browser Plug-In

Flash is easily the most ubiquitous browser plug-in. It became very popular relatively quickly because it was one of the few ways to reliably display video in the browser. Its first notable use was in 1996 when the MSN and Disney websites adopted it to serve video content, but what started out as a way to serve videos rapidly evolved into much more. Flash became the easiest way to expand the capabilities of web pages.

By the early 2000s, there were a multitude of websites using Flash as developers were making more and more elaborate video players, games, and animations. Flash website navigations, from the elegant to the nauseating, were very common, which meant there were entire websites unavailable to view unless you had the plug-in.

This was an age of web exploration and experimentation, and in many ways Flash defined a whole new set of features and *expectations* for the browser. Why shouldn't a browser be able to just play video? Why shouldn't there be interactive animation? Developers wanted to take these tasks seriously, and Flash allowed for it. Adoption of the plug-in skyrocketed, and by 2005 Macromedia claimed that more than 97% of Internet users had Flash installed. Macromedia's methodology might have been off, but Flash's footprint on the Web was undeniable.

Web 2.0

The rise of plug-ins and the discovery of different new applications for web pages caused a murmur throughout the Web during the first few years of the new millennium. In 2003, O'Reilly Media hosted a web conference that used the term *Web 2.0*. It wasn't the first use of the term, but Tim O'Reilly used the conference to talk about the future of the Web *as a platform*, where entire applications would be built intentionally in the browser as opposed to on desktops. User-generated content of all kinds was the future, so many said, and there's no place for it quite like the Web.

The term Web 2.0 went on to mean a general paradigm shift from the Web as a place that one visits to retrieve information and instead as a place to interact, a kind of massive participation platform. Blogs, wikis, and social networks sprung up like wildfire. Fortunes were made or lost trying to get users to stay, create, and interact with each other, usually while selling advertising real estate on the literal sidelines of pages. Exciting methodologies such as Asynchronous JavaScript and XML (Ajax) became prominent during this time.

Web 2.0 was a loaded term and the meaning depended on who you talked to, with no small amount of disagreement. It made a good buzzword, something that news outlets could talk about, and was liked enough to make the rounds for a few years. Web 2.0 didn't particularly describe any new technologies though, just new ways of thinking about the Web.

There was another group aside from all the standards writers, website creators, and media companies. The companies that actually built browsers had a very similar itch to scratch. Why *can't* a browser natively run video? If the Web can be a platform, how can the browser become the most capable enabler of that platform? Until now, browser vendors were at the mercy of third-party plug-ins and the standards writers, and at least one possible version of the Web's future was absent from the vision of the W3C.

HTML5

In 2004, a new group quietly formed, headed by individuals at Opera, Mozilla, and Apple. This browser-backed standards body called itself the Web Hypertext Application Technology Working Group, or WHATWG.

XML wasn't the future to the WHATWG, and neither were plug-ins. Browser vendors felt that the browsers ought to provide any functionality that is expected or common, and so (in a small snub to the W3C) they set off on their own path to write the future of the Web.

A specification called *Web Applications 1.0* slowly formed, later renamed *HTML5*. For years, the group was ignored by the W3C.

It is a bit too dramatic to ascribe emotions to organizations, but in some sense, those in power at the W3C must have had a crisis of confidence about their XML/XHTML path. In 2006, they agreed to abandon the XML path and instead adopt the WHATWG's new work as the starting point for a new HTML working group in the W3C.

What Exactly Is HTML5?

Specifications and sets of standards are nebular things. There's a bit of confusion about what exactly falls under the umbrella of HTML5 and what doesn't. What's more, since its inception, important parts of HTML5 have been spun off into their own standalone specifications.

HTML5 has become a catchall term that encompasses a large set of exciting browser technologies that will shape websites for some time to come, and because of this, it can be considered a de facto replacement for that old buzzword once used to describe new and exciting web pages, Web 2.0.

As mentioned before, Web 2.0 is a fuzzy term because it tends to be used to talk more about paradigms than specific technologies. HTML5, and this book, are about specific technologies, though just what technologies are included in HTML5 is often a question of whom you talk to and just how precise he or she wants to be.

Technically, this book encompasses HTML5 plus several other new web technologies, but the distinction is unimportant. The main aim of this book is not to be strict, it is to be useful, and if there are important new web technologies that are being implemented alongside HTML5, then they deserve to be included.

Developers are a crowd that tends to favor precision, but the rest of the world likes to keep things simple. So we have a term, HTML5, which means "next generation web technologies" to almost everyone. It's helpful to have a catchall term for these technologies, so the terminology we use for these additional features is simply *HTML5*.

With that in mind, literally speaking, HTML5 is the fifth revision of the HTML language itself. The complete HTML5 specification includes new content plus all older (nonobsolete) HTML, so it replaces (or subsumes) HTML4. There are also two HTML5 specifications, one maintained by the W3C and one by the WHATWG, so even speaking of "strictly"

HTML5 requires a few caveats. Figure 1.2 shows a graph of HTML5 features in both specifications and the associated technologies often considered alongside HTML5.

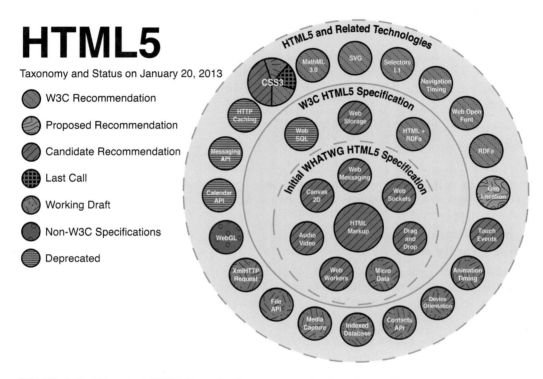

HTML5

Taxonomy and Status on January 20, 2013

W3C Recommendation

Proposed Recommendation

Candidate Recommendation

Last Call

Working Draft

Non-W3C Specifications

Deprecated

FIGURE 1.2   Diagram of HTML5 application programming interfaces (APIs) and related technologies. By Sergey Mavrody.

This era of HTML5 represents a lot of movements. It's an era of the native web, as browsers try to claw back functionality from plug-ins and place it into specifications. It's also an era of the open web, as anyone is allowed to join the WHATWG mailing list and contribute to the spec (membership in the W3C by contrast is small and not free). Countless good ideas have been adopted from all manner of sources. It could also be considered an era of the mobile web, as HTML5 enables technologies to build web applications that work across all manner of modern devices.

The Importance of HTML5

In spite of its beginnings in 2004, HTML5 is a term that casually entered ubiquity rather suddenly around 2010, largely due to a mass popularization push from both browser vendors and the media.

Thanks to the amount of data publicly available, we are able to peer back and witness the rise of HTML5 popularity rather accurately. Let's take a look using Google Trends, a service

Google offers to gauge the world's interest on search topics. Figure 1.3 shows the Google Trends graph for HTML5 and Web 2.0.

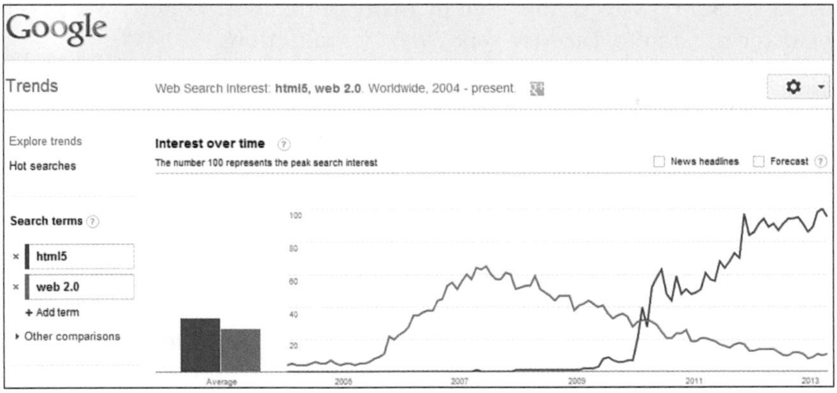

FIGURE 1.3   Google Trends graph for "HTML5" and "Web 2.0."

You can see that HTML5 has been around for some time, but it only gained relevancy in the Internet lexicon very recently, with a fast-paced explosion of activity at the start of 2010. You can also see that it took over as the dominant catchall Internet buzzword fairly quickly.

Using more nuanced phrases, we can see that as of mid-2011, HTML5 started to be considered a job skill. At the same time, we can observe the slow and steady decline of Flash. Figure 1.4 shows the Google Trends graph for "HTML5 developer" and "Flash developer."

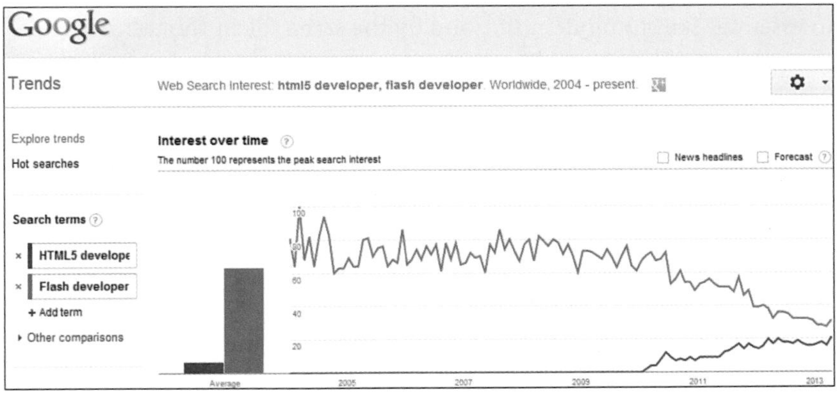

FIGURE 1.4   Google Trends graph for "HTML5 developer" and "Flash developer."

We see one good reason to care about HTML5: If you're a web developer or designer, you just might want it written on your résumé!

That's a little contrived of course. All web developers and designers ought to care about HTML5 because it has graduated from its old position as a set of avant-garde novelties. HTML5 technologies are supported by most modern browsers, with many of the technologies enjoying robust fallbacks. HTML5 is now used by many of the most popular websites in existence, from Google's search to *The New York Times'* visualizations.

To quell any questions about the certainty of HTML5's future, the W3C in December of 2012 declared the HTML5 specification stable and feature complete, assuring developers that HTML5 features represent a stable target for future web development.

Are Plug-ins Dead?

HTML5 doesn't spell the end of plug-ins, but it does make them much less necessary. Flash and Silverlight developers should consider JavaScript and HTML5 development. Even where Flash is capable on mobile devices, HTML5 canvas apps ought to generally be smaller in download size and consume less battery life, merely on account of less overhead in the platform.

The HTML5 canvas, audio, and video elements are future-proof replacements for plug-ins. Flash, after all, is a proprietary platform and has a much less-knowable shelf life. Apple's iOS platforms already forbid Flash, and for all we know, Adobe could end development of Flash tomorrow, or Chrome could stop bundling Flash by default tomorrow. The HTML elements that will replace Flash are far more of a "given" when it comes to what future browsers will implement or not.

Summary

All web developers and designers ought to care about HTML5 because HTML5, in simple terms, is the natural progression of web technologies. Whereas typing was a novelty in 1940, today it is an essential skill to modern life, and by the same token the technologies present under the umbrella of HTML5 will be necessary knowledge for developers and designers for years to come.

There are likely zero web apps that will endeavor to use *all* of the technologies of HTML5, but good developers and designers should at least be acquainted with all aspects of new web technologies like HTML5, if only to know what's now possible on the Web.

CHAPTER 2

Important Concepts for HTML5

This short chapter covers some important information to begin our path to HTML5 technologies. It explains some vocabulary used throughout this book that may be new to some readers, and also begins with a briefing on the recurrent goals you see throughout this book.

The Goals of HTML5

HTML5 was born out of visible needs in the browser ecosystem, and the aims of its specifications are all responses to these needs. This section details the three most prominent goals of HTML5, which can be thought of as themes that you see throughout the book.

Improving the Native Web

According to the World Wide Web Consortium (W3C) specification, HTML5 "introduces markup and APIs for emerging idioms, such as Web applications." More specifically, HMTL5 adds syntactic features to the Web that could previously only be accomplished with plug-ins. For instance, if serving video on the Web is a nearly ubiquitous expectation, web browsers ought to be able to accomplish it without additional help. The same goes for audio and other animated or dynamic content. Thus the `<audio>`, `<video>`, and `<canvas>` elements are some of HTML5's most important additions to the Web.

HTML5 doesn't just make plug-ins less necessary, it also increases the browser's functionality to be more in line with native mobile applications. Browser vendors and standards committees have begun work on application programming interfaces (APIs) that expose functionality of (mobile) devices within the browser. The most prominent example of this is the Geolocation API, which allows browsers to retrieve geographical location much like native phone apps do. There are several smaller niche APIs (such as one for device orientation) that also promise to afford more utility in the browser.

More Done with Less Code

One much more subtle feature of HTML5 is the ability to do more with less code. There are a lot of *de facto* standard web page features, such as placeholder text in forms, auto-focusing on a particular input element once the page loads, client-side validation of form input, date and time pickers, and so on.

All of these concepts are considered standard-issue stuff on a modern web page, but every one of them requires at least a little bit of JavaScript to work. Because of this, these concepts are implemented across websites in many different ways, and are at times buggy or inconsistent with each other.

HTML5 simplifies these common design patterns (and more) by creating standardized ways to accomplish them in HTML alone. This empowers designers and also reduces code maintenance and interoperability between platforms because the given feature's functionality can be more contextually handled by the browser.

The Semantic Web

The semantic web is a long-held dream of the Web's inventor, Tim Berners-Lee. He envisioned a web where content was not only readable by humans but also *understood* by machines. Just as we have to write carefully for humans to comprehend, it would also take a little footwork to make sure programs parsing web pages could pick up on meaningful content.

HTML5 represents the first big semantic push on the Web, and there are important semantic components discussed in Chapters 3 and 13 ("Getting Started with HTML5: Semantic Tags, Forms, and Drag and Drop" and "Microdata, Other Small Things, and Beyond HTML5," respectively). Now web pages can be marked up to be better understood and categorized by screen readers, search engines, and other web-crawling software. Chapter 13 also contains a brief history of web semantics and their current utility.

Requisites for HTML5 Development

This section covers a few important considerations for developing HTML5 web apps. These represent nothing new to a seasoned web developer but are otherwise important for understanding the rest of this book.

Modern Browser Developer Tools

Browser developer tools have matured rapidly over the past six years. For both developers and designers, it is strongly recommended that you familiarize yourself with them, as they are referenced occasionally in this book.

Specifically, this book utilizes the JavaScript console in many of its examples, which is used to log messages. This increases the simplicity of the book's code examples because we can create sample output without bothering with HTML page manipulation. We output to the console with the JavaScript method `console.log(someOutput)`.

Developer tools are typically launched via a Settings menu, or with the command Ctrl+Shift+I, or just F12 depending on the browser. The JavaScript console is found within most developer tools.

The developer console is very flexible, and can also be used to manipulate JavaScript on a page or merely for JavaScript experimentation. Writing directly into the console evaluates the statement and then provides its return value on the next line. Figure 2.1 shows the JavaScript console within the developer tools for Chrome and Firefox, with console-access buttons highlighted and a few commands entered.

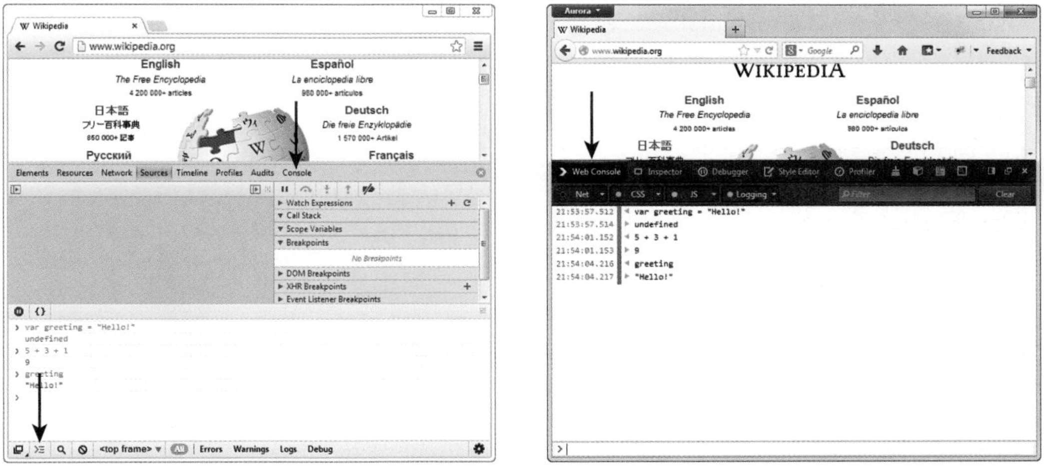

FIGURE 2.1   Chrome and Firefox with their developer tools open, with the console showing. Buttons to show/hide the console are indicated with arrows.

This book also mentions newer features of developer tools that specifically aid in debugging some HTML5 features, like local storage and web workers. These are referenced and explained in their respective chapters.

The importance of learning browsers' developer tools cannot be stressed enough. Familiarizing yourself with them is one of the most important job skills of web developers today. Chrome's developer tools are top notch, and Firefox has very recently (March 2013) debuted a huge amount of useful new functionality to its toolset.

HTML5 Fallbacks: Shims, Shivs, and Polyfills

You'll find the terms *shim*, *shiv*, and *polyfill* peppered throughout HTML5 resources. Where HTML5 is concerned, the three words represent roughly the same concept: a JavaScript library that provides HTML5-like functionality to older browsers, reproducing the native functionality as closely as possible.

In their most generous form, shims and polyfills are drop-in libraries that allow you to use HTML5 features without worrying about proper support for older browsers. The polyfill library detects these unsupporting browsers and attempts to re-create a particular HTML5 feature's functionality through JavaScript or other means. At the least, these libraries ensure that new HTML content is styled correctly on older browsers.

For a few years, the lack of support in older browsers stalled implementation of HTML5 features. Today, barring impossible-to-reproduce functionality in some features, HTML5 features can safely be used without fear of leaving older browsers in the dust.

Online, you will be able to find a good deal of these polyfill libraries and very good lists of such libraries, such as the one in the Modernizr project: https://github.com/Modernizr/Modernizr/wiki/HTML5-Cross-browser-Polyfills (the project itself is mentioned later in this chapter). Chapter 3 also contains a section on some of the most popular HTML5 polyfill libraries.

Feature Support and Detection

Not every HTML5 feature can be reasonably supported with a polyfill. For some features, such as complex canvas applications, it is necessary to support a different kind of fallback. In the case of canvas, that usually entails displaying an image instead of a dynamic animation or a "sorry, please consider upgrading your browser" message instead of interactive content.

How Do I Know What Features Are Supported?

Before you use any particular HTML5 feature, it's a good idea to look at a website of compatibility tables to see which browser versions currently support the feature. There are several of these websites, and the most popular ones are as follows:

- ▶ caniuse.com

- ▶ html5please.com

- ▶ mobilehtml5.org

Figure 2.2 shows a typical compatibility table from caniuse.com. You can see that all versions of Internet Explorer and many mobile browsers do not support WebGL, the 3D specification for HTML5 canvas (2D canvas is much more widely supported).

Always Use Feature Detection

Sometimes you'll want to use a feature even if some browsers do not support it and there is no reasonable fallback. Instead of attempting to detect particular unsupporting browsers, it is always better to detect the existence of features.

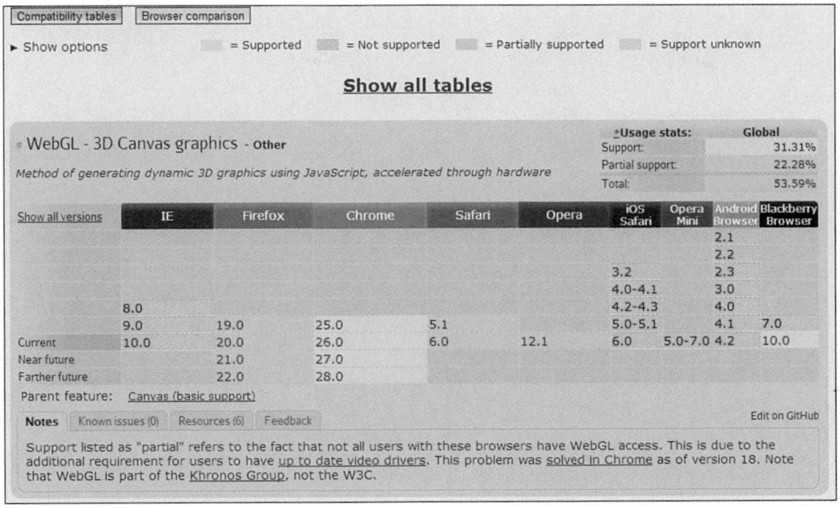

Compatibility tables | Browser comparison

▸ Show options   = Supported   = Not supported   = Partially supported   = Support unknown

Show all tables

WebGL - 3D Canvas graphics - **Other**

Method of generating dynamic 3D graphics using JavaScript, accelerated through hardware

±Usage stats:	Global
Support:	31.31%
Partial support:	22.28%
Total:	53.59%

Show all versions	IE	Firefox	Chrome	Safari	Opera	iOS Safari	Opera Mini	Android Browser	Blackberry Browser
								2.1	
								2.2	
						3.2		2.3	
						4.0-4.1		3.0	
	8.0					4.2-4.3		4.0	
	9.0	19.0	25.0	5.1		5.0-5.1		4.1	7.0
Current	10.0	20.0	26.0	6.0	12.1	6.0	5.0-7.0	4.2	10.0
Near future		21.0	27.0						
Farther future		22.0	28.0						

Parent feature: Canvas (basic support)

Notes | Known issues (0) | Resources (6) | Feedback   Edit on GitHub

Support listed as "partial" refers to the fact that not all users with these browsers have WebGL access. This is due to the additional requirement for users to have up to date video drivers. This problem was solved in Chrome as of version 18. Note that WebGL is part of the Khronos Group, not the W3C.

FIGURE 2.2 Compatibility table from caniuse.com showing WebGL support on major browser versions.

For instance, the HTML5 canvas element is not supported on Internet Explorer 8 or below. To test for its support, you could create a canvas element and then check for one of the methods that you would expect to exist:

```
var supportsCanvas = document.createElement('canvas').getContext != undefined;
```

The variable `supportsCanvas` will be true in Internet Explorer 9 and false in Internet Explorer 8. Using `document.createElement('canvas')` alone is not enough because it will successfully create an element of type `HTMLUnknownElement`. Instead, you check to see if the `getContext` method exists on the new element.

There are many other valid ways to test for canvas support (or most HTML5 features for that matter), and instead of bothering to find a working method for each, it is sometimes easier to use a library. The most popular feature detection library is Modernizr (modernizr.com), which can quickly detect all HTML5 and CSS3 (Cascading Style Sheets) features and enable you to respond by executing some appropriate JavaScript, or even conditionally loading different JavaScript and CSS files based on a feature's support.

Summary

The resources in this chapter were popular when this book was written, but there may be better (or more popular) libraries out there today. When considering any kind of library, it is always a good idea to do a fresh search to see what's most popular and why.

Now that you have the background and vocabulary needed for this book, it's time to explore the many features of HTML5.

## CHAPTER 3

Getting Started with HTML5: Semantic Tags, Forms, and Drag and Drop

Hᴛᴍʟ5 is such a large set of standards and application programming interfaces (APIs) that it's rare a developer would use every single one. We start by concerning ourselves with actual HTML elements, and this chapter covers the majority of new tags introduced in HTML5, which can be grouped into a few small feature sets.

The chapter begins with an important section on maintaining backward compatibility with the new HTML5 tags, then continues on to discuss HTML language differences and the new syntax available when authoring pages.

We then cover the new semantic tags: the structural page elements in HTML5 that better separate pages into logical parts. Then, we take a look at the exciting new form options that allow for more consistent presentation and validation of input that allow for page design with less custom code needed than ever before.

Finally, we peek at some JavaScript as we cover the new HTML element drag-and-drop API present in HTML5.

Ensuring Backward Compatibility with the New HTML Tags

As you see in this chapter, HTML5 introduces a wide range of new elements and attributes, none of which are present in older browsers (such as Internet Explorer 8). Thankfully, HTML degrades gracefully, and any unknown element will still be rendered as an inline element, with this inline element displaying whatever inner HTML content it has.

Programmers make use of this feature along with some very well-curated JavaScript to create realistic fallback options for HTML5 in the form of polyfill libraries. These fallback libraries allow us to use all of the new HTML tags (and many features) today without fear of building sites that might not function in older browsers.

The HTML5 Shim

As mentioned in Chapter 2, "Important Concepts for HTML5," these libraries are generally called shims, shivs, or polyfills. The most popular general-purpose one is the Webshims Lib (https://github.com/aFarkas/webshim), self-described as a "modular capability-based polyfill-loading library." It is built on top of jQuery, which needs no introduction, and Modernizr (http://modernizr.com), an extremely popular feature-detection library.

Loading the Webshims library is just a few lines of code. Because it depends on jQuery and Modernizr, using Webshims means we need to add script references to those libraries as well. Listing 3.1 shows the code needed.

LISTING 3.1   Loading the Webshims Library and Dependencies

```
<!-- dependencies: jQuery + Modernizr with yepnope
     Can be found bundled with webshims:
     http://afarkas.github.io/webshim/demos/index.html -->
<script src="js/jquery-1.7.1.js"></script>
<script src="js/modernizr-yepnope-custom.js"></script>

<!-- reference the base script -->
<script src="js-webshim/minified/polyfiller.js"></script>

<script>
  //implement all unsupported features or call polyfill before DOM-Ready
  // to implement everything as soon and as fast as possible
  $.webshims.polyfill();
  //or load only specific features you need
  //$.webshims.polyfill('forms json-storage');

  $(function(){
  //use all implemented API-features on DOM-ready
  });
</script>
```

Not only does the Webshims library enable the rendering of new HTML elements, but it also provides reasonable fallback implementations of newer JavaScript APIs such as Geolocation and Local Storage (which are detailed in later chapters).

The library is maintained and explained in more detail at its GitHub repository, found at https://github.com/aFarkas/webshim.

HTML5 Boilerplate

Another option for getting started with a cross-browser foundation is to use the HTML5 Boilerplate templates (http://html5boilerplate.com). This project maintains a set of HTML, Cascading Style Sheets (CSS), and JavaScript scaffolding that allows you to get started with making clean HTML5 pages with little hassle or worry about compatibility. It is extremely popular, with several big-name users such as Google and Microsoft.

The HTML5 Boilerplate project doesn't use a JavaScript shimming library to afford any backward compatibility. Instead, it simply takes advantage of Internet Explorer–specific CSS rules to turn the new elements into the appropriate default style, maintaining backward compatibility. Because of this different approach, HTML5 Boilerplate does not attempt to implement any HTML5 *functionality* in older browsers, it only ensures that your page elements will be positioned and seen. HTML5 Boilerplate documentation does, however, link to a comprehensive list of polyfills for various HTML5 components: https://github.com/Modernizr/Modernizr/wiki/HTML5-Cross-browser-Polyfills.

Although these two options are the most popular ways of addressing backward compatibility today, it would be wise to do a search to see if any alternatives have been written in the meantime that suit your needs better or more specifically.

Starting from the Top

HTML pages have a few mandatory pieces that have remained too arcane for too long. HTML5, as you soon see, begins with a mission of simplification: More will be done with less code.

Let's start with some syntax.

The Doctype

The Doctype declaration ought to be the first thing on any production HTML document. A Doctype statement is a declaration common in HTML and Extensible Markup Language (XML) documents that specifies what kind of Document Type Definition (DTD) the document is expected to use.

Doctypes in the past have been cumbersome. Before HTML5, a typical Doctype might look like one of the following:

```
<!DOCTYPE HTML PUBLIC "-//W3C//DTD HTML 4.01//EN"
➥"http://www.w3.org/TR/html4/strict.dtd">
<!DOCTYPE html PUBLIC "-//W3C//DTD XHTML 1.0 Transitional//EN"
➥"http://www.w3.org/TR/xhtml1/DTD/xhtml1-transitional.dtd">
```

The World Wide Web Consortium (W3C) has decided that Doctypes serve no purpose in the browser but are required for legacy reasons. The tag is still needed because some browsers render in standards-compliant mode or not (quirks mode) depending on its existence. With this in mind, the W3C has seen fit to simplify the Doctype to something actually memorable:

```
<!DOCTYPE html>
```

That's all you need. As long as that Doctype is present in the file, you're good to go. Welcome to an HTML5 page!

> **NOTE**
>
> The longer, older Doctypes were technically desired because HTML was based on a standard called SGML (Standard Generalized Markup Language), which requires a reference to a DTD. The W3C decided to depart from this standard when creating the HTML5 parsing rules. Extensible Hypertext Markup Language (XHTML) and XML, however, are still based on SGML.

Meta Character Encoding

The `<meta>` tag, placed inside the `<head>` tag, is used to provide additional metadata about a web page. Every page ought to at least have one meta element, specifying the character encoding. Before HTML5, these specifications looked like the following:

```
<meta http-equiv="content-type" content="text/html; charset=UTF-8">
```

In the same spirit of simplification, the most common character encoding declaration in HTML5 looks like this:

```
<meta charset="UTF-8">
```

Simple enough! The quotes around the encoding aren't strictly necessary, nor are the letters case sensitive.

HTML5 Syntax and Validation

HTML5 comes with a new approach to syntax and validation that can be (euphemistically) regarded as lenient. One of the primary reasons for this new syntax is simplification of validation, signifying a departure from XML/XHTML-style (very strict) validation.

In the past, it has been notoriously difficult to validate large web pages, which was often a bother to developers, causing many to simply forgo any attempt. Browsers never needed to parse HTML as if it were XHTML, and were typically interested in being as lenient as possible with parsing to allow as many pages to render as possible, even slightly malformed ones. The W3C in turn decided to loosen the rules to be more in line with what browsers are capable of dealing with. After all, if browsers don't care about being overly strict, why must developers?

This move to a more lenient syntax is somewhat controversial, as multiple permissible ways of writing the same thing is often seen as a bad thing. Several authors may write valid HTML in different ways, and it introduces yet another set of coding styles that a team should agree upon before working together.

The following is a list of examples of several common new syntax liberties, though it is not exhaustive:

▶ The `<script>` and `<link>` tags no longer need the `type="text/javascript"` and `type="text/css"` attributes, respectively.

▶ All HTML tags may be written in any letter case and will still validate without error. `<div>`, `<DIV>`, and `<dIV>` are equally valid, for instance.

▶ `<html>`, `<head>`, and `<body>` tags are not necessary to validate and can be implied.

▶ `<br />`, `<img />`, and other self-closing tags no longer need the self-closing slash.

▶ Many tags can get away without having a closing tag; for instance, you do not need to close `<li>` tags in a list. Writing `<p>blah<p>blah<p>blah` is also perfectly valid. In both of these cases, it is fairly apparent where the ending list item and paragraph tags ought to be placed.

▶ Quotations around attributes are now optional in far more cases, though there still exist cases where quotations are necessary; for instance, writing `<div class=classone>` is valid, but specifying two classes would necessitate quotes because multiple classes are separated with a space: `<div class="classone classtwo">`.

▶ Attributes with an empty value may be written as just the attribute name, omitting the equal sign and the value, even if it's not a Boolean attribute. For instance, `<video muted>`, `<video muted="muted">`, and `<video muted="">` all set the `muted` attribute to `true`.

▶ Attributes have to be separated by at least one whitespace character.

For those developers who are used to validating their code with the W3C's markup validation service, these new rules can make for somewhat surprising results. For instance, Listing 3.2 contains a small HTML5 page.

LISTING 3.2   A Poorly-Written-But-Valid HTML5 Page

```
<!DOCTYPE html>
<meta charset=utf-8>
<title>some title</title>
<link rel="stylesheet" href="myStyle.css">
<body>
```

```
<div>
<p>
  Forgot the paragraph end!<br>
</DIV>
<video autoplay muted="muted" controls="" src="myVideo.webM">
</video>
```

Listing 3.2 is enough to give strict HTML or XHTML authors a good cringe. The `<html>`
and `<head>` tags are completely omitted. The `<link>` tag doesn't contain a `type` attribute,
nor is it closed. The opening `<div>` tag is written in lowercase and its closing tag in all
capitals. The `<p>` tag is left unclosed, the `<br>` unslashed. Finally, the `<video>` has three
Boolean attributes written three different ways, all declaring the same thing (that the attribute is true).

Yet as Figure 3.1 shows, Listing 3.2 validates just fine as HTML5.

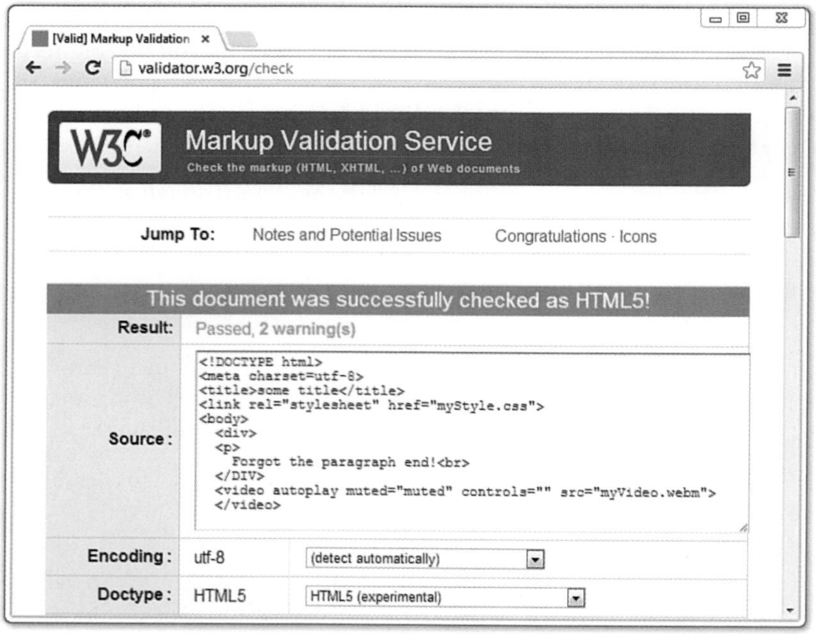

FIGURE 3.1   The W3C validator, validating Listing 3.2 with zero errors. One of the two warnings
is about using the experimental HTML5 Conformance Checker itself, the other about Direct Input
mode assuming UTF-8 regardless.

NOTE

The official validator can be found at http://validator.w3.org/, with the HTML5 validation
option listed as "experimental" because HTML5 is a living specification. A less-official validator, funded by the Mozilla foundation, can be found at http://html5.validator.nu/.

Just because you *can* write such HTML and still validate doesn't mean you should, but it's clear that the goal of validation has changed.

Some HTML authors have previously used the strict validators as a way to test for errors and enforce a rigid XHTML-like style. This is no longer possible, as HTML validation is now solely code validation and void of any stylistic checks. If it fails validation, it is because something is mechanically wrong and might cause an issue with an HTML parser. Everything else is fair game. This separation is useful for those who did not care about stylistic issues (or have a unique style) and just wanted to ensure their code was correct as a quality assurance step.

On the other hand, the ability to check for stylistic errors is an important tool. Because the new syntax is lax and the validator no longer covers coding style, many HTML authors have requested or sought to create tools that flag suspicious HTML use, or HTML that does not conform to their particular style. Such tools are usually called *linters*, and as of this writing the most popular one for HTML5 can be found at http://lint.brihten.com/html/. This particular linter has options that determine whether it should permit or flag quoted attributes, lowercase attributes, or the various methods of writing simple Boolean attributes.

> **NOTE**
>
> As with any online tool, you should always do a search to see if there are newer, more popular, or more correct tools that may serve you better than the ones mentioned in this text.

How You Should Write Your HTML

It is not the aim of this text to tell you how you should author your pages, but there are some convincing reasons for writing HTML with some stylistic restraint.

Always Write Tags and Attributes in Lowercase

Lowercase letters in tags and attributes are more common in existing HTML, and are generally considered easier to visually parse. All-capital lettering can be difficult to read, especially for nonnative English speakers. The glyphs of the lowercase alphabet have more differences in shape between each other than uppercase glyphs, making them easier to distinguish and therefore visually recognize. Consider, for instance, the differences of positions and heights of the letters in "height," where some glyphs are clearly taller than others or may hang lower than others, versus "HEIGHT," where all the glyphs occupy identically tall rectangles.

Always Use Quotations Around Attribute Values

Although the elimination of the requirement for quotes around attribute values minimizes characters needed, forgoing quotations introduces some inconsistency because there are times when quotes are always necessary, such as when writing multiple classes (`<div class="classone classtwo">`) or the attribute value is not very simple (the value `href="example.html?v=1"` needs quotations so the second equal sign parses properly). Because alternating styles can lead to confusion, it's probably best to always use quotes.

Boolean attributes can be written in several ways, even with quotes; for instance, all three of these enable the `muted` attribute of the video element:

```
<video muted>
<video muted="muted">
<video muted="">
```

It's arguable which one is the clearest, so the most important stylistic choice among these options is simply being consistent with yourself or your team.

Omit Tags, or Don't

The choice of omitting some tag closures is a stylistic gray area. Although it introduces some syntactical inconsistency to omit some closing tags, many consider doing so a coding benefit, as it may be easier to visually parse and maintain. Consider for yourself the visible difference between using closing tags or not in the following:

```
<ul>
   <li>Alcman
   <li>Alcaeus
   <li>Bacchylides
   <li>Pindar
</ul>

<p>The animated figures stand
<p>Adorning every public street
<p>And seem to breathe in stone
<p>Or move their marble feet!

<!-- versus -->

<ul>
   <li>Alcman</li>
   <li>Alcaeus</li>
   <li>Bacchylides</li>
   <li>Pindar</li>
</ul>

<p>The animated figures stand</p>
<p>Adorning every public street</p>
<p>And seem to breathe in stone</p>
<p>Or move their marble feet!</p>
```

For any of these, the sheer practicalities of working with other people (or their code) who use a different convention might be reason enough to do things one way or the other. Although the examples in this book intend to maintain a clean coding style, closing tags are never omitted in the text for the sake of consistency and familiarity with more developers.

Housekeeping

Keeping with the topic of old versus new, let's take a look at some of the differences in the HTML5 specification.

Several elements present in the HTML4 specification have been removed from HTML5. The following have been removed because they served no purpose but to alter presentation, a job which is almost completely handled by CSS nowadays:

- ▶ `<basefont>`
- ▶ `<big>`
- ▶ `<center>`
- ▶ `<font>`
- ▶ `<strike>`—Use `<del>` or `<s>` instead.
- ▶ `<tt>`

Frames and framesets are considered bad form, especially for accessibility, so the associated tags have been removed:

- ▶ `<frame>`
- ▶ `<frameset>`
- ▶ `<noframes>`

The `<iframe>` tag is still present, however, and very useful. Authors should continue to use it when they want to embed another page or sandbox certain content.

Finally, there are a few elements deemed rarely used or too confusing:

- ▶ `<acronym>`
- ▶ `<applet>`—Use `<object>` instead.
- ▶ `<dir>`—Use `<ul>` instead.
- ▶ `<isindex>`

More elements and attributes still are defined as obsolete in the specification, and "must not be used by authors." The nonstandard `<blink>` tag was never mentioned in previous HTML specifications, but has earned its place among the obsolete list. Disdain for the element is all but official, as we can see from the W3C's wiki page on the element, shown in Figure 3.2.

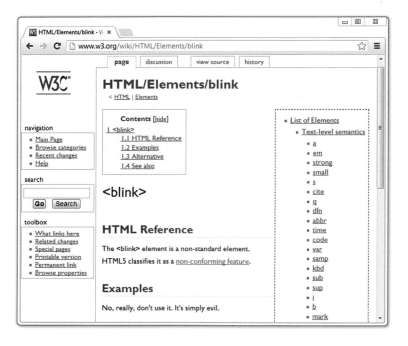

FIGURE 3.2   The blink element page in the W3C wiki.

Just because elements are removed from the specification does not mean that browsers will not render them. Although these elements are obsolete and authors should not use them, the specification requires browsers to implement them, and the document contains transition guidelines so that browsers may continue to appropriately handle many of the obsolete elements.

You'll notice that an obsolete feature that's still required for implementation sounds an awful lot like a deprecated feature. There's little difference between the concepts, so the W3C opted to remove the concept of deprecation entirely from the HTML5 spec. There are only features and obsolete features.

NOTE

The HTML5 specification details all obsolete features at http://dev.w3.org/html5/spec/obsolete.html. A list of all differences from HTML4 is also maintained at http://www.w3.org/TR/html5-diff/.

HTML5 Semantic Elements and Other Presentational Tags

Original web specifications, including HTML, were made long before anything remotely resembling the Web today was around. Since inception, it has been difficult to predict what kind of websites would be around, what their common design points might be, and what applications might arise to deal with them. The original web specifications were, at best, educated guesswork as to what might be desired, and what was desired in the early days was largely driven by the needs of the engineers and researchers who were to use it for research and documentation purposes. The `<img>` tag, after all, was not in the original HTML specification.

Older specifications and implementations also included many things we now consider in bad taste, such as the scrolling `<marquee>` element, the `<blink>` tag, and Comic Sans as a core web font. HTML also had many elements such as `<font>` and `<center>` that were useful at the time, but are no longer useful because ubiquitous CSS means we can cleanly separate the content of our pages from the styling of our pages.

HTML5 Semantic Tags

The Web has now been around for fair bit of time, and the new content in HTML5 is the result of the experience gathered from the data of countless developers, designers, and websites themselves. By looking at common conventions and structures, the HTML5 specification writers came up with a list of new semantic tags to replace some of these conventions.

Common HTML class and ID names typically found on divs have been turned into their own elements. For instance, `<div class="navigation">` and `<div id="article">` can now be written as the new tags `<navigation>` and `<article>`.

The purpose of these new tags is to separate HTML pages into semantic parts that are more definitively descriptive of their content, and this more semantic web confers several subtle advantages.

A typical news website might have an article page containing 50 divs, most of them related to structural positioning of headers, footers, captions, advertisements, and so on, with only one or two of them containing the true article content. If the div that contained article content was instead an `<article>` tag, machines and applications that parse that web page will have a much easier time finding the "real" content of the page to parse. Browsers can make text previews easier, and screen readers and other accessibility devices and programs can find the most important page content without guesswork. Web crawlers (like the ones that index pages for Google) can be directed to the most important page content to ensure that search engines better understand the important parts of a page to categorize and index it better.

It's important to remember that when we write HTML, we almost never expect anyone to read our pages as pure HTML; instead, users only ever see them as parsed documents. What we're doing with these new semantic tags is giving *guidance* to all of the programs and machines that parse the HTML pages, from browsers that want to display content in various fashions (such as a complete page render or a stripped-down readability mode), to crawlers that we never interact with directly. The more we can tell these parsers, the better job they can do for us.

Let's have a look at the major structural tags, each clearly filling a "role" on the page that might be relevant to a device or program. The majority of the time, these new tags will be used to replace `<div>` tags.

`<section>`

The `<section>` tag defines a section of a document, usually as a thematic grouping, and typically containing its own heading. The `<section>` tag should only be used when you would logically expect it to appear in an outline of a document, such as with the literal sections in the chapters of a book.

> **NOTE**
>
> Do not use `<section>` as a *generic* styling container—we still have `<div>` for that!

`<nav>`

The `<nav>` tag defines navigation for a document, representing a section of the document (or section) that contains links to other locations. There can be multiple `<nav>` tags on a page; for instance, there might be a `<nav>` tag around site navigation, one for footer links, and one for intrapage navigation.

With `<nav>` tags on a page, screen readers and other accessibility programs do not need to resort to guesswork when attempting to find navigation.

`<header>` and `<footer>`

The `<header>` and `<footer>` tags define the header and footer content of a document (or of a section of the document). These are for site (or section) related information such as navigation, logos, and contact information.

`<article>`

The `<article>` tag represents self-contained content in a web page. Like literal newspaper and magazine articles or blog posts, the purpose of the `<article>` tag is to encompass any content that could be otherwise removed from context of the rest of the page structure and stand on its own.

It's easy to see the utility of this tag with respect to apps and services that seek to summarize or preview content on a web page. If you were creating a news aggregation site that displayed snippets of many pages as a feed, you could search for `<article>` tags and, if present, display the first few sentences from each. Without `<article>` tags, you would have to either build an inference algorithm (that might be time consuming or kludgy) or else simply present the first text on the page, which may be something useless to a news summarizer, such as site navigation or an "about me" box, or other content not relevant to the particular article page.

`<aside>`

The `<aside>` tag defines portions of a page that consist of secondary content. Typically, this means content that is only tangentially related to the content around it. This includes content that is separate from the main content of the page, such as sidebar content like advertisements or author biography, or a blogroll (which is the most embarrassing term imaginable for saying "list of links").

The `<aside>` tag is also useful inside of articles, and HTML parsers are instructed to consider any such elements as directly related. The tag can be used inside an article for content pieces such as glossary definitions and pull quotes.

> **NOTE**
>
> Written text in parentheses is commonly referred to as an "aside," but the `<aside>` element is not intended to tag such content. It is only intended for content that is not part of the main document flow.

`<hgroup>`

The `<hgroup>` tag was created to contain several headers (`<h1>`, `<h2>`, etc.) and represents the heading of a section. The purpose of this tag is to collect two or more heading elements into one, for purposes of the document outline (which we discuss next). Typical usage looks like the following:

```
<hgroup>
  <h1>Slaughterhouse-Five</h1>
  <h2>Or The Children's Crusade: A Duty-Dance with Death</h2>
</hgroup>
```

Document Outlines in HTML5

Showing off these new semantic tags isn't particularly interesting on its own because it simply involves finding the appropriate, already existing divs on a given page and editing them to be the proper HTML5 tag instead. The fruits reaped by this labor are not directly visible. They do, however, play an additional role in HTML document outlines.

Document outlines are important, especially so for assistive devices and programs, and devices that might benefit from outlines or a logical separation of content (such as e-ink readers).

One of the big features of HTML5 is the ability for HTML parsers (such as browsers) and other apps or services to create much more sensible outlines for HTML documents. Previous versions had some capability for this in a very roundabout way: They could infer outlines by looking at divs with heading elements (`<h1>` though `<h6>` tags). This meant that a snippet of markup in HTML4:

```
<div id="someSection">
<h1>Rime of the Ancient Mariner</h1>
<p>
  How a Ship having passed the Line was driven by storms to
  the cold Country towards the South Pole
</p>
<div id="someSubsection">
<h2>Part I</h2>
<p>
  The Sun came up upon the left,
  Out of the sea came he!
  And he shone bright, and on the right
  Went down into the sea.
</p>
</div>
</div>
```

would lead to a simple outline:

```
1. Rime of the Ancient Mariner
    1.1 Part I
```

This is fine in such a small case, but you can imagine the trouble with making such an outline on a much larger page that contains all manner of divs and content that are wholly unrelated to the document. HTML4 outlining algorithms cannot definitively know if certain divs or headings are meant to participate in the outline of a page, or if they are only presentational.

Merging documents is also troublesome, as the rules for sectioning in HTML4 were based on heading values (<h1>, <h2>, and so on), so inserting one document in another leads to problematic outlines with improper nesting. With HTML5, the <section> tag removes the need to look for divs containing heading tags; instead, it can determine nesting on its own.

For a simple example, this HTML5 snippet:

```
<section>
  <hgroup>
    <h1>Slaughterhouse-Five</h1>
    <h2>Or The Children's Crusade: A Duty-Dance with Death</h2>
  </hgroup>
  <section>
    <h1>Introduction</h1>
    <p>(Content)</p>
  </section>
  <section>
    <h1>Chapter 1</h1>
```

```
    <p>(Content)</p>
  </section>
</section>
```

leads to this outline:

```
1. Slaughterhouse-Five
    1.1 Introduction
    1.2 Chapter 1
```

The `<hgroup>` tag allows us to use both `<h1>` and `<h2>` elements without making the `<h2>` into a subheading. The `<section>` tags allow us to use multiple `<h1>` tags in subsections, instead of starting a new, top-level section.

NOTE

The new `<aside>` tag has the additional purpose of defining sections to be *excluded* from the main outline, something not possible in HTML4 outlines.

Minor Semantic and Presentational HTML5 Tags

Several new tags are either too new to use or too minor to warrant their own sections, but are nonetheless worth mentioning for the sake of completeness.

`<menu>` and `<command>`

The `<menu>` tag defines an unordered list (just like the `<ul>` tag) that is expected to contain a set of actionable items, such as links or buttons. The `<menu>` tag generally carries the expectation that it will be used in web apps, and that items in the menu will perform a function in the app. This element should not be for page navigation. Instead, `<nav>` would be the better choice.

The `<command>` tag defines a self-closing element that represents a command that a user can invoke. It is intended to be used inside of menu elements, though it can exist anywhere on a page. It has an `icon` attribute that specifies an image, but can act as a check box or option button by specifying its `type`.

As of this writing, both of these elements are *very* sparsely implemented, and should not be used without first searching for current compatibility.

`<summary>` and `<details>`

The `<details>` tag describes a kind of widget that users can use to retrieve additional information. It must always contain a `<summary>`, which contains all the visible information the user sees by default. Users will be able to click on the summary (or an icon that the browser places nearby) in order to expand the details to reveal the rest of the information.

So the HTML:

```
<details>
  <summary>My principles</summary>
  <p>These are my principles. If you don't like them I have others.</p>
</details>
```

creates a details element with only the text "My principles" visible. Figure 3.3 shows the details and summary elements as they are currently implemented in Chrome, where an icon is automatically added that indicates the user can select the element.

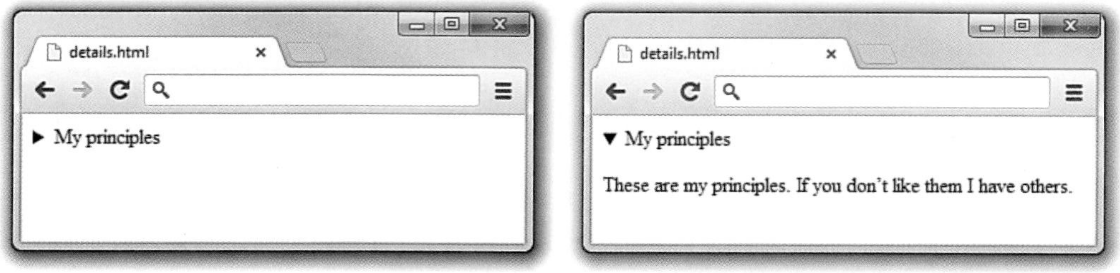

FIGURE 3.3 The `<details>` tag as currently implemented in Google Chrome, both collapsed (default) and expanded.

As of this writing, only Chrome has implemented support for the `<details>` and `<summary>` tags.

`<figure>` and `<figcaption>`

The `<figure>` and `<figcaption>` tags are new and widely implemented. The figure element is used to define self-contained content, such as images or code listings, and may include a caption in the form of the `<figcaption>` tag.

Typical usage may look like:

```
<figure>
    <img src="some-image.jpg" />
    <figcaption>Caption for the image</figcaption>
</figure>
```

`<mark>`

The `<mark>` tag defines marked (highlighted) text. This is used similarly to the `<em>` (or `<i>`) and `<strong>` (or `<b>`) tags, as the tags are wrapped around a passage of text.

Marking text is not the same as bolding it, and `<strong>` should continue to denote importance, whereas `<mark>` denotes relevance. For instance, when showing search results, a script could place `<mark>` tags around all text snippets that match the search term.

It has basic support on most browsers, and stylistically it usually adds a yellow background (like a traditional highlighting marker) to the text.

`<bdi>`, `<ruby>`, `<rt>`, and `<rp>`

The `<bdi>` tag, short for Bi-directional Isolation, isolates a part of text that might be formatted in a different direction from other text outside of it.

The `<ruby>`, `<rt>`, and `<rp>` tags are used for Ruby annotations, which are for showing pronunciation (or a short annotation) of East Asian characters.

These language aids are uncommon and sparsely implemented, but may be of use in the future.

`<time>`

The `<time>` tag allows authors to specify a time in both a human-readable and machine-readable format. This tag makes it easier for programs to date and index pages (and sections of pages), such as blog posts and news articles, without having to resort to guess-work. News aggregators and search engines may want to consider time stamps when choosing what content to display.

The `datetime` attribute indicates the machine-readable date and time of the element and must be a valid date or time (or both) string. The human-readable date and time goes inside of the time element tags. Let's see some examples:

```
<time datetime="22:00">10PM</time>
<time datetime="6-21">June 21st (of any year)</time>
<time datetime="1984">1984</time>
<time datetime="2012-11-22">22nd of November, 2012</time>
```

The dates can be flexible and fuzzy, using just a year or just a specific day or time, but unfortunately they cannot describe BC (or BCE) dates. The `datetime` value has several parsing rules, which are codified in the specification at http://www.whatwg.org/specs/web-apps/current-work/multipage/text-level-semantics.html#datetime-value.

> **NOTE**
>
> There was once a `pubdate` attribute, which other texts and websites may mention, but as of this writing it has been removed from the specification.

Visual HTML5 Tags: `<meter>` and `<progress>`

There are two minor visual elements added in HTML5, the `<meter>` and `<progress>` tags. These tags don't add especially new functionality to web pages; they just make the construction of these common design elements, once made with CSS and JavaScript, a good deal easier.

> **NOTE**
>
> HTML5 contains more major visual elements, such as `<audio>`, `<video>`, and `<canvas>`, which are the subjects of their own chapters.

`<meter>`

The meter element is a visual tool for representing any scalar value. It uses its `value`, `min`, `max`, `low`, `high`, and `optimum` attributes to determine an appropriately filled and colored meter. The `min` and `max` constrain the bounds of the measured range, which `value` must be in between. The other three obey commonsense rules (`low` must be smaller than `high` but larger than `min`, for instance).

The interplay between these attributes dictates the coloring of the meter. The `optimum` attribute does not need to be between `low` and `high`, and if it is between `high` and `max`, then the range from `high` to `max` is considered "preferred," working similarly for a low range.

Finally, like the other visual elements in HTML5, the inner HTML content of the `<meter>` tag is the place for fallback content in case a browser does not support the tag, and should not be left empty.

Let's see some examples:

```
<p>Engine Temperature:
  <meter min="0" max="500" value="205">205 degrees</meter>
</p>
<p>Theatre A Occupancy
  <meter low="60" high="80" optimum="100" max="100" value="49">49%</meter>
</p>
<p>Theatre B Occupancy
  <meter low="60" high="80" optimum="100" max="100" value="70">70%</meter>
</p>
<p>Theatre C Occupancy
  <meter low="60" high="80" optimum="100" max="100" value="100">Full!</meter>
</p>
```

These four meters produce Figure 3.4 in Chrome (other browsers look very similar). The first one would remain green regardless of value, whereas the next three, all with similar attributes except the `value`, look different depending on the `value`.

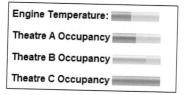

FIGURE 3.4   Four meters in Chrome.

`<progress>`

A famous writer once wrote, "Time is an illusion. Lunchtime doubly so." Progress bars were originally designed to give users an expectation of how much time remained before a task completed, but often leave users frustrated from inaccurate measurements and depictions of the time remaining.

Historically, progress bars have had a linear appearance mapping to a discrete value, including the visual element created by the `<progress>` tag. This has been problematic because the operations that make up the work a progress bar represents often proceed at an erratic and nonlinear pace. One of the most famous offenders historically was the old Windows file transfer progress bar, which would casually flip between "minutes" and "days" remaining as it churned along.

Even if a progress bar does accurately measure the relative time of a task, the utility of the bar is further confounded by the fact that people tend to have a nonlinear perception of time. After all, users are much more forgiving for the first 10 seconds of a wait than the last 10 seconds. If users simply *feel* a task with a progress bar is taking too long, they might simply quit the task.

User interface researchers at Carnegie Mellon found that arbitrarily accelerating the progress bar's movement toward the end of a task alone will make it appear to complete more quickly. So to make a progress bar that *feels* accurate and fair, lying to your users about the time remaining may be the best thing to do.

None of this means that using a progress bar is bad, but it is worth carefully considering if a progress bar is what you really want, as opposed to a more generic element that simply lets users know that work is still being done.

Usage of the `<progress>` tag is even simpler than the meter element, having just a `max` and a `value` attribute. The following tag produces the progress bar shown in Figure 3.5:

```
<progress value="66" max="100">66%</progress>
```

FIGURE 3.5   The progress element as seen in Chrome.

The big advantage of the `<progress>` tag over `<meter>` is the animation present in the bar. Even with all of the progress bar's faults, animation is important for users to know that work is being done and (perhaps) nothing has crashed or halted.

Because this animation serves a very useful purpose, instead of using a linear progress bar it has become increasingly popular on the Web to display an indefinite progress animation that merely evokes a sense of work being done. These are typically represented as a spinning wheel or object that disappears and reappears, and are either animated images or created in pure CSS.

It is not the aim of this book to tell you what to do, but it is worth considering what is available and popular (and why) before choosing what kind of progress indicator is appropriate to use. Both the progress and meter elements are rather basic compared with some of the impressive CSS-only inventions of designers that are available.

> **NOTE**
>
> As of this writing, Internet Explorer 10 supports the progress element but not the meter element, and no mobile browser supports either element.

HTML5 Forms

HTML5 has brought several exciting new features to the stuffy world of forms. Client-side validation has been accomplished in JavaScript for a long time to improve the user experience, and now HTML5 provides easy solutions for many common validations. New form input types also create more specialized controls (such as date and color picking) that are common on the Web but have (until now) been the domain of JavaScript libraries such as jQuery.

In case we haven't said it enough, one of the core missions of HTML5 is to reduce the amount of JavaScript code needed to create parts of pages that have become commonplace, and, as you soon see, most of the form additions reflect this.

Not everything in this section is widely supported yet, but the Webshims Lib (https://github.com/aFarkas/webshim) mentioned in the first section of this chapter implements several of the new features on older browsers. Additionally, nearly all of the content in this section can be thought of as an optional *extension* of forms as they exist today, and using these new features will not break older browsers.

Before we continue, it is important to mention that *validation on the client is in no way a replacement for server-side validation*. Client-side validation is wonderful because it gives immediate feedback to users filling in forms, helping them detect errors and save time. Client-side validation in no way protects against users (maliciously or accidentally) bypassing particular validations and submitting technically inappropriate data. So although we talk a great deal about validation in the coming section, we are really talking about upgrades to user responsiveness, and not final (server-side) validation of data.

Form Input Types

Many of the new input types bring presentational enhancements to their input elements. The ones implemented by browsers so far are quite useful, though slightly inconsistent between browsers, as the specification does not precisely detail how the controls should be presented. This is somewhat of a benefit because it allows browsers to tailor the look and feel of their controls to the OS and platform.

Let's take a look at the new form input types that have presentational differences: `number`, `range`, `search`, `datetime`, `datetime-local`, `date`, `month`, `week`, `time`, and `color`. Figure 3.6 shows these input fields with their default values in Chrome, Opera, and Firefox. As you can see, Firefox does not yet implement any of the new form types, and they all appear as standard input element boxes. You can see in Chrome, too, that the `datetime` input has yet to be implemented.

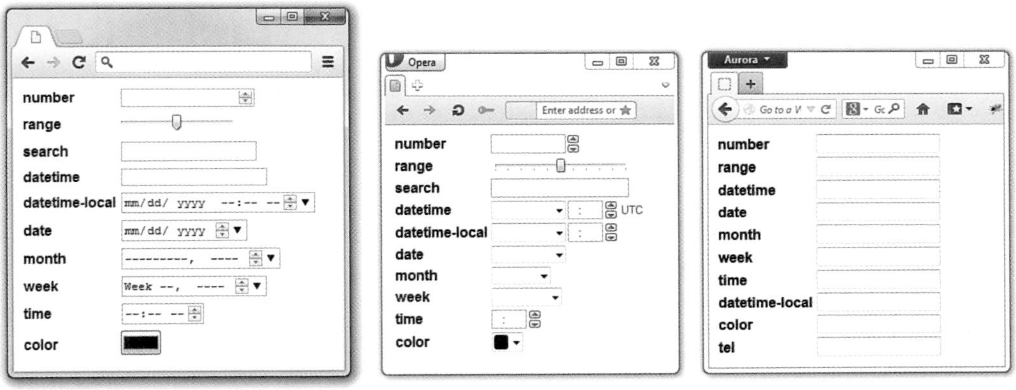

FIGURE 3.6   Several new input fields (labeled) with their default presentation in Chrome, Opera, and Firefox, respectively.

The new presentational form types enjoy nearly full support in Opera, Chrome, and iOS Safari, and partial support in a few other browsers, with Internet Explorer supporting the new presentational features starting with Internet Explorer 10.

The other new types, which have no presentational difference themselves, are `email`, `url`, and `tel` (though many mobile browsers use `email` and `tel` smartly, as you will see).

CSS Styling of Validation and Requirements

Validation is great during submission, but it's often even better to give the user visual feedback in real time as he or she is filling out the form. There are four new CSS pseudo-classes for forms: `:optional`, `:required`, `:valid`, and `:invalid`. These new classes allow you to style input elements according to their current state.

Required elements in forms are traditionally denoted using a red asterisk after the element or giving the box a red border, and styling such as this can now be done via CSS. HTML5 introduces a new `required` attribute on `<input>` tags that enforces the need for a value, and can be used in conjunction with the `:optional` and `:required` pseudoclasses to make styling automatic and easy.

The :valid and :invalid pseudoclasses can be used to instantly show a user when some input he or she is entering is appropriate or not, working with all of the new constraints that you soon see.

Let's make a short CSS snippet and take a look:

```
<style type="text/css">
/* Using both :required and :invalid will remove the border
   once a valid value is present */
input:required:invalid {
  border-color: red;
  border-width: 2px;
}

input:invalid {
  background-color: pink;
}

/* All inputs except the submit buttons */
input:not([type=submit]):valid {
  background-color: lightgreen;
}
</style>
```

We use this styling on two very simple forms:

```
Name:
<form>
  <input type="text" required>
  <input type="submit"/>
</form>
Email:
<form>
  <input type="email">
  <input type="submit"/>
</form>
```

The relevant inputs here are a "Name" and "Email" field, with the "Name" field being a plain text field sporting the required tag, and the "Email" field being an input of type email. Figure 3.7 shows both of these fields twice for comparison: in their default state on the left and with values entered on the right.

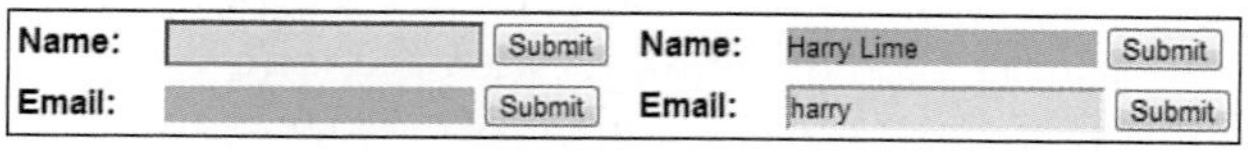

FIGURE 3.7   Two inputs using the aforementioned CSS and HTML and the same two inputs with values.

On the left, we have the default state of a "Name" text input field, which has the `required` attribute. Because it is required and no value is given, it matches both the `:required` and the `:invalid` CSS selectors, therefore having both a red border and a pink background. The "Email" input field on the left is of the new input type `email`, and does not have the `required` attribute, so an empty value is valid and, therefore, it matches the `:valid` CSS selector.

On the right side of Figure 3.7, we have the same two fields, this time with values entered. The "Name" field has a value, so it satisfies the `required` attribute, so it matches the `:valid` CSS selector, which removes the border it had from `:required` and changes the background color to a light green. The "Email" field, however, which was perfectly valid having no value, is now invalid because it contains a value that is not an email address.

> **NOTE**
>
> We discuss the `required` attribute and other new form attributes in the next section, "New Form Input Attributes and Elements."

number

The type `<input type="number">` has a presentational spinner (visually varies per browser/platform) alongside the control for incrementing and decrementing numbers. Validation of this control is bound by `min` and `max` attributes, and the increment of the stepper is described by the `step` attribute, which defaults to 1.

The following code creates a numerical input form that has no default value, and clicking the up or down arrows of the spinner allows it to reach only the values of 1, 3, and 5 because of the `step` of 2.

```
<form>
    <input type="number" min="1" max="6" step="2" />
    <input type="submit"/>
</form>
```

As shown in Figure 3.8 in Chrome, it is possible to manually enter values that are outside of the accepted range, and the browser shows an error.

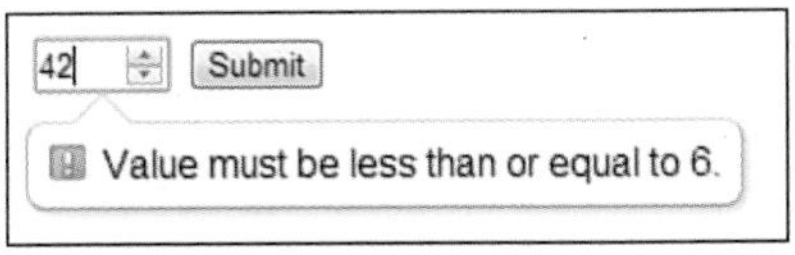

FIGURE 3.8   A numerical input, disallowing a value entered out of range.

NOTE

The spinner control works slightly differently across browsers that currently implement it. In the preceding example, clicking down on the spinner in Chrome changes the value from empty to 1, the lowest value. In Opera, clicking down on the empty numerical input changes it to 6, the highest value.

range

The type `<input type="range">` creates a slider that allows users to select a number. Like the number input type, it makes use of `min`, `max`, and `step`.

This time around, the input control takes the `step` a little more strictly. Using the element `<input type="range" min="1" max="6" step="2" />`, you are only able to drag the slider to the 1, 3, and 5 positions on most browsers. Opera is an exception, as it allows you to drag it to 6, but pops up an error message if you try to submit, as shown in Figure 3.9.

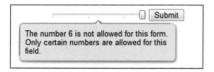

The number 6 is not allowed for this form. Only certain numbers are allowed for this field.

FIGURE 3.9   A range slider, with curious Opera error.

color

The type `<input type="color">` input allows users to select what the W3C calls a "valid simple color," which is a hex string describing an RGB color. Selecting alpha (transparency) values is not currently possible with the color picker.

In Opera, input type brings up a tiny color control with an option for more, which (in Windows) consists of the standard system color picker dialog box. Chrome opts to directly bring up the system color picker when selected. Figure 3.10 shows Opera's built-in color picker and the Windows system color picker.

Dates and Times

The `datetime`, `datetime-local`, `date`, `month`, `week`, and `time` input types are a delightful set of additions to forms that aim to bring some consistency to date and time picking in the browser. Countless websites need date pickers, for scheduling everything from bills to flights to events. Until now, these pickers have typically been implemented either haphazardly or using an off-the-shelf JavaScript plug-in.

In-house or JavaScript plug-in date/time pickers have the disadvantage of possible inaccuracies, such as accounting poorly for leap years. They also suffer from occasional localization issues such as displaying the date in an uncommon format. After all, some countries prefer MM/DD/YYYY, others DD/MM/YYYY, others still YYYY/MM/DD.

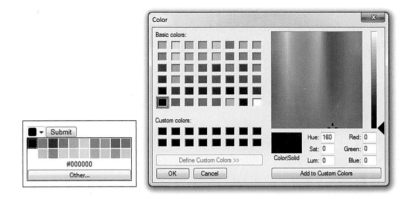

FIGURE 3.10 The built-in color picker in Opera after clicking, and the (system) dialog box that appears in Windows when "Other" is selected.

The HTML5 input types solve these problems by requiring the browser to provide standardized, simple ways of allowing users to select a date or time.

Figure 3.6 (earlier in this section) shows the default presentation of these input types in Chrome and Opera, and Figure 3.11 shows what they look like filled out in Chrome. Notice how weeks are numbered from 1 to 52, and Chrome's control tries to be very clear about which days are counted in each week.

FIGURE 3.11 The date and time input types in Google Chrome, with the calendar appearing for selecting a week.

Figure 3.12 shows an example of the native date picker in Chrome for Android. Because the browser controls the look and feel of the date picker, browser vendors can opt for much more canonical representations per platform to give them a more integrated (native) feel.

FIGURE 3.12   The date picker in Chrome (18) for Android (4.1).

> **NOTE**
>
> There's no `year` type, presumably because a `number` input type with appropriate `min` and `max` attributes would fill that role just fine.

email

The type `<input type="email">` input allows basic email validation. This is useful in catching user errors such as accidental spaces or other obvious hiccups.

Email validation is a tricky process that has caused developers to riddle the Web with erroneous JavaScript that fails to permit many valid emails, such as those with periods or plusses in the address. After all, `!#$%&'*+-/=?^_`{}|~@example` (no `.com` needed) is a valid email address, and there is no simple regular expression to capture all valid (and only valid) emails.

The `email` type attribute is a welcome addition because its availability means that developers do not have to do the (often erroneous) task of email validation themselves, saving both time and grief. Like the `tel` input type, using the `email` type will also bring up a context-dependent touch screen on mobile devices, typically manifesting as a keyboard with additional "@" and ".com" buttons.

Even the best client-side and server-side validation will not stop a misspelling (that results in an otherwise valid email), and the best validation in practice includes sending an email to whatever address was given, typically with an activation link to click.

> **NOTE**
>
> The (WHATWG) HTML5 specification for email validation uses a simplified regular expression that does not precisely match other email specifications. The regular expression used is:
>
> `[a-zA-Z0-9.!#$%&'*+-/=?\^_`{|}~-]+@[a-zA-Z0-9-]+(?:\.[a-zA-Z0-9-]+)*`
>
> In nearly all ways, this is permissive enough to work. The WHATWG explains their intended discrepancy: "This requirement is a willful violation of RFC 5322, which defines a syntax for e-mail addresses that is simultaneously too strict (before the "@" character), too vague (after the "@" character), and too lax (allowing comments, whitespace characters, and quoted strings in manners unfamiliar to most users) to be of practical use here."

Telephone Numbers

The type `<input type="tel">` input allows validation and integrated support for typing in telephone numbers. In many mobile browsers, such as Chrome for Android and Firefox mobile, selecting an input field of type `tel` brings up a number-pad input screen instead of the typical keyboard, as shown in Figure 3.13.

search

Lastly, we have the type `<input type="search">` for entering search strings. Values entered in search input type fields are saved and can be recalled across several pages or page loads. To facilitate this functionality, a new `autosave` attribute has been added that allows you to specify a unique category for the search. Giving this attribute a value (such as `<input type="search" autosave="my_searches">`) means that all searches belonging to fields with the same value will share the same search history.

New Form Input Attributes and Elements

Input elements also sport several new attributes, and not just for the new input types—many of these will see use on plain old `<input type="text">`. These attributes solve problems that previously had to be solved using JavaScript, so like many of the HTML5 features in this chapter, these attributes aim to lessen the burden when developing while standardizing common JavaScript hacks into native functionality.

After attributes, we cover the three new HTML form elements.

FIGURE 3.13   Although none of the new input fields are visually present in Firefox mobile yet, selecting the `tel` input field brings up an appropriate telephone-based touch input.

min, max, and step

As you saw in the `number` and `range` input types, `min` and `max` allow you to constrain the input in terms of stepping and validation. The `min` and `max` attributes also work for dates and times, where an attribute value such as `max="1999-12-31"` would constrain a `date` input to any date before the year 2000.

The `step` determines the amount for controls to increment or decrement numerical fields, and must either be a positive number or the string `"any"`. It also serves a function in the date and time types. For instance, the default `step` in the `time` input type is 60, for 60 seconds, and specifying a different value reveals a "seconds place" on the control in addition to the hours and minutes.

> **NOTE**
>
> All three of these attributes are commonly integers, but floating-point values are perfectly valid.

required

The `required` attribute (`<input type="text" required />`) requires a user to fill out a value to submit a form. This attribute saves the developer from having to write JavaScript demanding that a value exist in a given input element. Figure 3.14 shows the sort of error message that displays if a user attempts submission without filling in a required input.

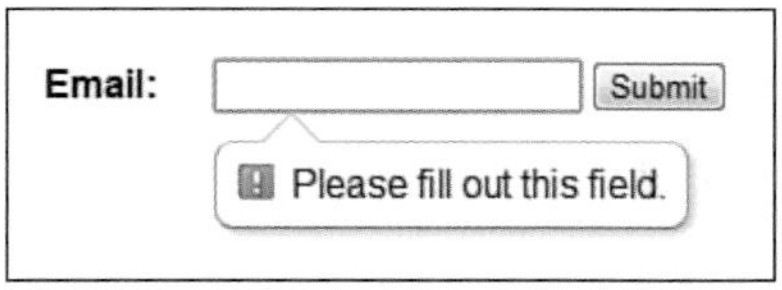

FIGURE 3.14   Attempting to submit a form with an input field using the `required` attribute, in Chrome.

As mentioned near the start of this section, inputs with this attribute can be styled with a special CSS pseudoclass, `:required`. The CSS pseudoclass that styles all nonrequired inputs is named `:optional`.

placeholder

Placeholder text typically exists as slightly faded prefilled values in input fields that disappears as soon as a user begins typing. This can be accomplished natively in HTML5 using the `placeholder` attribute: `<input type="text" placeholder="Placeholder Text!" />`.

Figure 3.15 shows an example of two fields using the `placeholder` attribute.

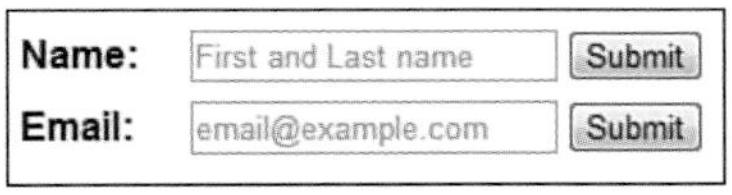

FIGURE 3.15   Name (text) and Email input fields with the `placeholder` attribute.

pattern

The `pattern` attribute allows you to specify a regular expression to check against the input field. If the input does not match the expression, the field does not validate. For instance, the following input:

```
<input type="text" pattern="[A-Za-z]*" title="Only Alphabetic characters!">
```

uses the `pattern` attribute to only allow alphabetic characters. Figure 3.16 shows an example of the kind of error that shows up. Note that the `title` attribute of the input element is displayed in the error. This is important for describing in human terms how to match the given expression.

FIGURE 3.16   An input field demanding only alphabetic characters.

`multiple`

The `multiple` Boolean attribute specifies whether or not a field can accept multiple values. So far, it is only used for the input types `email` and `file`. When a user inputs multiple values incorrectly, a relevant message appears, as shown in Figure 3.17.

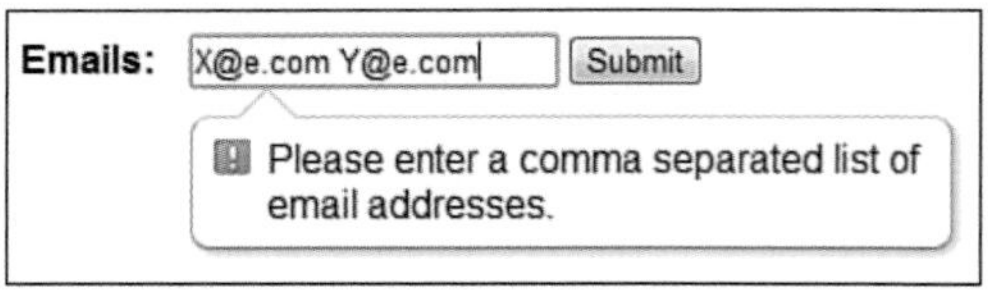

FIGURE 3.17   An email input field with the `multiple` Boolean attribute.

`form`

One of the long-standing annoyances of forms was that they need to have all of their input elements nested inside of the `<form>` tags:

```
<form>
  <input type="email">
  <input type="submit"/> <!-- I'm stuck inside the form tag -->
</form>
```

This presents a problem to designers who want to split up the form inputs in the DOM hierarchy for whatever reason. The common hack has been to wrap as much of the page as needed (sometimes the entire page) in the `<form>` tag. HTML5 introduces a `form` attribute for input elements to solve this problem. The attribute takes an element ID and, if that element is a form, associates itself with that form.

```
<form id="myForm">
  <input type="email">
</form>

<!-- After ten thousand years I'm free! -->
<input type="submit" form="myForm" />
```

The Submit button is now free to be placed anywhere, such as on a static sidebar so that a user can click it to submit the form (perhaps saving his or her work so far) at any time.

`autofocus`, `autocomplete`, and `autosave`

Autofocusing a specific input when the page loads has long been accomplished in several different ways with JavaScript. Some of these methods have been irritating to users, such as those on a timer or demanding page load completion, where a user may select a field and begin filling it out, then suddenly have the focus switched to another element. The `autofocus` Boolean attribute (`<input type="text" autofocus />`) grants this functionality natively, avoiding any implementation hiccups.

If two or more elements have the `autofocus` attribute set, the last one on the page is focused.

The `autocomplete` attribute is new on both input and form elements. This value indicates whether the controls can (by default) have their values stored by the browser. Setting this on an input element overrides any setting on the form itself. When this attribute is set to `off`, the browser does not automatically autocomplete entries. When set to `on` (the default), the browser may provide autocomplete options for the input.

The `autosave` attribute is only relevant to `search` input types, and specifies a unique category under which the search history is saved. A value such as `<input type="search" autosave="my_searches">` recalls the search history of only other search inputs with the `my_searches autosave` value.

Minor Form Input Attributes

Several other new form input attributes deserve a shorter mention:

- ▶ **novalidate (on form elements) and formnovalidate (on submit input elements)**— Boolean attributes that can be used to turn off validation for the form. These can be very useful if you want both a Save and a Submit button, and do not require all input elements to be valid when the user merely wants to save his or her work.

- ▶ **formaction**—An attribute that specifies a location (URL) for sending the form data on submission. This attribute (and the other `form...` attributes) does not add new functionality; it merely adds new specificity. This attribute overrides the form element's `action` attribute.

- ▶ **formenctype**—A new attribute for `submit` input types, used to specify the type of content that is used to submit the form to the server. Possible values are `application/x-www-form-urlencoded` (default), `multipart/form-data`, and `text/plain`. This attribute overrides the form element's `enctype` attribute.

- ▶ **formmethod**—An attribute that specifies the method for form submission, either `post` or `get`. This attribute overrides the form element's `method` attribute.

- ▶ **formtarget**—A name or keyword (such as `_blank`) telling the browser where to display the response from the form. Like the other `form...` attributes, this overrides the form element's `target` attribute.

- ▶ **spellcheck**—An attribute that can be set to `true`, `false`, or `default`, and (sensibly) indicates whether the input field checks for spelling, if the browser allows.

list and the <datalist>

The new `<datalist>` tag is used to specify a list of predefined options for most text-related input elements, and the `list` attribute is used to link an input to a given ID of a datalist element. Unlike using a `<select>` tag, this allows regular text-related inputs to provide additional *optional* predefined choices. For example, the following code produces Figure 3.18:

```
<input type="text" list="myList"  >

<datalist id="myList">
    <option label="Gluten free" value="Rosemary Chicken">
    <option label="Gluten free" value="Haddock and Potatoes">
    <option label="Vegetarian" value="Eggplant Parmesan">
</datalist>
```

FIGURE 3.18   Both the label and the value are shown in Chrome's datalist drop-down. Selecting a list item would place the `value` of that option into the input field.

NOTE

Unfortunately, you need to be careful how you use the `label` and `value` attributes of datalist options in practice. In Firefox, the values are not shown in the drop-down, only labels are, so the example seen in Figure 3.18 creates an unhelpful-looking list: A user sees only "Gluten free," "Gluten free," and "Vegetarian." Selecting an option in Firefox still places the `value` into the input, however, so selecting "Vegetarian" still correctly populates the text input with "Eggplant Parmesan."

`<output>`

The new `<output>` tag is designed to display the result of calculations, typically inside of forms. The output element is largely semantic in utility, and has only one unique attribute, `for`, which can specify a space-separated list of IDs of other elements that affect the calculation. The following code produces Figure 3.19, with the output element showing the result:

```
<form oninput="result.value=myRange.valueAsNumber+myNumber.valueAsNumber">
  0<input type="range" id="r1" name="myRange" value="50" />100 +
  <input type="number" id="n1" name="myNumber" value="25" /> =
  <output name="result" for="r1 n1"></output>
</form>
```

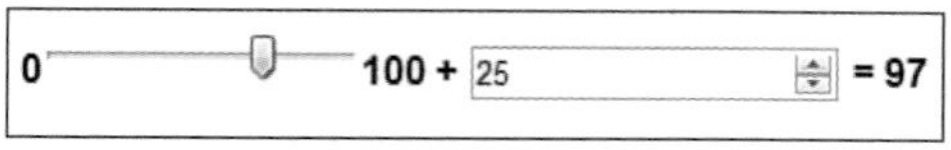

FIGURE 3.19   The value 72 is selected on the range, and the output displays the sum, 97.

`<keygen>`

The new `<keygen>` tag defines a key-pair generator for forms, for use in client authentication. When a form is submitted, the keygen element generates a public-private key pair, sending the public key to the server on form submission.

The keygen element has a very specific utility, and although it is new to the HTML specification, it has been around for some time. Unfortunately, it is not implemented in Internet Explorer 9 or 10, and the Internet Explorer team has suggested that any implementation in the future is extremely unlikely. Because it has a narrow utility and is new to HTML as a specification formality only, we do not cover this element in depth here.

Drag and Drop in HTML5

The ability to drag and drop arbitrary HTML elements has long been desired, and many popular scripts have arisen to fill the role over the years. As with most new HTML5 features, the HTML5 drag-and-drop API intends to incorporate this oft-used functionality into a native API.

Unfortunately for programmers, the drag-and-drop API is commonly considered the clumsiest part of HTML5. Several rants have been published about its somewhat confusing rules, which are loosely a product of reverse engineering Microsoft's drag-and-drop implementation that began with Internet Explorer 5. In spite of its odd nature, it has some support in every modern desktop browser, and certainly has enough use cases to warrant inclusion into HTML5.

As of this writing, browsers handle the components of drag and drop differently, sometimes with minor incompatibilities between themselves and the specification. As with any new feature, if you use the drag-and-drop API, you should be sure to test it on every browser you are targeting before using the code in production.

This section first covers the essentials of HTML drag and drop and ends with a complete code example.

The Basics

At its simplest, drag and drop allows a user to click and hold on certain HTML elements, drag the cursor elsewhere, and release. The drop location may be another page element, the address bar, or another application entirely.

Most browsers have several default drag operations built in. Typically, you can drag images to a folder to save them, drag text to select, and drag selections of text or links to copy them. With the HTML5 API, any arbitrary HTML elements are valid drag-and-drop targets.

To make an element draggable, you must fulfill two requirements:

▶ The element's `draggable` attribute must be set to `true`.

▶ The element must have a `dragstart` event defined.

Listing 3.3 shows a simple example.

LISTING 3.3   Dragging Requirements

```
<div id="myDragDiv" draggable="true">
  You can't select this text, but you can drag it!
</div>

<script type="text/javascript">
  var myDrag = document.getElementById('myDragDiv');
  myDrag.addEventListener('dragstart', function(e) {
    e.dataTransfer.setData("text/plain",
      "You can't select this text, but you can drag it!");
  });
</script>
```

This code produces a page with a single line of text, but the text is different in that you cannot select (highlight) it as usual. Instead, when you click on it and move the cursor, the entire line of text is dragged with it as if it were a single object. Figure 3.20 shows what this drag operation looks like in practice.

FIGURE 3.20   Dragging the sample div over an empty page and over the address bar of Firefox. Note cursor changes.

In Figure 3.20, you see that the cursor changes if it is over an acceptable drop location. The text can be dropped into the address bar, but not on the empty area of the page.

> **NOTE**
>
> In Firefox, you can select text in a draggable element by holding the Alt key. In Opera, double- and triple-clicking still allows word and paragraph selection. In some versions of Internet Explorer, the text is still selectable as normal, and more work is needed to get it to act like a single draggable object (sometimes with the use of <a> tags that link to nothing).

In Listing 3.3, we defined the `dragstart` event and called `e.dataTransfer.setData`, providing the method a copy of the text content of the div. This text is the content that gets dragged, not the text in the div (which just so happens to be identical for this example). The result of dragging this div places the `dataTransfer.setData` contents into whatever acceptable location is found, such as the address bar or a `<textarea>`. The first argument to `dataTransfer.setData` describes the type of data to be dragged, which we discuss in further detail shortly.

Any element can be draggable, though none are by default—except for links and images. You can set these to `draggable="false"` if you want, though doing so is often a loss for usability. You learn about custom dropping behavior later in this section.

Drag Data and Effects

All drag events have a property called `dataTransfer` that holds relevant information during the dragging process, including the drag data and associated drag effects.

Drag Data

During a drag event, data can be set and retrieved using the methods `event.dataTransfer.setData(MIME-type, data)` and `event.dataTransfer.getData(MIME-type)`, respectively. Data must be set to identify what is being dragged, and multiple types of data can be specified for a single drag.

When a drag begins on the `dragstart` event, all of the relevant data types should be set. During `dragenter` and `dragover` events, these types can be checked to see if any applicable data type is acceptable for a drop. When a drop occurs, the `drop` event listener should retrieve the appropriate data type and do its intended action.

Typical types of data set on the `event.dataTransfer` object are "text/plain," "text/uri-list," and "text/html." Less common as of this writing, some browsers (like Firefox) support image and file type dragging. Instead of direct image dragging, dragging images by URL (using the "text/uri-list" MIME type) is very common.

> **NOTE**
>
> In some versions of Internet Explorer, you must use the strings `"text"` and `"url"` instead of actual MIME type strings.

In setting our drag data, we need to be sure to call `setData` on the types in the order we want them to have priority. Let's see an example:

```
var myDraggableElement = document.getElementById('myDragDiv');
myDraggableElement.addEventListener('dragstart', function(event) {
  var data = event.dataTransfer;
  data.setData("text/uri-list", "http://example.com");
  data.setData("text/plain", "<strong>Some HTML!</strong>");
  data.setData("text/plain", "Text instead!");
});
```

In this case, dragging `myDraggableElement` (whatever element it might be) onto the address bar would drop the URL `"http://example.com"`, and dragging the element into a `<textarea>` would drop the `"Text instead!"` data because text areas only accept `"text/plain"` data.

It is important to set the data in the right order, typically from most specific data type to least, and to always provide a plain text alternative, especially when using browser-specific types such as images on Firefox.

NOTE

For some elements, some browsers may automatically populate "text/plain" or "text/ html" data for you, but this should not be relied on.

Attempting to set data twice with the same MIME type clears the old data. There is additionally an `event.dataTransfer.clearData(MIME_TYPE)` method to clear a specific type, or to clear all data types if no argument is given.

If by the end of your `dragstart` event, no data is set, then no drop occurs.

Drag Effects

Several different kinds of operations may be accomplished with dragging, so the drag-and-drop API allows for optional settable effects to hint at the proper behavior, and browsers appropriately create different visual cues to match.

During the `dragstart` event, the `event.dataTransfer.effectAllowed` property can be set to any of the following string values:

- ▶ `all`
- ▶ `none`
- ▶ `copy`
- ▶ `move`
- ▶ `link`
- ▶ `copyMove`
- ▶ `copyLink`
- ▶ `linkMove`

The default value is `all`, which allows for copy, move, and link operations. The other values are different combinations of the possible operation types.

Once you've dragged over an element, during that element's `dragover` event, you may set the related `dropEffect` property on `event.dataTransfer`. The valid values for `dropEffect` are `none`, `copy`, `move`, or `link`, and can be used to allow different elements (at different times or during different key presses) to limit the kinds of drag data they will receive.

Let's see an example. Listing 3.4 defines a `dragstart` event for one div and `dragover` event for another.

LISTING 3.4   `dragstart` and `dragover` Events

```
// startmove is a DIV with draggable="true"
var startmove = document.getElementById('startmove');
startmove.addEventListener('dragstart', function(e) {
  e.dataTransfer.effectAllowed = 'move';
  e.dataTransfer.setData('text/plain', "hello!");
}, false);

// endmove is our destination DIV for dragging
var endmove = document.getElementById('endmove');
endmove.addEventListener('dragover', function(e) {
  e.dataTransfer.dropEffect = 'move';
  e.preventDefault(); // This is necessary!
}, false);
```

Using different values of `effectAllowed` and `dropEffect` changes how browsers display the dragging operations. Figure 3.21 shows three instances of dragging operations, with the first using the JavaScript from Listing 3.4. The move effect is visible as the dragged div is largely transparent and the cursor changes to suit. The second set of divs in Figure 3.21 is using a copy effect instead, and the dragged div and cursor are visibly different to match. The third part of Figure 3.21 shows what a mismatch between the `effectAllowed` and the `dropEffect` looks like, with the typical "disallowed" cursor displayed.

FIGURE 3.21   Dragging divs with different `effectAllowed` and `dropEffect` values, as seen in the div text.

You don't actually have to set the `dropEffect` if you want it to always accept drags because the `dropEffect` starts out initialized to the effect of the drag operation that is occurring. When there is a mismatch between the `effectAllowed` and the `dropEffect`, drop events are prevented from occurring.

Drag Events

Seven events are raised during the course of a drag. In the order they occur during dragging, they are as follows:

- **dragstart**—Occurs on the draggable element where the drag starts, when the drag starts. Programmers need to set relevant drag data during this event.

- **dragenter**—Occurs when the cursor is moved over an element during a drag. This event is not essential to dragging but is often the appropriate place to do actions (such as custom highlighting or animation) indicating whether or not a drag is allowed. This event is essential to dropping because it must cancel its default action (by returning false or calling event.preventDefault()) in order for the drop event to fire. Most browsers no longer bother with this specification requirement for dragenter.

- **dragover**—Occurs when the cursor is over an element during a drag. This method typically does many of the same actions that dragenter might, but unlike dragenter, this event occurs constantly, even if the cursor is not moving. This event is essential to dropping because it must cancel its default action in order for the drop event to fire.

- **drag**—Happens constantly, even when the cursor isn't moving, so long as the drag is occurring. Unlike dragover, it occurs on the source element. In spite of its name, it is rarely used in drag operations.

- **dragleave**—Occurs when the cursor is moved off of an element during a drag. Like dragenter, this event is nonessential to dragging, but is the appropriate place to remove indicators of whether or not a drag is allowed.

- **drop**—Occurs when the cursor is released, and only occurs on an element that is an acceptable target.

- **dragend**—Occurs at the end of a drag, regardless of whether a successful drop occurred. Although this event is not essential to dragging, it is the appropriate place to reset cosmetic changes that were made during the dragstart event (such as making the source element semitransparent during a drag).

If you didn't catch it from the descriptions, the way to enable dropping on an element (or specify the element as an appropriate drop target) is to cancel the default action of both the dragenter and dragover events. You see examples of this later.

Event Oddities

When people refer to the HTML5 drag-and-drop specification as a clumsy API, they are typically referring to a series of odd requirements in the events. In no particular order, these issues among others are considered odd:

- Drag data must be set whether or not you intend to use it. Many valid uses of drag and drop have no need for the drag data.

▶ The arguments for drag data differ between Internet Explorer and the other browsers, with Internet Explorer not quite following the specification, even though the specification was originally modeled on Internet Explorer's drag and drop.

▶ According to the specification, you must cancel (call `return false` or `event.preventDefault()` during the event) both the `dragenter` and `dragover` events for the `drop` event to ever fire. Some argue that this is useful on `dragover` because that event could be defined on everything (or the entire document) and then the code inside the event may determine whether or not something is a valid drop target. The same excuse seems thin for `dragenter`, however, and most browsers have removed the requirement for its cancellation in spite of the spec.

▶ Some argue further that having both `drag` and `dragover` seems redundant. After all, there's no `mouse` and `mouseover`, just `mouseover`.

Drag and drop is arguably one of the most convoluted APIs in HTML5. More than any other topic in this book, you should be sure to search the Web for examples that closely resemble what you are trying to accomplish before you reinvent the common migraine on your own.

In Action

Let's set up a complete example. We will utilize every event except `drag`, which is usually reserved for running animations and other minor constantly occurring events.

In spite of using all the events but one, this is by no means a comprehensive example of drag-and-drop capabilities. Some browsers, especially Firefox, can do much more with drag and drop, such as drag files. It's always worth searching for novel examples on the Web, especially if you have a specific dragging task in mind.

Our goal here is to enable the reordering of draggable divs inside of container divs. We don't bother with divs swapping places, so we always need more container divs than draggable divs so that we have somewhere to move them when rearranging.

The Divs

The example consists of several container "dropzone" divs, inside of which one "draggable" div may rest. We use CSS classes to distinguish between the two types, and make sure that we are setting `draggable="true"` on the relevant divs:

```
<!-- four "dropzone" divs, three of them have "draggable" divs inside. -->
<div class="dropzone">
  <div class="draggable" draggable="true">Water</div>
</div>
<div class="dropzone">
  <div class="draggable" draggable="true">Coffee</div>
</div>
<div class="dropzone">
```

```
    <div class="draggable" draggable="true">Tea</div>
</div>
<div class="dropzone"></div>
```

We start with adding four dropzone divs, with three of them containing draggable divs. We add enough CSS to make the divs visually distinct, though the styling code isn't particularly important (it is present in the final code listing). We can see in Figure 3.22 that the "dropzone" divs are larger and blue.

FIGURE 3.22   Our four dropzone divs and three draggable divs.

The Necessary Events

For a complete drag-and-drop sequence to function, we need to define four events. We need dragstart on the draggable divs and dragenter (only *needed* for Internet Explorer), dragover, and drop on the "dropzone" divs.

Instead of finding all of the draggable divs and attaching a dragstart event to each, we simply add one event to the page's document. When the event fires, we disregard it (return) unless the target element is of the draggable class, in which case we save a reference to the element being dragged and set some drag data. We don't use drag data for this example, but it must be set nonetheless in order for a drag event to successfully occur. Listing 3.5 shows a no-frills dragstart event.

LISTING 3.5   dragstart

```
var dragged = null; // A reference to the element currently being dragged

document.addEventListener("dragstart", function(event) {
  if (event.target.className !== "draggable") return;
  // Some data must be set to allow drag
  event.dataTransfer.setData("text", "");

  // store a reference to the dragged element
  dragged = event.target;
}, false);
```

For the other three events, we add them directly to each relevant div instead of the document. We can find all of the "dropzone" divs using the new (in HTML5) method `document.getElementsByClassName()`, which takes a class name and returns a list of all elements of that class.

The `dragenter` and `dragover` events do their duty of canceling the default action, so that drop actually fires. The `dragover` event additionally checks to see if there's already a child inside of a dropzone, disallowing a drag (by not canceling the event) if it finds any child. Finally, the drop event removes the div saved from `dragstart` and places it in the target of the `drop` event. Listing 3.6 contains the definitions of the `dragenter`, `dragover`, and `drop` events.

LISTING 3.6   `dragenter`, `dragover`, and `drop`

```javascript
var dropdivs = document.getElementsByClassName('dropzone');

var l = dropdivs.length;
for (var i = 0; i < l; i++) {
  var div = dropdivs[i];
  div.addEventListener("dragenter", function(event) {
    // Requirement in some browsers, such as Internet Explorer
    event.preventDefault();
  }, false);

  div.addEventListener("dragover", function(event) {
    var t = event.target; // The object we are dragging over
    if (t.className !== "dropzone" || t.firstElementChild !== null) {
      // Disallow a drop by returning before a call to preventDefault:
      return;
    }

    // Allow a drop on everything else
    event.preventDefault();
  }, false);


  div.addEventListener("drop", function(event) {
    // prevent default action
    // (open as link for some elements in some browsers)
    event.preventDefault();
    // move dragged element to the drop target
    if (event.target.className == "dropzone") {
      dragged.parentNode.removeChild(dragged);
      event.target.appendChild(dragged);
    }
  }, false);
}
```

This gives us enough functionality for dragging and dropping our divs among containers, but without effects it is often difficult to tell just what's allowed and what isn't.

Adding Effects

Cosmetic effects are particularly important for drag-and-drop operations. When we create functionality in web pages or apps, it's all too easy for us authors to envision the functionality of different parts while forgetting that it might not be obvious or even discoverable for users who do not have the same prior knowledge of its workings.

The very first thing we should do is offer our users some instruction. For our example, a line of text telling users to "Drag and drop to rearrange the menu" will do.

The second thing we should do is look for some way to create an *affordance*. Affordances are cues built in to the design of physical or digital things that allow a user to discern that some action is possible. Knobs afford turning, and switches afford toggling. Handles on physical objects provide an affordance for holding or picking up an object. There are digital handles, too, such as those on the bottom-right of many windows, which aim to give an indication that the window can be resized.

Good design of draggable elements should have at least some sort of visual cue of what can be dragged (and what can't), at the least something to set it apart from other (undraggable) elements on the page. Our sample is too simple, so we don't have anything particularly interesting in the way of visual affordances other than different colored divs for the containers, but the concept is worth giving careful consideration to in practice.

Another visual cue, changing the cursor, is one of the best affordances we have. There's a built-in cursor well suited to the task, `cursor: move`. This should be set in our draggable class's CSS.

We also want to create visual cues during the dragging process itself. On the `dragenter` event, we check whether a dropzone contains an element or not and change its background color to either red or bright green, indicating any allowed zones:

```
div.addEventListener("dragenter", function(event) {
  // highlight potential drop target when the draggable element enters
  var t = event.target; // The object we are dragging over
  if (t.className !== "dropzone") return;
  if (t.firstElementChild !== null) {
    t.style.background = 'red';
  } else {
    t.style.background = 'lime';
  }
  // ...
}
```

We need to also define a complementary `dragleave` event that resets the effect:

```
div.addEventListener("dragleave", function(event) {
  // reset background of potential drop target
  if (event.target.className == "dropzone") {
    event.target.style.background = "";
  }
}, false);
```

We can also add effects to the dragged object in the `dragstart` and `dragend` events. In our example, we highlight the element with an added red border (code in the next section), but several other effects are popular. Common effects include giving any transparent background a semitransparent color (common when selecting and dragging icons), giving opaque backgrounds some transparency (done automatically with drag and drop in many browsers), and making the dragged element slightly larger or smaller, to stand out from the others.

All Together

With our mechanics and effects in place, we have a rudimentary but complete drag-and-drop sample, using every event but `drag` itself. Figure 3.23 shows stages in the complete process. The cursor changes to "move" as we hover over a draggable element, and changes appropriately as we drag over different dropzones, with our additional effects visible.

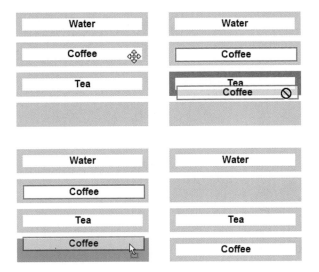

FIGURE 3.23   The dragging process in our sample. Note the cursor and effect changes.

Listing 3.7 contains the complete code for the sample.

LISTING 3.7   `dragdrop.html`—Complete Drag-and-Drop Example

```
<!DOCTYPE head>
<!--
  HTML5 Drag and Drop example
  based on an excellent Mozilla Developer Network (MDN) example
-->
<html>
<head>
  <title>Drag and Drop Example</title>
  <meta charset="utf-8">
  <style>
    .draggable {
      font: bold 16px sans-serif;
      width: 200px;
      height: 20px;
      text-align: center;
      background: white;
      cursor: move;
    }

    .dropzone {
      width: 200px;
      height: 20px;
      background: lightblue;
      margin-bottom: 10px;
      padding: 10px;
    }
  </style>
</head>

<body>
  <p>Drag and drop to rearrange the menu!</p>
  <!-- four "dropzone" divs, three of them have "draggable" divs inside. -->
  <div class="dropzone">
    <div class="draggable" draggable="true">Water</div>
  </div>
  <div class="dropzone">
    <div class="draggable" draggable="true">Coffee</div>
  </div>
  <div class="dropzone">
    <div class="draggable" draggable="true">Tea</div>
  </div>
  <div class="dropzone"></div>

<script>
```

```
var dragged = null; // A reference to the element currently being dragged

// This event should only fire on the drag targets.
// Instead of finding every drag target,
// we can add the event to the document and disregard
// all elements that are not of class "draggable"
document.addEventListener("dragstart", function(event) {
  if (event.target.className !== "draggable") return;
  // Some data must be set to allow drag
  event.dataTransfer.setData("text", "");

  // store a reference to the dragged element
  dragged = event.target;
  // Objects during drag will have a red border
  event.target.style.border = "2px solid red";
}, false);

// Below are events intended for the drop targets

// To get a list of all the divs of class 'dropzone', we'll use
// getElementsByClassName, a new method in HTML5!
// (getElementsByClassName originated in Opera 9.5)
var dropdivs = document.getElementsByClassName('dropzone');

var l = dropdivs.length;
for (var i = 0; i < l; i++) {
  var div = dropdivs[i];
  div.addEventListener("dragenter", function(event) {
    // highlight potential drop target when the draggable element enters
    var t = event.target; // The object we are dragging over
    if (t.className !== "dropzone") return;
      if (t.firstElementChild !== null) {
        t.style.background = 'red';
      } else {
        t.style.background = 'lime';
      }

    // Requirement in some browsers, such as Internet Explorer
    event.preventDefault();
  }, false);

  div.addEventListener("dragover", function(event) {
    // We call preventDefault to allow a drop
    // But on divs that already contain an element,
    // we want to disallow dropping
```

```
    var t = event.target; // The object we are dragging over
    if (t.className !== "dropzone" || t.firstElementChild !== null) {
      // Disallow a drop by returning before a call to preventDefault:
      return;
    }

    // Allow a drop on everything else
    event.preventDefault();
  }, false);

  div.addEventListener("dragleave", function(event) {
    // reset background of potential drop target
    if (event.target.className == "dropzone") {
      event.target.style.background = "";
    }
  }, false);

  div.addEventListener("drop", function(event) {
    // prevent default action
    // (open as link for some elements in some browsers)
    event.preventDefault();
    // move dragged element to the drop target
    if (event.target.className == "dropzone") {
      event.target.style.background = "";
      dragged.parentNode.removeChild(dragged);
      event.target.appendChild(dragged);
    }

    // If we were using drag data, we could get it here, ie:
    // var data = event.dataTransfer.getData('text');
    // Alas, for this simple example all we need are the event.target
    // and our saved "dragged" element
  }, false);

  div.addEventListener("dragend", function(event) {
    // reset the border
    event.target.style.border = "";
  }, false);
}

</script>

</body>
</html>
```

Next Steps

If you try this example in Internet Explorer 9, you'll notice that dragging is a tad fickle. You have to select some text in our example in order to initiate the drag. In the case of Internet Explorer 9, only `<a>` tags and `<img>` tags are draggable, so a bit of a hack is needed for proper function. In situations like our example, we would fulfill this requirement by surrounding our text content in `<a>` tags that do not link anywhere.

It's also worth noting that we were setting useless data just so the event would be considered a valid drag when we wrote `event.dataTransfer.setData("text", "")`. Without setting the data, no drag would occur on most browsers. Additionally, Internet Explorer demands `"text"` or `"url"` instead of a real MIME type for the first argument and (unlike other desktop browsers) cannot accept `null` as a second argument.

Good dragging that works across all browsers can be a very tricky process, depending on what you're trying to accomplish, and can often result in adding unintuitive code and styling to an app. As always, make sure that your page works as intended on all targeted browsers.

This is by no means a comprehensive example, and much more specific and useful examples abound on the Web. Before starting a drag-and-drop project, it would be wise to search for examples and samples from others who have attempted similar operations.

Summary

We've covered quite a bit here, and should have a firm grasp on the basics of HTML5 and the intended goals. We've seen several new elements that largely serve to better organize the Web, a boon to content creators and curators, especially search engines. In addition, we have covered a number of new elements and attributes in HTML5 that reduce the (JavaScript) code burden on getting modern page functionality (such as validation) up and running and introduce some new standardized visual elements for web pages.

Finally, we looked at our first API in HTML5, the DOM-element drag and drop. Although it's a bit of a black sheep (it's even in an odd place in this text), it's sure to find its uses on the Web.

With a library or two to ensure older browsers don't croak, nearly everything in this chapter is safely usable today.

We're nearly done with all of the small elements in HTML5, and the coming chapters focus in-depth on three of the most exciting HTML5 tags, `<audio>`, `<video>`, and `<canvas>`. After those, we take a look at more new JavaScript APIs, and finish up with other small mentions and future sightings.

Rich Media Tags: Video and Audio

Rich content on the Web has come a long way from the designs of the mid-1990s. Back then, most websites described as "rich" or "graphical" had been called so less for any added utility but rather because of superfluous odds and ends. This was an era of faux 3D GIFs, 8-bit background tunes that could be turned off only by turning off your speakers, and perhaps a video or two, if you were willing to download a plug-in (or two!).

If you have missed or forgotten this ungracious period of common web design, several sites (such as archive.org and reocities.com) have sought to chronicle the pages of decades gone by. In Figure 4.1, we have a specimen from a mirror of Geocities, a popular Yahoo!-owned site that let anyone create a (small) website for free.

In case you might miss them, the author saw fit to denote links using italic, underlining, red, and all-caps text, with an added "go" image at the end. In case you needed more distraction, four irrelevant GIFs dot the periphery with faux 3D animations and carrot chewing.

Even clean and professional sites from this era, as many of us may remember, looked quaint compared with common websites of the modern web era. Figure 4.2 shows an approximation of the Yahoo! main page in 1996.

FIGURE 4.1   A reocities.com mirror of an ancient Geocities page from a less-subtle era of web design.

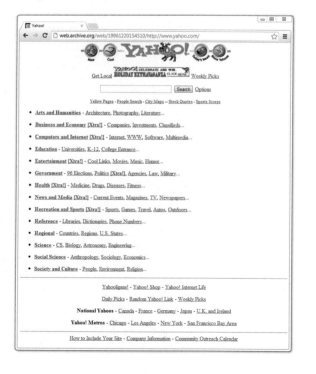

FIGURE 4.2   An archive.org mirror of the Yahoo! of yesteryear.

We've come a long way since the '90s. Websites today are generally cleaner, with design elements more understated, even down to the littlest parts. Times New Roman is out, sans-serif fonts rule the day. Links are no longer commonly underlined (except on mouse hover), and this generally holds true on even the more plain and stuffy sites such as Wikipedia. Perhaps most graciously of all, images tend to only move if they have good reason to, and background music is almost universally considered in bad taste. Autoplaying elements are reserved for advertising (which may still remain obnoxious for the foreseeable future, but has come a long way) and pages that solely serve media, like YouTube and music-centric websites.

Today the websites that are considered *dynamic* are ones with interactive elements, meaningful videos or animation, and user-generated content. An improvement no doubt, but although almost all past form and function graduated from the '90s, the delivery mechanism of audio and video did not. Almost imperceptibly, plug-ins have ruled web media for more than a decade.

HTML5—in its effort for a more native web—hopes to claw back this functionality from the grasp of plug-ins and return it to the domain of the browser. The new `<audio>` and `<video>` tags are very good developments in turning the Web into a natively rich experience and should be a driving force in bringing designers closer to developers.

As the HTML5 media tags become ubiquitous, the creators of the Web will no longer need a third set of plug-in-specific skills to display and style rich media. Thanks to the very reasonable fallback options that already exist, we can start creating native media sites today.

The Video Element

The new video and audio elements intentionally share a good deal of properties that carry out similar functions, so we cover them in an interwoven fashion, but before we can discuss the elements themselves, we need to take a look at the key differences regarding browser support and acceptable content formats.

Video Formats and Support

As of this writing, the video element enjoys near ubiquitous support. It is present in every modern browser, desktop and mobile, except Opera Mini.

Video *formats*, however, are not so universally present, and as of this writing you must host your videos in different formats for them to play in different browsers. When making media for the `<video>` tag, you need to consider three main video formats:

▶ **Mpeg-4/H.264**—Using the H.264 codec for its video stream and AAC for its audio stream. Mpeg-4 is often abbreviated as MP4, which lends itself to the typical file extension, `.mp4`.

▶ **Ogg/Theora**—Using Theora for video and Vorbis for audio. This typically uses the file extension `.ogv`.

▶ **WebM/VP8**—Using VP8 for video and Vorbis for audio. This uses the file extension `.webm`.

MP4

MP4 is one of the most popular video formats, but it is not royalty free. When plug-ins like Flash and Silverlight play video, they are almost always using this format. This is the format that powers most heavyweight video on the Web, such as YouTube, Vimeo, and iTunes videos.

At the time of writing, MP4 for the video element is supported by Internet Explorer 9, Chrome, Safari (and iOS), and Android's browser. Firefox and Opera (including Opera Mini) do not support this format.

The future of support for the MP4 format is unclear. Chrome is considering dropping support, citing principles of openness and disdain for the royalty and licensing requirements that come with the format. Firefox, on the other hand, is considering adding support for MP4, citing the simple practicality that users prefer a web that works *right now* over idealism.

As we discuss later, video content needs to be served in at least two formats for the time being. Thankfully, both Chrome and Firefox support the other two formats so the decision to include or drop MP4 support does not affect the overall practicality of the video element.

Theora

Ogg Theora is an open source alternative to MP4/H.264. It has been around since 2004, when a company called On2 donated a codec it developed (called VP3) to the open source community. Its age gives it a market share plus among the open source crowd and it has enjoyed serious use on Wikipedia, but its age also poses a hindrance to widespread adoption. Theora wasn't designed with modern demands in mind, such as HD streaming over broadband connections, and allegedly the codec would need substantial improvements before it could power large, streaming sites.

Theora is supported by Firefox, Chrome, and Opera, but not Internet Explorer 9 and Safari, and the format is not supported by a single mobile browser! Because WebM is a more modern open source competitor, Theora's long-term viability as a major video element format can be considered unlikely.

WebM

WebM is a high-quality, open source, royalty-free video format. Like Theora, the video codec (called VP8) was originally developed by On2, and it was subsequently purchased by Google with the intention of open-sourcing it to make a more modern royalty-free standard.

Video is now a major part of the Web, especially for Google in properties such as YouTube, Google Chat, and Google+, so making a modern (and open) video codec is highly relevant to their interests. Firefox and Opera have also joined in with formal support of the project and also sponsor its development.

WebM is currently supported by Chrome, Firefox, Opera (but not Opera Mini), and the Android browser. Although it isn't natively supported by Internet Explorer 9 and Safari, it works if the user has WebM codecs installed on his or her machine.

Codec Comparison

Table 4.1 gives a compatibility chart for the desktop browsers. Such a chart for mobile browsers is not as easy to produce because codecs can be both device specific and browser specific.

TABLE 4.1   Video Codec Support by Desktop Browser

	MP4	WebM	Ogg/Theora
Chrome	Yes[1]	Yes	Yes
Firefox	No[2]	Yes	Yes
Internet Explorer 9+	Yes	No[3]	No
Safari	Yes	No[3]	Yes
Opera	No	Yes	Yes

[1] Chrome has considered discontinuing support for MP4.

[2] Firefox has considered supporting MP4 in the future.

[3] Internet Explorer 9 and Safari will play WebM if a codec is installed manually.

If you're wondering which format to use, Table 4.1 provides the simple answer: More than one!

Realistically, you'll need to supply at least two formats for now, ideally MP4 and WebM, to ensure that every device is supported. Ogg Theora, at least currently, is simply not as widely used or web friendly as the other two because no mobile devices support it.

Some users may still want (or need) the Theora format and if you can afford the space and time to encode a third version of each video, then by all means you should provide it. Unless mobile browser vendors begin to show interest, though, its days are probably numbered.

The upcoming section titled "Encoding Your Media" covers how to create multiple video formats.

NOTE

What codec should I give preference to?

There are a multitude of essays, arguments, and benchmarks on the Web about WebM versus MP4, but we can summarize all of them.

They're approximately the same.

Well, except MP4 has more hardware accelerated support *for now*, and decoding video in hardware saves more battery life than decoding it in software. However, the turnover rate for mobile devices is very short, and this is unlikely to stay an issue for much longer.

Current Support

It is always best to check online to see if all platforms you are targeting have implemented the application programming interfaces (APIs) and formats you intend to use. Sites such as caniuse.com aggregate the HTML5 API and feature implementation status and aid you with the current status of the `<video>` tag, video format, and full-screen API support.

Regardless of what Internet resources tell you about each browser and platform, it's still good practice to test your videos (and pages) on every device available to you.

Testing for Support

Sometimes you might need to programmatically determine if a user supports the video element. You can accomplish this by attempting to create a video element and testing to see if a supported function of that video element exists.

```
// returns true if the HTML video element exists, false otherwise
function checkForVideo() {
  return (!!document.createElement('video').canPlayType);
}
```

Additionally, you might want to go deeper than just support for the video element. If you have an incomplete combination of video formats, you need to do further testing, perhaps providing a fallback in the case of a browser that can play HTML video but cannot play any of the supplied video formats.

The video element sports a method, `canPlayType`, that takes a MIME (Multipurpose Internet Mail Extensions) type, and optionally codecs, as a string and returns a string describing whether or not it supports that type or codec combination. Listing 4.1 provides the common type definitions used to test for support.

LISTING 4.1   Testing for Individual Video Format Support

```
var v = document.createElement('video');
var oggTest = v.canPlayType('video/ogg; codecs="theora, vorbis"');
var h264Test = v.canPlayType('video/mp4; codecs="avc1.42E01E, mp4a.40.2"');
var webmTest = v.canPlayType('video/webm; codecs="vp8, vorbis"');
// (Possibly do a custom action if browser can or cannot play a certain type)
```

The `canPlayType` method returns `"probably"` if the type is most likely to be supported.

The method returns `"maybe"` if it is less certain that the format can be played. This value is often the case if you only specify the MIME type and no codecs.

Finally, the method returns `""` (the empty string) if the browser does not think it can play the format at all.

The `canPlayType` method is typically only useful if you need to have a customized response to a user's inability to play any of your formats. If you already provide enough formats, you need not worry, and if you are unable to provide at least two formats, then there are libraries that can instantly embed a Flash player to provide video support. If the user cannot play your videos for any reason, the upcoming section titled "Supporting Older Browsers" details several fallback methods.

Using the Video Element

If you've used an `<img>` tag before, you can guess what a `<video>` tag might look like. At its simplest, you can specify a video and a `src` attribute:

```
<video src="video1.webm"></video>
```

This works, but because you need to specify multiple sources for multiple video files (each of a different encoding), creating a video on a page typically consists of the `<video>` tag in conjunction with one or more nested `<source>` tags. Here's a typical example:

```
<video>
   <source src="video1.webm" type="video/webm" />
   <source src="video1.mp4" type="video/mp4" />
   <source src="video1.ogv" type="video/ogg" />
</video>
```

The nested source elements allow you to specify multiple video formats. The browser looks through them in sequential order until it finds one that it can play.

That's all that's needed to get a simple video onto your page. Figure 4.3 shows a basic video on an otherwise blank HTML page.

FIGURE 4.3   A video element on a page. By default, it is difficult to tell that it is a video at all.

Because it is not obvious that the image on the page is actually a video, the video element has one practically essential attribute, controls. This attribute affords the element a standard set of video interface features, such as a Play/Pause button, a seek bar, a volume adjustment, and an indication of time elapsed or time remaining. The default controls allow web developers and designers to quickly get a video player up and running without any need to get involved in the JavaScript. Turning on these built-in controls is as easy as adding the attribute:

```
<video controls="controls">
  <source src="video1.webm" type="video/webm" />
  <source src="video1.mp4" type="video/mp4" />
  <source src="video1.ogv" type="video/ogg" />
</video>
```

Figure 4.4 gives an example of a video with the default controls added. The controls make it much more obvious that it is a video and not just a still image.

FIGURE 4.4   The video element from Figure 4.3 with the default controls activated.

The built-in controls for every browser are fairly clean and intuitive but they need not preclude you from building your own. If your site has the need for more fine-grained control of your video element or you want to integrate the feel and function of the video controls, the JavaScript API offers many attributes and methods for the observation and manipulation of the video state.

Always Specify the type Attribute of a Source Element

The type attribute of a source element is an additional hint to the browser about what file format is specified in the source. It's optional to specify but is a good practice to do so.

When you specify a MIME type, you are making a "promise" to the browser that allows it to intelligently determine which files it needs to download and which it can skip over, saving both the server and the client from spending unnecessary bandwidth.

If you promise that the first video is of type "video/webm," and the browser cannot play that format, it moves on to the next source, not bothering to download the WebM video file. The media tags aim to be clever: Not only do browsers not download the formats they cannot play, they also do not download additional formats once one is found that can be played.

As when making any promise, you had better be sure you're telling the truth! If you accidentally specify a type of `"video/mp4"` for a WebM file, `<source src="video1.webm" type="video/mp4;" />`, the incorrect type causes browsers that *cannot* play MP4 to think they cannot play the source file when they may be able to play WebM just fine. A mismatch like this means the browser doesn't download the potentially playable video—instead, an error is displayed, like the one shown in Figure 4.5.

FIGURE 4.5   Mind your MIME types!

The Audio Element

The new audio element is very similar to its video counterpart. They provide an almost identical set of problems, save for the visual part of video, and as you see in a later section, they share an almost identical set of attributes.

Audio Formats and Support

The story of audio formats is similar to video, except there are only two main formats you need to consider:

▶ **MP3**—The de facto standard for digital audio. Like MP4, the format is not royalty free, and as a result some browser vendors are refusing to support it in order to encourage a less royalty-encumbered web. MP3 typically uses the file extension `.mp3`.

▶ **Ogg**—The Ogg Vorbis codec, a royalty-free format. It typically uses the file extension `.ogg` or `.ogv`.

With just these two formats, we are able to play on every modern browser. There are two additional formats that may be of interest:

- **AAC**—A successor to MP3 and the audio component of MP4 video, this format was popularized by Apple with the iTunes store. Because YouTube uses MP4, this is also the standard audio format of YouTube videos. It typically uses the file extension `.aac`.

- **WAV**—An older, uncompressed audio file format developed by Microsoft and IBM. Because it lacks compression, it is fairly uncommon on the Web. It typically uses the file extension `.wav`.

Table 4.2 shows a compatibility chart for desktop browsers. Ogg and MP3 are the most widely supported, though you could get away with offering Ogg and AAC and still enjoy support on all modern desktop browsers.

TABLE 4.2   Audio Codec Support by Desktop Browser

	Ogg	MP3	AAC	WAV
Chrome	Yes	Yes	No	Yes
Firefox	Yes	No	No	Yes
Internet Explorer 9+	No	Yes	Yes	No
Safari	No	Yes	Yes	Yes
Opera	Yes	No	No	Yes

The compatibility of audio formats on mobile devices is trickier, as codec support is device dependent and not necessarily browser dependent. Nonetheless, if a device can play AAC, it can almost certainly play MP3, so having (at least) MP3 and Ogg makes for the safest set of formats to provide.

Current Support

As with video, it is always best to check online to see if all platforms you are targeting have implemented the APIs and formats you intend to use. Sites such as caniuse.com aggregate HTML5 API and feature implementation status and aid you with the current status of the `<audio>` tag and audio API support.

Testing for Support

In the same way as video, you can programmatically determine if a user supports the `<audio>` tag. You can accomplish this by attempting to create an audio element and testing to see if a supported function of that audio element exists.

```
// returns true if the HTML audio element exists, false otherwise
function checkForAudio() {
  return (!!document.createElement('audio').canPlayType);
}
```

If you have an incomplete set of audio formats and want to provide customized fallback depending on which types are supported or not, you can use the `canPlayType` method of the audio element. This method takes a MIME type (and optionally codecs) as a string and returns a string describing whether or not it supports that type or codec combination. Common tests for audio formats are shown in Listing 4.2.

LISTING 4.2　Testing for Individual Audio Format Support

```
var a = document.createElement('audio');
var oggTest  = a.canPlayType('audio/ogg');
var mp3Test  = a.canPlayType('audio/mpeg');
var aacTest  = a.canPlayType('audio/aac');
var waveTest = a.canPlayType('audio/wav');
// (Possibly do a custom action if browser can or cannot play a certain type)
console.log(mp3Test); // output whether or not this browser can play MP3s
```

As with the video element, the `canPlayType` method returns `"probably"` if the type is most likely to be supported, `"maybe"` if it is less certain that the format can be played, or `""` (the empty string) if the browser does not think it can play the format at all.

Testing for support programmatically may come in handy but you need not make your own solution. The "Supporting Older Browsers" section details a few simple ways to accommodate or notify users who cannot play HTML5 audio.

Using the Audio Element

Like the video element, the `<audio>` tag is typically accompanied by nested source files.

```
<audio>
  <source src="audio1.ogg" type="audio/ogg" />
  <source src="audio1.mp3" type="audio/mpeg" />
</audio>
```

Like video, you should always specify the MIME type via each source element's `type` so that the user need not download more than he or she has to in order to find a playable audio file.

Unlike the video element, a default audio element has no physical presence on the page. Adding the `controls` attribute to the tag declaration:

```
<audio controls="controls">
```

gives your audio element physical space and appearance in the page layout in the form of a Play/Pause button, seek bar, and total time or time remaining. Figure 4.6 shows typical audio controls, though the size varies by browser.

FIGURE 4.6   An example of default audio controls in Google Chrome, with a text sample to better demonstrate size. These controls are 300×30 pixels, but each browser sizes their controls differently.

Controlling audio ought to be natural and intuitive with the built-in controls, and additional `<audio>` tag attributes offer more very common options without having to author a bit of JavaScript. If you do feel the need to get fancier, custom controls are available through the JavaScript API.

Encoding Your Media

Because you'll need at least two video or at least two audio formats to effectively use the HTML5 media tags on all platforms, you may need to re-encode your existing audio or videos into a second or third format.

For the best results, you should always start the encoding from the original source audio track or video footage. When you are encoding your media into a new format, especially a web-optimized format such as WebM, you are tightly compressing it in a certain way and stripping out a lot of data in the process. Compression is a very fine thing, a small loss of quality comes with a large reduction in file size.

A problem arises when your just-encoded WebM file (as opposed to the original source) is used to produce an MP4 version. Both of these formats use *lossy* compression, meaning some of the source material is lost and the resulting file doesn't precisely represent the material it was generated from. As a result, any re-encoding results in additional loss and could reduce the quality of the subsequent encoding. Whereas a single encoding can have a very high quality, Figure 4.7 shows an example of the result of subsequent encodings.

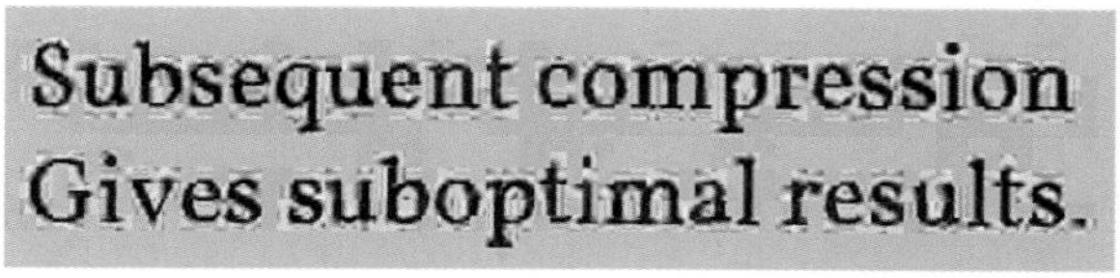

Subsequent compression
Gives suboptimal results.

FIGURE 4.7   An example of what happens when you recompress an already compressed file (several times). You do not want your video to look like this!

Conversion Tools

Although needing to provide multiple source formats is a bit of a bother, we are fortunate enough to live in an age where conversion tools flow freely from the fountains of the Internet. You can find multitudes of articles comparing different conversion programs, but unless you're very picky, opting for any of the most popular ones will do.

VLC (http://videolan.org) is an extremely popular cross-platform multimedia player that can play nearly any kind of audio or video file in common use. It can also convert files into a wide array of formats, including all relevant video element formats and most audio formats (but not AAC).

The **Miro Video Converter** (http://mirovideoconverter.com) can also convert nearly any file format into any of the relevant video formats and some audio formats. It also sports extra preset options for optimizing videos for different mobile devices, ensuring that the resulting files are of the correct format and size.

Miro and many of the other free video converters are based on a command-line tool called **ffmpeg** (http://ffmpeg.org), which affords vastly more options than VLC or Miro should you need more fine-grained control of the formatted output. If you plan on creating an audio or video sharing site, ffmpeg and similar command-line tools may come in handy as the encoding process could potentially be handled by a server instead of done by your users.

Supporting Older Browsers

The audio and video elements enjoy wide support in modern browsers, but you should never take their existence as a given. Most notably, versions of Internet Explorer before Internet Explorer 9 do not support the video element, and as of this writing, Opera Mini is the only major mobile browser that does not support the HTML5 media elements.

Although the `<audio>` and `<video>` tags do not exist in older browsers, HTML has a graceful way of degrading, and any unknown element is still rendered as an inline element. Conveniently, this inline element still contains (and displays) its inner HTML content.

Because the video element is made useful by displaying a video instead of nested HTML, and the audio element displays nothing unless controls are activated, any content inside of an `<audio>` or `<video>` tag can automatically work as fallback content on older browsers.

```
<!-- Example of providing fallback content,
     would work the same with an audio element. -->
<video>
  <!-- source tags are used by the audio and video element
       and are explained in the Basic Usage section. -->
  <source src="video1.webm" type="video/webm" />
  <!-- Fallback content goes here. You can provide a message,
       a Flash object, a download link, etc -->
  <p>
```

```
      Your browser doesn't support HTML5 video!
      Please upgrade to a modern browser.
    </p>
</video>
```

Depending on the importance of your audio or video, you have several options you could employ or suggest for your users as fallback:

▶ If you have a video of little importance, consider providing a simple image (or animated GIF) as fallback for video.

▶ Provide a Flash-based video or audio player fallback.

▶ Host a copy of the audio or video on a media sharing website (such as YouTube) and provide a link to the media, or embed the site's audio or video player.

▶ Suggest that the user install a modern browser or the Chrome Frame Internet Explorer extension.

▶ Provide a link to download one or many of the video or audio files to play instead on the local machine.

There are also more automatic fallback options in the form of JavaScript libraries. The open source HTML5 Media Project (http://html5media.info) is one such library that automatically conjures up a Flash-based fallback (using the open source Flash project Flowplayer) if the media element is not supported. Adding Flash fallback with this library is as easy as adding one line of code, the script element to your HMTL page, and it takes care of the rest.

Another popular fallback option is the `MediaElement.js` (http://mediaelementjs.com) library. Instead of merely providing fallback, this library aims to standardize the look and feel of browser controls across all platforms, using HTML5, Flash, or Silverlight (for Windows Media Video format) where appropriate. It provides several control styling templates that can be further customized.

Video and Audio Attributes

The video and audio elements share a host of attributes relevant to both tags. None of these attributes are necessary to function, but most of them can greatly reduce the amount of JavaScript needed to manipulate the video element in common ways.

Some browsers allow the user to toggle some of these attributes (such as `mute`, `loop`, and `controls`) via the context menu on the video or audio element.

Video-Only Attributes

While audio and video elements share most attributes, the physical nature of videos means there are properties only relevant to video elements.

width and height

The `width` and `height` attributes are familiar sights to those experienced with HTML. Just like the `width` and `height` attributes of the `<img>` tag, they specify a size in pixels to size the video player.

```
<!-- sets the video container to 320x240 -->
<video width="320" height="240">
```

If no `width` or `height` is specified, then the inherent size of the video source is used for the element. If a video source is not specified, fails to load, or cannot be found, the video element takes on its default size of 300×150, the same default size as the HTML5 canvas element.

Just like with other HTML elements that sport these attributes, setting only `width` or only `height` proportionally resizes the other dimension of the element so that the video fits neatly.

The `width` and `height` attributes do not stretch the video itself. Instead, they proportionally resize the video in its element container, as shown in Figure 4.8. This may leave empty space in the element on the sides of the video.

FIGURE 4.8   A rectangular video inside a video element with a square width and height. A red CSS border shows the dimensions of the video element, as opposed to the dimensions of the actual video.

Unlike the canvas element, you cannot stretch the video element by specifying the `width` or `height` as a tag attribute and a different CSS `width` or `height`. Instead, if you set both a CSS and a `<video>` tag attribute size, the CSS size simply takes precedence.

poster

The `poster` attribute works similarly to an image element's `src` attribute, specifying an image that displays while the video is downloading and until the video begins playback. Syntax is identical to an `<img>` tag's `src`:

```
<video poster="imagePreview.png">
```

Without a `poster` attribute set, most browsers display the first frame of the movie, which may not be particularly relevant to the content. For instance, in a how-to video, a poster of the finished product might be more representative of the content in the video, and in a theatrical video, the first frame is often black, telling the user nothing and possibly making the web page look less nice.

Unfortunately, the video's controls (if they are present—see the `controls` attribute in the next section) may block a portion of the poster image, so it is best not to put text or other relevant information at the bottom of the poster. Figure 4.9 shows how a poster might appear cut off by controls in Firefox, Chrome, Opera, and Safari. The odd one out here is Internet Explorer 9, which, as of this writing, displays the poster only until the video is done loading.

FIGURE 4.9   Four different browsers using a poster. Note that the last line of text, "THE FEATURE FILM," is difficult to see.

If the poster image is not the same size as the video element, it is proportionally scaled, larger or smaller, until it uniformly fits into the center of the video element.

muted

The `muted` attribute gives an easy way of setting a video to mute by default, requiring the user or JavaScript code to unmute it. This attribute is not yet supported in all browsers.

Because it is a Boolean attribute, `muted` takes advantage of the new HTML5 syntax for specifying tag attributes and can be set in a number of ways:

```
<!-- the audio tag has identical syntax -->
<video muted>
<video muted="muted">
<video muted="">
```

This attribute can be useful if the sound of the video is unimportant or need not be playing by default. Advertisements or websites demoing a physical product may be comfortable with an eye-catching video playing when the page loads, but not the associated audio, and this allows that without resorting to JavaScript.

> **NOTE**
>
> One big plus of native videos is a return of control over the context (right-click) menu to the browser. Right-clicking on a video element in any desktop browser raises a context menu that contains a "Mute" option among other options (that vary by browser).
>
> This means that, unlike unwanted Flash videos or advertisements that begin playing audio without your intention or consent, you can always right-click on an errant HTML5 video element to turn its sound off.

Attributes Shared Between Audio and Video

Because they carry out many common functions, most of the audio and video element attributes are shared and work similarly for both elements.

src

Like with the HTML image element, `src` specifies the uniform resource locator (URL) of an audio or video source file. Because audio and video elements typically need to specify many sources, the `src` attribute is rarely used. Instead, typical usage employs the new `<source>` tag:

```
<!-- the same nesting convention is used for the audio tag -->
<video>
  <source src="video1.webm" type="video/webm" />
  <source src="video1.mp4" type="video/mp4" />
  <source src="video1.ogv" type="video/ogg" />
</video>
```

The specifics of using the `<source>` tag with video and audio were detailed in the "Using the Video Element" and "Using the Audio Element" sections.

NOTE

In the future, we will be able to use the `src` attribute of an audio, video, or source tag to additionally specify a *playback range* for the media by appending a hash and a time description to the URL. It uses the following syntax, with the bracketed portions being optional:

```
src="filename.type#t=[startingTime],[endingTime]"
```

The following source element, for instance, would start the video at the 30-second mark, and has no specified ending time:

```
<source src="video1.mp4#t=30," type="video/mp4" />
```

These playback ranges only affect the first play-through, so a playback range of `#t=15,45` will start the media at the 15-second mark and end at the 45-second mark, where the audio or video pauses. Clicking Play resumes from the 45-second mark.

Unfortunately, this special suffix is only supported by Chrome and Firefox as of this writing. Safari and Opera ignore it, and using it causes Internet Explorer 9 to consider the source file erroneous, displaying a red X! For now, we have to use the JavaScript API to manipulate the start and end times.

---

controls

From the very beginning, there have been a large amount of Flash apps that existed for the sole purpose of playing audio or video in the browser. These Flash apps did nothing but play a movie and add a few standard controls, such as pause, play, and mute. These apps converged on a somewhat standardized way of displaying video controls on the Web, and almost no websites that display video (save for the ones that did nothing but) bothered to make their own controls. An off-the-shelf Flash app was just fine.

The HTML5 specification took this into account, and instead of leaving the onus on the user or JavaScript developers to create simple playback controls that almost everyone displaying a video might need, they have added it as a requirement for the browsers to implement. The audio and video element's attribute `controls` is a Boolean attribute that specifies whether or not the browser should display its built-in set of controls.

The control implementations differ between browsers, but all browsers sport the ability to play, pause, adjust volume, seek, and see either time remaining or time elapsed. For video, browsers that have so far implemented the full-screen API also have a full-screen button. Figure 4.10 shows what the default audio controls look like in different desktop browsers, and Figure 4.11 shows the default video controls.

FIGURE 4.10   The default audio controls in different desktop browsers.

FIGURE 4.11   The default video controls in different desktop browsers.

## 4

As is common in video players today, the controls hide themselves while the video is playing, and present themselves on a mouseover, a touch, or while paused.

Like other Boolean attributes, `controls` takes advantage of the new HTML5 syntax for specifying tag attributes and can be active by being set to a value or merely present. Any of these will activate the controls:

```
<!-- the audio tag has identical syntax -->
<video controls>
<video controls="controls">
<video controls="">
```

If you decline to use the built-in controls in favor of making your own alternative controls in JavaScript, you need not worry that the user blocking JavaScript will block video playback. The HTML5 specification states that if a user has JavaScript disabled, then the browser will present the default audio and video controls automatically, regardless of the status of the `controls` attribute.

> **NOTE**
>
> The appearance of the controls when no supported format is available differs between browsers. For the audio element, if no sources are provided or no playable source is found:
>
> ▶ **Chrome**—Displays controls with 0:00.
> ▶ **Opera**—Displays controls with 0:00.
> ▶ **Safari**—Displays controls without showing a seek bar or the time remaining.
> ▶ **Firefox**—Displays *nothing at all* if no playable format sources are listed, but does display controls with 0:00 for remaining time if no sources are listed.
> ▶ **Internet Explorer 9**—Opposite of Firefox; displays a black box with a centered red X instead of controls if no playable format sources are listed, but displays *nothing at all* if no sources are listed.
>
> Similarly, with video:
>
> ▶ **Chrome, Opera, Safari**—Display controls with empty video container.
> ▶ **Firefox**—If no playable format sources are listed, displays an empty video control with the message "No video with supported format and MIME type found." Does display controls if no sources are listed.
> ▶ **Internet Explorer 9**—If no playable format sources are listed, displays a black box with a centered red X. If no sources at all are listed, it displays controls (only visible on mouseover) in an empty video container.

autoplay

The video and audio tags have a Boolean `autoplay` attribute that tells the browser to automatically begin playing as soon as the source is ready. Because it is a Boolean attribute, it can be specified a number of ways:

```
<!-- the audio tag has identical syntax -->
<video autoplay>
<video autoplay="autoplay">
<video autoplay="">
```

Unless you're making an audio- or video-centric site, automatically playing a media element is generally considered distasteful. There are a few other inoffensive uses, such as playing informational or nonessential videos where sound is muted by default and the starting point of the viewing experience does not matter. For instance, autoplaying may be useful for short looping videos or slideshow videos on a page demoing a product.

Automatic playback makes good sense if the only point of being on a particular web page is to see a video or hear audio, as is the case with individual YouTube video URLs or Internet radio. Nonetheless, some video sites such as Vimeo—a popular, self-professed high-quality video sharing site—think it more courteous to wait for the user to click Play.

preload

The `preload` attribute takes one of three strings that describe what we think the browser ought to load, if anything, before the user attempts to play the media. There are three possible values:

```
<!-- the audio tag has identical syntax -->
<video preload="auto">
<video preload>          <!-- identical to "auto" -->
<video preload="">       <!-- identical to "auto" -->
<video preload="metadata">
<video preload="none">
```

The default value for `preload` is `auto`. With this value, media typically begins downloading as soon as the browser finds an acceptable source. This value should be used when there is a reasonable expectation that the user will want to watch or listen to the media at some point. This might not be the case, for instance, on a page that contains hundreds of audio samples.

The value is called `auto` because it defers to the browser or device to decide if preloading is prudent. Mobile platforms may want to conserve bandwidth and battery life, so the value of `auto` on some devices may only preload if the device is plugged in. Because the specification deems it best to allow the device/browser rather than the web page to have the final say, we can never *demand* that an audio or video file preload, only suggest that it should.

The `metadata` value fetches the associated metadata for the audio or video element's sources, downloading nothing further. On the video element, this retrieves information including the video dimensions and the first frame, which are useful in page presentation if no explicit size or `poster` attribute are set. The metadata additionally includes information such as total duration and tracks.

The `none` value simply suggests that nothing should be preloaded until the user (or JavaScript) activates the audio or video.

> **NOTE**
>
> If you use the `autoplay` attribute, any value given to the `preload` attribute has no effect.

loop

The `loop` attribute is another Boolean value that, if present, automatically replays the video upon reaching its end. Looping audio or video can be useful, but like `autoplay`, you should be careful not to annoy your users. Syntax is the same as other Boolean attributes, with several valid ways of setting it:

```
<!-- the audio tag has identical syntax -->
<video loop>
<video loop="loop">
<video loop="">
```

JavaScript API

The audio and video elements come with a near-identical JavaScript API that allows the elements to interact with the rest of the page. With JavaScript, you can create your own controls, manipulate and query the playback and network state, and fire events in response to various changes in the media state.

Remember that if you are creating your own custom controls or functionality with the JavaScript API, this functionality is exclusive to the HTML5 version of your site. You cannot expect any of it to work on older browsers or on any fallback content (such as a Flash video player) that users may see.

The API contains a decent amount of attributes but is pleasantly simple as the function of almost every part is obvious from its name alone. Table 4.3 contains the names of every attribute, method, and event in the HTML5 media element JavaScript API.

TABLE 4.3   HTML5 Media JavaScript API

Attributes

Error State	**Playback State**	**Controls**
error	currentTime	controls
	initialTime	volume
Network State	duration	muted
src	startOffsetTime	defaultMuted
currentSrc	paused	
crossOrigin	defaultPlaybackRate	**Tracks**
networkState	playbackRate	audioTracks
preload	played	videoTracks
buffered	seekable	textTracks
	ended	
Ready State	autoplay	**Video-Specific State**
readyState	loop	width
seeking		height
	Media	videoWidth
	controller	videoHeight
	mediaGroup	poster
	controller	

Methods

load()	play()	canPlayType(type)
	pause()	addTextTrack(kind, [label, language])

Events

loadstart	loadedmetadata	seeked
progress	loadeddata	ended
suspend	canplay	durationchange
abort	canplaythrough	timeupdate
error	playing	play
emptied	waiting	pause
stalled	seeking	ratechange
		volumechange

The World Wide Web Consortium (W3C) has a demonstration page of much of the API at http://www.w3.org/2010/05/video/mediaevents.html. There, you can quickly test different functions in various browsers, and observe the JavaScript state of the media elements as they are playing.

We provide a few examples of using the API to achieve interesting functionality, covering some of the media states available to us in the process.

The `readyState` and Starting at a Specified Time

Setting the `currentTime` property of a media element right away allows us to start a video at a specified time. We can't set the attribute until the video element has enough information to start playback, so we set the `currentTime` attribute when the video's `loadedmetadata` event fires.

```
<video id="myVideo" autoplay controls>
  <source src="video1.webm" type="video/webm" />
  <source src="video1.mp4" type="video/mp4" />
</video>

<script type="text/javascript">
  var video = document.getElementById('myVideo');
  video.addEventListener('loadedmetadata', function() {
    video.currentTime = 40; // start at the 40 second mark
  }, false);
</script>
```

If we just set the `currentTime` attribute, we risk running into an error because the video might not yet be available to seek through, so to stop a potential error, we need to wait for the media metadata (which tells us the media's duration) to load. To make sure we wait for the metadata, we only set the current time once the `loadedmetadata` event fires.

The `readyState` attribute tells us to what degree the audio or video element is ready to be rendered at the current position. The value from `readyState` will be an integer from 0 to 4, which corresponds to constants describing the state:

- ▶ **0: HAVE_NOTHING**—The media element has no information, including no data on the current playback position, and cannot set the `currentTime`, among other attributes.

- ▶ **1: HAVE_METADATA**—Enough of the data has been obtained to determine the duration of the media, and for videos, the `width` and `height` are also available. Attempting to seek or set the `currentTime` no longer throws an exception.

- ▶ **2: HAVE_CURRENT_DATA**—Data is available for the current playback position (the current frame), but no further.

- ▶ **3: HAVE_FUTURE_DATA**—Enough data is available to advance the media element in the direction of playback.

- ▶ **4: HAVE_ENOUGH_DATA**—Enough data is available and is becoming available at a rate where the current playback position, if it were to advance at the current playback rate, would not overtake the available data before it reaches the end of the media.

The `loadedmetadata` event fires as soon as the `readyState` reaches 1. If by the time our code is reached, the `readyState` happens to already have a value of 1 or greater, the `loadedmetadata` event never fires. To make a safer version of our previous script, we can check the `readyState` to see if we already have the metadata; otherwise, we use the event listener:

```
<script type="text/javascript">
  var video = document.getElementById('myVideo');
  // If we are already allowed to seek, set the current time,
  // otherwise set the current time as soon as we are able
  if (video.readyState >= 1) {
    video.currentTime = 40; // start at the 40 second mark
  } else {
    video.addEventListener('loadedmetadata', function() {
      video.currentTime = 40; // start at the 40 second mark
    }, false);
  }
</script>
```

If we had an audio or video sharing site and wanted users to be able to specify a starting time in the URL, we could incorporate the URL hash into setting the `currentTime`:

```
// This would allow a video at
// http://example.com/someVideo.html#90
// to start at 1:30 (90 seconds)
var time = parseInt(window.location.hash);
if (!isNaN(time)) video.currentTime = time;
```

> **NOTE**
>
> Because the metadata gives us enough information to request seeking in a media file, the `loadedmetadata` event is also an ideal time to enable any custom controls or user interface we have created.

The `playbackRate` and Time Control

Setting the `playbackRate` attribute of the API allows us to speed up, slow down, or (in some browsers) play the media backward. This has great practical utility; for instance, users could (slightly) speed up audiobooks and lectures as many listeners like to do in order to cover more material faster, or slow down videos for inspection such as footage made by security cameras.

Unfortunately, at the time of this writing, `playbackRate` is only supported by Webkit-based browsers.

Loading Videos Sequentially

We can use the JavaScript API to make a rudimentary playlist that automatically advances to the next video when one is finished playing.

We separate the functionality into two functions: loadVideo takes a number and sets the video's sources to the appropriate files and calls video.load(). The load function rescans the video sources and updates the element accordingly. We can use this function to arbitrarily set the video element to load any video in a list.

To update the list automatically, a second function is added to the ended video element event. When a video finishes playing, the ended event fires, calling our function that increments a saved number, recording the currently playing video and using that number to call loadVideo. Listing 4.3 contains the complete code needed for a simple playlist.

LISTING 4.3   A Simple Sequential Playlist

```
<video id="myVideo" width="400" controls>
  <source id="webm-source" src="video1.webm" type="video/webm" />
  <source id="mp4-source"  src="video1.mp4" type="video/mp4" />
</video>

<script type="text/javascript">
  // We could be cleverer if our videos have similar
  // naming conventions, but for the example
  // we'll keep it clear and simple.

  // Construct a list of videos and formats:
  var allVideos = [];
  allVideos[0] = ["video1.webm",
                  "video1.mp4"];
  allVideos[1] = ["video2.webm",
                  "video2.mp4"];
  allVideos[2] = ["video3.webm",
                  "video3.mp4"];

  // Loads the nth video in our list
  function loadVideo(n) {
    var webm = document.getElementById('webm-source');
    var mp4 = document.getElementById('mp4-source');
    webm.setAttribute("src", allVideos[n][0]);
    mp4.setAttribute("src", allVideos[n][1]);

    var video = document.getElementById('myVideo');
    video.load();
    // Start playing after loading:
    video.play();
  }
```

```
var currentVideo = 0;
var video = document.getElementById('myVideo');
// The 'ended' event fires every time a video reaches the end
video.addEventListener('ended', function() {
  currentVideo++;
  if (currentVideo > allVideos.length) currentVideo = 0;
  loadVideo(currentVideo);
}, false);
</script>
```

Custom Controls

The ability to create custom controls is a big plus to designers who want to integrate the look and feel of their video player into the rest of the page.

Although custom controls can add a lot to your website, we don't go over making your own controls in this book because making simple controls is trivial, and making good-looking controls is more of an exercise in design than using the media element's API. When all is said and done, a nice "Play" button with rounded corners, a glossy finish, shadows, fading out when not in use and so on, consists of 40 lines of CSS and just 1 line of JavaScript, a call to video.play() in the event handler.

If you are interested in creating your own custom controls, it is worth searching for existing open source controls, such as the projects Video.js (http://videojs.com) and MediaElement.js (http://mediaelementjs.com). These projects have given a good deal of effort in creating a professional feel that works across browsers and make a great resource for those who learn by example.

Advantages and Disadvantages of the HTML5 Media Tags Versus Flash

Flash's days may seem numbered, but it can still fulfill a few functions well that the HTML5 media tags cannot. This section details the pros and cons of both as they stand at the time of writing.

It's important to note that most of the criticisms of the HTML5 media elements are "not yet" issues. These issues are very likely to disappear over time, and if any of them are of concern to your projects, you should search online for their current status before making a decision to use the HTML5 tags or Flash.

Ease of Use and Extensibility

One of the most prominent advantages of the audio and video elements is that they are easy to use. The syntax for the <audio> and <video> tags are very simple compared with embedding a Flash object. If you already write HTML, you can use the audio and video elements with very little additional knowledge.

With the HTML5 media tags, there's also no need to pick through the various Flash media players until you find a suitable one because the browser has already provided built-in controls for you. The Boolean attributes also make for easy configuration of the basic scenarios for audio and video (looping, autoplaying, mute by default) without needing a single line of JavaScript.

Compared with Flash and associated plug-ins, the audio and video elements offer web designers and programmers more flexibility with the design and page interaction of the elements. They can be styled, scaled, and positioned with CSS. The creation of custom controls is merely an act of HTML and JavaScript, no third set of skills (ActionScript, in the case of Flash) and no proprietary software is needed.

The audio and video elements not only afford additional design, but they also offer additional functionality. Suppose, for instance, that you have several videos and want to arbitrarily position and synchronize them to play, pause, or mute at the same time. Using a Flash video player, you could very well be out of luck: You're at the mercy of whatever functions the Flash player exposes to JavaScript, if any at all.

With video elements, this can be done easily by using a JavaScript loop and a button on the page, or reusing whatever controls you might have made so far. Using the video element's JavaScript API, controlling several videos is just a simple loop:

```
// Play all videos on the page
var videos = document.getElementsByTagName ('video');
for (var i = 0; i < videos.length; i++) {
  videos[i].play();
}
```

Platform Support

Flash is not available on iOS devices (iPhone, iPod, iPad), and is deprecated in newer Android devices. Adobe has stated that it will no longer ship new versions of mobile Flash. If you want to support all mobile devices without building native apps, there's no question that HTML5 is the solution.

On the other hand, HTML5 video is not supported on older versions of Internet Explorer and may not offer a consistent experience across browsers. Flash fallbacks mitigate this, and, as mentioned earlier, there are several libraries such as the HTML5 Media Project (http://html5media.info) that make fallback for HTML5 elements as easy as adding a single <script> tag to your page.

Feature Support

Currently, Flash has better full-screen support as well as better webcam and microphone support. Both of these are in the works for browsers, as the Fullscreen API and WebRTC API specifications, respectively, but it may be some time before they are widely implemented.

Streaming support in HTML5 video and audio as of this writing is very weak. Adaptive streaming, the ability to adjust the quality of the stream based on the quality of the connection, is also not possible yet. Several large companies (including Google) have cited the lack of streaming capabilities (adaptive or otherwise) as one of the largest roadblocks to widespread HTML5 media support.

The HTML5 media elements have no finalized standard for media captioning, though the new WebVTT (Web Video Text Tracks) standard proposes a format that aims to be used for captioning HTML5 video.

The "Future Developments" section details several of these upcoming HTML5 media features.

Media Protection

When developers talk about media protection, they typically mean the ability for users to save the media that is playing and, therefore, potentially distribute it. Media cannot be "protected" as easily with the HMTL5 audio and video elements as it can be with Flash. As of this writing, there is no form of digital rights management (DRM) built in to the standard. In typical usage, downloading audio or video from an HTML5 media element is as easy as plucking it from the source, or in some browsers simply right-clicking the element and choosing the "Save (audio or video) As" option.

Flash is still the go-to plug-in for protecting your media. Of course, if you're playing audio or video on a user's machine, it is nearly impossible to prohibit the media from being recorded by out-of-browser applications, and it is worth weighing the real necessity (or not) of DRM. Unless you are bound by legal obligations, content protection may be a waste of your time.

We will almost certainly have DRM-capable (or otherwise protected) formats for the video element someday, but expecting widespread adoption is too far into the future to see as of this writing. Google, Microsoft, and Netflix have recently submitted a proposal to the W3C called "Encrypted Media Extensions," which aims to enable the playback of protected audio and video content in the HTML5 media elements. W3C editors were not thrilled when the proposal was initially introduced, as DRM flies in the face of the openness that HTML5 professes so far, but the practicalities of the matter will probably make it a reality.

Future Developments

There are several up-and-coming rich media web features that are not fully covered in this book due to their newness or lack of support. Nonetheless, they will be of great interest to some crowds, and some of them might have matured since this text was written. If any of these sound useful, you should investigate their current status.

WebRTC

WebRTC, short for Real-Time Communication, is a specification detailing functionality for media sharing in real time between browsers and allowing access to media devices.

In plainer terms, WebRTC seeks to make voice chat, video chat, and peer-to-peer (file) sharing native to the browser.

WebRTC is currently in working draft and supported by Google, Firefox, and Opera. Apple and Microsoft may come later to the table for WebRTC, as they have a vested interest in FaceTime and Skype, respectively, and catering to those platforms may be more of a priority. Microsoft has even gone forth and published its own competing proposal for the WebRTC innards. A compromise is more likely today than in web standards wars of the past, but as of this writing, there is no resolution between the W3C specification and Microsoft's proposal.

The technology is too nascent to use in production, but if you're interested in experimenting with the API, the official WebRTC site maintains a list of demos and instructions (http://www.webrtc.org/running-the-demos).

WebVTT and the `<track>` Tag

Accessibility for the HTML5 media elements is taken seriously by the W3C, and as such the captioning of video content has been given its own specification. The living standard is called WebVTT (previously, it was WebSRT because it is based on the SRT file format).

The primary purpose of WebVTT is captioning video content, allowing webmasters to provide subtitles for accessibility in the case of auditory impairment, such as a user who cannot hear or a device that cannot play sound, or for subtitling to give content a multilingual reach, or simply for transcription purposes.

WebVTT is used with the new HTML5 `<track>` tag and is nested alongside the video's source elements:

```
<video controls>
   <source src="video1.webm" type="video/webm" />
   <source src="video1.mp4" type="video/mp4" />
   <track label="English subtitles" kind="subtitles" srclang="en"
         src="video1-en.vtt" default>
</video>
```

The `.vtt` files themselves are simply UTF-8 encoded text files. Here's a simple example that contains two lines of captioning:

```
WEBVTT FILE

00:00:05.000 --> 00:00:08.000
This line of captioning appears between the 5 and 8 second mark

00:00:12.000 --> 00:00:17.000
Nothing is presented between 8 and 12 seconds
and then this line of text appears for 5 seconds.
```

Figure 4.12 shows an example of the captions in Chrome.

FIGURE 4.12   A captioned video of pea plants growing. The playing video is not entirely unlike the still image.

Unfortunately, as of this writing, only Chrome and Internet Explorer 10 support `<track>` and WebVTT. Thankfully, there are some very good fallbacks that work across all browsers if you need subtitling right away.

Using WebVTT Right Now

Playr (http://github.com/delphiki/Playr) is a small JavaScript library that adds subtitle support to all major browsers, supporting both VTT and SRT subtitle files. Enabling Playr is as easy as adding the JavaScript and associated style sheet, then adding a class to your video element:

```
<link rel="stylesheet" href="playr/playr.css" />
<script src="playr/playr.js"></script>

...

<!-- note the new class, needed for styling -->
<video controls class="playr_video">
  <source src="video1.webm" type="video/webm" />
  <source src="video1.mp4" type="video/mp4" />
  <track label="English subtitles" kind="subtitles" srclang="en"
        src="video1-en.vtt" default>
</video>
```

The Playr then parses any `<track>` tags that your videos contain.

The `MediaElement.js` (http://mediaelementjs.com) library, mentioned earlier in this chapter, also provides support for subtitles by making use of WebVTT files and has the added benefit of enabling video playback support for older browsers as well.

The Full-Screen API

The full-screen API is the relatively new and spottily supported method of allowing content (such as the video element or canvas element) to take up the entire screen. As of this writing, the browsers that do implement it do so differently, sometimes via prefixed methods. The following snippet attempts to enable Full-Screen mode on all browsers that support the full-screen API:

```
var elem = document.getElementById("myVideo");
if (elem.requestFullScreen) {
  elem.requestFullScreen();
} else if (elem.mozRequestFullScreen) {
  elem.mozRequestFullScreen();
} else if (elem.webkitRequestFullScreen) {
  elem.webkitRequestFullScreen();
}
```

In some versions of WebKit browsers, you must explicitly set the CSS of the element yourself:

```
:-webkit-full-screen #myvideo {
  width: 100%;
  height: 100%;
}
```

In the very near future, this will not be necessary, and is already not necessary in the desktop version of Google Chrome.

Esc and F11 exit Full-Screen mode by default. Full-Screen mode can also be exited via JavaScript with a call to `elem.cancelFullScreen()`.

As of this writing, Internet Explorer 9, older versions of Opera, and almost all mobile browsers do not support the full-screen API.

The Web Audio API

The Web Audio API is a working draft that extends the HTML5 media JavaScript API to allow for much finer-grained control over audio, including the processing and synthesizing of audio in the browser.

As of this writing, the Audio API has limited support in Firefox, Chrome, and Safari. Although the adoption is too sparse for production use, it has already seen a fair amount of demoing and experimentation. The Chromium project maintains a list of interesting samples and projects employing the API (http://chromium.googlecode.com/svn/trunk/samples/audio/index.html).

The Embed Element

Last, we have the final HTML5 rich media element, the `<embed>` tag. Its inclusion in HTML5 is a mere formality: The tag has been around for years, used as a de facto standard for embedding Flash content in almost every browser. Because it has existed for so long, we do not cover its use. Besides, outside the context of an external application or plug-in, it has no use!

The HTML5 specification decided to include the embed element, allowing pages that contain the tag to finally pass HTML validation tests. This inclusion can also be taken as recognition on the part of the W3C that plug-ins will realistically continue to be part of the future of browsers.

Summary

In this chapter, we covered the new `<audio>` and `<video>` tags, as well as their nested subordinates, the essential `<source>` tag and nascent `<track>` tag. These tags are not as full featured as Flash applications can be today—for instance, webcam and full-screen support is spotty. New functionality, however, is quickly being added to all major browsers and the current functionality will work for a wide range of audio and video sites.

These new multimedia elements make the biggest dent in returning formerly plug-in-specific functionality to the browser. With the additional use of a fallback library for older browsers, HTML5 audio and video are ready to use today.

CHAPTER 5

2D Canvas

Canvas is the most visible part of HTML5, and together with the audio and video tags we have the most important HTML elements that return rich web functionality from a world of plug-ins to a native experience.

Canvas has many immediate applications: It natively enables interactive movies, games, charts, diagrams, and other forms of dynamic visual content. You could even create an entire site in one canvas, just as many once did with Flash, though you probably shouldn't do this and we talk about why (and the limits of canvas in general) throughout this chapter.

The HTML5 canvas began as an Apple-made component added to WebKit, the rendering engine powering Safari and Google Chrome, in 2004. One year later, it was adopted in Firefox, and Opera adopted the component the year after that. It eventually found its way into the HTML5 specification and has since exploded in popularity. It is telling that the company to introduce it was also the first company to shirk Flash, which is not supported in Apple's iOS. Canvas, put simply, is the future of graphics on the Web.

Canvas is a low-level drawing surface with commands for drawing lines, curves, rectangles, gradients, images, and so on. There is very little else in the way of graphics drawing, which means programmers must create their own methods for several basic drawing functions, such as blurring, tweening, animation, management of state, and all interactivity. As of this writing, even drawing a dashed or dotted line is something that must be done by the programmer from scratch, though the specification has recently been updated to accommodate several more common drawing tasks such as this.

Canvas is an *immediate* drawing surface and has no scene graph. This means that once an image or shape is drawn to it, neither the canvas nor its drawing context have any knowledge of what was just drawn.

For instance, to draw a line and have it animate within the canvas, you cannot simply update a list of points. You must clear the canvas (or part of it) on every frame and redraw the line with the new points. Often in a complex app, this means keeping track of every object in your scene yourself and redrawing it all sequentially every time a piece changes.

This contrasts greatly with Scalable Vector Graphics (SVG), where the SVG element maintains a list of the line points for you, and to animate the line you would simply modify the SVG element's points and be done with it.

Canvas lets you peek and manipulate the pixel data of its bitmap, but if you were to draw a rectangle to the canvas, there is no stateful notion of a rectangle recorded anywhere unless you record it yourself. Put another way, the canvas does not remember the location or dimension of figures drawn, it simply executes drawing commands and that's it. Everything else is up to us. Many apps want to keep track of large amounts of drawing data, and the next chapter details canvas interactivity and management of drawing state.

This chapter covers the entire 2D canvas application programming interface (API), and alongside this coverage, we use practical examples and use cases derived from real-world canvas apps as well as common canvas questions and problems. In our exploration of the API, this chapter also covers several less-common drawing techniques that may be of interest to even experienced canvas programmers. As we cover various properties and methods, we touch upon performance issues, though a more comprehensive performance primer is the subject of Chapter 7, "Canvas Performance, Tips, and Peculiarities."

Browser Support

Canvas is available in all modern browsers, including all major mobile browsers. The specification, however, is still evolving and many new methods have been added in recent history. As of this writing, many of these newer methods are not even in the nightly builds of any browser, and Chapter 8, "The Future of Canvas and 3D Canvas," discusses them along with the future of canvas in general. Although almost none of these new properties and methods are available today, they are worth keeping an eye on for future use.

Regardless of the methods and properties you use, it is always important to test your canvas apps in every browser you are targeting. Implementations of the canvas element differ between browsers, especially where the specification is vague. There is no standardization of antialiasing or font measuring, for example. This means you cannot always expect your canvas apps to look identical across browsers, and if you are using text to measure objects or store data (such as the bounds of a block of text), then you cannot carry the expectation that your data will be consistent across browsers.

Internet Explorer

Canvas is supported in Internet Explorer 9 and above. To be perfectly clear, canvas is *not* supported in Internet Explorer 8 and below. There are two libraries, excanvas and FlashCanvas, which attempt to bring support for the canvas to older versions of Internet Explorer by emulating canvas commands in VML (Vector Markup Language, a Microsoft language similar to SVG) and Flash respectively. These libraries are best avoided, as unless your canvas app is very small, performance degrades quickly with both of these libraries, more so if animation is involved. These libraries do not (and cannot) completely emulate the functionality of canvas, and both of them have not been updated in some time. The excanvas library has been unchanged since 2009 and FlashCanvas since 2011.

Using a library to feign the existence of canvas in older browsers will never be on par with a real canvas app, and may leave your users with a sour impression of your (otherwise excellent) app.

If your app is small, it is best to make a Flash or VML version for Internet Explorer, or else attempt to provide reasonable fallback, rather than going through the headaches of working with excanvas and FlashCanvas. In the "Getting Started with Canvas" section, we cover the creation of appropriate fallback for the canvas element.

If you must support older versions of Internet Explorer, you could also consider directing your users to Google's Chrome Frame plug-in, which is designed for adding HTML5 support to older versions of Internet Explorer, and it does so by replacing the rendering and JavaScript engines of Internet Explorer with Chrome's. This allows the user to render all canvas applications in older versions of Internet Explorer, but like any other browser plug-in, you cannot force this on your users, only direct them to an installation page.

Testing for Support

The wonderful caniuse.com maintains a list of the major browsers and their support for canvas, and a list of most other modern browser features for that matter. At caniuse.com/canvas for 2D and caniuse.com/webgl for WebGL (3D), the site enumerates many browsers and which versions of them have support.

If you want to test for support programmatically, you can do so in a simple JavaScript function:

```
function supportsCanvas() {
  return (typeof document.createElement('canvas').getContext !== 'undefined');
}
```

If you need to test your website's functionality with canvas disabled, you can force Internet Explorer 9 and above into Internet Explorer 7 or Internet Explorer 8 Document mode. This feature can be turned on in Internet Explorer's developer console, as shown in Figure 5.1.

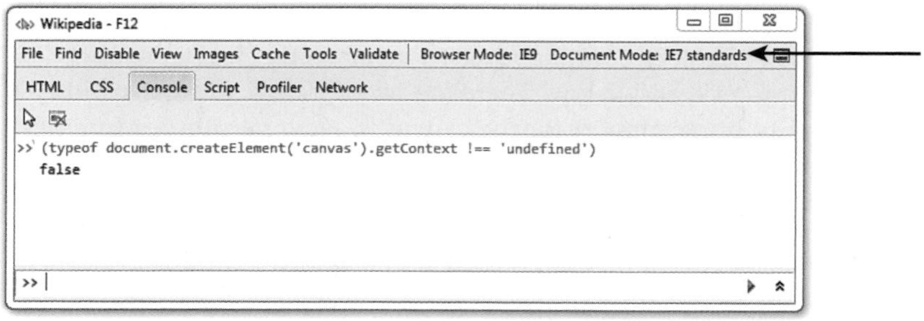

FIGURE 5.1   Like a time machine, the "Document mode" of Internet Explorer's developer tools allows us to travel back to the dark ages of the Web.

What Canvas Can and Cannot Do

Developers coming to canvas from Flash, Silverlight, or SVG may be shocked to find just how little is done for you with canvas. The most obvious differences are the total absence of animation support and the lack of built-in ways to keep track of canvas state. You must do both of these from scratch, or else use (and learn) a JavaScript library of someone who did.

Protecting your JavaScript app from copying or hacking is a bit more difficult than with Silverlight or Flash. The best you can do with JavaScript is obfuscate, booby-trap, and watermark your code and app. Depending on how you intend to deploy your application, you could leave some critical pieces of functionality up to a server so that the JavaScript alone will not constitute a working app.

Unlike the much more mature SVG specification, the behavior of canvas is browser dependent, and while the vast majority of functionality is identical across browsers, you will eventually come across one or two oddities or bugs that present themselves on one browser and not another. Flash, by comparison, ought to be consistent across all browsers and only differ by the Flash version.

On the other hand, canvas apps have the potential to carry much less overhead than SVG. Their payload is smaller than Flash or Silverlight, especially for small apps, and has the potential to work on all modern platforms where plug-ins like Silverlight and Flash might be snubbed. Canvas code is all JavaScript (or Google Dart if we're feeling bohemian), and therefore all debugging is pleasantly built in to the browser, and there is no need to learn a separate language or framework such as ActionScript or C#.

Canvas apps can more naturally and readily interact with the rest of the page compared with Flash or Silverlight. In many instances, canvas will replace Flash, but it's important to note that instead of being an embedded object in an HTML page, a canvas is a regular part of the HTML page and should be regarded as such.

Because a canvas is a regular HTML element and can easily fit into any part of a page layout and receive any number of page events, interactivity with the rest of the page is a breeze. Some web pages sport animated backgrounds using a canvas where graphical wisps gently follow the mouse, and there are doubtless more interesting and nuanced ways to weave canvases into web pages.

Others sites, of course, will take canvas use to an extreme and may end up distracting and disorienting their users. Whether this is their intention or an unfortunate side effect of a zealous designer, the JavaScript that runs any canvas can always be disabled, preferably on the spot such as with the popular NoScript, NotScripts, and ScriptNo browser plug-ins.

Whatever sort of app you are considering, you should at least be familiar with the most tenable substitute, SVG.

A Comparison with SVG

SVG is an alternative to canvas and in terms of choices for (native) rich graphics in the browser, the question often arises as to whether canvas or SVG would be a better fit for a particular project.

SVG, short for Scalable Vector Graphics, is another drawing technology available for web pages and is sometimes confused as part of HTML5. Even the w3.org website lists SVG on an HTML5 page for Graphics and Effects. In fact, SVG is more than 10 years old, though it wasn't until recently that all browsers displayed it well, and some of the more obscure features are still missing from major browsers.

Because SVG is quite old and not part of HTML5, this book does not cover it in depth, but the knowledge of the difference between canvas and SVG is important for determining which to explore as a potential platform for your web applications.

The two graphics systems have several basic differences. Canvas is bitmap based and SVG is vector based. Canvas is procedural, meaning the creation of objects is done through writing a series of instructions in JavaScript. SVG, on the other hand, is declarative, meaning you specify the shape to draw in the definition of an Extensible Markup Language (XML) object. The following SVG declaration creates a triangular figure:

```
<svg>
  <polygon points="100,10 150,140 60,110"
          style="fill:lime; stroke:purple; stroke-width:4" />
</svg>
```

An extremely similar figure drawn in canvas requires the following HTML and JavaScript:

```
<canvas id="canvas1" width="200" height="200"></canvas>

<script type="text/javascript">
var can = document.getElementById('canvas1');
var ctx = can.getContext('2d');
ctx.beginPath();
ctx.moveTo(100, 10);
ctx.lineTo(150, 140);
```

```
ctx.lineTo(60, 110);
ctx.closePath();
ctx.fillStyle = 'lime';
ctx.strokeStyle = 'purple';
ctx.lineWidth = 4;
ctx.fill();
ctx.stroke();
</script>
```

You can see the result of this SVG definition and the JavaScript canvas code in Figure 5.2. In spite of the different ways these figures are created, the SVG looks identical to its canvas counterpart.

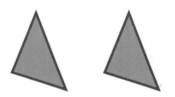

FIGURE 5.2   A figure made with SVG (left) and a similar figure made with canvas (right).

The definition of SVG as part of HTML documents also means that every SVG figure is also a DOM object. Maintaining all these references can be quite convenient when you want to update a given SVG element. In the previous example, all you need to do to move or reshape the SVG figure is to update the list of points, and the rendered SVG figure on the page will move or reshape accordingly.

Each SVG object's state exists as a DOM object and this can be helpful as it gives every SVG element many useful properties such as event handlers, making object detection and interaction very easy. Want to do an action when the mouse is over the SVG figure? Define onmouseover and do as you please.

Animation is also built in to SVG, and you can perform complex animations on your figures using either the declarative syntax or JavaScript.

Canvas has no such luxury. To update a point in the canvas figure, you must instead clear the canvas and redraw the entire figure with a new set of points. And if you want to do an action when the mouse is over your canvas figure, you must keep track of everything you draw, where it is, and define an onmouseover event for the entire canvas that runs through your list of objects in the appropriate z-order and manually does the math to see if you happen to be over a particular figure or not!

Canvas has no built-in animation. Everything animated in canvas depends on the programmer creating a timer and redrawing all relevant parts as they are expected to change. Animating a figure along a path in SVG involves very little code. Doing the same in canvas requires a nontrivial amount of math on the part of the programmer.

Why would anyone use canvas then, if SVG is seemingly more convenient and helpful?

Where Canvas Shines

The most obvious benefit of canvas is performance. Tens of thousands or even hundreds of thousands of objects can be drawn (and animated) with very little overhead in canvas. Although it is convenient that every single SVG element is a DOM object with event handlers and the like, all of this overhead can take a massive toll on performance. Particle effects in canvas, for instance, can be very powerful and beautiful. Ten thousand pixels flying around in canvas makes for a nice special effect. Ten thousand SVG objects is a nightmare.

Canvas performance, therefore, scales much better than SVG. With SVG, as the complexity of a scene increases, the complexity of the DOM increases, and anything that uses the DOM often is slow. With canvas, it is up to the programmer to ensure that his or her JavaScript code stays performant, but a more complex scene does not necessarily mean a slower app, and very little DOM interaction is necessary.

SVG may do just fine for a mapping application, working with small diagrams, static graphics, or simple animation, and SVG code is generally simpler to create and easier to read. But canvas is always a better choice when performance must be kept in mind, such as with games, dynamic diagramming, charting, data visualization, and other applications that might require complex animation or large numbers of objects and particles.

Canvas *can* be very fast, but it is up to the programmer to keep it that way. Many of the optimizations that might be taken care of by more advanced drawing frameworks must be done by the programmer. Speed becomes important, and any serious canvas developer should familiarize himself with the typical concepts of graphics performance, such as caching, invalidations, and viewports. Additionally, different drawing operations are faster or slower than others, and different methods of accomplishing the same task can take wildly different times. The third canvas chapter in this part is dedicated to performance, and some specific notes are mentioned throughout this chapter as we cover individual canvas parts.

Canvas is also a candidate for image and pixel manipulation. Canvases can draw images, modify them, and save the pixel data. SVG has no such pixel or image manipulation capabilities. Image analysis is possible with canvas, and you can make a miniature image editor or image forensics app. Image histograms, for instance, are relatively easy to create in canvas, and impossible in SVG.

When to Not Use Canvas

The specification advises against using canvas to render static content, and in general you shouldn't use it if typical image and text elements will suffice. If scripting is disabled on the client, the canvas will be useless. Text drawn on a canvas is not selectable, searchable, or crawlable by web spiders like the ones employed by search engines. Any use of canvas should bear in mind these accessibility issues, and no text-to-speech program is going to work with text drawn to a canvas.

Canvas is great for adding nice designs to a page, but static designs are best left static. If you are looking to simply stylize text or round off the edges of a text area, you should see if the desired effects (such as shadows or rounded corners) are possible with CSS3 before opting to use a canvas.

Canvas is not guaranteed to look the same on all browsers. The implementations of anti-aliasing (or not) differ, and other quirks can cause gradients, text, and scaled objects to look dissimilar. Both the specification and implementations of canvas should be considered slightly, yet constantly, evolving.

NOTE

The specification provides a long list of reasons detailing why the (re)implementation of text-editing controls in the canvas is a bad idea. Accessibility is a nightmare to implement and modern browsers have put a lot of effort into making sure it's done well. Below is an excerpt from the specification detailing some of the things that would need to be redone just to make the canvas as useful as other HTML text input options.

Authors should avoid implementing text-editing controls using the canvas element. Doing so has a large number of disadvantages:

- ▶ Mouse placement of the caret has to be reimplemented.
- ▶ Keyboard movement of the caret has to be reimplemented (possibly across lines, for multiline text input).
- ▶ Scrolling of the text field has to be implemented (horizontally for long lines, vertically for multiline input).
- ▶ Native features such as copy and paste have to be reimplemented.
- ▶ Native features such as spell-checking have to be reimplemented.
- ▶ Native features such as drag and drop have to be reimplemented.
- ▶ Native features such as page-wide text search have to be reimplemented.
- ▶ Native features specific to the user, for example custom text services, have to be reimplemented. This is close to impossible because each user might have different services installed, and there is an unbounded set of such possible services.
- ▶ Bidirectional text editing has to be reimplemented.
- ▶ For multiline text editing, line wrapping has to be reimplemented for all relevant languages.
- ▶ Text selection has to be reimplemented.
- ▶ Dragging of bidirectional text selections has to be reimplemented.
- ▶ Platform-native keyboard shortcuts have to be reimplemented.
- ▶ Platform-native input method editors (IMEs) have to be reimplemented.
- ▶ Undo and redo functionality have to be reimplemented.
- ▶ Accessibility features such as magnification following the caret or selection have to be reimplemented.

This is a huge amount of work, and authors are most strongly encouraged to avoid doing any of it by instead using the input element, the textarea element, or the `contenteditable` attribute.

Don't Use Canvas for General UI

Canvas is not a good choice for website navigation or UI (user interface) in general, with the exception of some in-app UI such as menus in a game. Even then, many opt to build their in-app UI as a layer of separate DOM elements that appear over the canvas.

The aforementioned text and accessibility problems ought to be a good enough reason on their own, but the complications brought about by using canvas as navigation don't stop there. Users with JavaScript disabled will be unable to navigate your site, and the unintuitive expectations of non-DOM navigation will disorient others, especially those on specialty devices that may not be able to click on the canvas as one would expect, but instead navigate by tabs or some other feature.

An extreme version of canvas-based UI would be creating an entire site in one canvas, which would make the site useless to web crawlers, other sites that wanted to link to specific content, the Back button, and so on.

Outside of apps, canvas should be considered a way to accent web pages and never a way to replace functionality. Some functionality is necessarily dynamic, such as charts and diagrams, and might be a good choice for canvas, but it is important to always remember your audience, and because canvas is not supported on every browser, you should always try to provide reasonable fallback content, even if it is just a notice that JavaScript may be disabled or the browser at hand may not have the canvas API. The next section discusses fallback content in more depth.

Getting Started with Canvas

In this section, we talk about what it takes to start drawing on a canvas and how to create fallback content for browsers that do not have the canvas element. We also create an extremely minimal HTML page that contains a single canvas. If you want to follow along on your computer as you read, you'll be able to use the HTML page in almost every section of the coming chapters to demo functionality. This HTML is absolutely not necessary—the book is written to be read without any need for a computer. Following along, however, may help those who learn by writing and learn by example, and with the JavaScript console, you will be able to experiment on a canvas in real time.

The first thing to note about canvas is that the properties and methods are split over two parts. There's the HTML canvas element, which is easy to define:

```
<canvas id="canvas1" width="200" height="200"></canvas>
```

You can get a reference to the canvas element just like any other element in JavaScript:

```
var canvas = document.getElementById('canvas1');
```

Then there is the canvas context, which is where all the drawing and state for the canvas is located. Depending on the browser, canvas can have more than one possible context available. Whenever a website mentions canvas without specifying a context, the 2D canvas context is typically implied. Once you have a reference to the canvas in JavaScript, you can get a reference to the 2D context using the `getContext` method:

```
var context = canvas.getContext('2d');
```

It's important to have the context separated from the canvas because the canvas describes an HTML DOM element that specifies a drawing area and the context describes the *kind* of drawing that is to be done on the canvas. This chapter and the following two concern themselves with only the 2D canvas. There is also a 3D context that is accessed with the string `"webgl"` or `"webgl-experimental"`. The 3D context is the subject of the final chapter in this part of the book.

> **NOTE**
>
> You can put any manner of HTML content inside of a canvas tag, but that content will only show if the canvas does not work!
>
> The inner HTML of the canvas tag (in other words, the HTML between the opening and closing tag of the canvas) is used to display fallback content if a browser does not support canvas.
>
> Depending on the type of app you are creating and your target audience, you will either want to encourage users to upgrade to a modern browser or provide a set of content that provides as much functionality as possible without using a canvas. For instance, if you have a dynamic diagram or chart, you might want to provide a static image. If the content is always generated dynamically, you could potentially create an image dynamically server-side (such as with the `node.js` library) and serve that to the user instead. The amount of fallback content you want to provide is up to you, but it's important to keep in mind your audience, their level of tech expertise, and the alternatives you can offer them.

The fallback content inside the `<canvas>` tag can be any arbitrary block of HTML. Keep in mind that this content can also be accessed by assistive technology and still exists in the default tab order of the DOM. This means that if you put, say, an `<input />` tag inside of the canvas, you can "tab" into it, modify its contents, and any events associated with it will fire. This can be useful if you want your canvas to have some functionality that corresponds to real HTML interactive inputs, and want those inputs to be seen by the user if the canvas element is unavailable in his or her browser.

Enabling screen-reading assistive technology is also possible via text placed inside of the canvas element, so by the same token, all fallback content is also content for special accessibility programs and devices.

Although the `<canvas>` tag doesn't exist in older browsers, HTML has a graceful way of degrading, and any unknown element will still be rendered as an inline element that still contains its inner HTML content. Because the canvas element is made useful by displaying a bitmap instead of nested HTML, any content inside of a canvas element is automatically considered fallback content on older browsers, and not shown on newer browsers. Listing 5.1 provides a simple example of fallback content nested inside the `<canvas>` tag.

LISTING 5.1   Canvas Fallback HTML

```
<canvas width="300" height="300">
  <p>
  You can't see these paragraphs if your browser supports HTML5 canvas.
  </p>
  <p>
  If you can see them, you should download a newer browser!
  </p>
  <p>
  This is where you might place a fallback embedded Flash object,
  or just an image, or provide a link to Chrome Frame.
  </p>
</canvas>
```

How much time you spend on fallback content is up to your own judgment, but it's worth noting that very little is expected of the average canvas app thus far. Most fallback content inside of the canvases today is of the simpler variety that just tells the user to upgrade his or her browser or turn on JavaScript. The least you could do to improve on this is to describe what *would* appear were a functioning canvas on the page, so that text-to-speech devices might have something more useful to say about the content of your page, and so that users of older browsers might be enticed to upgrade.

An HTML Page with a Canvas

Let's get an entire page set up that we can save and use to try out canvas commands. Listing 5.2 contains complete HTML for a well-formed page with a canvas element, including a script for easy access to the canvas and its context.

LISTING 5.2   `Example.html`—A Complete HTML Page with a Canvas

```
<!doctype html>
<html>
  <body>
    <canvas id="myCanvas" width="500" height="500"
            style="border: 1px solid black;">
      This text is displayed if your browser does not support HTML5 canvas
    </canvas>

    <script type="text/javascript">
      // We'll attach both of these to the JavaScript window object
      // so we can easily access them in the console
      window.canvas = document.getElementById('myCanvas');
```

```
    window.ctx = canvas.getContext('2d');
  </script>
  </body>
</html>
```

This makes for a clean, simple starting page. It's very small, but we could make an even smaller web page for our testing. Listing 5.3 is a minimalist version of Listing 5.2.

LISTING 5.3   `MinimalExample.html`—A Simpler HTML Page with a Canvas

```
<canvas id="myCanvas" width="500" height="500" style="border: 1px solid black;">
</canvas>

<script>
  window.canvas = document.getElementById('myCanvas');
  window.ctx = canvas.getContext('2d');
</script>
```

This works just as well, except in a certain browser we could name (you know the one) that reverts to Quirks mode and refuses to recognize the canvas. Either of these snippets works for our testing, but you should never leave out the `doctype`, `html`, and `body` tags in a production web page.

Saving either Listing 5.2 or Listing 5.3 as an HTML file and opening it in a browser produces a simple but convenient web page for testing canvas commands. You'll be able to use this for the rest of the 2D canvas chapter to try out methods and properties as we cover them. It's not essential that you follow along on your computer, and the following chapters are written to be read regardless of where you are, but having a similar file handy allows you to quickly experiment in the JavaScript console in real time.

In Listing 5.2 and Listing 5.3, we are saving a reference to the canvas to easily refer to it in the console, and we are also saving a reference to the canvas's 2D context. The canvas context is used often, and is typically referred to in code as `ctx` for conciseness.

You can use your browser's JavaScript console to follow along, trying commands live on your own machine as we go through each section of this chapter. If you've never used a JavaScript console before, you should know that it's part of the common developer tools that come with most modern browsers and I *strongly* recommend learning how to use one of them. The console is easily among the most delightful tools we have today for the debugging and development (and learning!) of JavaScript.

NOTE

There are three ways to create a canvas element, but in typical use you'll want to stick to only one of them.

```
<canvas id="myCanvas" width="500", height="500">Fallback content</canvas>
```

is the most proper way. You could also add the canvas to the DOM programmatically:

```
var canvas = document.createElement('canvas');
document.body.appendChild(canvas);
canvas.height = '500';
canvas.width = '500';
```

Or simply:

```
document.write("<canvas id='myCanvas' width='500', height='500'></canvas>");
```

The first way is preferable because it follows the rules of accessibility the best. If a user has JavaScript enabled or a previous JavaScript error has halted further JS execution, only the first one will actually display the canvas, and, therefore, will be the only one to display fallback content if it is defined.

The second method is still important for making in-memory canvases, which you learn about in the later section, "In-Memory Canvases."

All canvas drawing involves calling a set of commands that apply pixels or a drawing operation to the canvas. The canvas context method `fillRect`, for instance, draws a rectangle on the canvas. This particular call to `fillRect` draws a rectangle starting at the (x, y) coordinates (50, 60) with a width of 70 and a height of 80:

```
ctx.fillRect(50, 60, 70, 80);
```

If you've saved one of the above code listings as an HTML document and you open it in a browser, you will be able to type the `fillRect` command into the console and see the rectangle appear on your screen.

Canvas Attributes

The canvas itself has just a few JavaScript attributes.

The sizing attributes `width` and `height`, which default to 300 and 150 respectively, are often set in the HTML, but setting them programmatically is just as easy:

```
canvas.width = 500;
canvas.height = 500;
```

This achieves the same size as our code sample from the last section. It's important to note that setting the width or height of the canvas also completely resets the state of the canvas context, meaning that all context properties are set back to their defaults and anything drawn on the canvas bitmap will be cleared each time the `width` or `height` is set. In fact, a popular way to clear the screen is to set the width to itself, by calling `canvas.width = canvas.width;`.

NOTE

Setting the `width` and `height` attributes of the canvas is not analogous to setting a CSS width or height. Setting a size using CSS stretches and distorts the canvas bitmap. The only way to resize the real bitmap size of the canvas is by using the `width` and `height` attributes.

---

toDataURL

Often you'll want to turn the canvas bitmap into a URL:

```
canvas.toDataURL(type, options)
```

This function returns a string that is a `data:URL` for the image in the canvas. Both arguments are optional. The first one controls the type of image to be returned, with the default being `"image/png"` if the argument is omitted. The other common type is `"image/jpeg"`, which can take advantage of the second optional argument to specify JPEG quality on a scale of 0 to 1.0. It's possible that other image types will someday be supported, such as `"image/svg+xml"`, but for now PNG and JPEG are the only ones with wide support. If a type isn't supported, instead of throwing an error, `toDataURL` just returns a PNG.

```
canvas.toDataURL(); //returns a string describing a png
canvas.toDataURL("image/jpeg", 1); //returns a string describing a jpeg
```

In Google Chrome, the canvas `toDataURL` method also supports `"image/webp"` as an optional argument. WebP is an image format that can employ either lossless or lossy compression, and is considered a sister format to the WebM video container format. As of this writing, only Chrome and Opera support WebP, and only Chrome's canvas supports creating a WebP image with the canvas.

The string returned is a Base64 encoded image, and it typically follows the format:
`data:image/png;base64,[Base64 string here].`

NOTE

All modern browsers support several data URLs with Base64 images being the most common. It's possible to fit an entire tiny page into a data URL. For instance, you can type this into your address bar:

```
data:text/html;charset=utf-8,<style type="text/css">
➥body {font-size: 200px; }</style>Hello%20there
```

And it will spell out "Hello there" in very large print on the screen.

Data URLs of Base64 images can be very useful for reducing the number of requests that a page makes. Instead of having a separate request for an image (or many images), you could instead add the image to the HTML or CSS as a Base64 data URL, and the client will only have to make one request to the server instead of two or more.

Their other major use, in the context of canvas, is to have an easy way to send the contents of a modified canvas bitmap to and from the server. This is something of a powerful ability, and there are some security concerns with `toDataURL` that are addressed later, in the section about `ImageData` and pixel manipulation.

If you've never seen a Base64 string before, you might be surprised by the length. For instance, a canvas that's 50 by 50 pixels might return a string that is about 9,000 characters in length for a lossless PNG, or about 4,000 characters for the same image as a higher-quality JPEG, or 1,000 characters for the same image as a low-quality JPEG. Extreme character savings come at a cost, of course, and Figure 5.3 shows an example of quality reduction from JPEG compression.

FIGURE 5.3   Some castles may last hundreds of years, but will be ruined instantly at the hands of an overzealous JPEG compressor.

Context Methods and State

The real drawing that goes on in the canvas happens on the context. There is more than one possible context type, as mentioned before, and 2D is the sole concern of this chapter.

In spite of these different context types, all canvases only ever have one context. The first time `getContext` is called, a primary context is created with the specified type (2D or webGL), and all subsequent calls to the method simply return the primary context, regardless of the argument specified.

A Quick Look at the Properties and State Available

First, let's take a quick preview at the kind of state the canvas context holds.

If we load the HTML page we created in the "Getting Started with Canvas" section of this chapter, we can open the console in Google Chrome and type **ctx**. The console will return the reference, and if we click the arrow to the left of this reference, it will show us all of the attributes of the canvas context, as shown in Figure 5.4. Expanding the __proto__ would let us see all of the available context methods, too. Consoles in other browsers will produce similar results, though not all of them let us visually explore JavaScript objects as easily.

FIGURE 5.4   The Chrome console showing all properties of the canvas context and their default values.

If you look at the context state, you see several properties that are more or less intuitively named. We go over every property soon enough, but for now we start with the simple drawing methods and the properties that modify them.

Understanding Drawing, Starting with Rectangles

Drawing on the canvas is sort of like painting with a complicated paintbrush. Just as you dip your paintbrush into the pigment you want to paint, you load up your canvas context with certain state and possibly a path, and then you execute the command to draw it. If you want to fill a black rectangle as we did in the previous section, you would type:

```
ctx.fillRect(20,30,40,50);
```

And a black rectangle would appear.

NOTE

If you typed in the above command, you'd see a little black rectangle. It's important to remember that the bitmap of the rectangle is all there is to it. No additional state was created to remember where the rectangle was drawn. You can't select the rectangle or modify the rectangle in any way.

All you've done, like in painting, is place some paint upon your canvas. We can't move our paint, or change its color without adding more paint or clearing the paint. Because there's no state, simply moving the rectangle across the screen involves a lot of footwork. You see in the next chapter how to make canvas apps remember the useful and relevant bits of drawing to allow you to redraw, animate, and interact with the canvas.

The context method `ctx.clearRect` works just like `ctx.fillRect`, except instead of coloring in a rectangle, it clears the pixels in a rectangular region. There is no such thing as "not a pixel" on the canvas and a call to `clearRect` technically resets the pixels to the canvas default, which happens to be fully transparent black. Setting the canvas width equal to itself was one way we already learned to clear the entire canvas. Another way is by issuing the command:

```
ctx.clearRect(0,0,canvas.width, canvas.height);
```

There are some meaningful differences between these two approaches, which we detail later when talking about state and transformations.

fillStyle **and** strokeStyle

Let's take a look at some of the context state attributes. What if you wanted a red rectangle instead? To draw a red rectangle, you have to change the state of the context, specifically the `fillStyle`. Assigning the `fillStyle` almost any valid CSS color string sets a valid fill style:

```
ctx.fillStyle = 'red'; // red!
// identical to 'red', but represented as a hex value
ctx.fillStyle = '#FF0000';
// also identical to red, represented as an RGB value from 0 to 255
ctx.fillStyle = 'rgb(255, 0, 0)';
// also identical to red, represented as an HSL value
ctx.fillStyle = 'hsl(0, 100%, 50%)';
// also red but semitransparent!
ctx.fillStyle = 'rgba(255, 0, 0, 0.5)';
```

Frustratingly, setting many of the context attributes to an incorrect value does not produce an error but instead silently ignores the statement. As in so much of JavaScript, typos can be dangerous here. If your `fillStyle` was black and you want to set it to `"lightblue"` but accidentally type `"lightblerg"` (an invalid CSS string), you get no warning and the `fillStyle` simply remains black.

The context attribute `strokeStyle` is set in the exact same way and with the same possibilities. There are more to `fillStyle` and `strokeStyle` color options than just CSS strings, and we cover gradients and patterns in the later "Gradients and Patterns" section.

Paths

The context methods `fillRect` and `strokeRect` are convenience methods that carry out common path operations of creating a rectangle and stroking it or filling it. All nonrectangular shape drawing on the canvas is done by constructing a path using methods that add individual lines and curves. Finally, the path is realized on the canvas by calling the `stroke` or the `fill` method.

If you asked someone for instructions on how to draw a plus sign on paper, the directions would probably be as simple as remarking that you "just draw two lines crossing." As usual, in programming we need to be a lot more precise than common language, and in canvas there are a fair number of ways to draw two lines. Here is the smallest amount of code needed to make a plus symbol:

```
ctx.beginPath();   // This discards any old path and starts a new one
ctx.moveTo(50, 0);  // here we can position our "pen" at a starting point
ctx.lineTo(50, 100); // add a segment vertically
ctx.moveTo(0, 50);  // using moveTo a second time lets us pick up our "pen"
ctx.lineTo(100, 50); //add a segment horizontally
ctx.stroke(); // Draw the path we just constructed
```

The context commands that construct the path do not draw anything onto the canvas. Instead, they work on an invisible structure known as the *current path*. At any given time, there is only one path (or no path) "loaded" on the context. A path can have any number of *subpaths*, which are created by using the `moveTo` method.

The current path is not rendered onto the canvas bitmap until the programmer calls to the context methods `stroke` or `fill`, which use the `strokeStyle` or `fillStyle` values to render the path as an outline or as a filled figure. Stroking or filling a path does not clear or reset the current path, and forgetting to do so before moving on may lead to graphical defects in your canvas app! A call to `beginPath` is needed to discard the current path and start anew.

There's a subtle concept here that confounds a lot of canvas newcomers. In order to illustrate this, we set two state attributes on the canvas. If you're following along, clear what you've done so far to the canvas page by either refreshing the web page or setting the canvas width equal to itself in the console. Then set the following two attributes:

```
ctx.strokeStyle = 'rgba(0, 0, 0, 0.5)';
ctx.lineWidth = 20;
```

This code sets the stroke style to a half-transparent black and causes any paths stroked to be 20 pixels wide. If you enter those two lines into the console and then enter the code to make a plus again, you see a much thicker plus.

In the plus sign code from before, we make one path and stroke it, but that path consisted of *two* subpaths. Many who would want to write a plus might instead write it like this:

```
ctx.beginPath();
ctx.moveTo(50, 0);
ctx.lineTo(50, 100);
ctx.stroke(); // This time we stroke the first subpath right away
ctx.moveTo(0, 50);
ctx.lineTo(100, 50);
ctx.stroke(); // the second stroke
```

> **NOTE**
>
> If you're following along in a browser's developer console, remember to either reload the page or clear the canvas before trying the different blocks of code given here. Note that `ctx.clearRect` clears the canvas visually, but `canvas.width = canvas.width` clears the canvas and also sets all states (`fillStyle`, `lineWidth`, and so on) back to their defaults.

This intuitively looks right. After all, when you are drawing a plus sign on paper, you make two "strokes" with your pen. But unlike writing a plus sign on paper, this code strokes the vertical line twice. The first `stroke` command applies to the vertical line and the second `stroke` applies to both lines. This is because stroking a path does not automatically end or reset the current path. It's still there, waiting to be added to. So in this case, we add a second subpath and stroke a second time, and the second stroke applies, as it always will, to the entire current path.

Knowing this, there's yet another way to make a plus sign:

```
ctx.beginPath();
ctx.moveTo(50, 0);
ctx.lineTo(50, 100);
ctx.stroke();
ctx.beginPath();    // a new path
ctx.moveTo(0, 50);
ctx.lineTo(100, 50);
ctx.stroke();
```

Here, we make two separate paths, as opposed to our previous code that created a single path with two subpaths, and we stroke each path only once. This strokes the center of the plus sign twice, and is technically closest to what we do when we write a plus on paper because the two strokes we make with a real pen do overlap on paper, and if we wrote a plus lightly with a pencil we would expect the middle to be a little darker because the pencil crossed it twice. Figure 5.5 shows the result of all three code blocks, displaying the different outcome between these three plus-making methods.

FIGURE 5.5   From left to right: A plus made from one path with one stroke, a plus made from one path with two strokes (one intermediary), and a plus made from two paths.

> **NOTE**
>
> We get a glimpse of something deeper about the nature of paths in this code. When a path with many overlapping subpaths is stroked just once, none of the intersection points of the path have overlapping coloring. This is because the algorithm canvas used to "trace" a path for stroking treats any overlapping parts of a single path as a union, making sure they are stroked only once. You can see that clearly in the difference between the preceding three code blocks. Stroking one path (but two subpaths) causes the union of all the subpaths to be drawn as a clean plus. But creating two distinct paths in the third block does cause the intersection to be stroked.

So far, we've seen what `stroke` can do. As noted at the start of this section, the `strokeRect` command can be considered shorthand for a call to `rect` and a call to `stroke`.

```
ctx.beginPath();
ctx.rect(x, y, width, height);
ctx.stroke();
```

Similarly, the `rect(x, y, width, height)` is shorthand for the path commands:

```
ctx.moveTo(x, y);
ctx.lineTo(x + w, y);
ctx.lineTo(x + w, y + h);
ctx.lineTo(x, y + h);
ctx.closePath();
```

The `fillRect` command is the same shorthand, except `fill()` is implicitly called instead of `stroke()`.

Understanding the Canvas Coordinate System

If you've been following along on a computer, reload your simple canvas page and issue these commands in the console:

```
ctx.lineWidth = 1;
ctx.moveTo(0, 20);
ctx.lineTo(100, 20);
```

```
ctx.moveTo(0, 30.5);
ctx.lineTo(100, 30.5);
ctx.stroke();
```

This draws two lines, but you'll notice if you look carefully that the second one looks smaller and crisper. In fact, the first one appears slightly blurry. Why would this be? Enlarging the result gives us Figure 5.6, where we can see that the first line drawn is actually two pixels wide in spite of the lineWidth of 1.

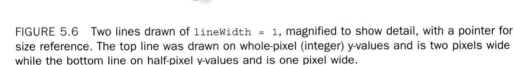

FIGURE 5.6   Two lines drawn of lineWidth = 1, magnified to show detail, with a pointer for size reference. The top line was drawn on whole-pixel (integer) y-values and is two pixels wide while the bottom line on half-pixel y-values and is one pixel wide.

To understand what's going on here, we have to consider what it means to draw a line from coordinates and what it means to be a pixel.

Pixels are little squares on a screen that are represented in the drawing system with x and y coordinates. Because they are not infinitely small points but instead little boxes, we have to pick a spot in that box to describe a given pixel's location. For the canvas coordinate system, the location of a pixel is its top-left corner.

This means that when we are specifying coordinates, we cannot use integers to specify the centers of pixels; instead, we can only use integers to point to the top-left corners of the square pixels that make up the screen, and, therefore, all integer coordinates actually specify the boundary (or corner) between two or more pixels. So (0, 0) may be considered the top-left *point* of the canvas and it is also the top-left *corner* of the first pixel of the coordinate system. The method fillRect(34, 56, 1, 1) paints the single pixel whose *top-left corner* is at (34, 56). Whenever we casually say a pixel is at an (x, y) location, we are really talking about the pixel whose top-left corner is located at (x, y).

Paths specified on the canvas, however, are very precise and if you draw a line from (0, 20) to (100, 20), it draws that line along the pixel boundary, starting from the top-left corner of the pixel at (0, 20) and ending at the top-left corner of the pixel at (100, 20). If the lineWidth is an odd number, then in drawing this line the context half-fills the pixels above and half-fills the pixels below the horizontal boundary at the y-position of 20. This leads to a line that is two pixels wide and those pixels are colored lighter to make up for it. Looking back at Figure 5.6, you can see that the first line, drawn on integer coordinates, is not only two pixels wide but also lighter than the line drawn on half-integer coordinates.

To see this a little more clearly, Figure 5.7 gives a representation of a pixel grid with each square representing a pixel. You can see the canvas coordinates marked on the grid lines, and two similar blue lines are again drawn, the first one at y = 1 and the second at y = 3.5. Because the line at y = 1 cannot draw directly on a row of pixels, it spreads a thinner blue across two pixel rows.

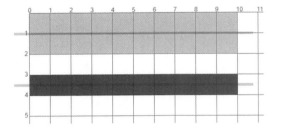

FIGURE 5.7   A representation of a pixel grid with two lines drawn of lineWidth = 1. The top line was drawn with a y-value of 1 and is two pixels wide while the bottom line was drawn with a y-value of 3.5 and is one pixel wide. Thin red lines mark these y-values.

With this knowledge, we can make nice and accurate lines on a canvas, such as the ones created in Listing 5.4, which form a clean grid.

LISTING 5.4   Simple Gridlines

```
var width = canvas.width;
var height = canvas.height;
for (var i = 0; i < width; i += 40) {
  ctx.moveTo(i - 0.5, 0);
  ctx.lineTo(i - 0.5, height);
}

for (var i = 0; i < height; i += 40) {
  ctx.moveTo(0, i - 0.5);
  ctx.lineTo(width, i - 0.5);
}
ctx.strokeStyle = 'gray';
ctx.stroke();
```

For performance reasons, in a real canvas application with a static grid as a background, it may be best to simply set the CSS background-image of the canvas element to a precomputed grid PNG.

Line Styles

The canvas context provides four properties to style stroked paths:

▶ lineWidth—A number attribute that allows you to customize the width of stroked paths. The default value is 1.0.

▶ lineCap—A string attribute that controls the looks of any open subpaths. butt, round, and square are valid values. The default value is butt.

▶ lineJoin—A string attribute that controls how corners look where two lines meet. miter, bevel, and round are valid values. The default value is miter.

▶ miterLimit—A positive number that controls the mitering ratio. The default value is 10.0.

The context attribute lineWidth sets the width of the path to be drawn. This means you can not only stroke paths of different widths, but you can also stroke the same current path many times with potentially many colors in many widths. The code in Listing 5.5 strokes a path repeatedly, changing its lineWidth and strokeStyle before each stroke. The result is shown in Figure 5.8.

LISTING 5.5   Stroking the Same Path Multiple Times

```
// If you're following along in the developer console and ran prior code,
// Remember to clear the canvas with canvas.width = canvas.width
// Or a page reload

// Construct a path
ctx.moveTo(40,40);
ctx.lineTo(100, 150);
ctx.lineTo(400, 40);

// stroke several times with a smaller line width
// and different color each time
for (var i = 5; i > 0; i--) {
  ctx.lineWidth = i*16;
  var blueValue = 255 - (i*32);
  var greenValue = i*32;
  ctx.strokeStyle = 'rgb(0, ' + greenValue + ',' + blueValue + ')';
  ctx.stroke();
}
```

Later, in the "Compositing" section, you see how to use different values of lineWidth to "hollow out" the middle of a large path.

The context method lineCap gets or sets how the ending point of each subpath is to be drawn. Figure 5.9 shows you the three possibilities.

FIGURE 5.8   A path created once and stroked repeatedly with different line widths and colors.

FIGURE 5.9   From top to bottom: Line caps of butt, round, and square, drawn to the coordinate marked by the gray line.

The default value "butt" extends the line to precisely where the end is defined and goes no further. Both "round" and "square" extend the line by half of the line width.

The lineJoin property gets or sets how corners are drawn when two line segments meet. Valid values are "miter" (the default), "round", and "bevel". Figure 5.10 displays the difference between the three when applied to a thick path elbow.

FIGURE 5.10   From left to right: Line joins of miter, bevel, and round.

When two segments join at acute angles and the lineJoin is set to miter, the path has the option to "stick out" to make an exceptionally pointy elbow. Just how far this point will extend is defined by the miterLimit. The miter *length* is the distance that the two segments could possibly extend if they kept going until the outer strokes of each touched.

The miter length could get awfully large if the angle between two line segments is small, so a path with a `lineJoin` of `miter` is constrained by the `miterLimit`. The `miterLimit` describes a ratio of the miter length divided by one half of the `lineWidth`. The default `miterLimit` is 10. The effect when the limit is reached is an abrupt cropping of any mitering, equivalent to a `lineJoin` of `"bevel"`, as shown in Figure 5.11.

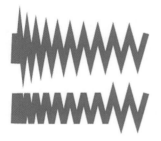

FIGURE 5.11   A path with the default miter limit of 10 is on top. Below is the same path with a miter limit of 4. When the miter limit is reached, the line joins become identical to a `lineJoin` of `"bevel"`.

Curves

The canvas context provides several methods for augmenting paths with curves:

- ▶ `arc(x, y, radius, startAngle, endAngle, counterClockwise)`

- ▶ `arcTo(x1, y1, x2, y2, radius)`

- ▶ `bezierCurveTo(cp1x, cp1y, cp2x, cp2y, x, y)`

- ▶ `quadraticCurveTo(cpx, cpy, x, y)`

arc

The context's `arc` method creates a sweeping arc from a given center point defined by the first two arguments. The third argument is the radius of the sweep, followed by two arguments defining starting and ending angles, in radians. The final argument is whether or not the path will be drawn counterclockwise.

> **NOTE**
>
> The last argument is technically optional but it's good form to write it anyway, as some browsers in recent history erroneously skipped the command if the argument was not there. If you assume your users have the very latest updates, then there ought to be no problem, but you shouldn't make that assumption!

The `arc` method makes drawing a circle simple:

```
ctx.beginPath();
ctx.arc(150, 150, 90, 0, Math.PI * 2, false);
ctx.fill();
```

The arguments for `arc` are enough to determine a starting point and ending point of a segment, unlike `lineTo`, which only describes an end point. Arcs are still connected to the current path, though, so calling the `arc` command with any previously existing current path makes a connection from the last point to the start of the arc. Sometimes this is wanted, but often it just looks strange, so you need to be extra mindful about using `beginPath()` or not before issuing the `arc` command. This extra line can often be useful, such as when constructing a pie slice.

The code in Listing 5.6 produces the pie slice shown in Figure 5.12.

LISTING 5.6   Making Pie

```
ctx.lineWidth = 4;
ctx.strokeStyle = 'magenta';

ctx.beginPath();
ctx.moveTo(50, 50);
ctx.arc(50, 50, 90, 0, 1, false);
ctx.closePath();
ctx.stroke();
```

FIGURE 5.12   A pie slice made with the `arc` command.

If we omitted the `moveTo` command, it would not have stroked the horizontal line, and if we omitted the `closePath` command, it would not have stroked the second (angled) line back to the center.

arcTo

Although arcs start and end at two points, the two points aren't explicitly given with the `arc` command. The context method `arcTo` is used to make an arc when you know where the arc ought to start and end. `arcTo` takes two points and a radius: `arcTo(x1, y1, x2, y2, radius)`.

The arguments to `arcTo` can be a little confusing. In many real-world uses of `arcTo`, it is fair to say that an arc is drawn from the first point to the second, but this would only be true at one radius value. After all, you can't draw an arc from (10, 10) to (2000, 2000) with a radius of only 50!

Technically, the arc created is the shortest arc that starts tangent to the line created from (x1, y1) and the previous point in the path. The arc ends on the point that is tangent to the line created from (x1, y1) and (x2, y2). If the previous point in the path does not equal the start of the arc, a line is drawn from the previous point to the start of the arc.

If this seems a tad confusing, then you're in good company. Even the canvas specification, which is sometimes a stuffy read, has in recent history provided a few diagrams to clear up confusion surrounding the workings of the arcTo method. Figure 5.13 shows the three examples provided by the specification.

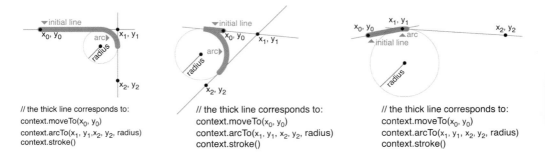

FIGURE 5.13   Three examples of the arcTo command from the WHATWG canvas specification.

The arcTo method is most popularly used for rounding the corners on rectangles. This is fairly simple to do, and because rounded rectangles are so common, we should make a function we can save and reuse anywhere. Listing 5.7 contains such a function and an example of its use.

LISTING 5.7   roundedRect, a Function for Producing Rounded Rectangle Paths

```
function roundedRect(ctx, x, y, width, height, radius) {
  // if the radius is larger than a side we have to reduce it
  if (width < 2 * radius) radius = width / 2;
  if (height < 2 * radius) radius = height / 2;
  ctx.beginPath();
  ctx.moveTo(x + radius, y);
  ctx.arcTo(x + width, y, x + width, y + height, radius);
  ctx.arcTo(x + width, y + height, x, y + height, radius);
  ctx.arcTo(x, y + height, x, y, radius);
  ctx.arcTo(x, y, x + width, y, radius);
  ctx.closePath();
}
```

```
// Sample usage:
roundedRect(ctx, 20, 20, 100, 100, 10);
ctx.stroke();
```

The sample page we constructed with Listing 5.2 already has a global context defined (ctx), but we want the method to work on other pages too, so we make the first argument a context on which to construct the path. Next, we have the four arguments describing a rectangle just as the context's rect method does. The last argument is the radius of the arc that makes up each rounded corner. To keep the method general, we don't want to call stroke or fill in the method itself; instead, it only loads the current path with a rounded rectangle. This also lets us use the constructed path for clipping, which you learn about in the "Clipping" section.

Setting the last argument of the roundedRect function to a value greater than half of the height and width of a square will draw a circle, though this would be an awfully round-about way of doing so.

Bezier Curves

Bezier curves are a common way of defining a curve that goes between two end points guided by one or more "control" points. They can curve in as many directions as there are control points, and canvas provides the two most common types of Bezier curves.

The context method bezierCurveTo(cp1x, cp1y, cp2x, cp2y, x, y) adds a *cubic* Bezier curve to the current path and takes two control points and an endpoint, with the first point of the curve being the last point in the subpath.

The similar method quadraticCurveTo(cpx, cpy, x, y) adds a quadratic Bezier curve to the current path and only takes one control point and one endpoint.

Both curves can be seen in Figure 5.14 with their control points highlighted. The cubic Bezier's two control points afford it the ability to bend in two directions, while the quadratic Bezier can only bend in one direction.

FIGURE 5.14   A quadratic Bezier (left) and cubic Bezier (right), with control points highlighted in red.

The math behind Bezier curves is fairly complex. The casual explanation is that the one or two control points "pull" the path to make the desired curve.

Without knowing any advanced math, we can still take a look at how Bezier curves are made and how to find their midpoints. Illustrating a quadratic Bezier curve is a little easier to visualize because there's only one control point, so let's make an example of one.

A quadratic curve is made of a start point (the last point in your path), one control point, and an endpoint. We can connect these three points with two lines. Using the midpoints of those two lines, we can make a third line. The midpoint of *that* line happens to be the midpoint of the quadratic curve! We can visualize this very easily with the code in Listing 5.8, which produces Figure 5.15.

LISTING 5.8   Bezier Curve Examples

```
var canvas = document.getElementById('myCanvas');
var ctx = canvas.getContext('2d');


// Convenience function for averaging two values
function mid(a, b) {
  return (a + b) / 2;
}


// The three points of our quadratic Bezier
var startX = 0;
var startY = 0;
var controlX = 150;
var controlY = 220;
var endX = 200;
var endY = 0;


// Draw the quadratic curve as a red path
ctx.lineWidth = 6;
ctx.strokeStyle = "red";
ctx.fillStyle = "rgba(0,0,0,0.9)";

ctx.beginPath();
ctx.moveTo(startX, startY);
ctx.quadraticCurveTo(controlX, controlY, endX, endY);
ctx.stroke();

// draw control point
// We subtract 3 from the x and y
// so the center of the rect is atop the relevant point
ctx.fillRect(controlX - 3, controlY - 3, 6, 6);

// Two blue lines:
// One from the start to the control point,
```

```
// and one from the end to the control point
ctx.strokeStyle = "rgba(0,0,250,0.3)";
ctx.beginPath();
ctx.moveTo(startX, startY);
ctx.lineTo(controlX, controlY);

ctx.moveTo(endX, endY);
ctx.lineTo(controlX, controlY);
ctx.stroke();

// Find the midpoints of the two lines
var ax = mid(controlX, startX);
var ay = mid(controlY, startY);
var bx = mid(controlX, endX);
var by = mid(controlY, endY);
 // Draw line midpoints for visual aid
ctx.fillRect(ax - 3, ay - 3, 6, 6);
ctx.fillRect(bx - 3, by - 3, 6, 6);

// One green line connecting the blue midpoints
ctx.strokeStyle = "rgba(0,240,0,0.5)";
ctx.beginPath();
ctx.moveTo(ax, ay);
ctx.lineTo(bx, by);
ctx.stroke();

// And now we have the Bezier's midpoint!
var midX = mid(ax, bx);
var midY = mid(ay, by);

// Show the midpoint with a rect
ctx.fillRect(midX - 3, midY - 3, 6, 6);
```

FIGURE 5.15   A quadratic Bezier curve in red, with blue lines showing the path from the start and end points to the midpoint.

Looking at Figure 5.15, we get an idea of how the curve is constructed. The frames in Figure 5.16 illustrate the continuous process of creating a quadratic Bezier curve.

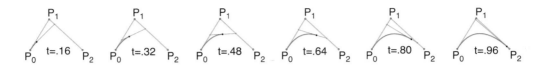

FIGURE 5.16   These frames depict the process behind a quadratic Bezier curve's construction.

The green line in Figure 5.16 can be considered moving, with its first point traveling from the start to the control point, and its second point traveling from the control point to the endpoint. It travels proportionally along each gray segment, so when one point is 20% along the first gray line, the second point will be 20% along the second gray line, and the green line can be said to have completed 20% of its journey.

At any given moment in the green line's journey, the point of the Bezier curve it is drawing is 20% along the green line. All of these metrics just so happen to line up nicely at 50% along so that you can calculate the midpoint with ease, but as you can see it's a bit more of a chore to calculate the whole thing!

When this green line is 20% done with its journey, the point of the Bezier curve it is drawing is 20% along the green line. The journey continues along to the end and so the curve is made. Because of this method of construction, a curve defined by just three points can scale indefinitely.

As you can imagine, Bezier curves are best illustrated with an animation and I encourage you to search for such an animation online. There are many interactive examples, too, including several made with canvas itself.

Ellipses

Until very recently, the canvas specification has left out an easy way to make ellipses. It is technically in the specification now, but at the time this book was written, no browser has implemented it. To have this functionality in the meantime, we give an example of how to make an approximation of an ellipse of arbitrary size using Bezier curves. Listing 5.9 creates a drawEllipse function, takes a rectangle describing a desired ellipse's area, and loads the current path with an ellipse. The result is shown in Figure 5.17.

LISTING 5.9   drawEllipse Function for Creating Elliptical Paths

```
function drawEllipse(ctx, x, y, w, h) {
  // For performance reasons I prefer to keep kappa stored
  // somewhere so it is only computed once. You could also
  // use a precomputed value such as 0.551784
  var kappa = 4 * ((Math.sqrt(2) - 1) / 3),
  cx = (w / 2) * kappa,
  cy = (h / 2) * kappa,
```

```
    right = x + w,
    bottom = y + h,
    xmid = x + w / 2,
    ymid = y + h / 2;

    ctx.beginPath();
    ctx.moveTo(x, ymid);
    ctx.bezierCurveTo(x, ymid - cy, xmid - cx, y, xmid, y);
    ctx.bezierCurveTo(xmid + cx, y, right, ymid - cy, right, ymid);
    ctx.bezierCurveTo(right, ymid + cy, xmid + cx, bottom, xmid, bottom);
    ctx.bezierCurveTo(xmid - cx, bottom, x, ymid + cy, x, ymid);
    ctx.closePath();
    ctx.stroke();
}

// Sample usage:
drawEllipse(ctx, 10, 10, 200, 60)
ctx.fillStyle = 'PaleTurquoise'
ctx.strokeStyle = 'MediumVioletRed'
ctx.lineWidth = 6;
ctx.fill();
ctx.stroke();
```

FIGURE 5.17   An ellipse generated with our `drawEllipse` function.

NOTE

In the "Transformation Matrix" section, you see another method of rendering ellipses.

Kappa is an irrational constant often used in conjunction with Bezier curves. Its value is needed to draw several shapes such as ellipses and sine waves. Here, it is used to get the appropriate offset for the control points, `cx` and `cy`. As the comment in the code mentions, it would be best if it is computed only once and the value stored, or if a constant is defined and used instead.

In the future, of course, we'll just call the context method `ellipse`, which will work very similar to the `arc` method. If you were enterprising, you could test for existence of the `ellipse` method on canvas and use it if it is there, and otherwise fall back on our custom Bezier-backed ellipse path-making method.

isPointInPath

The `isPointInPath` context method takes two arguments, `x` and `y`, and returns `true` or `false` depending on whether or not the point described is within the context's current path.

Because this method only works with the current path, it is not feasible to use with most real-world, hit-testing scenarios unless your app is small or otherwise has little going on, such as no animation or otherwise performance-dependent features. If this is the case, `isPointInPath` can save you some implementation time.

If you have several figures drawn and you want to test a point against all of them, you have to reconstruct the path on the canvas for each figure in order to use `isPointInPath`, which could get needlessly slow. If you need accurate hit detection or object picking, it is best to represent your figures with your own data structure and implement your own point-in-polygon method.

Recent changes to the specification have added paths as their own objects, independent of the canvas context. As of this writing, no browsers have implemented this functionality, but when they do, the `isPointInPath` method may become more efficient and useful than in current canvas implementations.

Path Filling—The Winding Number Rule

Often, you'll want a path that's more complicated than just a filled shape. Perhaps you want to make a figure resembling the silhouette of a window or frame. You need to make a hole, or "cut out" the glass panes from the frame.

Almost all drawing systems have either one or two ways to make holes in filled paths. Canvas uses an algorithm called the nonzero winding number rule to determine where holes in the path will be. The other algorithm you might encounter in drawing systems is called the even-odd rule, but canvas does not make use of it. SVG uses both.

Every time you draw a path, you are drawing in a direction. When you construct a rectangle, you start somewhere (`moveTo`), and then draw lines around in either a clockwise or a counterclockwise fashion to complete the shape. It can be said that a particular path is *winding* clockwise or counterclockwise relative to a particular point.

At its simplest, making a hole means making a subpath inside of another subpath that "winds" in the opposite direction, so that one subpath is going clockwise and the other one counterclockwise.

Listing 5.10 provides a framed rectangle example. The first subpath is constructed clockwise and the second (inner) subpath is counterclockwise. The result is shown in Figure 5.18.

LISTING 5.10   Drawing a Framed Rectangle from Two Subpaths

```
ctx.fillStyle = 'LightBlue';
ctx.beginPath();
ctx.moveTo(0, 0);
```

```
ctx.lineTo(100, 0);
ctx.lineTo(100, 100);
ctx.lineTo(0, 100);
ctx.closePath();

ctx.moveTo(10, 10);
ctx.lineTo(10, 90);
ctx.lineTo(90, 90);
ctx.lineTo(90, 10);
ctx.closePath();

ctx.fill();
```

FIGURE 5.18   A framed rectangle constructed from two subpaths and filled.

The "rule" in the nonzero winding number rule is fairly simple to understand. As we already said, any given subpath is drawn in a direction and can be said to wind either clockwise or counterclockwise relative to some point.

For any given piece of the figure, imagine a line extending from a point inside that piece outward in any direction. That line crosses at least one edge of the path. The algorithm counts the number of edges crossed and compares the number of clockwise edges crossed with the number of counterclockwise edges crossed. If the difference between one count and the other is zero, then that piece of the figure is unfilled. If the difference between the two counts is nonzero, then it is filled.

Put more succinctly, if the number of crossings in each category (clockwise and counter-clockwise) is the same, then that part of the shape is unfilled.

Let's see the nonzero winding number rule in action on a more complicated path. Listing 5.11 composes a figure out of three subpaths.

LISTING 5.11   Drawing a Complex Shape from Three Subpaths

```
ctx.lineWidth = 3;
ctx.fillStyle = 'rgba(0,255,0,0.5)';

ctx.beginPath();
ctx.moveTo(100, 0);
ctx.lineTo(200, 0);
ctx.lineTo(200, 200);
```

```
ctx.lineTo(0, 200);
ctx.closePath();

ctx.moveTo(20, 20);
ctx.lineTo(20, 180);
ctx.lineTo(170, 180);
ctx.lineTo(170, 20);
ctx.closePath();

ctx.moveTo(240, 100);
ctx.lineTo(240, 140);
ctx.lineTo(0, 140);
ctx.lineTo(0, 100);
ctx.closePath();

ctx.fill();
ctx.stroke();
```

The single path in Listing 5.11 produces a shape with several filled and unfilled sections, as shown in Figure 5.19.

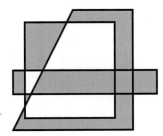

FIGURE 5.19   A shape constructed from three subpaths.

This is a bit complicated at first glance, so for the sake of clarity, we separate out the subpaths to get a better idea of the individual parts. If we make three separate paths by moving the coordinates of each shape, we would instead get Figure 5.20.

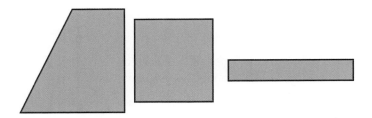

FIGURE 5.20   The three subpaths separated into three paths.

Figure 5.21 is the same shape again with red arrows superimposed showing the direction of each subpath. Drawing a few blue lines, we see that the rule holds true. The rightmost blue line is from a filled section and the crossings are both going the same direction. The middle section is unfilled and the two crossings are going in opposite directions.

Counting the clockwise and counterclockwise crossings from any point outward either leads to a zero sum of crossings—as clockwise and counterclockwise crossings cancel each other out—creating a nonfilled area, or else a nonzero sum of crossings, creating a filled area.

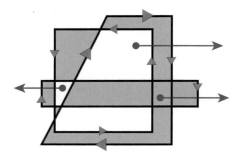

FIGURE 5.21   The same shape from Figure 5.19 with red directional arrows added and three blue lines showing crossings.

Although you don't need to understand the other common algorithm for filling areas in polygons, called the *even-odd rule*, you do need to keep in mind which one the canvas uses if you want to implement your own is-point-in-figure, hit-testing functions. Different drawing rules mean different sections are filled, and your hit-testing algorithm should match the drawing rule, so be sure any algorithms you might use are intended for shapes filled with the winding-number rule.

Summary of Context State So Far

Here's a quick recap of the canvas context methods and attributes we've covered so far:

▶ `fillStyle` and `strokeStyle`—Get or set the colors to apply on fill and stroke commands. They can accept most valid CSS color strings, but can also be set to gradients and patterns, as you see in the "Gradients and Patterns" section.

▶ `fillRect(x, y, w, h)`—Fills a rectangle with the current `fillStyle`.

▶ `strokeRect(x, y, w, h)`—Outlines a rectangle with the current `strokeStyle`.

▶ `clearRect(x, y, w, h)`—Clears the canvas context at the specified rectangle, returning the bitmap pixels to their default state of fully transparent black.

▶ `beginPath()`—Resets the current path on the canvas context. At any given time, there is only one path (or no path) "loaded" on the context. This is known as the current path. A path can have any number of *subpaths*.

▶ `closePath()`—Marks the current subpath closed, meaning a stroke connects the last point of the subpath with the first point. It also opens a new subpath, with the starting point equal to the first point of the last path.

▶ `stroke()`—Traces the current path with the color defined by `strokeStyle` and a thickness defined by `lineWidth`. Keep in mind that the current path still exists on the context, and only calling `beginPath()` again will clear that path.

▶ `fill()`—Fills the current path with the `fillStyle`. Open paths are implicitly closed for a fill, so making a V-shaped path fills a full triangle. Filling is done according to the nonzero winding number rule algorithm.

▶ `moveTo(x, y)`—Creates a new subpath, adding to (or starting) the current path, with the specified point as its starting point.

▶ `lineTo(x, y)`—Adds a line to the current subpath from the last point in the path.

▶ `rect(x, y, width, height)`—Creates a new subpath in the shape of a rectangle and closes that subpath. This is a convenience function that is equivalent to calling `moveTo`, `lineTo` three times, and `closePath` to make a rectangle.

▶ `quadraticCurveTo(cpx, cpy, x, y)`—Draws a quadratic curve with the given control point (`cpx`, `cpy`) to the given point (`x`, `y`).

▶ `bezierCurveTo(cp1x, cp1y, cp2x, cp2y, x, y)`—Draws a cubic Bezier curve described by the two given sets of control points and a given end point.

▶ `arcTo(x1, y1, x2, y2, radius)`—Draws an arc with the given control points and radius, connected to the previous point via a straight line.

▶ `arc(x, y, radius, startAngle, endAngle, [anticlockwise])`—Draws an arc described by the given arguments, starting at the `startAngle` and ending at the `endAngle`, going in the given direction and defaulting to clockwise if the last argument is omitted.

▶ `lineWidth`—Gets or sets the width of paths to be drawn when `stroke` is called. Default 1.

▶ `lineCap`—Gets or sets how the end of lines are to be drawn. Valid values are `"butt"`, `"round"`, and `"square"`. Default `"butt"`.

▶ `lineJoin`—Gets or sets how corners are drawn when two lines meet. Valid values are `"bevel"`, `"round"`, and `"miter"`. Default `"miter"`.

▶ `miterLimit`—Gets or sets the current miter limit ratio. Default 10.

▶ `isPointInPath(x, y)`—`True` if a given point is contained in the current canvas context path, `false` otherwise.

Saving and Restoring

The canvas context has two methods that can be used to save and recall the current state of the canvas at any time, `save()` and `restore()`.

When you call the `save` method, the context pushes its entire state onto an internal stack. This state includes all attributes but does not include the current bitmap (whatever is drawn to the canvas) nor does it save the current path that is constructed on the context.

> **NOTE**
>
> The canvas bitmap and current path are not considered part of the context state and persist regardless of any saving and restoring. If you need to save the canvas bitmap, you can do so by calling `drawImage` from one canvas to another.

The context method `restore` pops the most recently saved state off of the internal stack (if there is a state to pop) and sets the current context attributes accordingly. Let's see a very simple example of this functionality:

```
ctx.strokeStyle = 'red';
ctx.save(); // the state is saved, including all context attributes
ctx.lineWidth = 8;
ctx.strokeStyle = 'blue'; // overwrite our red strokeStyle
// Draws a blue rectangle with a lineWidth of 8:
ctx.strokeRect(20, 20, 20, 20);
ctx.restore(); // the state from before our "save" call is restored
// Draws a red rectangle with a lineWidth of 1:
ctx.strokeRect(50, 50, 30, 30);
```

Any changes that are made to the context in between calls to `save` and `restore` are discarded when the entire set of context attributes is replaced once `restore` is called. In our example, we saved the context when it had a `strokeStyle` of `'red'`, changed the strokeStyle to `'blue'`, and proceeded to draw one (blue) rectangle. Then, we called `restore`, which returned the `strokeStyle` back to `'red'`. Additionally, `lineWidth` was not set before `save` was called, but its default value of 1 was saved and so the value is 1 again when the context is restored.

> **NOTE**
>
> It's important to remember that setting the `width` or `height` of the canvas resets all of the context state, and that includes the `save` and `restore` stack. If you are using `canvas.width = canvas.width` to clear your canvas, your `save` and `restore` stack will be cleared with it.
>
> In fact, if you've been using `canvas.width = canvas.width` to reset your canvas context back to its original state, you can now use `save` and `restore` instead to reset all the state without having to reset the bitmap, too.

Saving and restoring the context state has many important uses that you see in later sections, especially in the next section on transformations. In general, the methods should be thought of as a way to "scope" all of the state of the canvas. Using `save` and `restore` is also currently the only way to reset the context's clipping region, aside from resetting all canvas state. You learn about clipping regions in the "Clipping" section.

As an example of "scoping" the state of the canvas, consider drawing in a complex canvas app where hundreds of rectangles are rendered. All of the rectangles follow a default set of rules, for example they might all be filled red with a thick black border. Additionally, each of the individual rectangles can be customized, so that one might be green with a thin violet border, another might be yellow with no border, and so on.

The drawing algorithm for such an app could set all of the default rules (`fillStyle` to `'red'`, `lineWidth` to `10`, `strokeStyle` left the default black) and draw nearly all of the rectangles with those settings. As it gets to a rectangle that has been customized by the user, it could save the context, set the appropriate differences for the nonstandard rectangle (a green `fillStyle`, and so on), and then restore the context once it is done drawing the special rectangle, ready to return to drawing the default rectangles.

Saving and restoring is also commonly present when objects on your canvas need to be positioned relative to other objects, as the canvas transformation matrix allows us to change the coordinate system origin on the fly, and `save` and `restore` allow us to easily change it back.

Transformation Matrix

An understanding of matrix math will help you wrap your head around transformations and the possibilities contained within their use, but I will assume as little prior mathematical knowledge as possible for this section.

The context methods `save` and `restore` have a lot of utility when dealing with transformations. Just like with other parts of canvas context state, saving and restoring can be used to keep track of the current transformation matrix.

translate

The origin of the canvas is the top-left corner by default, but it is often useful to have the origin moved around. Translating the origin can greatly simplify the work needed to draw complex figures such as a large path at many different locations.

Suppose we have a path such as a triangle that we want to draw. It's simple enough to draw it once, as the following code does to produce Figure 5.22.

```
ctx.beginPath();
ctx.moveTo(50, 50);
ctx.lineTo(100, 80);
ctx.lineTo(50, 80);
ctx.closePath();
ctx.lineWidth = 6;
```

```
ctx.fillStyle = 'orange';
ctx.fill();
ctx.stroke();
```

FIGURE 5.22   A triangle made from one path.

But what if we want to draw four or five of them next to each other? We could parameterize every x and y coordinate in the path, or we could simply use a `for` loop and one additional line of code, a call to `translate`:

```
for (var i = 0; i < 4; i++) {
  ctx.beginPath();
  ctx.moveTo(50, 50);
  ctx.lineTo(100, 80);
  ctx.lineTo(50, 80);
  ctx.closePath();
  ctx.lineWidth = 6;
  ctx.fillStyle = 'orange';
  ctx.fill();
  ctx.stroke();
  // translate the origin 50 pixels to the right
  // so the next triangle is drawn at a different location
  ctx.translate(50, 0);
}
```

And the desired effect is produced, as shown in Figure 5.23.

FIGURE 5.23   Four triangles produced from the same one-triangle path. The path was stroked and filled and then translated three times, restroking and refilling it each time.

Often, you want to build apps that hold a very large number of complex objects to be uniquely defined and positioned. `translate` allows you to separate the coordinates for defining those objects from the coordinates that locate them, making drawing and updating the objects a much easier task. And if you wanted to temporarily manipulate those figures, such as drawing all of them left-aligned to the canvas or in the middle of the canvas, you could do that without modifying (or needing to know) their location.

scale

The context method `scale(x, y)` scales the context's transform by the given values in their respective directions. This can be useful for a variety of reasons. Some examples of calling scale:

```
scale(0.5, 0.5); // figures drawn will be half the size
scale(2, 2); // figures drawn will be twice the size
scale(1, 5); // figures drawn will be stretched, but only in the Y direction
```

Canvas is a bitmap, but the paths themselves (and text) are vectors that can scale indefinitely, so you can still create paths and text on the canvas and expect a very accurate representation when the scale is set to large values.

Scaling the canvas and redrawing everything is how canvas apps can easily give the impression of zooming. Scaling can also be used to disproportionately distort the canvas or a piece of it, such as drawing very tall text. Next, we look at one important distinction in how scale applies when drawing paths.

Saving and Restoring Affect How Drawing Functions Act on a Transformed Canvas

Distorting the canvas is easy by setting a scale such as:

```
ctx.scale(2, 0.2);
```

But we need to pay careful attention to how this affects paths and stroking. Sometimes, we want to distort the stroke that is drawn from a path, and other times we merely want to distort the *path* yet still have the stroke drawn uniformly. We can differentiate between the two by choosing where the call to `restore` is placed. First, we have code that will distort both the path and the stroke:

```
// Draws a scaled circle (an ellipse)
// To draw a circle, omit the call to ctx.scale
ctx.save();
ctx.scale(2, 0.2);

ctx.beginPath();
ctx.arc(100, 120, 60, 0, Math.PI*2, false);

ctx.lineWidth = 12;
ctx.fillStyle = "lightblue";
ctx.fill();
ctx.stroke();

ctx.restore();
```

We scale the context, draw an arc that would otherwise be a circle but due to the scale distortion appears as a wide ellipse, and then stroke. Because the `save` and `restore` in this code block are at the very start and end of all relevant code, they don't actually do anything and could be omitted, but they are important to note to see the distinction later. The result of the code is shown in Figure 5.24, with the nonscaled circle for reference.

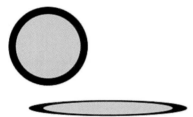

FIGURE 5.24   A circle drawn to the canvas, and the same circle drawn with `ctx.scale(2, 0.2)` applied before drawing.

The stroke created by scaling our drawing is very wide on the sides and very thin on the top. If we desire the elliptical effect on our circle but still want the stroke to be uniform, we have to call `restore` right after we finish defining the path instead of at the end:

```
ctx.save();
ctx.scale(2, 0.2);

ctx.beginPath();
ctx.arc(100, 120, 60, 0, Math.PI*2, false);

// The context is scaled for path creation
// but we will restore before we draw:
ctx.restore();

ctx.lineWidth = 12;
ctx.fillStyle = "lightblue";
ctx.fill();
ctx.stroke();
```

This scales the path so that the same shape is drawn, but the stroke for that shape is instead uniform, as shown in Figure 5.25.

FIGURE 5.25   A scaled circular path, but the call to `restore` before drawing allows the stroke to remain uniform instead of scaled.

Horizontal and vertical flips can also be achieved using the `scale` method. Calling `ctx.scale(-1, 1)` flips the context horizontally and `ctx.scale(1, -1)` flips it vertically.

There's one caveat though: Let's imagine for a moment that the canvas is represented by the right page of an open book, and that the page (like the canvas) is transparent except for the figures drawn. A horizontal flip achieved by calling `ctx.scale(-1, 1)` is just like flipping this right page over to the left side. You've flipped the objects on the page, but they're no longer in the location you want them to be!

To remedy this, we need to force the page to stay in place by first calling `ctx.translate(canvas.width, 0);`, so that when our imaginary page flip is executed, the page lands in the place it was before. Listing 5.12 gives an example of flipping the canvas horizontally and vertically, as seen in Figure 5.26. Canvas text is described in the "Using Text" section, but the commands used here should be intuitive enough.

LISTING 5.12   Flipping Figures Drawn to Canvas

```
// Normal
ctx.font = '32pt Georgia';
ctx.fillText('TIME', 50, 50);

// Flip context horizontally
ctx.fillStyle = 'blue';
ctx.save();
ctx.translate(canvas.width,0);
ctx.scale(-1, 1);
ctx.fillText('TIME', 50, 50);
ctx.restore();

// Flip context vertically
ctx.fillStyle = 'red';
ctx.save();
ctx.translate(0,canvas.height);
ctx.scale(1, -1);
ctx.fillText('TIME', 50, 50);
ctx.restore();
```

TIME ЭMIT

ᒣIᴎE

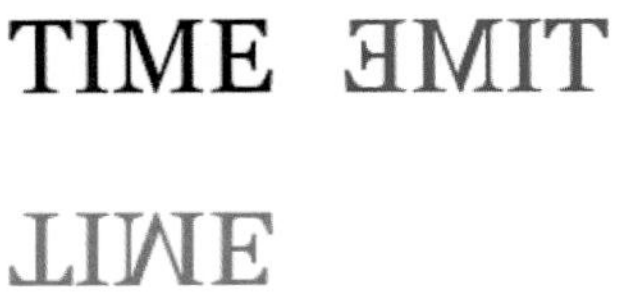

FIGURE 5.26   The word TIME is drawn, the context is flipped horizontally, and it is drawn again in blue, and then the context is flipped vertically and the text is drawn again in red.

> **NOTE**
>
> With proper knowledge of `save` and `restore` in mind, we can take advantage of transformations to disproportionately scale the current path, allowing us to draw an ellipse with the `arc` method.
>
> ```
> // x and y describe the center of the ellipse, not the top-left
> // r is the radius of base arc
> // w and h are the ratio of ellipse width.height to r
> function drawEllipse(ctx, x, y, r, w, h) {
>   ctx.beginPath();
>   ctx.save();
>   ctx.translate(x, y);
>   ctx.scale(w, h);
>   ctx.arc(0, 0, r, 0, Math.PI * 2);
>   ctx.restore();
> }
>
> // Sample usage:
> // Render an ellipse centered at 200,200 with a radius of 100
> // that is skewed to be twice as wide (200) as it is tall (100).
> drawEllipse(ctx, 200, 200, 100, 2, 1)
> ctx.fill();
> ctx.strokeStyle = 'red';
> ctx.lineWidth = 12;
> ctx.stroke();
> ```
>
> For simplicity's sake, the arguments are different than the ellipse function we created after discussing arcs and curves, but identical ellipses can be achieved, and this one doesn't require any Bezier math.

rotate

Rotation of the transformation matrix (and therefore context) is unintuitive for some, so for this section we introduce another HTML file in case you want to follow along and try out different transformations on your own.

In the section on canvas coordinates, we drew a grid. We modify that code and add it to our sample canvas HTML page to save as a new file. If you didn't make the sample HTML page from Listing 5.2 in the "Getting Started with Canvas" section, Listing 5.13 is very similar.

LISTING 5.13   `ExampleTransformations.html`

```
<!doctype html>
<html>
  <body>
```

```
    <canvas id="myCanvas" width="300" height="300"
        style="border: 1px solid black;">
    </canvas>

    <script type="text/javascript">
      // We'll attach both of these to the JavaScript window object
      // so we can easily access them in the console
      window.canvas = document.getElementById('myCanvas');
      window.ctx = canvas.getContext('2d');

      function degreesToRadians(degrees) {
        return degrees * (Math.PI/180);
      }

      // This is where we'll try out different transformation methods

      var width = canvas.width;

      var height = canvas.height;
      for (var i = 0; i < width; i += 10) {
        ctx.moveTo(i + 0.5, 0);
        ctx.lineTo(i + 0.5, height);
      }

      for (var i = 0; i < height; i += 10) {
        ctx.moveTo(0, i + 0.5);
        ctx.lineTo(width, i + 0.5);
      }
      ctx.strokeStyle = 'gray';
      ctx.stroke();

      ctx.beginPath();
      ctx.moveTo(-width*2, 0);
      ctx.lineTo(width*2, 0);
      ctx.moveTo(0, -height*2);
      ctx.lineTo(0, height*2);
      ctx.lineWidth = 8;
      ctx.strokeStyle = 'red';
      ctx.stroke();

    </script>
  </body>
</html>
```

As with all large code listings, this code is available on the Web at the companion repository mentioned in the introduction. It may be easier to navigate to that page and copy the code rather than typing it out.

Rather than dabbling in the console, it ought to be easier to modify the HTML file as we go through this section, so keep it open if you're following along.

The `rotate` command takes one argument, an angle of rotation, in radians. Radians can also be fairly unintuitive for some people, so Listing 5.13 contains a `degreesToRadians` function for convenience of conversion.

Let's edit our file at the `// "This is where"` line to rotate the context by 45 degrees:

```
// This is where we'll try out different transformation methods
ctx.rotate(degreesToRadians(45));
```

This produces the rotation shown in Figure 5.27, alongside the original, unrotated canvas.

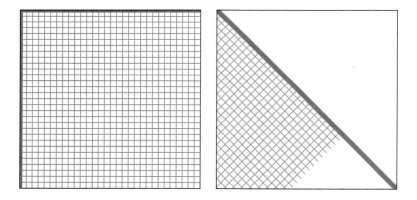

FIGURE 5.27   The original canvas and the same canvas with a 45-degree rotation applied before drawing.

We can see that the context was rotated about the top-left corner, but it's more accurate to say that the context has been rotated about its *origin*. It just so happens that the origin starts at the top left, but of course with `translate` we can move the origin to any location. Let's modify the file to additionally translate the origin to the center, resulting in Figure 5.28. If you added the `ctx.rotate` line above, remember to clear it out before replacing it with the following:

```
// This is where we'll try out different transformation methods
ctx.translate(150, 150);
ctx.rotate(degreesToRadians(45));
```

FIGURE 5.28   The canvas origin translated to the center and rotated 45 degrees.

Rotating the entire drawn scene isn't a particularly practical example, so let's look at rotating a figure about its center. Because we always rotate about the origin of the canvas, we want to modify the origin (using translate) to be the point in the figure that we want to rotate it about.

Suppose we have a triangle we want to rotate about its center. To do this, we must do the following:

▶ Find its midpoint

▶ Save the context

▶ Translate to the midpoint

▶ Rotate

▶ Translate *back*

▶ Draw

▶ Restore the context

To give it a try, let's draw a nonrotated triangular path and then rotate the same path and draw it a second time. Listing 5.14 was added to the end of the `<script>` tag in Listing 5.13 to create Figure 5.29.

LISTING 5.14   Two Triangles, One Drawn After the Context Was Rotated

```
ctx.lineWidth = 8;

ctx.beginPath();
ctx.moveTo(40, 40);
ctx.lineTo(120, 40);
ctx.lineTo(80, 120);
ctx.closePath();
```

```
ctx.strokeStyle = 'Magenta';
ctx.stroke();

ctx.translate(80, 80);
ctx.rotate(Math.PI);
ctx.translate(-80, -80);

ctx.beginPath();
ctx.moveTo(40, 40);
ctx.lineTo(120, 40);
ctx.lineTo(80, 120);
ctx.closePath();
ctx.strokeStyle = 'Lightblue';
ctx.stroke();
```

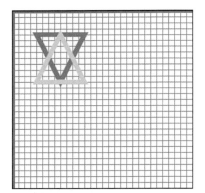

FIGURE 5.29   A magenta downwards triangle is drawn, then the context is translated and rotated, and the same downwards triangle (now rotated to point upwards) path is drawn in blue.

transform and setTransform

Translating, scaling, and rotating all operate on the canvas' transformation matrix, which is a matrix of six numbers that may look familiar. Figure 5.30 shows the typical written form of the 2D transformation matrix as well as its default (identity) values.

$$\begin{bmatrix} m11 & m21 \\ m12 & m22 \end{bmatrix} \begin{bmatrix} dx \\ dy \end{bmatrix} \quad \begin{bmatrix} 1 & 0 \\ 0 & 1 \end{bmatrix} \begin{bmatrix} 0 \\ 0 \end{bmatrix}$$

FIGURE 5.30   The transformation matrix written in typical mathematic fashion as a rectangular array, with the typical identifiers and default values shown.

The context's `transform` function takes the arguments from a transformation matrix that is to be applied to the context's current matrix, in the order: `transform(m11, m12, m21, m22, dx, dy)`.

With this, we can arbitrarily transform the current matrix. Applying a translation can be done with the translate command, as we have seen:

```
ctx.translate(40, 50);
```

Or by modifying the transformation matrix directly with the transform:

```
ctx.transform(1, 0, 0, 1, 40, 50);
```

Similarly, doubling the scale is analogous to doubling the values of `m11` and `m22`:

```
ctx.transform(2, 0, 0, 2, 0, 0);
```

Calls to `transform` always modify the existing matrix, though, and often we just want to set the matrix to some particular value. We can do that with the context method `setTransform`, which takes six arguments for the matrix: `setTransform(m11, m12, m21, m22, dx, dy)`.

Like with most properties, we often want to reset the transformation matrix back to the default without clearing the entire canvas state. To reset the transformation matrix, we can call `setTransform` with the default (identity) matrix:

```
setTransform(1, 0, 0, 1, 0, 0);
```

There is a new method in the canvas specification named `resetTransform`, but as of this writing, it is not implemented on any browsers, so `setTransform` with the identity matrix will have to do.

Most of the utility for `setTransform` otherwise is contained within knowing how a transformation matrix works. It may also be useful if you are keeping track of a string of transformations for various tasks and want to apply them all at once.

> **NOTE**
>
> You can temporarily reset the matrix to clear the canvas while still keeping track of all canvas state using `save` and `restore`.
>
> In general, there are three ways to clear a canvas. The first is a call to `clearRect`:
>
> ```
> ctx.clearRect(0, 0, canvas.width, canvas.height);
> ```
>
> The second is to set the canvas' width (or height) to itself:
>
> ```
> canvas.width = canvas.width;
> ```

Both of these have drawbacks. The first one does not work if the transformation matrix is not the default (identity) matrix, and the second one clobbers the entire canvas state, which can often be undesirable if you were trying to save or cache some state. Thankfully, we now have all the pieces of the puzzle needed to cleanly and quickly clear the canvas without erasing any state:

```
// I might have some complex transformation applied
ctx.save();
ctx.setTransform(1, 0, 0, 1, 0, 0);
// Now we will always clear the right space
ctx.clearRect(0, 0, canvas.width, canvas.height);
ctx.restore();
// I Still have my old transformation matrix
```

Keeping Track of Transformations

One of the common complaints of the canvas specification was that there is no way to get the current transformation. Thankfully, this often-requested feature has been implemented and there is a brand-new property in the specification, currentTransform, which allows you to get a copy of the current matrix. Unfortunately, almost no browsers support it as of this writing, so it can't be used in production apps for a while longer.

In the meantime, you can keep track of the transformation matrix separately with a small JavaScript class (it's technically not a class, there are no classes in JavaScript, but some JS developers get very good at pretending) that emulates the functionality of the matrix, allowing you to peek at the current transform. Listing 5.15 has the complete code for reproducing transforms so that you can keep track of the current matrix. You can use it alongside your context commands should you find a need to retrieve or save the current transformation matrix in your app.

LISTING 5.15   Transform.js—Helper for Keeping Track of the Current Transformation Matrix

```
// Simple class for keeping track of the current transformation matrix

// Usage example
// For instance:
//     var t = new Transform();
//     t.rotate(5);
//     var m = t.m;
//     ctx.setTransform(m[0], m[1], m[2], m[3], m[4], m[5]);

// Is equivalent to:
//     ctx.rotate(5);

// Or more concisely:
//     var t = new Transform();
```

```
//     t.rotate(5);
//     ctx.rotate(5);

function Transform() {
  this.reset();
}

Transform.prototype.reset = function() {
  this.m = [1,0,0,1,0,0];
};

Transform.prototype.multiply = function(matrix) {
  var m11 = this.m[0] * matrix.m[0] + this.m[2] * matrix.m[1];
  var m12 = this.m[1] * matrix.m[0] + this.m[3] * matrix.m[1];

  var m21 = this.m[0] * matrix.m[2] + this.m[2] * matrix.m[3];
  var m22 = this.m[1] * matrix.m[2] + this.m[3] * matrix.m[3];

  var dx = this.m[0] * matrix.m[4] + this.m[2] * matrix.m[5] + this.m[4];
  var dy = this.m[1] * matrix.m[4] + this.m[3] * matrix.m[5] + this.m[5];

  this.m[0] = m11;
  this.m[1] = m12;
  this.m[2] = m21;
  this.m[3] = m22;
  this.m[4] = dx;
  this.m[5] = dy;
};

Transform.prototype.invert = function() {
  var d = 1 / (this.m[0] * this.m[3] - this.m[1] * this.m[2]);
  var m0 = this.m[3] * d;
  var m1 = -this.m[1] * d;
  var m2 = -this.m[2] * d;
  var m3 = this.m[0] * d;
  var m4 = d * (this.m[2] * this.m[5] - this.m[3] * this.m[4]);
  var m5 = d * (this.m[1] * this.m[4] - this.m[0] * this.m[5]);
  this.m[0] = m0;
  this.m[1] = m1;
  this.m[2] = m2;
  this.m[3] = m3;
  this.m[4] = m4;
  this.m[5] = m5;
};
```

5

```
Transform.prototype.rotate = function(rad) {
  var c = Math.cos(rad);
  var s = Math.sin(rad);
  var m11 = this.m[0] * c + this.m[2] * s;
  var m12 = this.m[1] * c + this.m[3] * s;
  var m21 = this.m[0] * -s + this.m[2] * c;
  var m22 = this.m[1] * -s + this.m[3] * c;
  this.m[0] = m11;
  this.m[1] = m12;
  this.m[2] = m21;
  this.m[3] = m22;
};

Transform.prototype.translate = function(x, y) {
  this.m[4] += this.m[0] * x + this.m[2] * y;
  this.m[5] += this.m[1] * x + this.m[3] * y;
};

Transform.prototype.scale = function(sx, sy) {
  this.m[0] *= sx;
  this.m[1] *= sx;
  this.m[2] *= sy;
  this.m[3] *= sy;
};

Transform.prototype.transformPoint = function(px, py) {
  var x = px;
  var y = py;
  px = x * this.m[0] + y * this.m[2] + this.m[4];
  py = x * this.m[1] + y * this.m[3] + this.m[5];
  return [px, py];
};
```

One of the big advantages of having the current transformation matrix available is being able to handle your own saving and restoring of the matrix without saving and restoring the entire canvas context. The utility of this depends on your app, but saving and restoring only the information you need (instead of using the context's `save` and `restore`) may be beneficial to performance.

In-Memory Canvases

Often, you'll want to use a second canvas to prepare a complex figure that is to be drawn onto your primary canvas. You can create a canvas that is not part of the DOM, called an in-memory canvas, by using `createElement`:

```
var inMemoryCanvas = document.createElement('canvas');
```

In-memory canvases are one of the most versatile tools for making advanced graphics and effects. In-memory canvases can be used to temporarily save the bitmap of a canvas, to introduce the concept of "layers" that can be modified in any order and composited on the one primary DOM canvas, and to compound drawing operations in order to create figures that would otherwise be impossible to create on a single canvas.

In-memory canvases can aid performance by saving (caching) complex figures that were drawn with many commands. Instead of loading up a context with all the needed pieces of state (font, transformation matrix, `lineWidth`, etc.) each time the figure is drawn, this can be done only once and drawn to an in-memory canvas. Then, the programmer can draw the in-memory canvas to the real canvas over and over, allowing the complex figure to persist between redraws without redoing all the footwork of its initial creation.

> **NOTE**
>
> Canvas performance is the subject of Chapter 7. Be sure to read it if you're looking for a comprehensive collection of performance tips.

Let's take a look at one real-world use of in-memory canvases. Suppose you're making a drawing application where the user will draw lines in a freehand fashion with the mouse.

The lines can be drawn using three events: `mouseDown` records the starting location of the path to be drawn, initializes an array that will be used to keep track of the current path, and pushes the starting location to that path. It also needs to record that the mouse button has been pressed down.

Every `mouseMove` event checks to see if the mouse button has been pressed down; if not, it simply does nothing. If a `mouseDown` has occurred, the `mouseMove` function records the location of the mouse and pushes it to the list of points that constitutes our path. It then calls a function to draw the line because now we have at least two points in our path.

Finally, `mouseUp` draws the path one last time and records that the mouse button is no longer pressed down.

The code for this is fairly simple and we can add it to the HTML page we made in the "Getting Started with Canvas" section, Listing 5.2. Listing 5.16 contains the additions.

LISTING 5.16   Additions to Listing 5.2 for Making a Simple Drawing App

```
ctx.strokeStyle = 'rgba(205,0,100,.5)';
ctx.lineWidth = 5;

var path = null;
var down = false;

canvas.addEventListener('mousedown', function(e) {
    // grossly simplified mouse coordinates, don't use in production!
    // see chapter on making canvas interactive
    var x = e.clientX;
```

```
      var y = e.clientY;
      path = [];
      path.push([x,y]);
      down = true;
    }, true);

    canvas.addEventListener('mousemove', function(e) {
      if (!down) return;
      // grossly simplified mouse coordinates, don't use in production!
      // see chapter on making canvas interactive
      var x = e.clientX;
      var y = e.clientY;
      // add a new point to path, clear canvas, and draw complete path
      path.push([x,y]);
      drawPath();
    }, true);

    canvas.addEventListener('mouseup', function(e) {
      drawPath();
      down = false;
    }, true);

    function drawPath() {
      var l = path.length;
      ctx.beginPath();
      for (var i = 0; i < l; i++) {
      var p = path[i];
      if (i === 0) ctx.moveTo(p[0], p[1]);
      else ctx.lineTo(p[0], p[1]);
      }
      ctx.stroke();
    }
```

Drawing this way has a flaw that we can see when we run the code. The stroke is half-transparent, but we aren't getting transparent strokes.

The reason our strokes are not as transparent as we would like is because we are stroking the same path over and over as the mouse moves. A path with six points is stroked over a total of five times: The first line segment is stroked, then the second line segment is created and both segments are stroked, meaning the first one has now been stroked twice, and so on. These strokes quickly add up to make the entire line appear opaque.

The last one or two line segments are actually the half-transparent color that we want, which you might be able to observe if you whip your mouse across the screen quickly, or just set the alpha in the strokeStyle to a much smaller number.

There are a few ways to solve this problem. We could not draw a continuous path, meaning that on every new `mouseMove` we would draw a new path from the previous point to the current point, instead of drawing the entire path thus far. This is problematic because it disallows us from using canvas's built-in line joins and getting nice lines.

A cleaner way to solve the problem would be to clear the canvas before every restroke. This accomplishes the goal because clearing before each stroke means that the strokes won't ever "build up" to create an opaque line. This can be accomplished by adding one line to our `drawPath` method:

```
function drawPath() {
  ctx.clearRect(0,0,500,500);
  // ... (rest of method)
```

The problem with this second way becomes apparent as soon as we draw a second line. The first line we had drawn disappears! Because the canvas is cleared each time `drawPath` is called, we are erasing everything that we had on the canvas previously, not just the path that's currently under construction.

There are two ways to deal with this new problem. One is to keep not just a list of all the current line segments, like path does, but to keep a list of all the paths that have been drawn thus far on the canvas. Then we could redraw them all every frame and have our opacity and disappearing issues solved. But this would add up to a lot of state over time and might become terribly slow, and we want a much more performance-minded way of achieving the same thing.

This is where an in-memory canvas can come in to play, to save our previous canvas scene and draw it back as a kind of background to the current path construction. The changes needed are minor: We must create an in-memory canvas, and we must draw our regular canvas to the in-memory one during the `mouseUp` event in order to save the current canvas bitmap. Then, in our drawPath method, we can draw our in-memory canvas onto our regular canvas to restore all the previous lines that were drawn but cleared. Listing 5.17 has the complete code, wrapped up in a simple HTML page. Figure 5.31 shows the difference between this new method and the prior method of drawing.

LISTING 5.17   Drawing.html—Drawing App Making Use of In-Memory Canvas

```
<!doctype html>
<html>
<body>
<canvas id="myCanvas" width="500" height="500"
        style="border: 1px solid black;">
</canvas>

<script type="text/javascript">
  var canvas = document.getElementById('myCanvas');
  var ctx = canvas.getContext('2d');
```

```
ctx.strokeStyle = 'rgba(205,0,100,.5)';
ctx.lineWidth = 5;

// Make our in-memory canvas and set its size
var inMemCanvas = document.createElement('canvas');
inMemCanvas.width = canvas.width;
inMemCanvas.height = canvas.height;
var inMemCtx = inMemCanvas.getContext('2d');

var path = null;
var down = false;

// Fixes a problem where clicking in some browsers
// causes text selection on the page
canvas.addEventListener('selectstart',
  function(e) { e.preventDefault(); return false; }, false);

canvas.addEventListener('mousedown', function(e) {
  // grossly simplified mouse coordinates, don't use in production!
  // see section on making canvas interactive
  var x = e.clientX;
  var y = e.clientY;
  path = [];
  path.push([x,y]);
  down = true;
},  true);

canvas.addEventListener('mousemove', function(e) {
  if (!down) return;
  // grossly simplified mouse coordinates, don't use in production!
  // see section on making canvas interactive
  var x = e.clientX;
  var y = e.clientY;
  // add a new point to path, clear canvas, and draw complete path
  path.push([x,y]);
  drawPath();
},  true);

canvas.addEventListener('mouseup', function(e) {
  drawPath();
  down = false;
  // save canvas to our in-memory canvas
  inMemCtx.clearRect(0,0,500,500);
  inMemCtx.drawImage(canvas, 0, 0);
},  true);
```

```
function drawPath() {
    ctx.clearRect(0,0,500,500);
    // put what was previously there back:
    ctx.drawImage(inMemCanvas, 0, 0);
    ctx.beginPath();
    var l = path.length;
    for (var i = 0; i < l; i++) {
        var p = path[i];
        if (i === 0) ctx.moveTo(p[0], p[1]);
        else ctx.lineTo(p[0], p[1]);
    }
    ctx.stroke();
}
</script>
</body>
</html>
```

FIGURE 5.31   The difference in drawing between the original code and modified code is apparent. The modified code allows the display of proper transparency.

We use the `drawImage` command to draw the bitmap of `inMemCanvas` onto our regular canvas. We go over that command in the next section.

Using an in-memory canvas instead of keeping track of all paths ever drawn is much more efficient, and continues to be efficient as the number of lines drawn increases. If you tried to keep track of every line ever drawn, you'd eventually have an array of enormous size, and you'd need to construct all of those paths every time. But if you use an in-memory canvas, you'll be saving a bitmap that stays the same size regardless of how many lines have already been drawn.

> **NOTE**
>
> There are additional practical examples of using an in-memory canvas in the "Gradients and Patterns" section, the "Compositing" section, and the "Image Data and Pixel Manipulation" section.

Using Images and Other Canvases

The canvas context has one method for drawing images, `drawImage`, but it is loaded with functionality. It isn't just for drawing HTML `<image>` elements—you can also use it to draw frames of a `<video>` element or even draw another canvas onto the canvas.

Even if you don't think of your app as one drawing any images to the canvas, the `drawImage` method can still come in very handy. For performance reasons, you might find yourself making in-memory canvases and drawing portions of them to your screen or vice versa, like in the previous section. You can even use `drawImage` to draw the same canvas onto itself, which can be useful when you want to make a mini map or overview effect in your application.

Drawing images onto the canvas is relatively fast, almost always faster than drawing paths and text. Image drawing speed stays good even when some manipulation is required, as the `drawImage` method comes with a large list of optional arguments to scale and crop on the fly. Let's take a look at the three possible ways to call `drawImage`:

```
drawImage(image, dx, dy)
drawImage(image, dx, dy, dw, dh)
drawImage(image, sx, sy, sw, sh, dx, dy, dw, dh)
```

All three of them take an image, which can be an `HTMLImageElement`, an `HTMLVideoElement` (rather, the current frame of one), or an `HTMLCanvasElement`.

Because the first argument is a resource that might or might not be loaded, this method runs the risk of attempting to draw something that isn't on the client's machine yet. If that's the case, then nothing is drawn, and a little later we'll deal with how to make sure we avoid any mishaps with loading resources.

The `dx` and `dy` parameters in `drawImage` specify the destination location on the canvas context. Often you don't need to scale an image, but when you do, the `dw` and `dh` parameters allow you to force the image to be a specific size on the destination. Using these four arguments, you can draw an image onto any location and scaled in any manner, with no canvas context transformations needed.

The four corresponding `s-` arguments, `sx`, `sy`, `sw`, and `sh`, specify a source location and size, so instead of drawing the entire image to a canvas, you can opt to draw a smaller (cropped) part of it. Figure 5.32 gives a visual explanation of the source and destination rectangle.

The `s-` arguments can be used to crop the source image and are often used to make sprite maps or tile sets useful on the canvas. A sprite map is a single image file that contains many smaller images. Often when working with multiple small images, developers combine them into one large image and then specify a position inside the large image in order to draw only a portion of it. This reduces the number of requests that a user sends to the server, meaning only one image has to get served instead of 20 or 30 small images. Positioning sprites is done in CSS with the `background-position` property, and in canvas the `s-` arguments to `drawImage` are used for the same purpose. Figure 5.33 shows an example of a sprite map, the one used for YouTube.

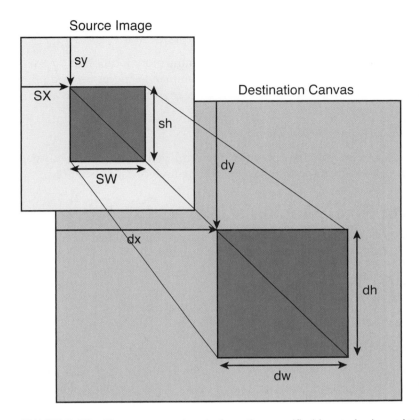

FIGURE 5.32   The source rectangle from the specified image is drawn into the destination rectangle on the canvas. If the destination width and height differ from the source height, the image content will be scaled.

FIGURE 5.33   A sample sprite map from YouTube, housing many of the buttons and logos used on the site.

Double Buffering

Often in our canvas apps, we can imagine ourselves needing to clear a canvas and redraw the entire scene with some small thing, such as an animated figure, changed. On many graphics systems, this causes a flickering or a tearing effect because the user can see for a split second that the canvas is cleared before the scene gets redrawn to it.

To combat this, developers often draw the new scene to an in-memory location and then draw that in-memory scene onto the page so that no clear command is necessary and no flicker occurs. You can imagine how this would be done with an in-memory canvas and drawImage.

If you're thinking about implementing double-buffering, don't.

Browsers do this on the canvas for you. Implementing buffering yourself is a waste of time that will do nothing but decrease your performance by adding unnecessary operations.

Image Data and Pixel Manipulation

Canvas has three methods with a few different argument sets relating to direct image pixel manipulation for advanced editing and storing of the canvas bitmap:

▶ getImageData(sx, sy, sw, sh)

▶ createImageData(width, height)

▶ createImageData(imagedata)

▶ putImageData(imagedata, dx)

▶ putImageData(imagedata, dx, dy, dirtyX, dirtyY, dirtyWidth, dirtyHeight)

getImageData

The context method getImageData takes four arguments describing a rectangle on the canvas bitmap and returns an associated ImageData object, which describes the pixel data for the given rectangle. ImageData contains three properties that we care about: width and height, which describe how large it is, and data, which is a one-dimensional sequential array describing every pixel in the rectangle. Every pixel must be described by four numbers, the values of red, green, blue, and the alpha (transparency), so each pixel increases the length of data by four. Pixels are arrayed in rows, from left to right.

There's a difference in the type of pixels we are dealing with when talking about image data. Some browsers and devices distinguish between CSS pixels and device pixels, and very high-resolution displays may have more device pixels than CSS pixels, so a 1×1 CSS pixel might be rendered onto a 2×2 square of device pixels.

The width and height of the ImageData object are always in device pixels, so you can use this number to determine if there is a discrepancy between CSS pixels and device pixels. Because of this discrepancy, often you will want to work with the ratio of ImageData width or height divided by canvas width or height. For many devices, for now at least, this ratio is usually 1 to 1.

Using the sample page we made in the "Getting Started with Canvas" section, we can easily see getImageData in action. Because pixel data can get rather large, we are only going to use a 2-by-2 rectangle, and because looking at a blank ImageData is not very interesting, we're going to fill three of the four pixels first. We can type Listing 5.18, which paints just three pixels, into the browser's console. It's difficult to see the three colored pixels at the top-left of the canvas, so the result is seen magnified in Figure 5.34.

LISTING 5.18   Image Data

```
ctx.fillStyle = 'red';
ctx.fillRect(0, 0, 1, 1);
ctx.fillStyle = 'rgba(0, 0, 255, 0.4)';
ctx.fillRect(0, 1, 1, 1);
ctx.fillStyle = 'lime';
ctx.fillRect(1, 1, 1, 1);
console.log(ctx.getImageData(0, 0, 2, 2));
```

FIGURE 5.34   The code paints one pixel red, one lime, and one half-transparent blue pixel. The top-right pixel is left as the canvas default, fully transparent black.

The console returns an ImageData object, which we could have saved to a variable and explored using a for loop, but instead we use the visual inspector that some browsers have. Figure 5.35 shows what the ImageData looks like in Chrome when the data is expanded.

Figure 5.35 shows the data for all four pixels in the ImageData array. If we separate them out, they are, sequentially, in [R,G,B,A] notation:

```
[255, 0, 0, 255]
[0, 0, 0, 0]
[0, 0, 255, 162]
[0, 255, 0, 255]
```

There's our red pixel (full red, full opacity) first.

Next is our unfilled pixel. It's interesting to note here that the default state of the canvas isn't white or even transparent white, as it might casually seem since most web pages have a white background. Instead, the default pixels are, in fact, fully transparent *black*.

Next is the pixel we filled with rgba(0, 0, 255, 0.4). As we can see, it converted the alpha from a scale of 0–1 to 0–255.

Finally, we have the lime pixel, which is full-on green. In RGBA, the CSS color "green" is actually only *half* brightness green, or [0, 128, 0, 255].

```
> ctx.fillStyle = 'red';
  ctx.fillRect(0, 0, 1, 1);
  ctx.fillStyle = 'rgba(0, 0, 255, 0.4)';
  ctx.fillRect(0, 1, 1, 1);
  ctx.fillStyle = 'lime';
  ctx.fillRect(1, 1, 1, 1);
  console.log(ctx.getImageData(0, 0, 2, 2));
  ▼ImageData {height: 2, width: 2, data: Uint8ClampedArray[16]}
    ▼data: Uint8ClampedArray[16]
        0: 255
        1: 0
        2: 0
        3: 255
        4: 0
        5: 0
        6: 0
        7: 0
        8: 0
        9: 0
        10: 255
        11: 102
        12: 0
        13: 255
        14: 0
        15: 255
      ▶buffer: ArrayBuffer
        byteLength: 16
        byteOffset: 0
        length: 16
      ▶__proto__: Uint8ClampedArray
      height: 2
      width: 2
    ▶__proto__: ImageData
< undefined
>
```

FIGURE 5.35 The commands entered into the Chrome console, and the resulting `ImageData` explored.

NOTE

The `toDataURL()`, `toBlob()`, and `getImageData()` methods check an internal flag, called the origin-clean flag, and throw a `SecurityError` exception rather than leak cross-origin data. This is detailed in the section "Image Security on the Canvas."

createImageData

You don't have to use the current canvas bitmap to make an `ImageData` object. You can create a blank one instead with the `createImageData` method. To use this method, you must either specify a width and height or pass in an existing `ImageData` object. Passing in an existing `ImageData` does *not* copy the data contents of the `ImageData` itself. Instead, it only creates a new blank `ImageData` that has the same size as that of the argument.

```
// Sample usage
// Both return an ImageData describing 400 transparent black pixels
var imagedata = ctx.createImageData(20, 20);
var imagedata2 = ctx.createImageData(imagedata);
```

putImageData

Exposing these pixels as an array has a wide array of uses when paired with `putImageData`. Often we want to loop through all of the pixels, which we'll detail, but first let's discuss the reverse function, `putImageData`.

The method putImageData(imagedata, dx, dy) does what you'd expect: It takes an ImageData object and a location (dx, dy) and replaces a chunk of canvas pixels with ones from the ImageData. Simple enough!

The seven-argument version of the function, putImageData(imagedata, dx, dy, dirtyX, dirtyY, dirtyWidth, dirtyHeight), is a little more nuanced. The four optional arguments describe a *dirty* rectangle, which can be thought of as a source rectangle for the imageData itself. The dirty rectangle is specified in device pixels.

Unlike the optional arguments to drawImage, the dirty rectangle for putImageData still allows you to draw using an offset as if you were drawing the entire width and height. The dirty rectangle doesn't crop the ImageData; instead, it just *limits* what actually gets drawn back.

To illustrate the dirty rectangle, we can use the following HTML page. Note that there aren't the usual <doctype>, <html>, and <body> elements for the sake of conciseness. We can be lazy when testing. Listing 5.19 is an HTML page that produces Figure 5.36.

LISTING 5.19   ImageData.html

```
<canvas id="canvas1" width="100" height="100" style="border: 1px solid black;">
</canvas>
<canvas id="canvas2" width="100" height="100" style="border: 1px solid black;">
</canvas>

<script>
var can = document.getElementById('canvas1');
var ctx = can.getContext('2d');

var can2 = document.getElementById('canvas2');
var ctx2 = can2.getContext('2d');

ctx.fillStyle = 'DarkSlateGray';
ctx.fillRect(30, 30, 50, 50);
ctx.fillStyle = 'MistyRose';
ctx.fillRect(70, 50, 50, 50);
ctx.fillStyle = 'Thistle';
ctx.fillRect(50, 70, 50, 50);
ctx.fillStyle = 'MediumSlateBlue';
ctx.fillRect(40, 10, 5, 80);

var imgData = ctx.getImageData(0, 0, 100, 100);
ctx2.putImageData(imgData,
   0, 0,        // destination location
   30, 30, 50, 50); // dirty rect
</script>
```

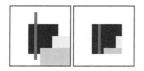

FIGURE 5.36   Image data is retrieved from the left canvas and placed on the right canvas.

As you can see in Figure 5.36, our destination location is (0, 0) but the copied content starts at (30, 30) because all of the content drawn with putImageData is still implicitly offset by the entire size of the ImageData. To do the same thing with drawImage, we'd have to set both the source location and the destination location to (30, 30):

```
// gives an identical outcome
// you can substitute this for the putImageData above
ctx2.drawImage(can,
    30, 30, 50, 50,  // source rect
    30, 30, 50, 50); // destination rect
```

The putImageData method can be thought of as always placing the entire ImageData onto the context, and the dirty rectangle can be thought of as a clipping region because only that part of the ImageData is shown.

Of course, the previous example is just an illustration and would be silly in real usage because we can do the same operation with drawImage, and drawImage would accomplish it much faster. In fact, getImageData and putImageData are among the slowest methods on the context, and should be used only when you need manipulation of pixels that other effects cannot achieve.

> **NOTE**
>
> Because working with image data is slow, if you merely want to change the color of a single pixel dynamically and don't need to know what color was there before, you will almost always want to use fillRect instead. A call to fillRect is extremely fast in comparison with creating image data, editing it, and calling putImageData.
>
> But there's another side to this story. If you want to fill several individual pixels in one go, then using putImageData quickly becomes faster than the hundreds of calls to fillRect.
>
> You should always do your own benchmarking for your pages and apps, but here's a general estimate to keep in mind:
>
> ▶ Filling a single pixel with fillRect is roughly 30 times faster than doing the same with putImageData.
>
> ▶ Filling a 20×20 area (400 pixels) with putImageData is roughly 10 times faster than 400 calls to fillRect.
>
> You shouldn't use image data to save the contents of a canvas for redrawing later. Using drawImage to save the canvas to and from an in-memory canvas is always a faster alternative.

Access to the pixel colors means that we can produce a wide array of effects and filters, from desaturation (grayscale) of an image to creating complex blurring algorithms. Let's create some real pixel manipulation examples with image data. Listing 5.20 shows examples of how to reduce the number of colors, desaturate, and tint and invert colors. The results of each of these effects on an image can be seen in Figure 5.37. To get such an effect in your own code, you would draw your image or content and then add one of the code blocks from Listing 5.20 to your code afterward.

LISTING 5.20   Several Examples of Bitmap Manipulation

```
// This listing is not meant to be run by itself, it is for reference
// What follows are several blocks of code each starting with
// getImageData and ending with putImagedata. They are intended
// to be used independently, to manipulate content that already exists
// on a canvas. For simplicity's sake they all modify the contents
// of a 250x150 canvas area, in-place.

// Since there needs to be something drawn on the canvas to manipulate,
// these code blocks by themselves don't do anything

// reduce to 8-bit color!
var imgData = ctx.getImageData(0, 0, 250, 150);
var data = imgData.data;
var length = data.length;
for (var i = 0; i < length; i += 4) {
  data[i]     = data[i] - (data[i] % 32);
  data[i + 1] = data[i + 1] - (data[i + 1] % 32);
  data[i + 2] = data[i + 2] - (data[i + 2] % 32);
  // don't change alpha!
}
ctx.putImageData(imgData, 0, 0);

// desaturate!
var imgData = ctx.getImageData(0, 0, 250, 150);
var data = imgData.data;
for (var i = 0; i < length; i += 4) {
  var average = (data[i] + data[i + 1] + data[i + 2]) / 3;
  data[i]     = average;
  data[i + 1] = average;
  data[i + 2] = average;
  // don't change alpha!
}
ctx.putImageData(imgData, 0, 0);
```

```
// tint green!
var imgData = ctx.getImageData(0, 0, 250, 150);
var data = imgData.data;
for (var i = 0; i < length; i += 4) {
  data[i]     = data[i];
  data[i + 1] = Math.min(data[i + 1]*1.9, 255);
  data[i + 2] = data[i + 2];
  // don't change alpha!
}
ctx.putImageData(imgData, 0, 0);

// every other vertical line turned blue
// Appears tinted all the same. Note that you could do this
// without image data by creating a path of lines
var imgData = ctx.getImageData(0, 0, 250, 150);
var data = imgData.data;
var flip = true;
for (var i = 0; i < length; i += 4) {
  flip = !flip;
  if (flip) continue;

  data[i]     = 0;
  data[i + 1] = 0;
  data[i + 2] = 255;
  // don't change alpha!
}
ctx.putImageData(imgData, 0, 0);

// invert!
var imgData = ctx.getImageData(0, 0, 250, 150);
var data = imgData.data;
for (var i = 0; i < length; i += 4) {
  data[i]     = 255 - data[i];
  data[i + 1] = 255 - data[i + 1];
  data[i + 2] = 255 - data[i + 2];
  // don't change alpha!
}
ctx.putImageData(imgData, 0, 0);
```

In-place colors aren't the only thing we might want to manipulate. Modifying image data also enables us to create interesting effects, such as blurring, dithering, embossing, noise generation, and so on. There are showcases of many great effects online, so be sure to search before you go reinventing the JavaScript wheel if you desire one.

FIGURE 5.37   An image of the author (on the right) with several effects applied using image data.

For many effects, we might have to clobber some of the image data as we go, which we can avoid by using `createImageData` to store the results on a separate `ImageData` object. Listing 5.21 contains a function that takes an `ImageData` and returns a new one scaled to a given width and height using nearest-neighbor interpolation, which makes for a very "blocky" or pixelated zoom, as opposed to the default image scaling on the canvas, which uses a smoother and more blurry interpolation algorithm. The algorithm in Listing 5.21 is used to create Figure 5.38.

LISTING 5.21   A Function for Blurring Image Data Using Nearest-Neighbor Interpolation

```
// This listing is not meant to be run by itself,
// it is a function to be used for reference if your canvas
// app needs this kind of image blurring.

// resizing by nearest neighbor interpolation
// based on Araki Hayato's ImageFilters.js
// This kind of resizing looks more "pixely" and less
// blurry than bicubic, and generally makes
// pixel art look better when scaled up
```

```
// imgData: the image data to resize
// returns a new ImageData that is the size of resultWidth, resultHeight
function resizeNearestNeighbor(imgData, resultWidth, resultHeight) {
  var data = imgData.data;
  var data        = imgData.data,
      srcWidth    = imgData.width,
      srcHeight   = imgData.height,
      srcLength   = data.length,
      dstImageData = ctx.createImageData(resultWidth, resultHeight),
      dstPixels   = dstImageData.data;

  var xFactor = srcWidth / resultWidth,
      yFactor = srcHeight / resultHeight,
      dstIndex = 0, srcIndex,
      x, y, offset;

  for (y = 0; y < resultHeight; y += 1) {
      offset = ((y * yFactor) | 0) * srcWidth;

      for (x = 0; x < resultWidth; x += 1) {
          srcIndex = (offset + x * xFactor) << 2;

          dstPixels[dstIndex]     = data[srcIndex];
          dstPixels[dstIndex + 1] = data[srcIndex + 1];
          dstPixels[dstIndex + 2] = data[srcIndex + 2];
          dstPixels[dstIndex + 3] = data[srcIndex + 3];
          dstIndex += 4;
      }
  }
  return dstImageData;
}

// Sample usage, assumes something is on the canvas sized 250x150:
var imageData = ctx.getImageData(0, 0, 250, 150);
// 250x150 to 1000x600 = scaling four times as large:
var result = resizeNearestNeighbor(imageData, 1000, 600);
ctx.putImageData(result, 0, 0);
```

FIGURE 5.38 A sprite "smoothly" scaled by a factor of 4 with `drawImage` (left) compared with the same sprite scaled by image data manipulation using the nearest-neighbor algorithm (right).

NOTE

The specification has recently added a property called `imageSmoothingEnabled`, which defaults to `true` and determines if images drawn on noninteger coordinates or drawn scaled will use a smoother algorithm (like bicubic or bilinear interpolation). If it is set to `false`, then nearest-neighbor is used, producing a less-smooth image and instead just making larger-looking pixels. Using this new property produces the same effect as the nearest-neighbor algorithm described previously.

Image smoothing has only recently been added to the canvas specification and isn't supported by all browsers, but some browsers have implemented vendor-prefixed versions of this property. On the context, there exists `mozImageSmoothingEnabled` in Firefox and `webkitImageSmoothingEnabled` in Chrome and Safari, and setting these to `false` stops smoothing from occurring. Unfortunately at the time of this writing, Internet Explorer 9 and Opera have not implemented this property, vendor prefixed or otherwise.

Image Security on the Canvas

There's a common point of confusion regarding when you can use the canvas context's `getImageData` method and the canvas's `toDataURL` method. Certain operations use these methods to throw a security error instead of functioning normally, so that no image data and no data URL can be made.

The rules for what you can and cannot do are laid out in the canvas specification, though the reasoning behind them isn't immediately obvious. The most typical violation is when a programmer calls the `drawImage` method with an image that is from a different domain than the page that the canvas is on, or called with an image that is on the local file system, even if it is in the same directory as the HTML file. When `drawImage` is called with an image that has a different location like this, the canvas internally sets its `origin-clean` flag to `false`.

From the moment a canvas has its `origin-clean` flag set to `false`, you are not allowed to use the `getImageData` and `toDataURL` methods of that canvas; instead, the security error is thrown. There are a few more cases where the `origin-clean` flag is set to `false`, but almost all of them rest upon a cross-domain image being drawn to the canvas somehow. The only other action that sets the `origin-clean` flag to `false` is calling `fillText` or `strokeText` when a font from a different origin is set.

The reason for this security is to prevent something called information leakage. To understand why this is a security issue, consider the following hypothetical situation:

Say you are on a work network and so you have access to internal, private company sites and your (private!) hard drive. The private sites might be something like www.internal.myCompany.com and your hard drive would typically be accessible from your browser in the form of a URL, such as `file:///C:/SomeOfMyPhotos/`.

Now suppose you visited a website with an in-memory canvas and while you were browsing the site that canvas was silently churning away some JavaScript. This script wouldn't do anything the user sees; instead it would constantly call `drawImage` onto the in-memory canvas with URLs that it was guessing might exist. These URLs would be things like an image on the private subdomain:

```
www.internal.myCompany.com/secret/secret-plans.jpg
```

Or an image on one of your local disks:

```
file:///C:/SomeOfMyPhotos/thatEmbarassingPhoto.png
```

The malicious site could keep trying different combinations of private-to-you URLs until it found one that was actually a file. Then it would draw it to the canvas. Then it would retrieve the image data from the canvas using `getImageData` or `toDataURL` and send it off to the server.

Voila! The malicious site owner now has your secret plans and your embarrassing photos—without your consent.

Now we know that the previous scenario is not very probable: In the real world, secret plans are almost always in PNG format, whereas embarrassing photos are typically in JPG format! But it stands that situations like this *could* happen and so the security implications of canvas must take this into account.

CORS

In common practice, it is the case that websites *do* want to allow image access from other domains or subdomains. After all, just because your app is on example.com shouldn't mean that you can't use images from the public subdomain you created, images.example.com.

Luckily, there is a specification for allowing images to be marked as truly open access and using it allows you to keep the `origin-clean` flag of the canvas in its default true state. This specification is called Cross-Origin Resource Sharing, or CORS, and it was created to allow content that is meant to be publicly accessible by scripts such as our canvas code to be used without security restrictions.

Enabling CORs is platform specific, so what you must do depends on what kind of server technology you're using. Searching the Web is still the best way to find the appropriate configuration for your server, though the webpage enable-cors.org maintains a simple list of a few common server technologies and how to enable CORS on each of them. It also has a tool for testing whether or not a site is CORS-enabled, though you could build one yourself with what you know now. To do so, simply draw an image to a canvas and see if calling `getImageData` throws an error or not!

But I Want to Test My Image Data Code Locally!

The image security rules can be a bit of a pain if you have code that involves `getImageData` or `toDataURL` that you want to debug locally. Thankfully, some browsers allow local file access without restriction as long as some rules are met.

bibliotheca SelfCheck System

Customer ID: 2904115212**

Items that you checked out

Title: HTML5 unleashed / Simon Sarris.
ID: 947085207815
Due: Wednesday, November 29, 2017

Total items: 1
Account balance: $0.00
11/8/2017 6:13 PM
Ready for pickup: 1

Thank you for using the bibliotheca
SelfCheck System.

Firefox allows you to use `getImageData` if the images drawn to the canvas are in the same directory as the file. Internet Explorer 9, Opera, and Safari (on Windows) are a little more lenient and let you do as you please as long as both files are local, regardless of where they are in the local file system. Google Chrome doesn't make a distinction for local files, but you can add the `--allow-file-access-from-files` flag when starting Chrome and it then ignores the associated security issues. In the interest of being safe, you should probably create a second shortcut to Chrome with this flag and only use that instance for testing, not general use.

Gradients and Patterns

So far, the only values we've covered for `strokeStyle` and `fillStyle` have been strings. In addition to specifying most valid CSS strings for these styles, we can also specify special gradient objects.

Gradients are used nearly everywhere in graphic design. Buttons, icons, logos, and backgrounds all see gradients in common use. In fact, gradients have become so ingrained in graphic and web design that Microsoft's Metro or "Modern UI" styling, their cornerstone of the Windows 8 look and feel, is considered risqué because the design team decided to largely forego the use of gradients!

Although gradients are very common elements in UI, logo, and poster designs, weighing whether to use them is something for you to decide. I do, however, encourage you to take a good look at the common web pages and programs you use and keep an open eye out for gradients. If you're not accustomed to thinking about visual styling elements, you might be surprised.

There are two types of gradients that can be created using a canvas context:

▶ `createLinearGradient(x1, y1, x2, y2)`

▶ `createRadialGradient(x1, y1, radius1, x2, y2, radius2)`

Both of these methods are called on the context and return a `CanvasGradient`. The `CanvasGradient` then has a method to modify the gradient, `addColorStop`.

Creating gradients demands a few parameters that specify a location for the gradient. For linear gradients, we specify "from" and "to" spots that describe where the gradient will start and end. For radial gradients, we specify "to" and "from" circles, with their own center and radius.

Linear Gradients

Let's create a linear gradient, the result of which can be seen in Figure 5.39.

```
// Create a vertical gradient going from the top of the canvas to the bottom
var gradient = ctx.createLinearGradient(0, 0, 0, canvas.height);
gradient.addColorStop(0, 'Black');
gradient.addColorStop(0.15, 'Black');
```

```
gradient.addColorStop(0.2, 'DarkSeaGreen');
gradient.addColorStop(0.4, 'DarkSeaGreen');
gradient.addColorStop(0.7, 'Goldenrod');
gradient.addColorStop(0.8, 'DarkOrange');
gradient.addColorStop(1, 'GhostWhite');

ctx.fillStyle = gradient;
ctx.fillRect(0,0,canvas.width, canvas.height);
```

FIGURE 5.39   A linear gradient with several color stops.

The `addColorStop` method takes two arguments: a number between 0 and 1, representing what point along the gradient the stop is located, and a CSS color string, representing the color for that stop. So in the previous gradient definition, we see:

```
gradient.addColorStop(0.7, 'Goldenrod');
gradient.addColorStop(0.8, 'DarkOrange');
```

This means that the part of the gradient between 70% from the start and 80% from the start will be a transition from Goldenrod to DarkOrange. Put another way, 10% of our gradient is spent blending these two colors.

Looking at the code, it's apparent that we not only list the colors we want in the gradient, but we also occasionally list the same colors twice. Using multiple stops of the same color in a row gives you control of how hard or soft of a transition you want. In the gradient we constructed, we wanted a lot of black, so we made the first 15% of the gradient completely black and then have a pretty abrupt transition from Black to DarkSeaGreen. Then we have solid DarkSeaGreen for 20% of the gradient (between 0.2 and 0.4), ending with a rather smooth transition from DarkSeaGreen to Goldenrod, and so on.

We could have made this gradient go in the opposite direction by flipping the y-arguments:

```
ctx.createLinearGradient(0, canvas.height, 0, 0);
```

Similarly, we could change the direction from left to right, or perhaps a diagonal because the two points in the parameter list can describe any line to follow.

We don't have to fill the entire canvas, of course, even though the gradient does. Instead of filling the entire canvas by calling `fillRect` with the entire area, we could use the same gradient and draw a few smaller shapes. The result of the following code is seen in Figure 5.40.

```
// Create a vertical gradient going from the top of the canvas to the bottom
var gradient = ctx.createLinearGradient(0, 0, 0, canvas.height);
gradient.addColorStop(0, 'Black');
gradient.addColorStop(0.15, 'Black');
gradient.addColorStop(0.2, 'DarkSeaGreen');
gradient.addColorStop(0.4, 'DarkSeaGreen');
gradient.addColorStop(0.7, 'Goldenrod');
gradient.addColorStop(0.8, 'DarkOrange');
gradient.addColorStop(1, 'GhostWhite');

ctx.fillStyle = gradient; // using same gradient as before
ctx.fillRect(30, 30, 30, 30);
ctx.fillRect(90, 10, 30, 150);
ctx.beginPath();
// Circle at the bottom left with a radius of 50
ctx.arc(0, 200, 90, 0, Math.PI * 2, false);
ctx.fill();
```

FIGURE 5.40   The same gradient with a few smaller shapes filled instead of the entire canvas.

Radial Gradients

The method for creating a radial gradient takes six arguments, `createRadialGradient(x1, y1, radius1, x2, y2, radius2)`. The first three describe a circle's center and radius and the next three define a second circle in the same way. All radial gradients on the canvas context can be thought of as going from one circle to another.

Once they're made, radial gradients work much the same way as linear gradients. We must add color stops using the same arguments and these stops span from the first circle to the second. Like linear gradients, we don't need to show the entire gradient when using it because any arbitrary path can be filled. Listing 5.22 contains three examples, with the result of these gradients shown in Figure 5.41.

LISTING 5.22   Examples of Radial Gradients

```
// Create a centered gradient and fill a rectangle
var radgrad = ctx.createRadialGradient(60, 60, 10,
                                        60, 60, 50);
radgrad.addColorStop(0, 'rgba(255,0,0,1)');
radgrad.addColorStop(0.8, 'rgba(228,255,0,.9)');
radgrad.addColorStop(1, 'rgba(228,255,0,0)');

ctx.fillStyle = radgrad;
ctx.fillRect(0, 0, 500, 500);


ctx.translate(100, 0);


// Create a radial gradient and fill a triangular path with it
var radgrad = ctx.createRadialGradient(65, 65, 10,
                                       50, 50, 50);
radgrad.addColorStop(0, 'Magenta');
radgrad.addColorStop(0.6, 'Blue');
radgrad.addColorStop(0.8, 'Blue');
radgrad.addColorStop(1, 'rgba(0,0,255,0)');

ctx.fillStyle = radgrad;
ctx.strokeStyle = 'rgba(0,0,0,.3)' // Triangle border
ctx.beginPath();
ctx.moveTo(50,0)
ctx.lineTo(100,100)
ctx.lineTo(0,100)
ctx.closePath();
ctx.fill();
ctx.stroke();


ctx.translate(100, 0);


// Create a radial gradient with an offset center and fill a rectangle
var radgrad = ctx.createRadialGradient(25, 45, 10,
                                       50, 50, 50);
radgrad.addColorStop(0, 'PaleGoldenrod');
radgrad.addColorStop(0.4, 'Olive');
radgrad.addColorStop(0.7, 'Sienna');
radgrad.addColorStop(1, 'rgba(140,0,0,0)');
ctx.fillStyle = radgrad;
ctx.fillRect(0, 0, 500, 500);
```

FIGURE 5.41   Three radial gradients. The middle gradient was used to fill a triangular path, which was also stroked gray.

In typical usage, the first circle is usually defined as being inside of the second circle in both location and size. Having the two circles at nonconcentric (outside of each other) may result in some very strange brushes, and these odd cases may not look the same across all browsers. If you define a radial gradient in a strange way but still want to use it, make sure it looks as you'd like on all platforms you're targeting.

> **NOTE**
>
> If you need to blur a canvas or part of a canvas, searching online will yield many algorithms and libraries that use canvas image data to accomplish a blur.
>
> Working with image data, however, can be relatively performance intensive, and if you need to draw a blurred circle, then you can accomplish your goal by simply drawing a *rectangle* that has a radial gradient instead.

Gradient Performance and Reuse

Gradients aren't particularly slow but there are some performance considerations with their use. Often you'll want to draw the same gradient in several places to make many similar figures, for instance to make a stack of buttons that have a gradient backing.

Using the same gradient many times poses a problem: Because gradients are defined as being between two points or two circles, you can run into trouble when you want to use identical gradients for figures located in different places.

A naïve solution to this problem is given in Listing 5.23. A new linear gradient, with new start and end points, is defined inside of the loop, once per button.

LISTING 5.23   A Poor Way to Fill Multiple Objects with the Same Gradient

```
// For example only!
// This code shows a poor method of using the same gradient for many figures
function loadGradientColors(gradient) {
  gradient.addColorStop(0, 'WhiteSmoke');
  gradient.addColorStop(0.5, 'SkyBlue');
  gradient.addColorStop(1, 'DodgerBlue');
}
```

```
// An array that describes the [x, y] location of each button
var locs = [
  [30, 30],
  [30, 70],
  [30, 110],
  [30, 150]];

ctx.font = '12px verdana bold';
for (var i = 0; i < locs.length; i++) {
  var loc = locs[i];
  var grad = ctx.createLinearGradient(loc[0], loc[1], loc[0], loc[1] + 30);
  loadGradientColors(grad);
  ctx.fillStyle = grad;
  ctx.fillRect(loc[0], loc[1], 70, 30);    // Draw the gradient
  ctx.strokeRect(loc[0], loc[1], 70, 30); // Draw a black outline
  // Draw button text
  ctx.fillStyle = 'black';
  ctx.fillText('Button ' + i, loc[0] + 6, loc[1] + 20);
}
```

This code produces the visual of four buttons that all use the same gradient, as seen in Figure 5.42, but in order to do it we had to create a new gradient for each button. This is highly undesirable because the creation of additional `CanvasGradient` objects could become a performance concern. It clearly doesn't scale as well as it might because every new button we have means another new JavaScript object we must create alongside it.

FIGURE 5.42   Four buttons with backgrounds made from gradients.

To fix this, we create a more nuanced version of the button drawing code, shown in Listing 5.24. This time, we only create one `CanvasGradient` object, at the very start, and use the canvas origin as a reference for the two points in the `createLinearGradient` call. We then reuse the same gradient for every figure by translating the canvas for each button we draw.

LISTING 5.24   A More Efficient Way to Fill Multiple Objects with the Same Gradient

```
// This time we create the gradient only once, at the start,
// and it is defined to start at the canvas origin
var gradient = ctx.createLinearGradient(0, 0, 0, 30);
```

```
gradient.addColorStop(0, 'WhiteSmoke');
gradient.addColorStop(0.5, 'SkyBlue');
gradient.addColorStop(1, 'DodgerBlue');

// An array that describes the [x, y] location of each button
var locs = [
  [30, 30],
  [30, 70],
  [30, 110],
  [30, 150]];

ctx.font = '12px verdana bold';
for (var i = 0; i < locs.length; i++) {
  var loc = locs[i];
  ctx.save();
  // Our gradient is defined at the origin,
  // so we can move the origin and draw everything from there!
  ctx.translate(loc[0], loc[1]);
  ctx.fillStyle = gradient;
  ctx.fillRect(0, 0, 70, 30);
  ctx.strokeRect(0, 0, 70, 30);
  // Draw button text
  ctx.fillStyle = 'black';
  ctx.fillText('Button ' + i, 6, 20);
  ctx.restore();
}
```

This code is much more efficient and scalable because drawing 5,000 buttons doesn't mean creating 5,000 gradients, instead we still just have created the original one! This code is a little cleaner, too, as the variable that changes each loop is referenced in only one location, in the call to `ctx.translate`.

Patterns

Canvas has some built-in functionality for drawing patterns and repeating textures with ease. Like gradients, patterns are represented with a special object, `CanvasPattern`, which is created via a method on the context, `createPattern(image, repetition)`.

The first argument is the same as that for `drawImage`. That is, it can be an actual instance of an `Image`, or a current frame of an HMTL5 video element, or another canvas.

The second argument is a string that accepts the following values: `repeat`, `repeat-x`, `repeat-y`, and `no-repeat`. These options do what you'd expect: Either the pattern repeats endlessly in both axes, one axis, or does not repeat at all.

The last option, `no-repeat`, may not seem useful at first but remember that patterns work identically to gradients. Although you cannot set `fillStyle` or `strokeStyle` to an image, you *can* set them to a pattern. If you want to fill, say, some text with an image, then it's possible you aren't concerned about repeatability, you just want to take advantage of using an image as a fill.

Listing 5.25 gives an example of using a pattern to fill text with an image. We take an image of the Large Magellanic Cloud, a "nearby" galaxy, and use it as a nonrepeating pattern and fill text with the stars. The result of this code is shown in Figure 5.43.

LISTING 5.25   Using a Pattern to Fill Text with an Image

```
var img = new Image();

img.onload = function() {
  ctx.fillStyle = ctx.createPattern(img, "no-repeat");
  // We cover text in a later section,
  // so don't worry if these commmands look unfamiliar
  ctx.font = 'bold 60pt georgia';
  ctx.fillText('Large', 0, 72);
  ctx.fillText('Magellanic', 0, 72 * 2);
  ctx.fillText('Cloud', 0, 72 * 3);
}

// An image from the "Star" article on Wikipedia
// of the Large Magellanic Cloud
// (you'll have to supply your own image)
// The big font used assumes your image is very large,
// otherwise you might not see all the text!
img.src = 'Starsinthesky.jpg';
```

Large
Magellanic
Cloud

FIGURE 5.43   We are all made of star-stuff, and with canvas patterns text can be, too.

Some of the greatest utility of patterns comes from the ability to make your own patterns from scratch on the canvas itself, defining your own figures on the fly. If you want to make a repeating leaf pattern, for instance, you can do it procedurally on an in-memory canvas and then use that in-memory canvas as the pattern source. Listing 5.26 does just that, resulting in Figure 5.44.

LISTING 5.26   Creating a Pattern on an In-Memory Canvas

```
// set up an in-memory canvas to use as a pattern
var pattern = document.createElement('canvas');
pattern.width = 40;
pattern.height = 40;
var pctx = pattern.getContext('2d');

// construct a canvas to be repeated
// We use two quadratic curves to look like a leaf
pctx.beginPath();
pctx.moveTo(2, 2);
pctx.quadraticCurveTo(40,0, 38,38);
pctx.quadraticCurveTo(0,40, 2,2);
pctx.closePath();
pctx.fillStyle = "LightGreen";
pctx.strokeStyle = "SeaGreen";
pctx.lineWidth = 2;
pctx.fill();
pctx.stroke();

// Now we can use our in-memory canvas to construct a pattern
var pattern = ctx.createPattern(pattern, "repeat");
ctx.fillStyle = pattern;
ctx.beginPath();
ctx.arc(100,100,90,0, Math.PI*2, false);
ctx.fill();
```

FIGURE 5.44   A pattern created on one canvas and used as a `fillStyle` to fill a circle on another.

In the circle of Figure 5.44, using `repeat-x` or `repeat-y` instead of `repeat` would display only the first row or column of leaves, respectively.

There are several ways to fill or stroke a shape with an image, and a pattern is one good way. Another simple way is to use a clipping region of a path, which we talk about in a later section, but clipping regions does not allow us to fill text with an image as we have just done. One of the most useful properties of patterns, therefore, is not using them as patterns at all, but simply taking advantage of the fact that you can use them to fill any path or text with an image easily, without having to resort to clipping or compositing.

Shadows

Shadows are among the most subtle design tools in many of the programs we use and visual elements we see. Just like with gradients, in most operating systems almost all visual elements (windows, cursors, menus, widgets, icons, etc.) have their own shadows. They're such a subtle part of design that many people don't notice they exist until pointed out.

Shadows aren't necessary, but they give subtle cues that let us perceive the mouse cursor as a thing that is actually floating, or icons as actually 3D. This understated visual pop gives extra texture and dimension to what are otherwise very flat elements. They play with the human mind to make objects on a 2D screen "feel" 3D to the user.

Just like setting any other styling property, you set the shadow properties before you render something to the canvas, and subsequent drawing commands are then drawn with the defined shadow. Specifying a shadow is easy:

▶ `shadowOffsetX` and `shadowOffsetY` specify the offset in pixels from the figure that the shadow is to be drawn.

▶ `shadowBlur` is a number that specifies the level of shadow blurring. The lower the value, the sharper the edge of the shadow will be.

▶ `shadowColor` is any valid CSS color string. Unlike `fillStyle` and `strokeStyle`, `shadowColor` cannot be a gradient or pattern.

All three of the numerical properties default to zero, and turning shadows on or off is a matter of specifying these values. There's no explicit way to tell the canvas not to draw shadows. Instead, you must either set all three of the numerical values to zero or you set the `shadowColor` to fully transparent; otherwise, some form of shadow is drawn. The `shadowColor` default is transparent black, `'rgba(0, 0, 0, 0)'`.

Shadows are unique among context drawing methods in that they ignore the transformation matrix. This is very convenient because if you want to draw many figures with shadows and these figures were drawn with various transformations of angle and scale, the shadows themselves will still all remain on the appropriately offset side of each figure so that it correctly looks as if a consistent light source was used. Figure 5.45 shows an example of a square drawn and that same square rotated. In both cases, the shadow offset is unaffected by the rotation.

This means that if you were to rotate the square 180 degrees, the shadow would be in the exact same place as if the square were not rotated at all. There is an advantage to having shadows drawn unaffected by the transformation matrix. If you draw several objects, some rotated and some not, you typically want the shadows to all stay in the same direction, giving the proper illusion of a light source. If the shadows were affected by the transformation matrix, it would look as if there is no singular light source, but instead shadows going in every direction!

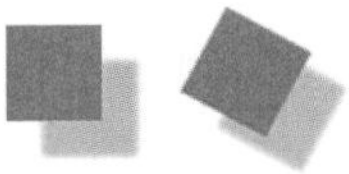

FIGURE 5.45   A square drawn with a `shadowOffsetX` and `shadowOffsetY` of 15. The shadow is drawn evenly 15 pixels offset in both axes. To the right is the same square drawn with the same `shadowOffsetX` and `shadowOffsetY`, but the context was rotated about the square's center.

> **NOTE**
>
> Due to some oddities in implementation, browser vendors have requested that the specification change such that shadows are not drawn unless the `globalCompositeOperation` is the default value, `source-over`. Regardless of whether the spec changes, it is probably best if all objects drawn with shadows use the default value for `globalCompositeOperation`.

Shadows do have a few visual hang-ups that canvas programmers should be aware of. Although they are intelligent with respect to transforms, they are not so intelligent with respect to clipping regions. If you are clipping part of your drawing in order to create a different looking figure, you will also unfortunately be clipping the shadow. This can be solved by using an in-memory canvas as an intermediary step. Simply draw the clipped figure to the in-memory canvas, and draw from the in-memory canvas to your shadowed primary context. Figure 5.46 shows some clipped text both with and without taking this intermediary step.

Halftext
Halftext

FIGURE 5.46   Top: Text drawn to the canvas with a shadow and clipping region. Bottom: Text drawn to an in-memory canvas with a clipping region, and then drawn to the primary canvas, which has a shadow but no clipping region.

There's another common problem with shadows directly related to their smartness. If you're scaling the transformation matrix to give the impression of zooming in and out of your app, your shadows may appear a bit odd as you scale. Because they are not affected by the transformation matrix, the `shadowOffsetX` and `shadowOffsetY` will be constant regardless of your zoom (scale) amount. Many users may expect that when you zoom a figure to be four times as large, the shadow would be four times as large as well, and just as *proportionally* offset as before, but this isn't the case. Although your figures may get larger, the shadows start to look very minute. You can solve this issue by multiplying the shadow offsets by the total zoom scale that a given figure is to be drawn with.

Compositing

All drawing operations are affected by two compositing attributes on the canvas context, `globalAlpha` and `globalCompositeOperation`.

The `globalAlpha` property is the current alpha (opacity) value applied to rendering operations. It can be set in the range between 0 (fully transparent) and 1 (fully opaque), inclusive. A value of 1 does not mean that the content drawn will be fully opaque—it merely means that there will be no *additional* transparency, so if a rectangle is drawn with a `fillStyle` set to `'rgba(255, 0, 0, 0.5)'` and a `globalAlpha` of 1, you can still expect to see a half-transparent rectangle.

Like many context attributes, values of `globalAlpha` that are outside of the range do not throw an error—they are simply ignored.

The `globalCompositeOperation` property is an attribute that dictates how shapes and images drawn onto the canvas interact with the existing canvas content. It may seem odd that there are ways to render to a bitmap other than simply putting the new parts on top, but there are a lot of complex drawing operations that would otherwise require pixel manipulation without these different modes of compositing. We give a few code examples of the uses of `globalCompositeOperation` after we go over what each of them does.

Here is a list of all the possible values for `globalCompositeOperation`. In the following descriptions, "existing content" is defined as any pixels that were already drawn and not previously transparent.

- ▶ `source-over`—The default. New content is drawn over existing content.

- ▶ `source-in`—New content is only drawn where existing content was nontransparent.

- ▶ `source-out`—New content is drawn only where there was transparency.

- ▶ `source-atop`—New content is drawn only where it overlaps existing content.

- ▶ `destination-over`—Opposite of `source-over`. It acts as if new content is drawn "behind" existing content.

- ▶ `destination-in`—Opposite of `source-in`. Existing content is drawn only where new content is nontransparent.

- ▶ `destination-out`—Opposite of `source-out`. Existing content is drawn only where new content is transparent. Acts as if existing content is drawn everywhere except where the new content is.

- ▶ `destination-atop`—Opposite of `source-atop`. New content is drawn, and then old content is drawn only where it overlaps with new content.

▶ `lighter`—Where new content overlaps old content, color is determined by adding the color values.

▶ `copy`—New content replaces all old content.

▶ `xor`—New content is drawn where old content is transparent. Where the content of both old and new is not transparent, transparency is drawn instead.

In Figure 5.47, a blue square is drawn to represent shapes already existing on a canvas, then the `globalCompositeOperation` is set to the specified value and a red circle is drawn.

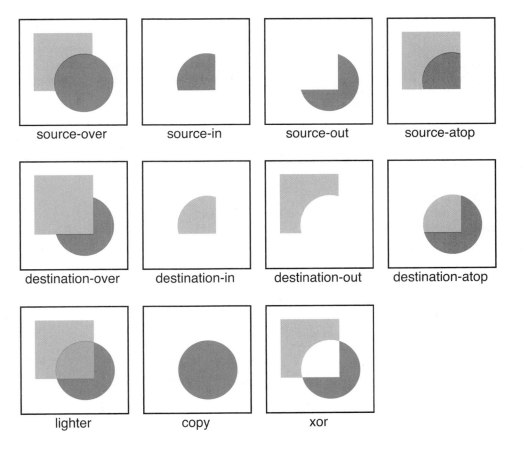

FIGURE 5.47   Every value of `globalCompositeOperation`.

The `globalCompositeOperation` property is often ignored by canvas newcomers because it isn't immediately apparent how it could be of any use, so we provide two practical examples. Although this property isn't used for many common applications, it's good to always keep its existence in the back of your mind as you're developing a canvas app. As soon as you come across a drawing operation that is seemingly impossible, come back to this section and give it some thought in the context of what `globalCompositeOperation` can do.

Compositing Examples

It is easy to use a pattern or gradient on a filled or stroked path by simply setting the `fillStyle` or `strokeStyle` of the context before we draw it. If we want to use a gradient or path to fill an arbitrary image with transparency, however, we have to be a little cleverer because `drawImage` never depends on filling or stroking.

One way to accomplish the task of filling an image with a gradient or pattern is to use a compositing. With the `source-in` compositing operation, the only new pixels drawn are in the place of already existing pixels, so if we want to draw a gradient or pattern (or anything, really) in the shape of an image, we can simply draw the image to the canvas, change the `globalCompositeOperation` to `source-in`, and draw the gradient or pattern in a rectangle across the entire image. Listing 5.27 accomplishes this, resulting in a gradient in the shape of the image, as seen in Figure 5.48.

LISTING 5.27   Using Compositing to Fill the Opaque Portions of an Image

```
// Draw our initial image.
// myHTML5Logo is a reference to an Image element
// The logo is from http://www.w3.org/html/logo/
// such as:
// http://www.w3.org/html/logo/downloads/HTML5_Logo_256.png
ctx.drawImage(myHTML5Logo, 0, 0);

// Gradient setup:
var grad = ctx.createLinearGradient(0, 0, 0, 256);
grad.addColorStop(0, 'Black');
grad.addColorStop(0.2, '#E34C26'); // Dark Orange
grad.addColorStop(0.6, '#F06529'); // Light Orange
grad.addColorStop(1, 'Black');
ctx.fillStyle = grad;

// Cover the image with our gradient
ctx.globalCompositeOperation = 'source-in';
ctx.fillRect(0,0,500,500);

// Don't forget to set it back to default!
ctx.globalCompositeOperation = 'source-over';
```

Although compositing is a good way to fill an image with a gradient or pattern, doing the opposite operation (filling a path or text with an image) is best done using patterns of the clipping region, both of which are almost always faster than compositing.

FIGURE 5.48 The World Wide Web Consortium's (W3C's) HTML5 logo image alongside our gradient-filled version of the same image.

Another compositing use is to draw paths that have a hollow or "cut-out" center. Paths can be of any thickness, but getting a path to also have an inner "hollow thickness" is a bit more nuanced. Using clipping won't work easily because the part of the path that we don't want is in the middle of the path, not the other way around. To accomplish this with clipping, we'd have to make a complex path that contained only the edges of the thick path and not the to-be-hollow center, and a fair bit of math would be involved. Instead, we can accomplish the hollowing-out of a path very easily with the destination-out value set for the globalCompositeOperation.

Like many uses of globalCompositeOperation, we want to do our work on an in-memory canvas and then transfer the result to our primary canvas. This ensures that the already-drawn content on our primary canvas does not interfere with our compositing operation.

To make a hollow path, we load the in-memory canvas context with a path and stroke it twice, first with the total thickness of the path, and a second time with the globalCompositeOperation set to destination-out and the lineWidth set to the inner hollowing amount. Listing 5.28 uses this technique to create Figure 5.49.

LISTING 5.28   Using Compositing to Make a Hollow Path

```
// Construct an in-memory canvas:
var inMemCan = document.createElement('canvas');
inMemCan.width = canvas.width;
inMemCan.height = canvas.height;
var inMemCtx = inMemCan.getContext('2d');

// Put some sample content on the primary context
ctx.fillStyle = 'orange';
ctx.fillRect(50, 50, 300, 300);
ctx.fillStyle = 'lightblue';
ctx.fillRect(80, 30, 30, 250);
```

```
// Load up the in-memory context with our path
inMemCtx.beginPath();
inMemCtx.moveTo(25, 25);
inMemCtx.quadraticCurveTo(50, 50, 80, 180);
inMemCtx.quadraticCurveTo(100, 250, 280, 180);

// Draw the thick path on our in-memory context:
inMemCtx.lineWidth = 35; // Our total line width
inMemCtx.stroke();

// The same current path is still on our context,
// we're going to reuse it!
// Change compositing and lineWidth to draw the hollowing path:
inMemCtx.globalCompositeOperation = 'destination-out'
inMemCtx.lineCap = 'square'; // I'm an important detail! Read the text!
inMemCtx.lineWidth = 20; // Our hollow line width
inMemCtx.stroke();

// Draw the in-memory canvas back to our primary canvas:
ctx.drawImage(inMemCan, 0, 0);
```

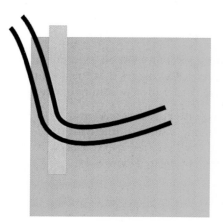

FIGURE 5.49   A path of thickness 35 with a hollow thickness of 20, drawn onto a primary canvas that had preexisting content.

A crucial part of making this technique look good is setting the lineCap to round or square for the hollow stroking. This ensures that the hollowing part of the path strokes beyond the end of the thicker path. Otherwise, a thin line might exist at the ends of the path due to antialiasing.

Clipping

The clipping region is one of the most important concepts in canvas drawing. All drawing on the canvas is constrained by a special context path called the clipping region, with the default clipping region consisting of the entire canvas.

The clipping region is remembered in the canvas state and constructed just like a normal rendered path. To set it, construct a path on the context and call clip() instead of fill() or stroke() and the clipping region will be set to the intersection of the current clipping region and the current path. Because it uses the intersection of these two paths, successive calls to clip can only make the clipping region smaller.

The function of the clipping region is similar to the two globalCompositeOperation options source-in and source-atop. Both of those options only allow you to draw content inside of or on top of existing content, and by the same token the clipping region only allows you to draw inside of the defined path. Of course, the clipping region doesn't require anything to be on the screen nor does it leave any visual traces behind, but you see at the end of this section how the source-in globalCompositeOperation can make custom, complex clipping paths.

One of the most common practical uses of the clipping region is to draw an image with rounded corners. To do this, we create a path with rounded corners, call the clip method, and draw the image normally. The image is then constrained to the path. Listing 5.29 gives the general function for creating rounded rectangle paths and applies it to a clipping region so that we can draw an image with rounded corners, and Figure 5.50 shows an example.

LISTING 5.29   A Function for Creating Rounded Rectangle Paths

```
// This function constructs a path on the
// context in the shape of a rounded rectangle.
// If this looks confusing to you, see the section on curves and arcs.
function roundedRect(ctx, x, y, width, height, radius) {
  // if the radius is larger than a side we have to reduce it
  if (width < 2 * radius) radius = width / 2;
  if (height < 2 * radius) radius = height / 2;
  ctx.beginPath();
  ctx.moveTo(x + radius, y);
  ctx.arcTo(x + width, y, x + width, y + height, radius);
  ctx.arcTo(x + width, y + height, x, y + height, radius);
  ctx.arcTo(x, y + height, x, y, radius);
  ctx.arcTo(x, y, x + width, y, radius);
  ctx.closePath();
}

var img = new Image();
```

```
img.onload = function() {
  roundedRect(ctx, 20, 20, 140, 140, 30);
  ctx.clip();
  ctx.drawImage(img, 20, 20);
}

// At the time of this writing this website serves up
// an image of a kitten in the desired /width/height
// The actual image shown is from the public domain
img.src = 'http://placekitten.com/140/140';
```

FIGURE 5.50   A square image of a kitten drawn with a rounded rectangle clipping region.

If you were so inclined, you might be able to emulate the functionality of a clipping region using the `source-in` option for `globalCompositeOperation`. You could fill the above rounded rectangle path onto an in-memory canvas, set the composite operation, draw the image, and you'd have the result of an image with rounded rectangles that you could then draw onto your primary canvas. *Do not do this.* Clipping is faster in every single browser, sometimes thousands of times faster, even if you don't use an intermediary in-memory canvas.

There's still one situation where we would want to use `source-in` instead of a proper clipping region. In the "Compositing" section, we showed an example of using `source-in` to fill an image with a gradient, pattern, or solid color. Because clipping regions are defined as paths only, we can use `source-in` as a sort of clipping region to clip to any arbitrary image. In fact, that's exactly what we did in the compositing example: We used an image with transparent regions as a clipping region when drawing a gradient!

For most applications, it is best to stick to proper clipping regions, and if you need to clip to an image often in a performance-heavy application, then you might want to look for ways to precompute and save the resulting images you are generating, as drawing an image is always faster than compositing on the fly.

Clearing Nonrectangular Areas

Another prominent use of clipping regions is clearing nonrectangular areas. The context's `clearRect` method is one of the few methods that can clear pixels, in other words make them more transparent than they were previously. There are other ways, namely fancy uses of `globalCompositeOperation` and image data, but these are nowhere near as performant. Efficiently clearing a nonrectangular area, therefore, is accomplished by using a clipping path in conjunction with `clearRect`. To clear a circular area, we merely have to create a clipping path out of an arc and call `clearRect` over the entire arc. Only the space that occupies the clipping path will be cleared.

It's important to note that the clipping region is affected by the transformation matrix and being mindful of this can lead to performance gains. If we were writing a drawing application, we might want to make a circular eraser tool, which would clip and clear a circular region as the user moved his or her mouse or touch device. One way to accomplish this would be to save the context, create a clipping region, call `clearRect` on that region, and then restore the context. On every mouse move or touch move, you'd have to repeat that process, though, and this might slow things down on less-powerful devices.

In performance-minded apps, the saving and restoring abilities of the context are to be avoided, as are the creation of multiple paths and multiple calls to `clip`. Instead of doing it the previous way, we could instead create the clipping region just once, at the origin, and then translate the context to move the clipping region around as the mouse or touch device moves. We have an example of this functionality in Chapter 6, "Making Canvas Interactive and Stateful."

As of this writing, the clipping region can only ever get smaller. The only way to make it larger (or reset it for that matter) is to use the `save` and `restore` methods on the context or reset the entire context by setting the width or height of the canvas. This can hurt performance as saving and restoring the context adds up computationally, and it hinders the caching of context attributes that might be slow to set. Thankfully, the specification has recently added a `resetClip` method to the context, but it may be some time before all the major browsers implement it.

Clipping has a host of other uses, such as aiding in the drawing of some complex shapes. If you want to draw some rectangular portions of a circle, for instance, drawing the rectangles in a clipping path and then drawing the circle is a lot easier than trying to figure out the complex path that would be necessary to do the same thing. Such a shape is seen in Figure 5.51.

FIGURE 5.51   This figure would be very difficult to construct with just a normal path, but is very easy to make using the clipping region. It is a clipping region of several thin rects and a regular path made of a single filled arc.

Making stencils that the user cannot draw out of, successively constraining nested shapes, and applying filters to only a portion of the screen are other common uses of the clipping region.

Using Text

The canvas specification has a bit of a quirky API for text. The text API has just a handful of parts but a fair bit of nuance and caution is needed if you're to use it well. This is not to say using the text methods is bad—in fact, they are almost always useful and you'd be hard pressed to find a substantial canvas app (outside of some games) that does not render text.

Some enterprising individuals (and enterprising enterprises) have even seen fit to create entire text-editing applications inside of the canvas. This is usually regarded as a folly, though, and even warned against in the specification. One of the most prominent text-centric canvas apps was made by Mozilla. This app, called Bespin and later Skywriter, was a web-based framework for code editing that you could embed into your own projects.

Due to all the difficulties encountered and minor browser features that we take for granted, the Bespin/Skywriter project eventually abandoned its canvas ambitions and merged with the Ace project, which uses traditional HTML elements such as divs instead. Although the abandoned project should stand as a warning to all about the creation of text editors in canvas, the code for the project is fairly simple to understand for its size and it is worth reviewing that code if your app involves any substantial amount of text manipulation.

Before we cover how to use the context's text methods and properties, let's clear the air.

First the Bad Parts

Text on the canvas comes with a host of accessibility problems. Any text rendered on the canvas is not searchable and is not readable by text-to-speech devices or programs. Because of this, if you are merely using the canvas to prettify some text in a way that was not commonly possible with CSS styling alone, I urge you to instead consider using the new CSS3 abilities for text styling, which include many new effects such as transformations, shadows, and animations.

> **NOTE**
>
> There is a more comprehensive warning about the difficulties of trying to reimplement native text controls on the canvas (including some notes from the specification) in the "When to Not Use Canvas" section near the beginning of this chapter.

Text drawn on the canvas is not guaranteed to look identical to the same text (with the same font) rendered in the DOM. In some browsers, the antialiasing and subpixel rendering between the canvas and DOM text vary, and the properties of text rendered onto the canvas varies between browsers, too.

While all text is rendered as a vector that scales indefinitely, using transformations with the text does not necessarily produce a clean result. It used to be the case that a few browsers would produce miserable-looking text when anything other than simple scaling was involved, but large bugs do still remain in some browsers. One such bug can be seen in Figure 5.52.

scepter
scepter

FIGURE 5.52   An example of text inconsistency. The word scepter drawn to a canvas in 120pt sans-serif font (top) and the same word drawn on in 10pt sans-serif font with scale(12, 12) applied to the context. This used to be problematic with a few browsers, but as of this writing this problem is only present in Opera.

Transformations pose another problem as proper kerning, the adjusting of letter spacing in words, begins to vary wildly on many browsers as the text is scaled. Figure 5.53 shows an example, comparing a string drawn with a large font to a supposedly identically sized string drawn with the default font and a scale transformation.

Dermatology
Dermatology

FIGURE 5.53   The word Dermatology rendered twice and magnified to show detail. The top rendering used a default canvas scale and a larger font size. The bottom rendering used the default font size and a scaled context.

Note in Figure 5.53 the inconsistent spacing between the "rm" and "ma" letter pairs, making the word longer even though the letter glyphs are all the same size. What's worse, this kerning behavior changes inconsistently as the scale of a canvas changes. This can be disastrous if you want a user to smoothly zoom on some text element rendered to the canvas. The visual effect of letters popping in and out of proper kerning as the scale changes produces a jarring effect.

In addition to not looking the same on every browser, text measured using the context's own `measureText` method often produces different results on different browsers. This discrepancy gets larger as the font size increases. This means that text as a measurement tool for positioning is unreliable and should be avoided.

In short, the text API was the last piece of the canvas specification implemented on almost every browser, *and it shows.*

Drawing Text

The context has three methods and three properties related to text. Two of the methods render text to canvas:

▶ `fillText(textString, x, y, [maxWidth])`

▶ `strokeText(textString, x, y, [maxWidth])`

If you are familiar with `stroke` and `fill`, then these methods do as you'd expect: `fillText` renders a string of text at a specified location using the `fillStyle` and `strokeText` outlines a string of text at a specified location using the `strokeStyle`. The optional argument specifies a maximum width and is rarely used.

Text can be filled or stroked with anything that paths can, including solid colors, gradients, patterns, and images. It bears repeating that the easiest way to fill or stroke with an image is making a pattern out of that image and setting that as the fill or stroke style, and there is an example of this in the section on patterns.

Like the `stroke` method, `strokeText` takes into account whatever `lineWidth` is set and strokes the outline of the text accordingly.

The coordinates specified for the two methods do not indicate the top-left corner of the block of text, as some may think after using the `fillRect` and `strokeRect` methods. Instead, the coordinates specify the alphabetic baseline of the text, which can casually be thought of as the bottom-left point of the first glyph in the text string.

The horizontal line in the next image shows the location of the alphabetic baseline. Note in Figure 5.54 how the x and y coordinates do not necessarily specify the bottom of the rendered text, as many text glyphs can descend below the alphabetic baseline.

Later, we see that we can change the baseline to be drawn on with the context's `textBaseline` property.

The optional argument in the two text-rendering methods is supposed to specify an optional maximum width, but the specification isn't very precise on its definition. It states that if a block of to-be-rendered text is longer than the maximum width, the canvas must "change *font* to have a more condensed font (if one is available or if a reasonably readable one can be synthesized by applying a horizontal scale factor to the font) or a smaller font."

FIGURE 5.54   The word Jelly rendered using `fillText`. The x and y coordinates of `fillText` were also used to make the two red lines.

The "or" that the specification inserted has caused two interpretations. Most browsers take the spec to mean that setting a `maxWidth` should simply scale the width of the font to condense it. So Firefox and Chrome, upon trying to render a 100px font with a `maxWidth` set, keep the text 100 pixels high and it is scaled (squished) to fit the width horizontally only. Opera and Opera Mobile, on the other hand, opt simply for a smaller font, making the rendered text look less squished and more proportionally correct. At least for now, if consistency is your goal, `maxWidth` is not your ticket.

Fonts

The `font` property gets or sets the font to be drawn with calls to `fillText` and `strokeText`. It is settable to any valid CSS font string. The default is `10px sans-serif`.

Note that getting the font does not always return the same value that you set. Setting the font to something complicated may be valid, but the context may only save a simplified version of the string. Here are a few examples:

```
// Technically a valid font string
ctx.font = "normal normal normal 12pt/normal Georgia"
console.log(ctx.font)
// "12pt Georgia" in Internet Explorer 9 and Firefox
// "normal normal normal 12pt/normal Georgia" in Chrome

ctx.font = "12px/14px Arial, helvetica"
console.log(ctx.font)
// "12px Arial,helvetica" in Internet Explorer 9 and Firefox
// "12px/14px Arial, helvetica" in Chrome
```

The `font` property will be looking for five CSS properties in the string: `font-style`, `font-variant`, `font-weight`, `font-size`, and `font-family`. An example of using all of them might be `"italic small-caps bold 72px Georgia"`. There's one more CSS font option, `line-height`, but it is ignored in canvas because there is no native multiline text support. Figure 5.55 shows several examples of text filled on the canvas with various font strings.

> **NOTE**
>
> As of this writing, Firefox does not support the small-caps font variant when rendering canvas fonts.

30px sans-serif

Italic Small-caps bold 32px Georgia

normal normal normal 32px Verdana

normal Small-caps 700 32px Verdana

400 32px Arial, Helvetica, sans-serif

24px "Comic Sans MS", "Some other horrible font"

Small-caps 32px serif

32px "Times New Roman", serif

22px "Lucida Console", Monaco, monospace

700 32px "Gill Sans", sans-serif

900 22px "Gill Sans", sans-serif

FIGURE 5.55   Examples of filling text with various valid font strings. The font strings were also used as the text argument to `fillText`.

In common practice, most people only use weight, size, and family, but regardless of which ones we decide to use, we should always be careful to set them in that respective order; otherwise, some browsers will interpret the string incorrectly. For instance, setting font to `"72px Georgia bold"` renders correctly in Chrome and Internet Explorer 9 as bold-weighted Georgia at 72 pixels. But the same string instead renders a default serif font—not Georgia, but presumably the browser's default—in Firefox and Internet Explorer 9 at 72 pixels, and renders the default context font instead (sans-serif) at 72 pixels in Opera.

To get the font to render correctly across all browsers, you must specify it with the weight first, in this case as `"bold 72px Georgia"`.

> **NOTE**
>
> The fonts specified can be web-safe fonts, but some browsers can also render embedded and linked fonts (from style sheets) to the canvas. You should always test every browser you are targeting to ensure that your font selection looks good and that it contains a reasonable web-safe backup.

textBaseline

Positioning the text you want to draw is a matter of specifying the x and y coordinates in a `fillText` or `drawText` command, which specify the baseline, but you can also change the text baseline to one of several attributes.

For positioning text, some people find it easier to have the x and y coordinates specify the topmost part of the characters instead of the alphabetic baseline. The context's `textBaseline` property lets us achieve this. The valid values for `textBaseline` are the strings:

- ▶ `top`
- ▶ `hanging`
- ▶ `middle`
- ▶ `alphabetic` (the default)
- ▶ `ideographic`
- ▶ `bottom`

As of this writing, the baselines are not always consistent across browsers. Not all values of `textBaseline` are supported on all browsers, and results may vary with the font used. Some browsers place more space at the top of the character for `top` and `hanging`, and Webkit-based browsers (Chrome and Safari) place `ideographic` and `bottom` at the same y-position, while the other major desktop browsers place `ideographic` and `alphabetic` at the same y-position. If you use a `textBaseline` other than the default `alphabetic`, be sure it works consistently on all platforms you're targeting. Figure 5.56 shows a simple comparison of the baselines in Firefox 14.

FIGURE 5.56   The characters "Ag" drawn with the same y coordinate, represented by the red line. The baselines are, from left to right: `top`, `hanging`, `middle`, `alphabetic` (in red, the default), `ideographic`, and `bottom`.

textAlign

The context's `textAlign` property controls where on the x-axis the text is drawn. These names may look familiar as almost every text editor has text alignment options for left, right, or center. The canvas context is a bit more nuanced, and there are five possible values:

▶ `start` (the default)

▶ `end`

▶ `left`

▶ `right`

▶ `center`

In practice, the default value `start` is seemingly identical to `left` and `end` is seemingly identical to `right`. The difference is only apparent if the `dir` attribute of the canvas is switched from `ltr` to `rtl`, then `start` becomes the same as `right` and `end` becomes the same as `left`. Using `start` and `end` are therefore a bit nicer than using `left` and `right` because they allow your app to automatically switch when a right-to-left language is specified. If you need it to be more absolute than that, then the `left` and `right` options can be used.

Figure 5.57 shows the difference of drawing the same word at the same x coordinate with different values of `textAlign`.

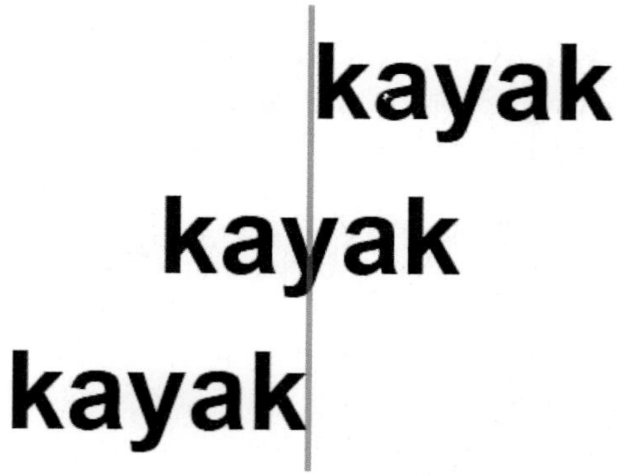

kayak

kayak

kayak

FIGURE 5.57   Three lines of text drawn at the same x coordinate, with `textAlign` values of `start`, `center`, and `end` from top to bottom. A red line denotes the x coordinate of the `fillText` command.

Measuring Text

The context has one method for measuring text, `measureText`, which takes a string and evaluates its size based on the current `font` attribute. It returns a `TextMetrics` object that contains only a single property, `width`, which expresses the width of the string in pixels. Because there is only one property on the `TextMetrics` object (for now!), common usage might look like this:

```
var stringWidth = ctx.measureText("Some string").width;
```

As I mentioned in the beginning of this section, measuring text is highly discrepant between browsers. The three strings, "A text", "Block", and "a Text Block", when measured for width, produce different results on almost every browser. Measuring the width of each of the three strings produces the respective values:

▶ 31, 25, 58 in Chrome

▶ 27, 25, 53 in Chrome Mobile

▶ 30, 25, 57 in Firefox

▶ 31, 25, 58 in Opera

▶ 27, 25, 54 in Opera Mobile

▶ 29, 24, 55 in Internet Explorer 9

▶ 31, 25, 58 in Safari

This means you shouldn't rely on the measured width of strings for any information that is expected to be consistent across browsers, such as the width or height of visual elements that need to be precisely positioned or located.

> **NOTE**
>
> Not only is the measured width of text different per browser, it's also not necessarily precise. Often you'll find that the width is a few pixels longer or shorter than the rendered string that you might be measuring. Font glyphs have a lot of leeway in their components, and it's possible for them to wildly "spill out" of their em square, especially if you're using non-web-safe fonts that mimic cursive handwriting, or complex accent marks that might extend beyond a normal em square.

The lack of text height in the `TextMetrics` was a deliberate choice by the specification owner. Producing text-oriented apps was not a priority for the specification.

In the meantime, people typically either precompute the heights of their fonts or approximate it, such as by taking the width of a capital *M* for a height value.

Performance

Text is slow. Very slow. Not just drawing the text, setting the font and measuring text are slow enough to be carefully avoided when possible. In fact, simply *setting the font* is often slower than creating and stroking a path to the context!

There are several optimizations to be had when drawing text, including caching fonts, caching font heights, or turning oft-drawn renderings of text into images. Chapter 7 focuses on canvas performance and possible solutions if text performance becomes an issue in your app.

Canvas Context Recap

This chapter ends with a recap of all the canvas context methods and attributes in the form of a quick reference guide.

Styling

▶ `fillStyle` **and** `strokeStyle`—Get or set the colors to apply on fill and stroke commands. They accept most valid CCS color strings as values, as well as `CanvasGradient` and `CanvasPattern` objects.

▶ `createLinearGradient(x0, y0, x1, y1)`—Returns a `CanvasGradient` object describing a linear gradient. The arguments specify a start and end point to the gradient.

▶ `createRadialGradient(x1, y1, radius1, x2, y2, radius2)`—Returns a `CanvasGradient` object describing a radial gradient. The arguments specify two circles that form the gradient.

▶ `addColorStop(offset, color)`—Adds a color stop to the gradient of the specified color at a given stop between 0 and 1; a method on `CanvasGradient`.

▶ `createPattern(image, repetitionRule)`—Returns a `CanvasPattern` object. The first argument is any image element, video element, or canvas element. The `repetitionRule` supports the string values `repeat` (default), `repeat-x`, `repeat-y`, and `no-repeat`.

Shadows

▶ `shadowOffsetX`—Gets or sets the shadow's x-offset. Default 0.

▶ `shadowOffsetY`—Gets or sets the shadow's y-offset. Default 0.

▶ `shadowBlur`—Gets or sets the amount for a shadow to blur. Default 0.

▶ `shadowColor`—Gets or sets the shadow color. Accepts valid CSS strings. Default is transparent black, `rgba(0, 0, 0, 0)`.

State

▶ `save()`—Saves the canvas context state, pushing it onto an internal stack

▶ `restore()`—Pops the most recent canvas context state from the internal stack and restores all context state values

Rectangles

▶ `fillRect(x, y, w, h)`—Fills a rectangle with the current `fillStyle`

▶ `strokeRect(x, y, w, h)`—Outlines a rectangle with the current `strokeStyle`

▶ **clearRect(x, y, w, h)**—Clears the canvas context at the specified rectangle, returning the bitmap pixels to their default state of fully transparent black

Paths

▶ **beginPath()**—Resets the current path on the canvas context. At any given time, there is only one path (or no path) "loaded" on the context. This is known as the current path. A path can have any number of *subpaths*.

▶ **closePath()**—Marks the current subpath closed, meaning a stroke will connect the last point of the subpath with the first point. It also opens a new subpath, with the starting point equal to the first point of the last path.

▶ **stroke()**—Traces the current path with the color defined by strokeStyle and a thickness defined by lineWidth. Keep in mind that the current path still exists on the context, and only calling beginPath again will clear that path.

▶ **fill()**—Fills the current path with the fillStyle. Open paths are implicitly closed for a fill, so making a V-shaped path will fill a full triangle. Filling is done according to the nonzero winding number rule algorithm.

▶ **clip()**—Intersects the current clipping region with the current path. The default clipping region is the entire canvas.

▶ **moveTo(x, y)**—Creates a new subpath, adding to (or starting) the current path, with the specified point as its starting point.

▶ **lineTo(x, y)**—Adds a line to the current subpath from the last point in the path.

▶ **rect(x, y, width, height)**—Creates a new subpath in the shape of a rectangle and closes that subpath. This is a convenience function that is equivalent to calling moveTo, lineTo three times, and closePath to make a rectangle.

▶ **quadraticCurveTo(cpx, cpy, x, y)**—Draws a quadratic curve with the given control point (cpx, cpy) to the given point (x, y).

▶ **bezierCurveTo(cp1x, cp1y, cp2x, cp2y, x, y)**—Draws a cubic Bezier curve described by the two given sets of control points and a given end point.

▶ **arcTo(x1, y1, x2, y2, radius)**—Draws an arc with the given control points and radius, connected to the previous point via a straight line.

▶ **arc(x, y, radius, startAngle, endAngle, [anticlockwise])**—Draws an arc described by the given arguments, starting at the startAngle and ending at the endAngle, going in the given direction and defaulting to clockwise if the last argument is omitted.

▶ **lineWidth**—Gets or sets the width of paths to be drawn when stroke is called. Default 1.

▶ **lineCap**—Gets or sets how the end of lines are to be drawn. Valid values are "butt", "round", and "square". Default "butt".

▶ `lineJoin`—Gets or sets how corners are drawn when two lines meet. Valid values are `"bevel"`, `"round"`, and `"miter"`. Default `"miter"`.

▶ `miterLimit`—Gets or sets the current miter limit ratio. Default 10.

▶ `isPointInPath(x, y)`—True if a given point is contained in the current canvas context path, false otherwise.

Image Drawing

▶ `drawImage(image, dx, dy [dw], [dh])`—Renders an image to the context at location (`dx`, `dy`). The two optional arguments represent a destination width and height for optional scaling. The image can be an image element, video element, or canvas element.

▶ `drawImage(image, sx, sy, sw, sh, dx, dy, dw, dh)`—Renders a portion of an image described by the source (`s-`) arguments to a rectangle of the context described by the destination (`d-`) arguments.

Transformation

▶ `translate(x, y)`—Translates the origin of the context

▶ `scale(x, y)`—Scales the context

▶ `rotate(angle)`—Rotates the context by `angle` radians

▶ `transform(m11, m12, m21, m22, dx, dy)`—Applies an arbitrary transformation to the current transformation matrix

▶ `setTransform(m11, m12, m21, m22, dx, dy)`—Replaces the current transformation matrix with the specified matrix

Compositing

▶ `globalAlpha`—Gets or sets the additional alpha value to apply to rendered objects. Default 1.

▶ `globalCompositeOperation`—Gets or sets the composite operation to apply for all subsequently rendered objects. Default `source-over`.

Text

▶ `font`—Gets or sets the current font style to use when rendering text. Default `10px sans-serif`.

▶ `textAlign`—Gets or sets the alignment being used when drawing text. Possible values are `left`, `right`, `center`, `start`, and `end`. Default `start`.

▶ `textBaseline`—Gets or sets the baseline used when drawing text. Possible values are `top`, `hanging`, `middle`, `alphabetic`, `ideographic`, and `bottom`. Default `alphabetic`.

► `fillText(string, x, y, maxWidth)`—Renders text with the current `fillStyle` at the specified location. The optional argument `maxWidth` restricts the width of the font by horizontally scaling the font or using a smaller font.

► `fillText(string, x, y, maxWidth)`—Renders an outline of text with the current `strokeStyle` at the specified location.

► `measureText(string)`—Returns a TextMetrics object with one attribute, `width`, that describes the pixel width of the specified string.

Image Data

► `canvas.toDataURL(type, args)`—Returns a string describing the canvas bitmap as a data URL, in Base64. The `type` argument is a string specifying desired image type such as `image/png` or `image/jpeg`. If the image type is JPEG, the second optional argument describes the desired quality level on a scale of 0 to 1, inclusive. This method is bound by canvas security rules and may throw an exception if the canvas has been tainted. Note that this is a canvas (not context) method.

► `createImageData(w, h)`—Returns an empty `ImageData` object of the specified size.

► `createImageData(imageData)`—Returns an empty `ImageData` object of the same size as the specified `ImageData` object. This method does *not* copy the image data of the argument, only the size.

► `getImageData(x, y, w, h)`—Returns an `ImageData` object that describes the given rectangle on the canvas. This method is bound by canvas security rules and may throw an exception if the canvas has been tainted.

► `putImageData(imageData, x, y)`—Places the specified `ImageData` onto the context. This method ignores the transformation matrix.

► `putImageData(imageData, x, y, dirtyX, dirtyY, dirtyWidth, dirtyHeight)`— Places only a specified rectangle of the specified `ImageData` onto the context.

Summary

Canvas offers a native way of providing rich dynamic content reminiscent of Flash and Silverlight. Its popularity grows by the day and at the current rate we can reasonably suspect it will replace nonnative plug-ins (like Flash) as the default graphics rendering platform of the Web.

In this chapter, we covered all methods and attributes for the HTML5 canvas and its 2D context. You should have a good idea of what it is capable of accomplishing, what might not be, and what might not be just yet!

Chapter 6 covers examples of the interactivity possibilities of the canvas as well as examples of usage in a real app and keeping track of state. Chapter 7 deals with real-world canvas performance, and Chapter 8 discusses the most recent additions to the canvas API and the future of the canvas element.

Making Canvas Interactive and Stateful

Now that we've covered the entire canvas API, we take a look at animating the canvas and making it interactive.

Nearly all interactive canvas applications are event driven, typically by a combination of mouse, touch device, or keyboard events. Retrieving coordinates from input devices is not always an intuitive exercise, so we examine our options for handling mouse and touch events in the canvas.

This chapter then talks about the JavaScript options for animation, covering some relatively new JavaScript methods in the process. We give examples of how to draw at a specified frame rate and implement time-based animation.

Lastly, we create a full canvas app to showcase interactivity. This also serves as an exploration of (simple) state management.

Canvas Coordinates—Mouse and Touch

Finding the location a user has clicked or touched on the canvas element can be an irksome process, especially when HTML borders, paddings, and margins are involved. The canvas specification makes little mention of input events, presumably with the expectation that it ought to be similar to performing the same task on any given HTML element.

Because there's no mention in the specification, there's no method of getting mouse or touch coordinates on a canvas that is considered canonical. Instead, programmers typically rely on any of several InputEvent attributes from the `mousedown, mouseup, mousemove, touchstart, touchend, touchmove,` and `click` event listeners.

These events have various attributes, such as `clientX, clientY, screenX, screenY, pageX,` and `pageY`. The attributes represent various coordinate sets locating where the event occurred, such as where a mouse was clicked in relation to the page or element. Unfortunately, none of these coordinate pairs themselves describe precisely where the event occurred relative to the top-left corner of the drawable region of the canvas. We take a look at two methods that use event and element attributes to determine proper mouse and touch input positions. Importantly, there's no "right" way to get input coordinates on a canvas, and the two ways discussed in this chapter are very different but equally valid.

The code in this section often assumes a reference to the canvas element exists with the variable name `canvas`. If you want to start with (and modify) a complete HTML page example, you can use the code in the "Canvas Interactivity Example: Making and Moving Shapes" section in this chapter (Listing 6.11).

getBoundingClientRect

First, let's take a look at very simple mouse code wrapped in its own function. The function takes a mouse or touch `InputEvent` and returns a JavaScript object with x and y defined. It uses the HTML element method `getBoundingClientRect`, the event's client coordinates, and the canvas's width and height. Listing 6.1 contains the code for this position-getting function.

LISTING 6.1   `getPos`—Simple Mouse and Touch Position

```
// Simple coordinates from a mouse or touch event
// Does not work if there is a border, padding, or margin on the canvas
function getPos(e, canvas) {
  var bbox = canvas.getBoundingClientRect();

  return {
    x: e.clientX - bbox.left * (canvas.width / bbox.width),
    y: e.clientY - bbox.top * (canvas.height / bbox.height)
  }
}
```

We call this `getPos` function by passing it a mouse or touch `InputEvent`:

```
canvas.addEventListener('click', function(e) {
  var position = getPos(e, canvas);
  alert(position.x + ',' + position.y);
}, false);
```

This position method is simple and short, and will suffice in many common cases. However, this code does not account for situations where a canvas has border, padding, or margin values. It also does not account for situations where the canvas is scaled by CSS (Cascading Style Sheets) to be a different width or height from its attributes.

Figure 6.1 shows a canvas with four points drawn on it in red using `fillRect` and `fillText`. The canvas element has several CSS rules applied: a blue background, a black border, and margin on the top, pushing it downward from its parent div (yellow with a red border) and padding on (only) the left side of the canvas. The padding is why the (0, 0) coordinate is not all the way to the left, and we see that the point (-7, 70) is partially "cut off," which illustrates that the canvas padding is not a drawable area, even though it shares the blue background. Using `getPos` on this canvas and clicking on the (50, 50), the point (84, 65) is returned.

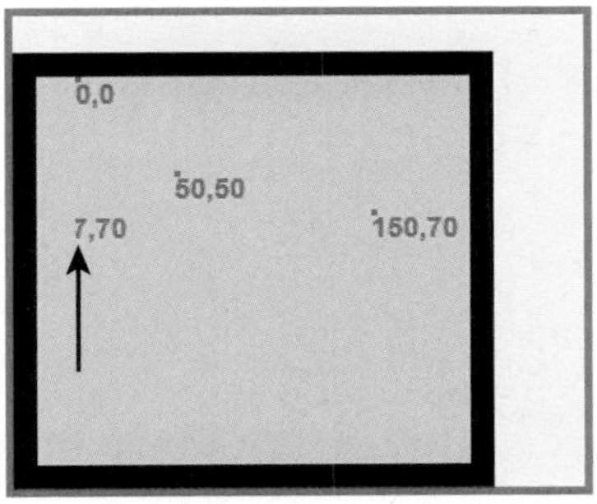

FIGURE 6.1   An example of a canvas with a blue background, black border, top margin, and left padding applied. Note that (0, 0) is not in the top-left corner of the blue area due to left-side padding, and the point (-7, 70) is "cut-off" in drawing (see arrow) because we cannot draw onto the padding. Our simple `getPos` method will not work with these padding, border, and margin rules.

With a bit of labor, we could fix these problems in the `getPos` function in Listing 6.1, but instead we focus on accomplishing these goals in a second (faster but more complicated) method.

Computing Element Offset

Our second method is a good deal longer but will work with CSS-styled canvas elements, and has the additional benefit of being roughly 50% faster in WebKit-based browsers (and modestly faster in others) as of this writing.

This second method, which we call `getPos2`, does not need to account for margin by design, and explicitly offsets border and padding, as well as accounting for any offset in the `<html>` tag itself. The last consideration is rare, but can fix issues on pages with toolbars that work by positioning themselves above the `<html>` tag. This method also computes and accounts for any difference between the CSS width and height and the canvas attributes `width` and `height`, though we comment this part out by default because it is not typical, and we want to present something fast that works in the most common cases.

Because computing the sizes of these CSS properties can be slow, we only want to do it once, outside of the `getPos2` function. The `getPos2` function then computes a total offset and uses it against `pageX` and `pageY`. Although this loop could be cached, it is typically faster than the `getBoundingClientRect` used in the previous `getPos` function as it is written, and we want our code in both methods to be general enough to work in the case that elements on the page resize or move around. Listing 6.2 has the code for `getPos2`.

LISTING 6.2   `getPos2`—Faster and More Comprehensive Mouse and Touch Position

```
// This code is outside the getPos2 function, because
// we only want to compute it once
// This code requires a reference to the canvas element, used here as "canvas".
var stylePaddingTop = parseInt(
  getComputedStyle(canvas, null).getPropertyValue('padding-top'));
var stylePaddingLeft = parseInt(
  getComputedStyle(canvas, null).getPropertyValue('padding-left'));
var styleBorderLeft = parseInt(
  getComputedStyle(canvas, null).getPropertyValue('border-left-width'));
var styleBorderTop = parseInt(
  getComputedStyle(canvas, null).getPropertyValue('border-top-width'));

// The total padding width and height are only needed
// if your canvas is scaled by CSS:
var stylePaddingRight = parseInt(
  getComputedStyle(canvas, null).getPropertyValue('padding-right'));
var stylePaddingBottom = parseInt(
  getComputedStyle(canvas, null).getPropertyValue('padding-bottom'));
var paddingWidth = stylePaddingLeft + stylePaddingRight;
var paddingHeight = stylePaddingTop + stylePaddingBottom;

var html = document.body.parentNode;
var htmlTop = html.offsetTop;
var htmlLeft = html.offsetLeft;


function getPos2(e, canvas) {
  var element = canvas, offsetX = 0, offsetY = 0, mx, my;

  // Compute the total offset. Additional caching may be possible here
  if (element.offsetParent !== undefined) {
    do {
      offsetX += element.offsetLeft;
      offsetY += element.offsetTop;
    } while ((element = element.offsetParent));
  }
```

```
// Add padding and border style widths to offset
// Also add the <html> offsets in case there's a position:fixed bar
offsetX += stylePaddingLeft + styleBorderLeft + htmlLeft;
offsetY += stylePaddingTop + styleBorderTop + htmlTop;

mx = e.pageX - offsetX;
my = e.pageY - offsetY;

// Enable this if the CSS sizing is different than the canvas width/height:
//mx *= canvas.width / (canvas.clientWidth - paddingWidth);
//my *= canvas.height / (canvas.clientHeight - paddingHeight);

return {x: mx, y: my};
}
```

The `getPos` and `getPos2` methods will work pleasantly with both mouse and touch inputs. We simply pass them both a relevant event:

```
// Assuming "canvas" is a reference to a canvas element
canvas.addEventListener('mousedown', function(e) {
  var coords = getPos2(e, canvas);
  // Do something with coords
}, true);

canvas.addEventListener('touchstart', function(e) {
  if (e.targetTouches.length > 0) getPos2(e.targetTouches[0], canvas);
  // Do something with coords

  // perhaps stop other touch functionality, like panning the page:
  e.preventDefault();
}, true);
```

The final section of this chapter contains a full example of mouse and touch events making use of canvas coordinates.

> **NOTE**
>
> There are some important differences between the expectations of mouse events and touch events. Double-clicking with a mouse typically selects text near a mouse, and so most canvas apps cancel the `selectstart` event on the canvas by calling `preventDefault` on the event argument. Double-tapping on a touch device often zooms the canvas and is often more difficult to cancel, as different mobile browsers implement the action differently.
>
> Simply swiping with a mouse click does not typically indicate any action, except when selecting text or while hovering over a draggable object on a page, such as an image or text selection. Swiping on touch devices, on the other hand, typically means that the user

wants to pan the page. When constructing touch events for our canvas apps, we must be careful to call `preventDefault` on all of the touch events we are taking control of, and possibly ensuring that we do not call `preventDefault` on any of the touch events that are OK to pass on to other elements or the browser.

Canvas Animation

Animation is an essential part of most canvas uses, but there is nothing new in the canvas specification itself for animation, so we construct animation loops as we would in any animated JavaScript application. For JavaScript animation itself, however, we have an exciting new method to employ.

The old way of animating JavaScript was to use either the `setInterval` or the `setTimeout` function. The first repeatedly invokes a method every given number of milliseconds, while the second invokes a method only once after a specified millisecond delay. These functions are widely used but are not ideal for animation. The millisecond arguments represent only an approximation of the time to wait before executing the draw loop again, and they only allow you to guess as to when you should draw the next animation frame. In almost every application, it is better if the browser is able to tell you when it is ready and able to (re)draw canvas content, and so some browsers have implemented a more modern animation method.

Letting the Browser Take Control with `requestAnimationFrame`

The new method of animating for the HTML5-era is `requestAnimationFrame`. This method lets you tell the browser that you want to perform an animation, and rather than doing it after a specified time, the browser will animate as soon as it can, on the next animation frame.

This new method attempts to select an optimal frame rate, typically capping itself at 60 frames per second for foreground browser tabs, while background tabs will be throttled based on conditions that the browser decides. A simple implementation of `requestAnimationFrame` looks like the following:

```
function draw(time) {
  // Immediately queue another frame
  // by making another call to requestAnimationFrame.
  requestAnimationFrame(draw);

  // draw loop code goes here

  // ...
}


requestAnimationFrame(draw); // Initial call to requestAnimationFrame
```

Rather, a simple implementation *would* look like that, if every browser supported it. We're going to have to be more clever before we can use `requestAnimationFrame`.

Support for `requestAnimationFrame`

Because `requestAnimationFrame` is relatively new, it is not supported in all browsers. It exists on various browsers in one of three forms:

▶ `requestAnimationFrame`—Internet Explorer 10

▶ `webkitRequestAnimationFrame`—Chrome, Chrome Mobile, Safari 6, and iOS Safari 6

▶ `mozRequestAnimationFrame`—Firefox and Firefox Mobile

The function is not supported at all in Opera (as of this writing) or in Internet Explorer 9 and previous versions. It is also not currently present in the Android browser or Opera Mobile. Nightly browser builds offer more support, but of course we cannot expect our users to run them—we can only safely know that wider implementation is on the horizon.

In the meantime, we have a slightly large but fairly clean polyfill that will afford us a fallback on any browser that does not have `requestAnimationFrame`. Inserting this code in your script before `requestAnimationFrame` is used allows you to call the method without worrying about whether it is prefixed, or whether it exists at all! When the function doesn't exist, it falls back on a simple `setInterval` timer.

Listing 6.3 contains the code for the most popular `requestAnimationFrame` polyfill, with due credit in the opening comment.

LISTING 6.3   requestAnimationFrame Polyfill

```
// requestAnimationFrame polyfill by Erik Moller
// fixes from Paul Irish and Tino Zijdel
// Source and revisions: https://gist.github.com/1579671

(function() {
    var lastTime = 0;
    var vendors = ['ms', 'moz', 'webkit', 'o'];
    for(var x = 0; x < vendors.length && !window.requestAnimationFrame; ++x) {
        window.requestAnimationFrame = window[vendors[x]+'RequestAnimationFrame'];
        window.cancelAnimationFrame = window[vendors[x]+'CancelAnimationFrame']
                                 || window[vendors[x]+
➥'CancelRequestAnimationFrame'];
    }

    if (!window.requestAnimationFrame)
        window.requestAnimationFrame = function(callback, element) {
            var currTime = new Date().getTime();
            var timeToCall = Math.max(0, 16 - (currTime - lastTime));
            var id = window.setTimeout(function() { callback(currTime +
➥timeToCall); },
```

```
                timeToCall);
            lastTime = currTime + timeToCall;
            return id;
        };

    if (!window.cancelAnimationFrame)
        window.cancelAnimationFrame = function(id) {
            clearTimeout(id);
        };
}());
```

This solution standardizes the name if a prefixed version exists and otherwise defines a fallback function if no `requestAnimationFrame` function exists. After execution, this lets us use just the nonprefixed `requestAnimationFrame` function on any browser.

Syntax
The `requestAnimationFrame` function takes one argument, a callback function, and executes that function as soon as the browser is ready to render another frame. This callback can optionally employ one argument, a millisecond time stamp that denotes when the function was called.

cancelAnimationFrame
The `requestAnimationFrame` function returns an integer ID that uniquely identifies the callback that is queued to run. As we can see in the polyfill code, there's also a `cancelAnimationFrame` function, which currently enjoys slightly less support than `requestAnimationFrame`, and is itself sometimes prefixed (such as `webkitCancelAnimationFrame`).

If you would like to cancel a callback you have set with `requestAnimationFrame`, the `cancelAnimationFrame` function can be called with the return value ID of `request AnimationFrame`. Because the `cancelAnimationFrame` implementation is currently spottier than the `requestAnimationFrame` implementation as of this writing, you may want to code any needed frame cancellation manually for the near future to ensure proper functionality.

Animation and Timing
The `requestAnimationFrame` method is useful for allowing the browser to animate as fast as it can, but often we want our animations more structured. Two common cases where using `requestAnimationFrame` requires some thought: animation based on frames per second and animation based on time differences.

Animating Objects Based on Frames Per Second
The `requestAnimationFrame` function is rather low level, and there is no built-in way to limit drawing (or other operations) to a particular frame rate. Because `requestAnimationFrame` does not let you choose a frame rate, but rather attempts to maintain 60 frames per second when the browser tab is active, some extra footwork is required to draw at a specified frame rate.

Listing 6.4 shows one simple method of updating the drawing at a constant frame rate. We use the time stamp provided to the callback function as an argument to determine the time that has elapsed since the last requested frame, and only draw after a certain amount of time has passed.

LISTING 6.4   Using `requestAnimationFrame` to Update at 8 Frames Per Second

```
// Remember: Depending on browser you may need the polyfill
// in Listing 6.3 for requestAnimationFrame to work

function update(ts) {
  requestAnimationFrame(update);
  elapsed += ts - lasttime;
  lasttime = ts;

  // Draw at 8 frames per second (draw every 125 milliseconds)
  if(elapsed > 125) {
    elapsed -= 125;  // reset the elapsed counter
    // Our canvas updating code would go here
  }
}

// Initial call:
var elapsed = 0;
var lasttime = new Date().getTime();
requestAnimationFrame(update);
```

There are many solutions to limiting the drawing to a specific frame rate, but the preceding code is general enough to work in most cases and has the performance advantage of creating no new objects.

Animating Objects at Different Times

Another common scenario is updating objects based on time instead of frame rate. Often we want objects to be at a consistent location regardless of any disruptions in frame rate, temporary or otherwise, such as in time-synchronized animations that overlay a video or a real-time multiplayer game. This type of animation is similarly solved by using the `requestAnimationFrame` callback's argument to determine how much time has elapsed.

Listing 6.5 contains an example of drawing three squares on the canvas at different speeds, updating their positions based on the time between subsequent calls to `requestAnimationFrame`. Unlike last time, the variable `elapsed` refers to the amount of time since the last call, instead of cumulative time after several calls.

Because the `elapsed` variable refers to the amount of time between two calls to `requestAnimationFrame`, we could additionally use it to determine our frame rate with the expression `(1000 / elapsed)`.

LISTING 6.5   Animating Three Squares at Different Speeds Based on Elapsed Time

```
// Remember: Depending on browser you may need the polyfill
// in Listing 6.3 for requestAnimationFrame to work

// Keep track of the x location of three squares:
var mx1 = 0;
var mx2 = 0;
var mx3 = 0;

var time;
function draw(now) {
  requestAnimationFrame(draw);
  var elapsed = now - (time || now);
  time = now;

  // move the squares by some (very small) number of pixels per millisecond
  mx1 += 0.2 * elapsed;
  mx2 += 0.1 * elapsed;
  mx3 += 0.05 * elapsed;

  // Drawing the squares:
  ctx.clearRect(0,0,300,300);
  ctx.fillStyle = 'red';
  ctx.fillRect(mx1, 40, 20, 20);
  ctx.fillStyle = 'green';
  ctx.fillRect(mx2, 80, 20, 20);
  ctx.fillStyle = 'blue';
  ctx.fillRect(mx3, 120, 20, 20);

  // Reset the squares' positions to zero when they go offscreen
  if (mx1 > 300) mx1 = 0;
  if (mx2 > 300) mx2 = 0;
  if (mx3 > 300) mx3 = 0;
}

// Initial call:
requestAnimationFrame(draw);
```

The result of this code can be seen in Figure 6.2. Three squares all began at an x position of zero and raced to the right at their own paces. Disruptions in frame rate do not modify the consistency of their travel.

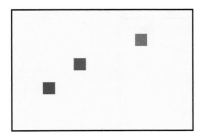

FIGURE 6.2   The three animated squares moving at different "speeds" after one second has elapsed.

> **NOTE**
>
> Because canvas apps may be run on everything from powerful desktops to mobile phones, animation performance should not be taken lightly. The next chapter is devoted to canvas performance, nearly all of which implicitly concerns animation performance.

Canvas Interactivity Example: Making and Moving Shapes

In this sample app, we cover how to use a few data structures to store and modify the state of shapes on an HTML5 canvas. We create selectable, movable objects that the user can interact with using the mouse or a touch interface.

In the interest of keeping our examples short and functional, this app doesn't appear particularly flashy, but should give a decent foundation to begin your own interactive projects. Figure 6.3 shows what our finished web app looks like.

If you are the kind of person who prefers to try out each code snippet or learn by example, then I encourage you to start by loading up the complete code at the end of this section (Listing 6.11). It is intentionally heavily commented, so every working piece is explained inline in addition to in the chapter text. If you encounter something confusing or don't understand its purpose, come back and look at the text of the relevant section.

If you are the kind of person who prefers to learn by narrative explanation, read on!

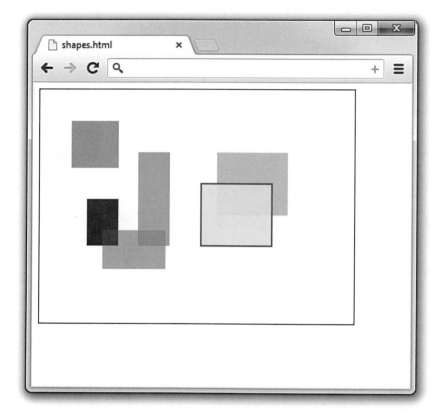

FIGURE 6.3   The finished example. The shape with a red border is the currently selected object.

Getting Started

For this example, the only HTML element we need on our page is a `<canvas>` tag. Because the page is otherwise blank and we want to know where the canvas edges are located, we add a border using inline CSS styling. Because this is a sample app, we keep the fallback to a minimum, having just a sentence of text to display in case canvas is not supported. In production apps, we should always be much more accommodating to our users.

```
<canvas id="myCanvas" width="400" height="300" style="border:1px solid black;">
   Your browser does not support HTML5 Canvas!
</canvas>
```

As we saw in the last chapter, canvas drawing doesn't retain any information: When you execute a drawing command, the canvas retains no memory of what was just drawn or where. Because there is no built-in state management, we need to keep track ourselves of all the shape colors and locations that we want to draw (and redraw) each frame.

We also need to make use of our stored shape information to handle our own mouse and touch events, as we will be doing our own hit detection (also called object picking) to determine what is at the mouse pointer or touch location or when an input event occurs.

To create our web app with canvas, we need to add the following functionality in JavaScript:

▶ Code for keeping track of drawn shape state

▶ Code for keeping track of canvas state

▶ Code for handling mouse and touch events

▶ Code for drawing the objects as they are made and moved around

The Shapes We Draw

Our example draws simple rectangles, and we create a `Shape` class to represent these rectangular objects, keeping track of size, location, and color.

JavaScript is a prototype-based language and doesn't technically have classes, but that isn't a problem because JavaScript programmers are very good at playing pretend. To accommodate as many backgrounds as possible, our example is coded in an object-oriented style of programming: We have a `Shape` "class" and create `Shape` instances with it.

What we are really doing is defining a function named `Shape` and adding functions to the `Shape` prototype. When we make new instances of the function `Shape`, all instances share the methods defined on the `Shape` prototype. Playing pretend with JavaScript classes can become complicated when inheritance is involved, but our canvas sample app does not use inheritance.

Listing 6.6 has the code for our `Shape` constructor and the two methods defined on its prototype, which are roughly comparable to instance methods.

LISTING 6.6   Shape Constructor and Prototype Methods

```
// Constructor for Shape, an object to hold all data for drawn rectangles
function Shape(x, y, w, h, fill) {
  // All we're doing is checking if the values exist.
  // "x || 0" is a simple way of saying:
  // "if there is a value for x, use that. Otherwise (it's undefined), use 0."
  this.x = x || 0;
  this.y = y || 0;
  this.w = w || 10;
  this.h = h || 10;
  this.fill = fill || '#AAAAAA';
}

// Draws this shape to a given context
Shape.prototype.draw = function(ctx) {
```

```
  ctx.fillStyle = this.fill;
  ctx.fillRect(this.x, this.y, this.w, this.h);
}

// Determine if a point is inside the shape's bounds
Shape.prototype.contains = function(mx, my) {
  // All we have to do is make sure the Mouse X,Y fall in the area between
  // the shape's X and (X + Height) and its Y and (Y + Height)
  return  (this.x <= mx) && (this.x + this.w >= mx) &&
          (this.y <= my) && (this.y + this.h >= my);
}
```

The Shape constructor as written has some rudimentary capability to handle no given arguments, default to a 10×10 gray rectangle at (0, 0).

Calling the draw method of a Shape instance sets the fillStyle of the canvas and draws a rectangle corresponding to the measurements of that Shape onto a given context.

We also have a contains method that takes input coordinates and returns whether or not the given point is located within the Shape. We call this method for hit detection.

> **NOTE**
>
> If we were making a canvas library (or simply wanted to be more careful coders), we might want to be more strict with the input to our constructors and methods. For instance, in the Shape constructor, we could add code to make sure that all given measurement arguments really are numbers and that the given width and height are not negative. We would want to throw a sensible error if a programmer inputs otherwise.

Keeping Track of Canvas State

In this section, we create a second class (function) called CanvasState. We only need one instance of this function and it holds all of the state in this tutorial that is not associated with the Shape instances.

The CanvasState holds a reference to the canvas, its dimensions, and its context. We also compute and save the border and padding (if there is any) of the canvas element so that we can ensure accurate mouse coordinates.

In the CanvasState constructor, we also initialize a collection of state relating to the objects on the canvas and the current status of dragging. We make an array of shapes (shapes) to keep track of what's been drawn so far, a flag called dragging that will be true while we are dragging, a reference to which object is selected (selection). We also keep track of where in an object we click so we can update its position as we drag by the appropriate point.

```
function CanvasState(canvas) {

  // ...
  // Setup code not shown for conciseness
  // See the full source at the end

  // **** Keep track of state! ****

  this.valid = false; // when set to true, the canvas will redraw everything
  this.shapes = [];   // the collection of shapes to be drawn
  this.dragging = false; // Keep track of when we are dragging

  // the current selected object.
  // In the future we could turn this into an array for multiple selection
  this.selection = null;
  this.dragoffx = 0; // See mousedown and mousemove events for explanation
  this.dragoffy = 0;

  // ... (rest of constructor)
```

Our app draws on a simple `setInterval` timer that executes a draw every 30 milliseconds, so our `CanvasState` also has a `valid` flag that lets the timer know if a redraw is needed or not. Our timer causes the canvas to clear everything and redraw the scene only when `valid` is set to `false`. This stops the canvas from needlessly redrawing every 30 milliseconds; instead, it only redraws when a change occurs that sets the `valid` flag to `true`, such as a selection or a mouse-move during a dragging event, as both of these would visibly change the scene.

It is important to note that the `setInterval` function is not ideal for animation and is only used for its conciseness in the example's source code; real canvas animation should always attempt to use `requestAnimationFrame` if it exists. See the previous section in this chapter ("Canvas Animation") for details.

This process is sometimes called drawing invalidation or scene invalidation. It is not strictly needed in this shape-moving example because instead of a timer we could just redraw the scene after every event that changes something—because selection, deselection, or a shape's drag are the only events to modify the scene in this example. Although it isn't necessary here, it would be in more complex apps and may be if we wanted to extend this sample to include things such as animation or timed effects. We talk more about the importance of this concept in Chapter 7, "Canvas Performance, Tips, and Peculiarities."

Mouse and Touch Events

Continuing with the `CanvasState` constructor, we add events for `mousedown`, `mouseup`, and `mousemove` that control when an object starts and stops dragging. We also disable the `selectstart` event, which stops double-clicking on a canvas from accidentally selecting text on the page. We want at least rudimentary touch (mobile) device support, so we also include touchstart, touchend, and touchmove events that call the same CanvasState methods as their mouse counterparts: doDown, doUp, and doMove.

Finally, we add a double-click (dblclick) event that creates a new Shape and adds it to the list of shapes on the CanvasState. Listing 6.7 shows the code for the events, all of which is initialized in our CanvasState constructor.

LISTING 6.7   Canvas Events

```
// ... continued from constructor (function CanvasState)

// The following myState var is an example of a closure!
// Right here "this" means the CanvasState,
// but we are making events on the Canvas itself,
// and when the events are fired on the canvas,
// the variable "this" is going to mean the canvas!
// Because we still want to use this particular CanvasState
// in the events, we have to save a reference to it.
var myState = this;

//fixes a problem where double-clicking causes text selection on the page
canvas.addEventListener('selectstart',
  function(e) { e.preventDefault(); return false; }, false);

// For dragging we need:
// mousedown/touchstart, mousemove/touchmove, and mouseup/touchend
canvas.addEventListener('mousedown', function(e) {
  myState.doDown(e);
}, true);
canvas.addEventListener('mousemove', function(e) {
  myState.doMove(e);
}, true);
canvas.addEventListener('mouseup', function(e) {
  myState.doUp(e);
}, true);

canvas.addEventListener('touchstart', function(e) {
  if (e.targetTouches.length > 0) myState.doDown(e.targetTouches[0]);
  e.preventDefault();
}, true);
canvas.addEventListener('touchmove', function(e) {
  if (e.targetTouches.length > 0) myState.doMove(e.targetTouches[0]);
  e.preventDefault();
}, true);
canvas.addEventListener('touchend', function(e) {
  if (e.targetTouches.length > 0) myState.doUp(e.targetTouches[0]);
```

```
    e.preventDefault();
}, true);

// double-click to make new shapes
canvas.addEventListener('dblclick', function(e) {
    var mouse = myState.getPos(e);
    // Add a green 20x20 shape, centered over the mouse position:
    myState.addShape(
        new Shape(mouse.x - 10, mouse.y - 10, 20, 20, 'rgba(0,255,0,.6)'));
}, true);
```

As you can see, both `mousedown` and `touchstart` call the `doDown` method, which begins by calling the (yet-discussed) `CanvasState` method `getPos` to return the position of the mouse or touch. The method then iterates through the array `this.shapes` on `CanvasState` to see if any of them contain the mouse position, calling the `contains` method of each `Shape`. We search through the list backward because they are drawn forward, and we want to select the one that appears topmost, so we must find the potential shape that was drawn last.

If we find a shape, we select it: We save the offset between the input coordinates and the shape's top-left corner, save a reference to that shape as the `this.selection` of our `CanvasState`, set `this.dragging` to true, and set the `this.valid` flag to `false` because we want to redraw with a selection border denoting the newly selected object. Already we've used most of our state variables!

Finally, if we don't find any objects, we need to see if there was a selection saved from earlier. Because we clicked on nothing, we obviously didn't click on the already selected object, so we want to deselect and update the `this.selection` reference, setting it to `null`. Clearing the selection means we have to clear the canvas and redraw everything without the selection ring, so we set the `this.valid` flag to `false`.

The `doMove` and `doUp` methods are much simpler. The `doMove` method checks to see if we are dragging, and if we are, it updates the `Shape` referred to by `this.selection` of the `CanvasState`. The `doUp` method simply ends dragging. Listing 6.8 has the code for all three input methods.

LISTING 6.8   doDown, doMove, and doUp

```
CanvasState.prototype.doDown = function(e) {
    var pos = this.getPos(e);
    var mx = pos.x;
    var my = pos.y;
    var shapes = this.shapes;
    var l = shapes.length;
    for (var i = l-1; i >= 0; i--) {
        if (shapes[i].contains(mx, my)) {
            var mySel = shapes[i];
```

```
      // Keep track of where in the object we clicked
      // so we can move it smoothly (see doMove)
      this.dragoffx = mx - mySel.x;
      this.dragoffy = my - mySel.y;
      this.dragging = true;
      this.selection = mySel;
      this.valid = false;
      return;
    }
  }
  // If we haven't returned it means we have failed to select anything.
  // If there was an object selected, we deselect it
  if (this.selection) {
    this.selection = null;
    this.valid = false; // Need to clear the old selection border
  }
}

CanvasState.prototype.doMove = function(e) {
  if (this.dragging){
    var mouse = this.getPos(e);
    // We don't want to drag the object by its top-left corner,
    // we want to drag it from where we clicked, so we use the offset
    this.selection.x = mouse.x - this.dragoffx;
    this.selection.y = mouse.y - this.dragoffy;
    this.valid = false; // Something's dragging so we must redraw
  }
}

CanvasState.prototype.doUp = function(e) {
  this.dragging = false;
}
```

Getting Input Coordinates

Our code for getPos, the method that calculates and returns the position of our input coordinates, is very similar to code from the first section of this chapter, and is explained in detail there.

This method takes the JavaScript event from either a mouse or touch and returns a JavaScript object with x and y attributes defined. Listing 6.9 has the complete code for the getPos method.

LISTING 6.9   Getting the Input Coordinates with `getPos`

```
// Creates a JavaScript object with x and y defined,
// set to the mouse (or any input) position relative to the state's canvas
CanvasState.prototype.getPos = function(e) {
  var element = this.canvas, offsetX = 0, offsetY = 0, mx, my;

  // Compute the total offset
  if (element.offsetParent !== undefined) {
    do {
      offsetX += element.offsetLeft;
      offsetY += element.offsetTop;
    } while ((element = element.offsetParent));
  }

  // Add padding and border style widths to offset
  // Also add the <html> offsets in case there's a position:fixed bar
  offsetX += this.stylePaddingLeft + this.styleBorderLeft + this.htmlLeft;
  offsetY += this.stylePaddingTop + this.styleBorderTop + this.htmlTop;

  mx = e.pageX - offsetX;
  my = e.pageY - offsetY;

  // We return a javascript object with x and y defined
  return {x: mx, y: my};
}
```

Drawing

The last line of our `CanvasState` constructor initializes our draw loop with a call to `setInterval`:

```
setInterval(function() { myState.draw(); }, 30);
```

Now we're set up to draw every 30 milliseconds, which allows us to continuously update the canvas so it appears like the shapes we drag are smoothly moving around. *As stated previously, `setInterval` is only used for its conciseness in the example's source code, and real canvas animation should always attempt to use `requestAnimationFrame` if it exists.* See the previous section in this chapter ("Canvas Animation") for details.

We need to clear the canvas before each redraw—otherwise, we would be drawing over our already drawn shapes, and dragging would look very odd. Because redrawing in a complex application can get expensive, we only draw when we're certain something has changed, which is why `CanvasState` has the `valid` flag mentioned earlier.

After the scene is redrawn, the `draw` method *validates* (sets the `valid` flag to `true`). Then, once we do something like add a new `Shape` or try to drag a `Shape`, the state gets *invalidated* (sets the `valid` flag to `false`) and the `draw` method clears, redraws all objects, and finally validates again. Listing 6.10 contains the code for the `CanvasState draw` method.

LISTING 6.10   Drawing the Shapes

```
// While draw is called as often as the INTERVAL variable demands,
// It only ever does something if the canvas gets invalidated by our code
CanvasState.prototype.draw = function() {
  // if our state is invalid, redraw and validate!
  if (!this.valid) {
    var ctx = this.ctx;
    var shapes = this.shapes;
    this.clear();

    // ** Add stuff you want drawn in the background all the time here **

    // draw all shapes
    var l = shapes.length;
    for (var i = 0; i < l; i++) {
      var shape = shapes[i];
      // We can skip the drawing of elements that have moved off the screen:
      if (shape.x > this.width || shape.y > this.height ||
          shape.x + shape.w < 0 || shape.y + shape.h < 0) continue;
      shapes[i].draw(ctx);
    }

    // draw selection ring
    // right now this is just a stroke along the edge of the selected Shape
    if (this.selection != null) {
      ctx.strokeStyle = this.selectionColor;
      ctx.lineWidth = this.selectionWidth;
      var mySel = this.selection;
      ctx.strokeRect(mySel.x,mySel.y,mySel.w,mySel.h);
    }

    // ** You would add content you want drawn on top all the time here **

    this.valid = true;
  }
}
```

Complete Canvas Interactivity Example

All our infrastructure is complete. From here, we simply need to construct an HTML page of the code covered. Listing 6.11 contains the complete code for the interactivity example.

LISTING 6.11   `shapes.html`—Canvas Interactivity Example

```
<canvas id="myCanvas" width="400" height="300" style="border:1px solid black;">
  Your browser does not support HTML5 Canvas!
</canvas>

<script type="text/javascript">

// Constructor for Shape, an object to hold all data for drawn rectangles
function Shape(x, y, w, h, fill) {
  // All we're doing is checking if the values exist.
  // "x || 0" is a simple way of saying:
  // "if there is a value for x, use that. Otherwise (it's undefined), use 0."
  this.x = x || 0;
  this.y = y || 0;
  this.w = w || 10;
  this.h = h || 10;
  this.fill = fill || '#AAAAAA';
}

// Draws this shape to a given context
Shape.prototype.draw = function(ctx) {
  ctx.fillStyle = this.fill;
  ctx.fillRect(this.x, this.y, this.w, this.h);
}

// Determine if a point is inside the shape's bounds
Shape.prototype.contains = function(mx, my) {
  // All we have to do is make sure the Mouse X,Y fall in the area between
  // the shape's X and (X + Height) and its Y and (Y + Height)
  return  (this.x <= mx) && (this.x + this.w >= mx) &&
          (this.y <= my) && (this.y + this.h >= my);
}

function CanvasState(canvas) {
  // **** First some setup! ****

  this.canvas = canvas;
  this.width = canvas.width;
  this.height = canvas.height;
```

```
this.ctx = canvas.getContext('2d');
// This complicates things a little but but fixes mouse coordinate problems
// when there's a border or padding. See getPos for more detail
this.stylePaddingLeft = 0;
this.stylePaddingTop  = 0;
this.styleBorderLeft  = 0;
this.styleBorderTop   = 0;
if (window.getComputedStyle) {
  this.stylePaddingLeft = parseInt(
    getComputedStyle(canvas, null).getPropertyValue('padding-left'));
  this.stylePaddingTop  = parseInt(
    getComputedStyle(canvas, null).getPropertyValue('padding-top'));
  this.styleBorderLeft  = parseInt(
    getComputedStyle(canvas, null).getPropertyValue('border-left-width'));
  this.styleBorderTop   = parseInt(
    getComputedStyle(canvas, null).getPropertyValue('border-top-width'));
}
// Some pages have fixed-position bars at the top or left of the page.
// (i.e., the stumbleupon.com bar)
// They will break mouse coordinates unless we also account for this offset:
var html = document.body.parentNode;
this.htmlTop = html.offsetTop;
this.htmlLeft = html.offsetLeft;

// **** Keep track of state! ****

this.valid = false; // when set to false, the canvas will redraw everything
this.shapes = [];    // the collection of shapes to be drawn
this.dragging = false; // Keep track of when we are dragging

// the current selected object.
// In the future we could turn this into an array for multiple selection
this.selection = null;
// Keep track of where in the object we clicked
// See doDown and doMove for explanation
this.dragoffx = 0;
this.dragoffy = 0;

// **** Then events! ****

// The following myState var is an example of a closure!
// Right here "this" means the CanvasState,
// but we are making events on the Canvas itself,
// and when the events are fired on the canvas,
// the variable "this" is going to mean the canvas!
// Because we still want to use this particular CanvasState
```

```
// in the events, we have to save a reference to it.
var myState = this;

//fixes a problem where double-clicking causes text selection on the page
canvas.addEventListener('selectstart',
  function(e) { e.preventDefault(); return false; }, false);

// For dragging we need:
// mousedown/touchstart, mousemove/touchmove, and mouseup/touchend
canvas.addEventListener('mousedown', function(e) {
  myState.doDown(e);
}, true);
canvas.addEventListener('mousemove', function(e) {
  myState.doMove(e);
}, true);
canvas.addEventListener('mouseup', function(e) {
  myState.doUp(e);
}, true);

canvas.addEventListener('touchstart', function(e) {
  if (e.targetTouches.length > 0) myState.doDown(e.targetTouches[0]);
  e.preventDefault();
}, true);
canvas.addEventListener('touchmove', function(e) {
  if (e.targetTouches.length > 0) myState.doMove(e.targetTouches[0]);
  e.preventDefault();
}, true);
canvas.addEventListener('touchend', function(e) {
  if (e.targetTouches.length > 0) myState.doUp(e.targetTouches[0]);
  e.preventDefault();
}, true);

// double-click to make new shapes
canvas.addEventListener('dblclick', function(e) {
  var mouse = myState.getPos(e);
  // Add a green 20x20 shape, centered over the mouse position:
  myState.addShape(
    new Shape(mouse.x - 10, mouse.y - 10, 20, 20, 'rgba(0,255,0,.6)'));
}, true);

// **** Options! ****

this.selectionColor = '#CC0000';
this.selectionWidth = 2;
setInterval(function() { myState.draw(); }, 30);
}
```

```javascript
CanvasState.prototype.doDown = function(e) {
  var pos = this.getPos(e);
  var mx = pos.x;
  var my = pos.y;
  var shapes = this.shapes;
  var l = shapes.length;
  for (var i = l-1; i >= 0; i--) {
    if (shapes[i].contains(mx, my)) {
      var mySel = shapes[i];
      // Keep track of where in the object we clicked
      // so we can move it smoothly (see doMove)
      this.dragoffx = mx - mySel.x;
      this.dragoffy = my - mySel.y;
      this.dragging = true;
      this.selection = mySel;
      this.valid = false;
      return;
    }
  }
  // haven't returned it means we have failed to select anything.
  // If there was an object selected, we deselect it
  if (this.selection) {
    this.selection = null;
    this.valid = false; // Need to clear the old selection border
  }
}

CanvasState.prototype.doMove = function(e) {
  if (this.dragging){
    var mouse = this.getPos(e);
    // We don't want to drag the object by its top-left corner,
    // we want to drag it from where we clicked, so we use the offset
    this.selection.x = mouse.x - this.dragoffx;
    this.selection.y = mouse.y - this.dragoffy;
    this.valid = false; // Something's dragging so we must redraw
  }
}

CanvasState.prototype.doUp = function(e) {
  this.dragging = false;
}

CanvasState.prototype.addShape = function(shape) {
  this.shapes.push(shape);
  this.valid = false;
}
```

```javascript
CanvasState.prototype.clear = function() {
  this.ctx.clearRect(0, 0, this.width, this.height);
}

// While draw is called as often as the INTERVAL variable demands,
// It only ever does something if the canvas gets invalidated by our code
CanvasState.prototype.draw = function() {
  // if our state is invalid, redraw and validate!
  if (!this.valid) {
    var ctx = this.ctx;
    var shapes = this.shapes;
    this.clear();

    // ** Add stuff you want drawn in the background all the time here **

    // draw all shapes
    var l = shapes.length;
    for (var i = 0; i < l; i++) {
      var shape = shapes[i];
      // We can skip the drawing of elements that have moved off the screen:
      if (shape.x > this.width || shape.y > this.height ||
          shape.x + shape.w < 0 || shape.y + shape.h < 0) continue;
      shapes[i].draw(ctx);
    }

    // draw selection ring
    // right now this is just a stroke along the edge of the selected Shape
    if (this.selection != null) {
      ctx.strokeStyle = this.selectionColor;
      ctx.lineWidth = this.selectionWidth;
      var mySel = this.selection;
      ctx.strokeRect(mySel.x,mySel.y,mySel.w,mySel.h);
    }

    // ** You would add content you want drawn on top all the time here **

    this.valid = true;
  }
}

// Creates a JavaScript object with x and y defined,
// set to the mouse (or any input) position relative to the state's canvas
CanvasState.prototype.getPos = function(e) {
  var element = this.canvas, offsetX = 0, offsetY = 0, mx, my;
```

```
  // Compute the total offset
  if (element.offsetParent !== undefined) {
    do {
      offsetX += element.offsetLeft;
      offsetY += element.offsetTop;
    } while ((element = element.offsetParent));
  }

  // Add padding and border style widths to offset
  // Also add the <html> offsets in case there's a position:fixed bar
  offsetX += this.stylePaddingLeft + this.styleBorderLeft + this.htmlLeft;
  offsetY += this.stylePaddingTop + this.styleBorderTop + this.htmlTop;

  mx = e.pageX - offsetX;
  my = e.pageY - offsetY;

  // We return a JavaScript object with x and y defined
  return {x: mx, y: my};
}

// Sample initialization:
function init() {
  var mycan = document.getElementById('myCanvas');
  var state = new CanvasState(mycan);
  state.addShape(new Shape(40,40,60,60)); // The default is gray
  state.addShape(new Shape(60,140,40,60, '594F4F'));
  // Let's make some partially transparent
  state.addShape(new Shape(80,180,80,50,  'rgba(84, 121, 128, .5)'));
  state.addShape(new Shape(125,80,40,120, 'rgba(69, 173, 168, .7)'));
  state.addShape(new Shape(225,80,90,80,  'rgba(157, 224, 173, .9)'));
  state.addShape(new Shape(205,120,90,80, 'rgba(229, 252, 194, .9)'));
}

init();
</script>
```

Figure 6.4 shows the final code, with one element selected.

Now that we have the basic structure of an interactive example, we can easily imagine extending it to handle other kinds of objects, though different objects may need their own state and special cases. Using images, for instance, would need extra code to invalidate the content as soon as they finish loading. Using polygon paths would need a more complicated contains (hit testing) method and additional state to keep track of segments.

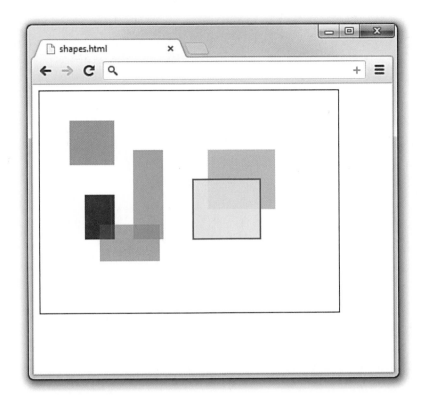

FIGURE 6.4   The finished example, as produced by the final code.

Canvas is clearly capable as a platform for user interaction, but the low level of canvas means that the implementation of interactivity and state is our responsibility. With so many details to manage, writing clean and efficient canvas code is imperative. The next chapter covers canvas performance in detail.

Summary

In this chapter, we covered the basics of handling canvas inputs and animation with some practical and reusable code.

We covered two reasonable methods of getting input (mouse and touch) coordinates in the canvas, and explored a new method (`requestAnimationFrame`) that attempts to create a smarter animation environment in the browser. Finally, we examined a very simple example of cleanly keeping the state of drawn objects and updating that state along with a canvas to reflect the changes.

The examples in this chapter merely scratch the surface of canvas functionality, but should nonetheless serve as a good starting point for creating your own interactive and animated canvas applications.

CHAPTER 7

Canvas Performance, Tips, and Peculiarities

Many would-be canvas programmers come from backgrounds such as Flash, Silverlight, and other graphical development environments. Fortunately, they need not learn all of HTML and JavaScript to create effective canvas apps. In fact, you can get away with near zero HTML knowledge and still create superb canvas tools, visualizations, and games.

But as with any new drawing system that rests on a potentially new (to the developer) platform, canvas has its own list of cautions and caveats. The first section of this chapter deals with very common issues that arise among newcomers to canvas, mostly platform related, that might put programmers in a bind regardless of prior graphical experience. Few of these issues are serious, but most are irksome, and if you are new to canvas you should be able to save yourself some time and trouble by reading it.

The second section of this chapter concerns itself with canvas performance, both general and specific. We are fortunate to live in an age where JavaScript is fast, and although the HTML canvas element is fast too, the onus is on the programmer to keep it that way. Performance is crucial for rich apps such as games and apps targeting lower-powered mobile devices.

The second section is important for all canvas developers, but especially so for those who have never been in the mind-set of creating efficient graphical apps. Programmers are trained to be thorough and efficient, but graphical performance often means making technical trade-offs, and getting away with rendering and checking as little as possible.

The two sections in this chapter are written to stand alone, so if you read this chapter from beginning to end, you'll find there's a bit of overlap. Additionally, both sections expect a rudimentary familiarity with the canvas application programming interface (API), and additional information and examples can be found on many of the topics in Chapter 5, "2D Canvas."

Canvas Peculiarities and Tips

This section acts as an introductory guide, addressing a lot of common problems that new-to-canvas programmers stumble upon. Many of these are mentioned throughout the initial canvas chapter (Chapter 5), deep in their respective topics, so if you have read the canvas part so far like a novel, then you should be in good shape. In case you didn't give a complete read of the previous sections, or if you just want a refresher before you head off to make great canvas apps, here are the principal peculiarities for you to heed.

> **NOTE**
>
> All of these are visited in more detail in the initial canvas chapter (Chapter 5), in their respective sections.

CSS Width and Height

One of the most common mistakes that people make when starting with canvas is setting the width and height of the element using Cascading Style Sheets (CSS). Canvas is unusual among HTML elements in that its width and height are set by using `width` and `height` attributes on the HTML tag itself, and not with CSS rules.

This makes a canvas that is 100 pixels wide and 100 pixels tall:

```
<canvas id="myCanvas" width="100" height="100"></canvas>
```

This, however, makes a canvas that is the default size (300 pixels wide and 150 pixels tall), but is then transformed (scaled) by CSS to be 100 by 100 pixels:

```
<canvas id="myCanvas" style="width: 100px; height: 100px;"></canvas>
```

The canvases look identical at first. They occupy the same space on a page, but the difference is apparent as soon as you draw something to them. Figure 7.1 shows a canvas defined with HTML width and height of 100 versus a canvas defined using CSS width and height of 100, with a call to `fillRect(20, 20, 50, 50)` on each.

Paths or Images Look Blurry

There are a few common causes of unwanted blurring on the canvas element. The coordinates that we use to draw objects affect how antialiasing (or not) is done, with differences between paths and images.

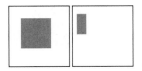

FIGURE 7.1   A 50×50 rectangle will draw correctly as a square on the first canvas, but the scaled nature of the second (CSS-sized) canvas is apparent.

Blurred Paths

As is discussed in the canvas path and coordinates section, path drawing can sometimes appear blurry or thicker than the context `lineWidth` specifies. This is because a line drawn on integer coordinates is drawn on half-pixels, and it is not possible to accurately represent an odd-width line when it is spread across an even number of pixels, so instead the canvas draws a lighter color line along two rows of pixels. Figure 7.2 shows one line drawn on integer coordinates and another with y-values ending in 0.5.

FIGURE 7.2   A line drawn at y = 20 is blurred across two rows of pixels, while a line drawn at y = 30.5 is drawn neatly across only one row.

Using an odd `lineWidth`, such as 1, the first line appears blurred and the second one looks pixel-perfect. Using an even `lineWidth` makes the opposite true: Drawing along integer coordinates produces a pixel-perfect line.

How you choose to remedy this drawing problem (if you see it as one) is highly dependent on your application. If you are using odd stroke widths with nothing but right-angle paths in integer coordinates, one easy solution is to translate the canvas by (0.5, 0.5) from the start.

Blurred Images

Blurred images suffer from the opposite problem. Instead of drawing on half-pixels, images look the sharpest if they are always drawn on integer coordinates.

Drawing images on noninteger coordinates causes the browser to smooth the image pixels, meaning that images might appear blurred. This is fine for some applications, but can be irksome when working with detailed pixel sprites or animation. When a sprite is slowly animated along a line, you can visibly see it "pop" in and out of blurring because of the coordinates occasionally becoming integers as they increase.

Scaled images suffer from a similar blurring, as the resizing algorithm attempts to do a smooth interpolation, which might not be what you want.

To fix the first issue, you can simply avoid drawing on noninteger coordinates. This can be done by applying `Math.round`, `Math.floor`, or the bitwise OR operator such as `(x | 0)` to floor x or `((x + 0.5) | 0)` to round x. Bitwise operators are often faster than calls to `Math.round` or `Math.floor`, but do not work with numbers larger than 2,147,483,647 (the largest 32-bit signed integer).

A second fix to blurring, more pertinent to image scaling, exists as an emerging canvas context property. Toggleable image smoothing has recently been added to the specification as the property `imageSmoothingEnabled`. Unfortunately, this is not widely implemented as of this writing, additionally Firefox and Webkit (Chrome and Safari) have prefixed their implementations (for now) to be `mozImageSmoothingEnabled` and `webkitImageSmoothingEnabled`, respectively.

Setting this property to `false` causes the canvas to draw images with a nearest-neighbor algorithm instead of a smoother interpolation algorithm. Instead of trying to smoothly scale an image, the nearest-neighbor algorithm simply makes pixels appear larger, which often gives a more accurate representation of scaled sprites and pixel art. Unfortunately, at the time of writing, Internet Explorer and Opera have not implemented this property, vendor prefixed or otherwise.

> **NOTE**
>
> If you can't wait for all browsers to implement the `imageSmoothingEnabled` property, you can implement your own nearest-neighbor interpolation algorithm in canvas. Note, however, that a custom implementation needs to use image data, which is very slow, so animated applications are out of luck, but it can be used well for image scaling (and the result cached). We provide a sample implementation of nearest-neighbor interpolation in Chapter 5 (Listing 5.19).

The Methods `save` and `restore`

One of the common occurrences you will encounter when reading or reviewing canvas code in the wild is the habitual overuse of the context methods `save` and `restore`. Many programmers wrap every discrete block of context commands with these two methods and it often serves no purpose. What's worse, because the entire context state is saved and restored, using them unnecessarily can be detrimental to performance. Even many otherwise well-written tutorials abuse these methods.

The presence of needless `save` and `restore` calls may additionally prevent you from being able to cache properties that are time consuming to set. The setting of the context's `font` property, as you see in the "A Performance Primer" section later in this chapter, can take a nontrivial amount of time to set and being able to cache it can lead to performance gains. Unnecessary `save` and `restore` calls, however, make it much harder to cache because a font set after a call to `save` will be reset once `restore` is called. If the next canvas figure needs to use the same font, then we have to set the `font` property all over again.

You should give serious consideration when using `save` and `restore`. You do not need to wrap blocks of commands in the two calls without good reason, and when most programmers are thinking that they need to reset "everything" at the start of a draw, they usually only need to reset one thing, the transformation matrix, which can be reset by calling `ctx.setTransform(1, 0, 0, 1, 0, 0)` instead.

When Are Save and Restore Useful?

The common case is the construction of compound figures, where the state of each object is kept in a treelike structure, for instance a canvas app where custom "panels" can house other objects, including additional panels.

These nested objects may all have their own locations relative to their parents, or other more complex transformations (such as rotations) applied. In such a situation, the panel would need to transform the context to draw itself at the right location. Then, a panel's children may need to additionally transform the context to draw themselves and then transform the context *back* so that subsequent children of the panel may use the panel's transform as a starting point. Such recursive drawing structures may necessitate the use of `save` and `restore`, but even then there are performance optimizations to be had, as you see in the next section.

Another common case is to reset the clipping region, which (as of this writing) can only be reset either by using `save` and `restore` or by clearing the entire context state. This in itself is a peculiarity.

> **NOTE**
>
> It could be argued that `save` and `restore` have no place at all in performance-minded canvas apps, except for when needed to reset a clipping region. The `save` and `restore` methods (and the alternatives) are covered more in the performance section of this chapter.

Clipping Regions Can Only Get Smaller and Cannot Be Reset

This is one canvas oddity that isn't obvious at first. Out of all of the canvas context state, the clipping region is the only property that cannot be reset to default on its own.

The clipping region is implemented in such a way that it can only get smaller and never larger. To be precise, the `clip` method creates a new clipping region by calculating the intersection of the current clipping region and the area described by the current path on the context. The default clipping region is the entire canvas.

In other words, you cannot define a clipping region of `rect(50,50,50,50)` and then define a larger one of `rect(0,0,200,200)`. The clipping region will still be the rectangle defined by `(50,50,50,50)`.

The rule itself, that clipping regions can only get smaller, is fine. But this means that you cannot use a clipping region and then reset it back to the default state on its own. Instead, you have two options: Resetting *all* canvas context state, for instance by setting the width of the canvas equal to itself or by using the context's `save` and `restore` methods to restore the clipping region.

In sufficiently complex canvas applications, resetting the clipping region is typically desirable via `save` and `restore` instead of clobbering all state, to allow more caching of the context state (such as the context's `font` property).

There is a brand-new method in the canvas specification, `resetClip`, that allows the programmer to reset the clipping region without modifying any other state, but as of this writing, it is not implemented in any browser.

Security Exceptions, Cross-domain Images, and Image Data

Another frustration to canvas newcomers involves attempting to use the image data of a canvas that has been tainted with cross-origin data. Several actions on a canvas stop further usage of the canvas's `toDataURL` method and the context's `getImageData` method. These actions are said to set the `origin-clean` flag of the canvas to `false`.

Most of these actions depend on drawing an image to a canvas from a different (sub-) domain, or origin, than the canvas itself is located.

So if you have a canvas located at http://example.com/page.html, you can draw images located elsewhere on example.com as long as the subdomain and protocols match. This means that any of the following are not considered as the same origin and, therefore, set the `origin-clean` flag to `false`:

- **http://example.com:8080/image.png**—Because it is a different port
- **https://example.com/image.png**—Because it is a different protocol (https)
- **https://internal.example.com/image.png**—Because it is a different subdomain
- **http://wikipedia.org/image.png**—Because it is a different site altogether
- **file:///C:/SomeFolder/someResource.png**—Because it is a resource private to you

It is possible to use images from other (sub-) domains and protocols if the server is configured to be more permissive by enabling Cross-Origin Resource Sharing (CORS), a specification made to allow better access to content that is explicitly meant to be more public.

> **NOTE**
>
> See the "Image Security on the Canvas" section in Chapter 5 for more details about your options when dealing with cross-domain images.

Transformations Affect Drawing in Addition to Paths

When modifying the canvas's transformation matrix, we must not only be careful of how we modify it, but when. If we have a path that we want to skew, we need to do three things: path construction, transforming and untransforming, and drawing. The order of these three operations changes the drawn effect.

If we want to scale the entire figure, we need to apply the transformation, execute our path commands, and then draw. Presumably after drawing we would undo the transformation, by using `restore` or otherwise.

If we want to scale the path but not skew the stroke of the path, we need to apply the transformation, execute the path commands, and then restore the transformation. Then, when we stroke, the context's path will still be skewed but the stroke will draw along the path uniformly.

> **NOTE**
>
> An example of this is given in Chapter 5 in the "Saving and Restoring Affect How Drawing Functions Act on a Transformed Canvas" section (page 143).

A Performance Primer

Performance on the Web is important, and graphical performance is more important than ever before. There's a set of expectations carried over from Flash's performance, as well as the general expectations that games should be fast and animation should be smooth, so canvas better be up for the job.

Canvas is in a fairly unique position, especially among game platforms, where it is expected to run smoothly not only on newer high-end machines but also on less-powerful devices, including netbooks, tablets, and smartphones. Since the early days of HTML5, there have been many allegations that canvas is too slow.

Canvas performance on most browsers has improved greatly in just a few years, especially with the introduction of hardware-accelerated canvases by default on all major modern desktop browsers. There is no doubt that canvas outshines the other cross-platform options when performance is crucial because Scalable Vector Graphics (SVG) and other DOM-related solutions introduce far more overhead. With canvas, just how much overhead exists is up to your code and the libraries you choose to use, so performance has the potential to be very good, but it's up to us to keep it that way.

Different drawing operations on the canvas are faster or slower than others, and different methods of accomplishing the same task can take wildly different times. With graphical rendering and the associated app or game logic, it's not about what you need; it's about what you can get away with.

If you're new to programming graphics and animation, you'll find that you become a sort of magician. People want to see Rome, but you shouldn't be building Rome; you should be building Hollywood sets. The more corners you can cut, the smoother you can display the rest of the perceived world.

Some of the canvas tips in this section may become obsolete as improvements are made to various canvas implementations, or as portions of the canvas specification are updated.

Tools of the Trade

If you want to be serious about canvas performance, you need to be familiar with the developer tools that come with browsers. Specifically, you ought to be well versed in the performance profilers available with browsers, so that you may use them to discover and modify problematic code.

JavaScript profilers are browser features or add-ons that allow you to run a section of code and get feedback on what methods or properties are particularly time consuming or not. They can be used to help identify unnecessary or extraneous code that needs to be refactored, or to benchmark two or more ways of accomplishing the same task, or to determine if a suspected effect or code block is the reason for an app's poor performance.

Not all browsers have easily accessible performance profilers, especially browsers on mobile platforms, so in addition to these tools developers ought to be familiar with benchmarking within JavaScript itself. This is sometimes done by hand using the JavaScript `Date` object, but using a library saves a lot of time in the long run and can return more accurate results. There are several benchmarking libraries, the most popular of which is `Benchmark.js`, so we discuss a small performance example using it and its sister site, `jsPerf.com`. Afterward, we discuss browser profilers more in depth.

Benchmark.js

`Benchmark.js` (http://benchmarkjs.com) is an open source cross-platform JavaScript benchmarking library that makes constructing timed tests a little easier for the programmer. There's no fussing with `Date` objects and it has a few options for including higher-resolution timers by using a Java applet to expose a nanosecond timer, and by using Google Chrome's built-in microsecond timer.

The `Benchmark.js` library is used most notably on `jsPerf.com`, a site where anyone can create public JavaScript benchmarks to test and share. We see a little usage of that in a moment, but first let's see a simple example of `Benchmark.js` on its own.

Suppose we are making a canvas app, and we have a hunch that drawing lots of text is slowing down our app. Suppose further that we are in the convenient position where many or all of our calls to `fillText` *could* be replaced with calls to `drawImage`, using images of premade text, with no visible difference to the user. Having this luxury would typically be possible if we had a finite number of text strings to draw, and ideally if those strings didn't move or animate, as the antialiasing rules for text and images are different for each browser.

We want to quickly test our hypothesis that drawing images might be faster than drawing text and using `Benchmark.js` makes that possible in just a few lines of code. For the sake of constructing the test even quicker, we don't use any of the code from our (fictional) app, we just grab a small image off the Web and substitute text with a sample string. Once we see the results, we can decide if there's further investigation to be had. After all, what if `fillText` is extremely fast compared with `drawImage`? If that were the case, making a very detailed test would be a waste of our time!

Listing 7.1 contains the HTML page needed to run our sample. It links to the `benchmark.js` library file, so you'd need to download it (benchmarkjs.com) if you are to run the code yourself.

LISTING 7.1   `ImageVsText.html`—Comparing `drawImage` with `fillText`

```
<!DOCTYPE html>
<canvas id="myCanvas" width="500" height="500"></canvas>

<script src="benchmark.js"></script>

<script>
var can = document.getElementById('myCanvas');
var ctx = can.getContext('2d');
ctx.font = '72px Verdana';

var img = new Image();

img.onload = function() {
  var suite = new Benchmark.Suite;
  // add tests, chaining commands as we go
  suite.add('Draw Image', function() {
    ctx.drawImage(img, 0, 0);
  })
  .add('Fill Text', function() {
    ctx.fillText('lala', 100, 100);
  })
  // add listeners to see results
  .on('cycle', function(event) {
    console.log(String(event.target));
  })
  // announce a winner
  .on('complete', function() {
    console.log('Fastest is ' + this.filter('fastest').pluck('name'));
  })
  // run the benchmark
  .run();
}

// At the time of this writing this website serves up
// an image of a kitten in the desired /width/height
// This image may not load, and you may need to
// replace it with a 100x100 image of your own
img.src = 'http://placekitten.com/100/100';
</script>
```

We have to make sure that the image is loaded before we start the test. Otherwise, the test might not be accurate because if the image isn't fully loaded, then many or all of the drawImage calls might happen instantly because the canvas is supposed to do nothing when drawImage is called with a not-fully-loaded image.

If we save the listing and open it in a browser, we can observe the results in a JavaScript console. The console output will look like this:

```
Draw Image x 406,280 ops/sec ±66.46% (61 runs sampled)
Fill Text x 67,259 ops/sec ±160.21% (38 runs sampled)
Fastest is Draw Image
```

Drawing images is clearly faster!

Right?

Well, maybe, but maybe not. Being the careful scientists that we are, we can't honestly conclude that drawing images is always faster than drawing text from such a simple example. It might *only* be true for this size of text and image, or perhaps only for the particular browser we used to test. It may additionally be the case that drawImage is only faster on hardware-accelerated machines or high-end machines.

It's important to stress that the amount we can conclude from a single test is often very little, and we should always do performance testing in every browser we expect to target (both desktop and mobile), and preferably on both fast and slow machines.

We should also take simple tests not as the law of the land but as a reason to investigate further. This test has shown that drawImage is seemingly quite fast, and now we should construct a test that emulates the real conditions that our app uses to draw.

Now that we understand Benchmark.js, let's have a look at jsPerf.com, the site that uses the same library.

jsPerf.com

Using the Benchmark.js library may sometimes be preferable, especially if you decide to read the API and use some of the finer points of the library. For simple tests, however, it is often easier to use the website that is run by the Benchmark.js developers, called jsPerf.com.

Using jsPerf.com is fairly straightforward, and to make a similar test to the previous example, we can reuse almost all of the code. The preparation code might look like this:

```
<canvas id="canvas1" width="500" height="500"></canvas>

<script>
var can = document.getElementById('canvas1');
var ctx = can.getContext('2d');
var img = new Image();
// At the time of this writing this website serves up
// an image of a kitten in the desired /width/height
```

```
img.src = "http://placekitten.com/100/100";
ctx.font = '72pt Verdana';
img.onload = function() {
  // draw the image so we know it's done loading
  // don't start the test until the image loads!
  ctx.drawImage(img, 0, 0);
}
</script>
```

And the two test cases would be the same one-line tests that were used in Listing 7.1, `ctx.drawImage(img, 0, 0);` and `ctx.fillText('lala', 100, 100);`. Once the test is created, we can share the jsPerf link, and the jsPerf test at http://jsperf.com/images-versus-text contains the code from this section.

The jsPerf website has several advantages over using the `Benchmark.js` library alone. The results are stored and tabulated on their website, with graphical representations should you want them. Every test is given a uniform resource locator (URL), so that you can share tests easily with other people and load the test quickly on several devices. It's much faster, after all, to simply whip up a jsPerf test page and enter the URL on the tablets and smartphones that you need to test.

Running our newly created jsPerf test on multiple devices produces the results shown in Figure 7.3.

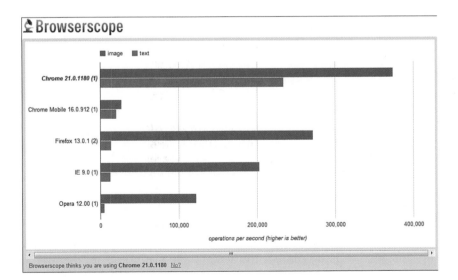

FIGURE 7.3   A screenshot of the test results from jsperf.com.

The aggregate results are more telling than our single test. Depending on the browser, `drawImage` ranges from twice as fast to 20 times as fast as `fillText`! It looks fairly close on

Chrome Mobile, though, which may suggest that they are much more equal on devices that do not have much (if any) power or hardware acceleration.

If you run a jsPerf page on the same machine across many browsers, you can also use the data to prove that one browser is faster than another with respect to a particular method. Be careful not to take the results as a universal truth, though. Chrome and Firefox have been iterating their development very rapidly lately, and the results from these browsers can change wildly from month to month, or even from week to week if you're using the beta or nightly versions.

Browser Performance Profilers

Although `Benchmark.js` and jsPerf make the creation of accurate tests very easy, they do take additional setup time. With the browser-based JavaScript profilers, there's no need for special code or any setup phase. All you need to do is start the profiler, let your application execute some code, then stop and take a look at the results.

The profilers for most browsers can be found in the developer tools, which differ among browsers but are all typically accessed by pressing F12 or Ctrl+Shift+I. Because each profiler functions a little differently, we just cover what can and should be done with profilers in general.

Profilers have a few large advantages over constructing your own benchmarks. Without knowing what the source of any slowness might be, they can be run in an attempt to gather enough data to find something actionable. Simply letting the profiler run while your app is in use and looking at the results can be very enlightening.

Perhaps you find that the figures you draw with shadows account for 50% of the time in your entire draw routine, or perhaps the profiler makes it apparent that some function is being called far more often than you thought it was, pointing out a performance-related bug in need of investigation.

Just like with benchmarking libraries, profilers can be used to benchmark multiple ways of accomplishing the same task, and can point out in more fine-grained detail just which piece of a complex function is slow. Several profilers also tally the number of times each function is called and the average duration of each function.

Figure 7.4 shows a typical set of data captured from a performance profiler.

Profilers should typically be used on near-complete applications as a holistic approach to optimization. Their use lets you prioritize your time better than benchmark libraries by pointing out the slowest bits for you, letting you know what may need to be further benchmarked. Profilers can be used *instead* of benchmarking libraries, but benchmarking libraries have the advantage of working consistently across more platforms. Just because a profiler says that one thing is slow in Internet Explorer does not mean that the same operation is slow in Firefox or Opera!

Profilers are also useful when testing the impact of mouse, touch, and page load events, which are harder to benchmark in JavaScript benchmarking libraries. Most profilers also afford you the luxury of being able to start a profiler before the page (and any JavaScript) is loaded.

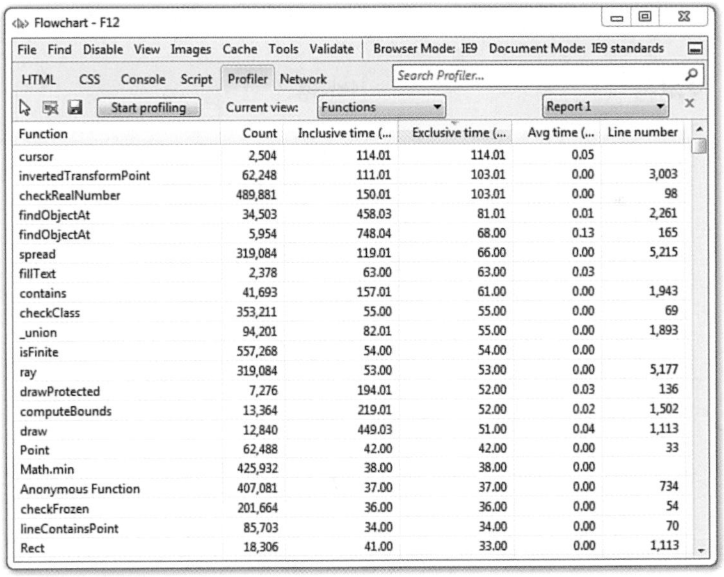

Function	Count	Inclusive time (...	Exclusive time (...	Avg time (...	Line number
cursor	2,504	114.01	114.01	0.05	
invertedTransformPoint	62,248	111.01	103.01	0.00	3,003
checkRealNumber	489,881	150.01	103.01	0.00	98
findObjectAt	34,503	458.03	81.01	0.01	2,261
findObjectAt	5,954	748.04	68.00	0.13	165
spread	319,084	119.01	66.00	0.00	5,215
fillText	2,378	63.00	63.00	0.03	
contains	41,693	157.01	61.00	0.00	1,943
checkClass	353,211	55.00	55.00	0.00	69
_union	94,201	82.01	55.00	0.00	1,893
isFinite	557,268	54.00	54.00	0.00	
ray	319,084	53.00	53.00	0.00	5,177
drawProtected	7,276	194.01	52.00	0.03	136
computeBounds	13,364	219.01	52.00	0.02	1,502
draw	12,840	449.03	51.00	0.04	1,113
Point	62,488	42.00	42.00	0.00	33
Math.min	425,932	38.00	38.00	0.00	
Anonymous Function	407,081	37.00	37.00	0.00	734
checkFrozen	201,664	36.00	36.00	0.00	54
lineContainsPoint	85,703	34.00	34.00	0.00	70
Rect	18,306	41.00	33.00	0.00	1,113

FIGURE 7.4 What a performance profiler report looks like in Internet Explorer 9.

Occasionally, you'll want to start the profiler at a seemingly inconvenient time. For instance, if you wanted to start a profiler during a mouse dragging operation, then it would be impossible to click the Profile button simultaneously. Fortunately, many profilers can be started and stopped programmatically with calls to built-in functions. `console.profile(name)` takes an optional name and begins the profiler, and `console.profileEnd()` stops the profiler and in some browsers prints a report.

Before We Get to Canvas

To keep canvas fast, you need to take care to use good programming practices and always employ the fastest parts of JavaScript. This isn't a book on programming practices or the finer points of JavaScript, but we very quickly cover some common canvas-related principles and parts of the language.

For starters, you should always avoid repeating work. You should define complex objects as little as possible and try not to create unnecessary objects (or allocate memory) inside of loops. You should be careful not to make any unnecessary function calls, such as superfluous calls to the canvas context's `save` and `restore` methods. You should avoid accessing deeply nested prototypes or object attributes often.

Loops

You should avoid `for-in` loops, as JavaScript creates extra overhead for each looped element.

In loops, accessing a single attribute over and over can be a performance penalty. For instance, this is slower:

```
for (var i = 0; i < list.length; i++) {
  // some code
}
```

because the `length` attribute is accessed in every iteration of the loop, even though it never changes. If the length is 99,999, then the property is accessed 99,999 times. With a list of such length, this loop iteration can be 10% to 20% faster by storing the length in its own `var`:

```
var len = list.length;
for (var i = 0; i < len; i++) {
  // some code (that does not modify the list length!)
}
```

In general, frequently accessed attributes should be stored because object literals and variables are typically faster than object properties and array items. If a function calls `canvas.width` and `canvas.height` repeatedly and they do not change value, then they should be declared as local variables and referred to that way:

```
var width = canvas.width,
    height = canvas.height;
```

Scope

Variables in a local scope are faster than variables in a global scope, though several modern JavaScript implementations make efforts to optimize this. Accessing anything outside of the local scope is slower in general, which is why you should avoid the JavaScript `with` statement, as it introduces an additional scope.

Math

Use the bitwise `OR` operator to floor or round numbers:

```
(x | 0); // instead of Math.floor(x)
((x + 0.5) | 0); // instead of Math.round(x)
// Typical usage:
ctx.drawImage(myImg, x | 0, y | 0)
```

The `Math.floor` and `Math.round` function calls require more overhead than bitwise `OR`, which (as used above) simply removes any fractional portion of a number.

Avoid using `Math.sin`, `Math.cos`, and `Math.sqrt` whenever possible. These are all computationally expensive, and numbers involving them that function as constants in your app should be computed only once. The `Math` object also has many constants such as

`Math.SQRT2`, which is the precomputed square root of 2, so that you do not have to compute some common constants each time.

The distance between two points is given by a formula that contains a square root:

```
var x = (x2 - x1) * (x2 - x1);
var y = (y2 - y1) * (y2 - y1);
var dist = Math.sqrt(x + y);
```

Often in canvas apps or games, we do not need to determine precise distance, but instead compare two distances, such as determining which of two objects are closer to something. In such cases, instead of using the distance of the objects, we can just compare the *distances squared*, so that we do not need to call `Math.sqrt`. For example:

```
var x = (x2 - x1) * (x2 - x1);
var y = (y2 - y1) * (y2 - y1);
var distSquared = (x + y); // no square root!
var otherDistSquared = otherDist * otherDist;
if (distSquared > otherDistSquared) {
   // Do something with the knowledge that distSquared is greater
}
```

Other Considerations

After all the code is complete and ready to ship, consider using a JavaScript minifier in production, such as the Google Closure Compiler, as it may further optimize your code, and will certainly reduce the size of your JavaScript files, helping larger apps to load faster.

Whatever performance optimizations you choose to use or not use, you may want to consider creating an in-app options menu that allows the user to disable special effects. Some platforms, especially mobile phones, cannot cope with large amounts of special effects such as large sets of particles and shadows. Giving options to reduce or eliminate these effects has been common practice in video games for a very long time and is worth considering if it means more devices can run your canvas app.

Further Reading

This is by no means a comprehensive list of JavaScript language tips. If you're not already a JavaScript expert, it would be worth searching for and reading a few articles (or picking up a book) on JavaScript performance.

7

The DOM and Canvas

We should take care to "touch" the DOM as little as possible. Almost everything dealing with the DOM is slow compared with the canvas context and running pure JavaScript, so one of the best performance rules is to simply avoid it.

When you change something in the DOM, you can cause a cascade of side effects that need to recalculate layouts, access style sheets to recompute looks, and reposition children, firing up HTML and CSS parsers along the way. Simply changing the `innerHTML` of a DOM object causes the browser to play many hidden games of musical chairs that are best avoided.

Modern browsers have taken great pains to make JavaScript fast and efficient, but using JavaScript to manipulate the DOM crosses a divide that has to consider an enormous set of rules that cannot be optimized in the way that the JavaScript language alone can.

It used to be the case that even setting the width of the canvas to itself was slow because you were updating the size of a DOM element. Thankfully, almost all browsers have since fixed this, and setting the canvas width equal to itself is now generally fast.

Resizing the canvas constantly, however, or using DOM elements atop the canvas that often change their size or location, may negatively impact performance. Depending on the app, positioning some elements atop a canvas can be good and natural, such as when making a heads-up display. But if you're designing with animated DOM elements atop the canvas, it is usually best to move those elements into the canvas drawing code itself.

Avoiding the DOM not only means avoiding the manipulation of DOM elements, but setting properties on the canvas context that need to use the CSS parsing rules (setting colors and fonts) can also add up to a performance penalty. We can remedy some of that with caching.

Caching Context Properties

Often the best way to use a canvas context, too, is to touch it as little as possible!

Because CSS parsing is used to determine the validity for the context's `fillStyle`, `strokeStyle`, and `font` properties, setting them can be rather slow. Further, setting them to the same value over and over should be avoided.

If a `fillStyle` is set to `"blue"`, it might be reasonable to assume that setting it to `"blue"` again would result in a quick statement that does nothing at all, but this is not the case. For one, setting the `fillStyle` to blue does not necessarily mean the value of `fillStyle` will actually remain `"blue"`:

```
ctx.fillStyle = 'blue'
console.log(ctx.fillStyle) // outputs "#0000ff", not "blue"!
```

Similarly, setting a `font` to something complex can result in the same font string being saved in some browsers, but others modify the string:

```
// Technically a valid font string:
ctx.font = "normal normal normal 12pt/normal Georgia"
console.log(ctx.font)
// "12pt Georgia" in Internet Explorer 9 and Firefox
// "normal normal normal 12pt/normal Georgia" in Chrome

ctx.font = "12px/14px Arial, helvetica"
console.log(ctx.font)
// "12px Arial,helvetica" in Internet Explorer 9 and Firefox
// "12px/14px Arial, helvetica" in Chrome
```

Regardless of what the browser does, you should cache the `font` attribute as it is one of the slowest properties to set on the context.

Caching the `font` and color styles can be as easy as checking against the current value, but this is not optimal:

```
// This is how caching should NOT be done
function setFontSlow(newfont) {
  // Only set if it is not equal to the new font
  // using ctx.font to check is slow in itself
  if (ctx.font !== newfont) {
    ctx.font = newfont;
  }
}
```

Instead, you should save the `font` and color styles somewhere else, either in their own object (as shown below) or on the context in a new property that you add to the context, such as `ctx.cachedFont`. We occasionally refer to these saved values as our "cache state."

```
// Our  "cache state"
// Keep track of previously set values:
var myCache = {
  font: '',
  fillStyle: '',
  strokeStyle: ''
}

// The proper way to cache a font
function setFontFast(newfont) {
  // Only set if it is not equal to the new font
  // We use the myCache object to save the previous font
  if (myCache.font !== newfont) {
    ctx.font = newfont;
    myCache.font = newfont; // set the cache
  }
}
```

Effective caching is best achieved when you are able to reorder the objects you draw so that all the objects drawn with a particular color, gradient, or font are drawn sequentially. Of course, z-ordering of objects may not allow for this possibility.

The performance gains of such operations are browser dependent, but in general caching the `fillStyle` and `strokeStyle` properties is 10 to 100 times as fast as setting them redundantly, and caching the `font` property can be 100 to 1,000 times faster than setting it redundantly!

If you change less-common properties often, such as `shadowColor`, you may want to consider caching them as well, or at least testing to determine if there are performance gains to be had from caching them.

Clearing the Canvas in a Cache-Friendly Manner

Setting the canvas width equal to itself is an easy and convenient method of clearing the canvas, but it also clears the rest of the context state, invalidating our cache. In other words, setting the canvas width equal to itself sets the `fillStyle` back to `"black"`, resets the clipping region, clears out the context's current path, and so on. The `clearRect` method should generally be used instead to clear the canvas. This typically entails saving the transformation matrix beforehand if necessary, setting it to identity (`ctx.setTransform(1, 0, 0, 1, 0, 0)`) so that the right space is cleared, clearing the canvas (`ctx.clearRect(0, 0, canvas.width, canvas.height)`) and then optionally restoring the transformation.

Stop Using `save` and `restore`

The `save` and `restore` methods create a state stack of every canvas context property. This can be awfully handy, and we saw a few real-world uses in Chapter 5, but for apps where performance matters, these methods are vastly overused and best avoided. In fact, unless you're using clipping regions, you probably don't need to *ever* use `save` and `restore` in your apps.

It is essential that you do not (or very rarely) use `save` and `restore` if you want to get the most out of caching. After all, every time you call `restore`, you would need to either reset your cache state or set the context menu's properties that were cached back to the cache state because the `restore` method overwrites every context property, invalidating the cache.

A large percentage of `save` and `restore` usage is derived from the need to traverse a "tree" of transformations, for instance when drawing complex objects. Because we are saving and restoring everything, and not just the transformation matrix, the `save` and `restore` calls can be avoided in favor of simply keeping track of the transformations we do and reversing them ourselves. If our needs are more complex, we could keep track of the entire transformation matrix ourselves. A small class to do just that is provided in Listing 5.13 of Chapter 5 (page 146).

Because the only way to reset a clipping region is to reset the canvas state, either by using `save` and `restore` or by setting the canvas width equal to itself, some usage of the methods may still be warranted. In the future, the context's `resetClip` method will fill this purpose. It has been recently added to the specification, but as of this writing, no browser has implemented it yet.

Caching with Images and In-Memory Canvases

Often on the canvas we typically draw objects that are a combination of paths, text, and images, and these objects can be thought of as discrete entities. An example might be a fancy button in a menu that is drawn with rounded rectangles, a gradient background, and some text. Nothing in this object changes, so it is a good candidate for "caching" the entire object as an image.

Drawing images is vastly faster than drawing even mildly complex paths, and drawing images is worlds faster than drawing text. Whenever you have a complex object, consider making an image of it instead. This type of caching-by-image is also known as *prerendering*.

Cached images can be created with canvas commands and saved either as image files or computed on the fly. Computing images dynamically can be done by saving complex objects to in-memory canvases and using `drawImage` with the in-memory canvases as a source, or else outputting those canvases to data URLs.

An example of this would be caching nonmoving obstacles in a 2D game (such as the walls of a level). We would create an in-memory canvas the size of the normal canvas and draw all of the static elements to it, instead of our regular canvas. Then in the draw loop, we use `drawImage` to draw the in-memory canvas onto our real one.

The objects we are caching in such an example could be paths, text, or even just several smaller images. Regardless, all the drawing in subsequent animation frames is "flattened" into just one `drawImage` call using this in-memory prerendered canvas. Parts of menus, heads-up displays, and backgrounds are other good candidates for this sort of scene prerendering.

The more complex your objects, the more performance will be gained by caching (prerendering) them to images. With text, even a single call to `fillText` is much slower than a call to `drawImage`, so it's almost always beneficial to cache drawn strings if they do not change or move often, and caching text to an image has the added benefit of no longer needing to set the `font` attribute.

It's important to note that rendering with some animated objects may cause undesired smoothing effects because animated images may not look identical to animated paths and text. Additionally, if your canvas app gives the impression of "zooming" by scaling all drawn objects, cached images drawn at a scale will lose fidelity while rendered canvas paths and text would draw more appropriately as scalable vectors.

> **NOTE**
>
> Caching images in memory isn't free in terms of space and time, and you should always try to cache using the smallest image or canvas needed.

Images

As we have seen in caching, much of the performance utility from images comes from the fact that they are fast. Using them wherever possible to replace long chains of complex drawing operations may be the single biggest performance improvement in a given app.

Drawing on Integers

In many browsers, drawing images on integer coordinates can lead to a modest boost in rendering speed. As we covered in the "Before We Get to Canvas" section, `Math.floor` and `Math.round` are not the fastest ways to create integers; instead, it is better to use the bitwise OR operator:

```
(x | 0); // instead of Math.floor(x)
((x + 0.5) | 0); // instead of Math.round(x)
// Typical usage:
ctx.drawImage(myImg, x | 0, y | 0);
```

Drawing on integer coordinates can be faster because the browser does not need to apply a smoothing algorithm to the image. The new context property `imageSmoothingEnabled` controls this algorithm, but is not yet universally supported.

Scaling with the Optional Arguments of `drawImage`

In some browsers, using the optional arguments of `drawImage` to scale an image will be slightly faster than using a transformation.

```
// this takes a 100x100 image and scales it 2x
ctx.drawImage(img, 0, 0, 100, 100, 0, 0, 200, 200);

// use a transformation to do the same thing
ctx.scale(2, 2);
ctx.drawImage(img, 0, 0);
// we would also need to set the scale back here
// or otherwise reset the transformation
```

Text

Drawing text on the canvas is slow. Measuring text on the canvas is slow. Even setting the font on the canvas is slow! Thankfully, there are some considerations that may lessen the burden of text rendering in our canvas apps.

We should be careful to conserve our use of text in performance-minded apps, which often means caching text strings as images, measuring rarely, and forgoing the drawing of text if it will not be legible anyway.

Caching

Caching text as images is an easy way to gain a performance benefit because you avoid both `drawText` and setting `font`. Unfortunately, it is infeasible in many situations, such as those with dynamic text, animation, or zooming.

Greeking

Very generally, "Greeking" is the act of rendering something unreadable in the place of text. The name is a reference to the (Shakespeare-derived) phrase "It's Greek to me," implying that something isn't understood. In web design, the concept is often employed with "Lorem Ipsum" filler text, where the words themselves are not meant to be sensible. The term has a similar rendering connotation.

If your canvas app draws text with the possibility of scaling objects or zooming the scene, there may be a point where some drawn text is too small to be legible or meaningfully visible. If your app is created in such a way that you can determine the absolute size of the strings drawn, then when the font size drops below 3 pixels instead of drawing a text string, you could opt to "greek" the text by drawing a line instead of the text. This looks somewhat visually very similar and also allows you to draw scenes, such as zoomed-out diagrams with hundreds of nodes, without wasting performance rendering hundreds of text strings that would not be readable anyway.

There are other situations that are more app specific where drawing such a degenerate object may be just as good as drawing the real thing. The same principle could be applied to gradients, for instance. You could save an object's dominant color alongside its gradient and draw only the flat color if the screen bounds of the object are just a few pixels in size.

Measuring Text

Measuring text isn't particularly fast, but precomputing text width and height values is a relatively easy optimization to make. Even if your strings change a good deal, calculating and saving the height of oft-used font strings may be beneficial.

Precomputing values for text has the added benefit of reducing differences in the measurement of drawn objects across browsers. Many browsers return different numbers for the measurement of strings, typically off by a pixel or two, but if you are using precomputed values from just one browser, then you can maintain consistency if the text sizes are used in object placement or layout.

Shadows

Shadows are slow. *Very* slow. As a general rule, they should be avoided in canvas apps that are expected to run as fast as possible.

If true shadows in your canvas application are desirable and you have reason to be performance conscious, you can always add a menu option to disable their drawing so that users of fast machines see a prettier app and users of slower machines have all the retained functionality of a fast (but not as pretty) app.

Shadows are great effects and can really make visual elements feel like they have a depth and tangible presence, so if you want shadow effects without hurting performance, there are a couple of reasonable alternatives to explore.

Precomputing Shadows

The first thing to consider is precomputing your shadows and turning them into images, or using in-memory canvases if the figures are dynamic. The general idea is discussed in the previous section on caching with images. This method is extremely fast compared with using true shadows, but is unsuitable for animated objects.

Faking It

It is worth considering using gradients, especially radial gradients, to *approximate* shadows. Gradients are not as fast as images but they can certainly be used to add variable-sized shadows to objects on the fly, and they are still much faster than using true shadows. The effectiveness of this method is more platform dependent than using images, and as usual you should benchmark your approximated shadows against using real shadows.

If your shadows aren't blurring at all, then simply substituting shadows with semitransparent rectangles (or the figure's same path, semitransparent and translated slightly) will suffice!

Blur Affects True Shadow Performance

There is relative slowness among true shadows. The larger the value of `shadowBlur`, the slower the shadow will be. Figure 7.5 shows the same shadowed object drawn with three different blur values.

FIGURE 7.5   The same shadowed object drawn with a `shadowBlur` of 40, 4, and 0, respectively.

A `shadowBlur` of 4 has hardly any blur at all, but it will only be 1.2 times faster than a `shadowBlur` of 40. A `shadowBlur` of 0 is equivalent to drawing a red rectangle and is about 4 times faster than a `shadowBlur` of 40. Drawing a cached image of a shadow, by contrast, is more than 100 times faster than a `shadowBlur` of 40. The slowest shadow here is also the easiest to replace by approximating it with a radial gradient instead.

Gradients

Gradients aren't terribly slow, but they are slower than solid styles and if you use them often there are a few things to keep in mind to make sure they aren't a performance hindrance.

As a general rule, you should be seeking ways to create as few new instances of objects as possible, especially in loops. Many gradients can be created just once, at initialization time, and reused as often as needed. Because gradients are defined as being between two points or two circles, you'll run into trouble when you want to use the identical gradient for figures located in different places. The solution to this is to always define gradients as if they started at the origin and to translate the gradient (and figures that are to be drawn) so that you can reuse the single gradient in multiple locations. A detailed example of this is given in the section "Gradient Performance and Reuse" in Chapter 5 (page 177).

If you are drawing blurred circles with radial gradients, keep in mind that you do not have to use a circular path (arc) to draw them—a single `fillRect` command will suffice. After all, the shape being drawn doesn't matter as long as it contains the entire gradient.

Paths

Aside from caching, most path optimizations involve taking care to create as few new paths as possible.

Consider the task of making 100 circles drawn at random locations on the canvas. A simple way would be as follows:

```
// Slow! Creates a new path for every single arc
var x = 0, y = 0;
for (var i = 0; i < 100; i++) {
    x = Math.random()*200 + 10;
    y = Math.random()*200 + 10;
    ctx.beginPath();
    ctx.arc(x, y, 10, 0, Math.PI*2, false);
    ctx.fill();
}
```

If all of our to-be-drawn path components are the same color, we can "flatten" all of our paths into one:

```
var x = 0, y = 0;
ctx.beginPath();
for (var i = 0; i < 100; i++) {
    x = Math.random()*200 + 10;
    y = Math.random()*200 + 10;
    ctx.moveTo(x+10, y);
    ctx.arc(x, y, 10, 0, Math.PI*2, false);
}
ctx.fill();
```

This accomplishes the same drawing operation much faster. Only one new path is created, and only one call to `fill` is made. Note, though, that we had to insert a `moveTo` command because the `arc` method draws a line from the end of one circle to the start of the next circle otherwise, and, instead, we want to open a new subpath.

This sort of optimization isn't limited to figures of the same shape, and it should be considered for any arbitrary set of paths that could be drawn as a single path with a set of subpaths instead. This is important when deciding how to write your state organization and drawing code: You should take care to allow sequential objects that could benefit from being drawn as a single subpath to do so.

NOTE

A word of caution: If the `fillStyle` used in the previous two snippets was partially trans-parent, the resulting renders would be very different. The first one fills each circle indi-vidually because they are all separate paths. The second code snippet, however, fills the *union* of the entire path, so no transparency overlap would be seen for circles sitting atop each other.

Nuanced path rules such as this are discussed in Chapter 5.

`fillRect` Is Faster Than Making a Rectangular Path, But...

When drawing single rectangles, you should use the context method `fillRect`, as it is faster than beginning a new path, calling `rect`, and filling that path.

However, if you intend to draw hundreds or thousands of rectangles, perhaps as part of a game or particle engine, then performance is better if you create one path, call `rect` for each rectangle, and call `fill` just once to draw the very large path.

Multiple Canvases

If a site is using several canvases on a page, such as with an image gallery, you should take care to conserve the total number of canvases. There might be hundreds of images in a gallery page, but the performance will be notably improved if there only exist `<canvas>` tags for the currently visible images on screen, which might total 20 or so. If you're making a gallery site or app, try to cap the number of canvases you have and reuse them as different images come onto the screen.

It's not always bad to have more rather than fewer canvases. Sometimes a canvas app will have distinct drawing layers, such as a foreground, background, and middle-ground. If the middle-ground constantly changes but the fore- and background are relatively static, it may be best to use three canvases overlaid atop each other. Doing this allows you to take hundreds or thousands of canvas commands that make up the background, and replace them with a canvas that rarely (if ever) needs to redraw.

It may be better still to draw a prerendered "background scene" of all background figures, cache it to an image or in-memory canvas, and simply draw that image first before the foreground. This way, you are taking the hundreds or thousands of canvas commands that make up the background and replacing them with a single call to `drawImage`.

The performance gains from separating your drawing into multiple canvas layers depend on your app's needs and implementation. Which method is better varies too much by scenario to definitively say, but as a default it's best to stick with using a single in-DOM canvas and prerendering backgrounds. Keeping the DOM and your event code cleaner is a big plus, and it ought to be easier to transition your code to multiple canvases (if need be) than to make modifications to the code the other way around.

> **NOTE**
>
> If your background is just an image or a truly static set of figures that never changes, then you can greatly simplify this optimization by setting the image as the CSS `backgroundImage` of the canvas. You may have to make an image from the figures, but that can be precomputed into a regular image to host on your site, or simply computed once by the canvas on initialization and saved as a data URL.

Keeping Track of Objects

One of the big advantages of SVG over canvas is that it keeps a reference to every object you create and offers the native ability to attach events to all sorts of shapes. One of the big advantages of canvas, on the other hand, is that you often do not need or want to keep track of every line, speck, and thimble that gets drawn to the screen!

Both games and enterprise apps have a lot of effects, animations, and figures that do not need to participate in hit testing of any kind, and it's important that you remember to only run hit testing on objects that are actually relevant.

You might make virtual layers or categories to organize your objects, reducing the set of objects that participate in hit testing. If you are keeping track of the rectangular bounds of each object, then one natural set to maintain would be the set of all objects currently visible on the screen. Knowing the bounds of every object drawn, you could forgo drawing all objects off the screen, and exclude them from participating in mouse or touch hit-testing algorithms.

If we have tens of thousands of objects and few of them move at a time, it may be beneficial to separate our canvas (and hit testing) into logical quadrants, so a mouse click on a given location may only have to search through 25% of the objects in the canvas. Instead of all the work being done on hit testing, the work is instead shifted to updating which quadrant an object is in when it moves.

Specific apps may have specific methods of organizing, so although there are no catchall performance improvements here, it is worth giving serious thought to how your objects might best be organized.

Hit Testing

Hit testing (or hit detection, or object picking) is the act of determining if a given point or object intersects another object.

The canvas method `isPointInPath` tests if a given point is in the path currently loaded onto a canvas context. This is slow to use in practice, as you have to reconstruct that path on the context of every object you want to test. It is always faster to implement your own point-in-polygon algorithm to suit your needs.

It's important to remember that with the vast majority of shapes, you can get away with rectangular or circular hit testing, even if the shapes are not perfectly rectangular or circular. In the case of very elaborate figures or images, you can create a hit box (or wireframe) consisting of a very simple path or a few rectangles and then check the point against the simplified shape instead.

Rectangular hit testing is a fairly obvious and fast procedure:

```
// Determine if a point x,y is inside the rectangle's bounds
function pointInRect(x, y, rx, ry, rw, rh) {
  return  (rx <= x) && (rx + rw >= x) &&
          (ry <= y) && (ry + rh >= y);
}
```

Circular hit testing allows for some nuance. We test if a point is in a circle by taking the distance between the two points and comparing that distance with the radius. This raises an optimization opportunity because determining the distance between two points involves a square root, and the square root function is slow. To avoid this, we can write a function that measures the distance between the two points *squared* and compares it with the radius *squared*. We don't actually care about the true distance; we are just comparing two values, so we can just as easily compare two squared values:

```
// We could write this as a one-liner
// but it's expanded to illustrate what's going on
function pointInCircle(x, y, cx, cy, radius) {
  // We aren't using Math.sqrt so this is
  // the distance between the two points squared
  var distsq = (x - cx) * (x - cx) + (y - cy) * (y - cy);
  // Because of this, we must compare it to the radius squared:
  return distsq <= radius * radius;
}
```

Using this circle, hit-testing code is about 20% to 50% faster than using one with `Math.sqrt`.

Several available point-in-polygon algorithms are available online that may suit your needs for path hit testing. It is important when implementing an algorithm to keep in mind that paths drawn on the canvas follow the nonzero winding number rule, not the even-odd rule, and your hit-testing algorithm needs to match this rule to properly test subpath intersections.

Approximations

When performance is at stake, cutting corners becomes a bit of a virtue. Instead of perfectly hit testing against a very complex path or a semitransparent image, it is often permissible to simply specify an approximate hit-testing region, either using a series of rectangles, or circles, or a reduced-complexity path, that results in "good enough" hit testing or collision detection. Figure 7.6 shows two such examples.

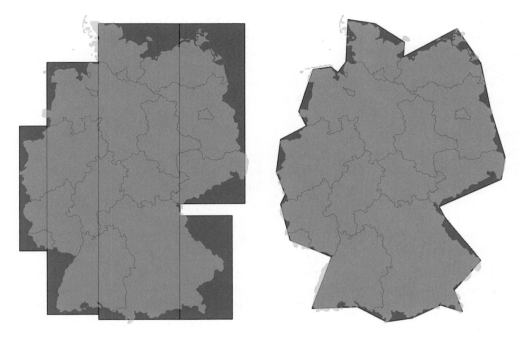

FIGURE 7.6   A map of Germany overlaid with two possible hit-testing approximation regions: a series of five rectangles and a simplified border path.

Pixel-Perfect Hit Testing

If you do need pixel-perfect hit testing, as in the case of hit testing fonts or images with some transparency, you must take a look at the image data. The typical way of doing this is to draw each object as you go to an in-memory canvas and get the image data of the pixel at a given x and y for that location: `getImageData(x, y, 1, 1)`. If the single-pixel image data is not 100% transparent, then you've hit something. If it is completely transparent, then you can draw the next object in the object list and try again. If you're stopping once you find the first hit object, there's no need to clear the in-memory canvas between drawn objects.

Although the above method gets the smallest amount of image data possible on your in-memory canvas, there is a second method to consider that does not create new image data during an app's normal execution. If you only have a handful of relatively small objects that need pixel-perfect hit testing, you could save a copy of their image data along with the rest of the object state and test against that saved image data instead.

For instance, if you have a 40×40 semitransparent image, on initialization you could create a 40×40 in-memory canvas, draw the image to the canvas, get the image data, and save a reference to it. Then, when it is time for hit testing, you only have to translate the location to be tested by the image's top-left position, and test the resulting x and y coordinates against your array of already-saved image data. This way, image data is created only once, on initialization, and not constantly during the app's normal execution.

Even if you are doing pixel-perfect hit testing, you should first check to see if your tested point is within the rectangular bounds of the object before you bother to peek at any image data. There might be 90 objects drawn to the canvas that need to be tested, but if the bounds of only 3 of them intersect with the point, then it's just a maximum of three calls to `getImageData` instead of 90. This principle of checking the rectangular bounds first is generally a good idea for all types of hit testing.

Size Matters

It should come as no surprise that smaller canvases are better for performance and reducing your memory footprint. This is one good reason to keep a canvas a small fixed size (such as 640×480) and scale it larger with CSS. This is typically only permissible with games, especially games made in retro styles, as canvas text (among other things) scaled in such a way isn't going to look very good. The speed may or may not be worth it, but it should certainly be a consideration if you need all the CPU time you have for other complexities, such as physics.

With scrolling canvas apps or games, you should never have a canvas that is larger than your screen, or hide part of your canvas. Instead, you should maintain a logical "viewport" that is the visible portion of your app, and translate objects onto or off of it accordingly. In most cases, care should be taken to keep track of what is and isn't currently viewable, as you should only be drawing objects that are actually in the viewport. Some browsers optimize some offscreen drawing calls, but you should not rely on this behavior.

Only Clear and Draw What's Changed

For many applications, it is overkill to redraw the entire scene on every animation frame. Clearing and redrawing only a small portion of the canvas is almost always faster, though not always straightforward if there are overlapping or antialiased objects in the scene.

One of the most common ways to manage redrawing is to maintain a list of *dirty rectangles*, which describe all areas in need of redrawing when the scene is next rendered. For instance, if we had a scene with several thousand objects and you moved one object from location A to location B, the object's old and new bounds would be the dirty rectangles. When it's time to redraw, we would begin the process by creating a clipping region that contained both dirty rectangles.

Upon clearing the canvas to begin redrawing, thanks to the clipping region, only the two rectangular regions would be cleared. Afterward, we can redraw the necessary objects, but instead of drawing all (several thousand) of them, we check each object's rectangular bounds to see if they intersect one of the dirty rectangles, and only draw the object if there is such an intersection.

Checking these bounds intersections and only drawing a handful of objects is typically far faster than blindly redrawing all objects. Because the clipping region still exists when drawing, no visual defects will occur when only the objects that intersect the dirty rectangle are redrawn.

The advantages of this method are highly application dependent, and implementations can become complicated. If large portions of the screen need to be redrawn or there are too many dirty rectangles to consider, the benefits can diminish. Nonetheless, the concept of selective clearing and redrawing is one of the most widely used optimizations throughout most graphical systems.

Because clipping is involved, you have to use `save` and `restore`, and potentially clear any cached canvas attributes. However, because you are only clipping once per frame, before all drawing, caching fonts and colors during the redrawing process will still work, it just won't carry over to the next frame.

As an alternative to using any clipping at all, you could use an in-memory canvas that is the same size as your primary canvas. Instead of making a clipping region on the primary canvas, you'd use `clearRect`, draw the intersecting objects to the in-memory canvas, then draw the relevant rectangles from that canvas onto your primary canvas. This achieves the same effect as clipping, though the performance difference between the two methods is too situational to conclude.

Summary

There are a handful of extremely common canvas missteps that beginners take, and if you're new to canvas, reading the first section of this chapter should put you on a more confident path to making your first apps.

Canvas implementations are improving performance rapidly, but canvas programmers should chiefly be concerned with the thing they can control: their own code. The second section of this chapter covered a comprehensive list of performance considerations that will prepare you to maintain fast and smooth canvas applications.

In the next chapter, we discuss the future of 2D canvas, the latest additions to the specification, and the 3D API.

## CHAPTER 8

The Future of Canvas and 3D Canvas

The HTML5 canvas specification has evolved a good deal since its inception, and will continue to do so for the foreseeable future. It has so far gone through a few major updates and several minor ones, with the most recent major update containing several exciting (but yet-to-be-implemented) features that we cover in this chapter.

Alongside the 2D canvas specification, another standards body (the Khronos Group) maintains a 3D canvas application programming interface (API) called WebGL. Although this 3D API is far too complex to cover here, several interesting libraries have been created around it that vastly simplify 3D development, and are worth a look even if you have no 3D experience.

The Future of 2D Canvas

Canvas is important enough that every browser vendor has been keen to aim for swift and complete implementation, and the specification editor aided in this endeavor by halting large additions to the specification for some time. When asked in late 2009 why measuring text on the canvas only returned the width and not the height of the text, the editor replied, "I'd rather we waited for browsers to catch up and implement <canvas> well before adding yet more things for them to get wrong. :-)".

Current implementations of canvas aren't perfect, but it's stable enough to use on every modern browser. The specification editor must have thought so too, and in March of 2012 he decided to define several new methods and attributes that were in the works.

We can expect these methods to be implemented in the coming years, and we can additionally expect (as has been happening) that browsers will continue to add new features on their own that may eventually get absorbed into the specification.

Although this section is a showcase of new features in the canvas API that are yet-to-be widely implemented, it's very possible that by the time you read this, some of them are well supported. If you like a feature, try it out!

New in the Specification

Although the majority of new features in the March of 2012 update are yet to be implemented in any browser, it's worth taking a look at the exciting bits of the spec that will be usable in our future canvas projects.

Fill Rules

There's a new attribute on the context, `fillRule`, which defaults to `"nonzero"` with the option of `"evenodd"`. This allows paths to be filled according to the even-odd rule as opposed to the nonzero winding number rule. This is a necessary addition if the canvas context is to render Scalable Vector Graphics (SVG) paths faithfully, as their specification allows either fill rule.

> **NOTE**
>
> The difference between the nonzero winding number rule and the even-odd rule is touched upon in Chapter 5, "2D Canvas."

Path Primitives and SVG Paths

Instead of creating paths by issuing canvas commands to the context, loading up its current path, paths can now be created as their own separate objects and saved for redrawing or hit testing without using the context's current path at all.

Path primitives are constructed just like building current paths on the context, by using `moveTo`, `lineTo`, `bezierCurveTo`, etc. For example, a simple line `Path` could be defined like this:

```
var p = new Path();
p.moveTo(0, 0);
p.lineTo(50, 50);
context.stroke(p);
```

To support this new primitive, the canvas context methods `fill`, `stroke`, and `isPointInPath` all now take an optional `Path` argument. Path primitives should greatly enhance the utility of `isPointInPath` because you would no longer need to reload every path you wanted to test onto the current context just to use it.

The `Path` constructor also has two optional argument sets: `Path(path)` and `Path(svgDOMString)`. The first one copies a given `Path`, and the second one creates a path out of all the subpaths in a given SVG path string.

In other words, we could write the constructor argument:

```
new Path('M 100,100 1 50 50 1 250 -100');
```

to create a path with two line segments.

The SVG path notation makes for some convenient shape creation, especially because many will not have to convert their SVG path strings if they are making a transition to canvas. In addition, there is currently no (easy) way to create SVG-style arcs with the canvas context path commands, and there is currently no simple way to write path commands relative to the last point, as there is with SVG path strings.

Path primitives have several methods for adding paths or text (as a series of subpaths) onto the `Path` object:

- ▶ `addPath(path, transformation)`

- ▶ `addPathByStrokingPath(path, styles, transform)`

- ▶ `addText(text, styles, transform, x, y, [maxWidth])`

- ▶ `addPathByStrokingText(text, styles, transform, x, y, [maxWidth])`

- ▶ `addText(text, styles, transform, path, [maxWidth])`

- ▶ `addPathByStrokingText(text, styles, transform, path, [maxWidth])`

There's a new `DrawingStyle` object that acts as a container for all possible style attributes, such as `lineWidth`, `lineCap`, `font`, `textAlign`, and so on. This is used to store a set of drawing styles that may be applied to portions of a new `Path` object, and is used as the `styles` argument in the previously listed methods. The `styles` method also accepts a reference to any context.

The `transform` argument must be `null` or an `SVGMatrix` object, and will be applied to the path or text before being added to the `Path` object.

These new `Path` objects are one of the most welcome additions to the canvas specification. Their existence allows easier stateful persistence of shapes as "objects" on the canvas because only a reference to a `Path` object needs to be saved instead of a potentially long list of drawing commands. Performance should see a boost too because programmers will be able to make a single call, `context.stroke(myPath)`, instead of having to call hundreds of path methods (`lineTo`, `bezierCurveto`, and so on) to reload a particular shape onto the current path during every drawing loop.

Ellipses

In the past, the specification only allowed for the drawing of primitive arcs with the `arc` and `arcTo` commands. This was a tad shortsighted, as it's a bit complicated to make ellipses or elliptical curves from arcs, though it is doable with some careful transformations.

The specification has seen fit to add an `ellipse` method, `ellipse(x, y, radiusX, radiusY, rotation, startAngle, endAngle, anticlockwise)`, and an upgrade to `arcTo` with two new optional arguments (in square brackets): `arcTo(x1, y1, x2, y2, radiusX [, radiusY, rotation ])`. These bring the canvas specification closer to the abilities of SVG paths.

> **NOTE**
>
> In spite of these additions, there is nothing (yet) that quite mimics the SVG `arc` command present in SVG paths, though technically they are possible to accomplish using just the old `arc` command and a fair bit of math involving transformations.

Dashed Lines

Dashed lines have been an oft-requested feature since the early days of canvas, and they've finally landed in the specification. What's more, some browsers have already implemented line dashes and offsets, albeit in slightly different ways.

There are two line dash methods and one attribute, `setLineDash()`, `getLineDash()`, and `dashOffset`. The method `setLineDash()` takes a list of distances to alternate the line drawing on and off, such as `[2, 4, 2, 2]`. If a list with an odd length is supplied, the list is simply doubled. The `dashOffset` sets the "phase" of the line, and can be constantly incremented or decremented in an animation to create animated dashed lines with the "marching ant" effect.

Dashed lines are already implemented well in at least Chrome and Firefox, though the methods differ slightly for now. Firefox uses `context.mozDash` as an attribute instead of the two methods, and `mozDashOffset` instead of `dashOffset`. If you're interested in using this feature in the near future, it may be worth creating a shim that appropriately detects and sets any prefixed possibilities for the dashes. An example of such a shim (containing only the browsers that work as of this writing) might look like this:

```
// Line of 2, space of 3, line of 4, space of 5, repeat!
var myLineDash = [2, 3, 4, 5];
// Typically a value that changes with animation to get
// the "marching ant line" effect
var myLineDashOffset = 0;
setLineDash(myLineDash, myLineDashOffset)

// Simple shim for setting line dash
// note that the specification uses a function (setLineDash) but
// the browser prefixed ways use an attribute
```

```
function setLineDash(lineDash, lineDashOffset) {
  if (context['setLineDash'] !== undefined) {
    context['setLineDash'](lineDash);
    context['lineDashOffset'] = lineDashOffset;
  } else if (context['webkitLineDash'] !== undefined) {
    context['webkitLineDash'] = lineDash;
    context['webkitLineDashOffset'] = lineDashOffset;
  } else if (context['mozDash'] !== undefined) {
    context['mozDash'] = lineDash;
    context['mozDashOffset'] = lineDashOffset;
  } else {
    // no native support!
    // We could implement our own here,
    // depending on the kind of shapes we intend to draw.
  }
}
```

Text Along a Path

Like in SVG, programmers will be able to draw text along a path. A simple example would look like:

```
var p1 = new Path('M 100 350 q 150 -300 300 0');
var p2 = new Path();
var styles = new DrawingStyle();
styles.font = '20px sans-serif';
p2.addText('Hello World', styles, null, p1);
context.fill(p2);
```

This is a very welcome addition, as doing this sort of operation manually involves a lot of mathematical footwork.

Hit Testing (Hit Regions)

The only built-in hit testing that the canvas context has is in the form of `context.isPointInPath([path], x, y)`. This method receives an enormous boost in utility thanks to its new optional `Path` argument, which means we can test against saved paths and not just whatever is loaded onto the current path of the context.

Nonetheless, it takes a bit of work to create a managed hit-testing system, and the specification editors have seen fit to add two new methods, `context.addHitRegion(options)` and `context.removeHitRegion(regionID)`, that manage hit regions for a canvas context.

The `options` argument is an object with several optional members:

▶ **path**—A `Path` object that describes the hit region. If not specified or null, the context's current path is used.

▶ `id`—A string to identify the region. This is used in `MouseEvent` events on the canvas and can be accessed through `event.region`. This defaults to an empty string and is also the ID used in `removeHitRegion`s.

▶ `parentID`—ID of a parent region, for accessibility. The default is null.

▶ `cursor`—A pointer (mouse) cursor to display when over the region. The default is `"inherit"`. Any valid Cascading Style Sheets (CSS) cursor string should work.

▶ `control`—An element that is a descendent of the canvas to which events are to be routed for access by accessibility tools. The default is `null`.

▶ `label`—A text label for accessibility tools. This defaults to `null`.

▶ `role`—An ARIA (Accessible Rich Internet Application) role for accessibility tools to determine how to represent this region if no `control` is given. This defaults to `null`.

As you can see from the arguments, a lot of hit regions utility lies in accessibility. But they also make hit detection easier in general, as it affords an automatic way to determine hit regions in mouse events, automatic cursor control, and an automatic way to route events.

Unfortunately, we can only speculate on what the performance will be compared with creating your own hit-testing algorithms, but it should make for some potential improvements, at least in development time and canvas app prototyping.

Transformation Matrix

Although we could modify and set the transformation matrix before, there wasn't actually any way to retrieve the current transformation. To remedy this, many programmers opt to keep track of the transformation matrix themselves, but now the ability to retrieve the matrix is finally on the context as `context.currentTransform`, which returns an `SVGMatrix` object.

There is additionally a new `context.resetTransform()` function that returns the current transformation to the identity matrix, but this is just a convenience function, and was easily accomplished before by using `context.setTransform(1, 0, 0, 1, 0, 0)`.

> **NOTE**
>
> We show how to keep track of the transformation matrix yourself in Chapter 5, so that you can retrieve the matrix any time should you need this ability today.

The new specification also allows us to apply transformations to `CanvasPattern` objects. The `CanvasPattern` now has a `setTransform` method that, unlike the context's `setTransform`, which takes six numbers describing a matrix, takes an `SVGMatrix`:

```
var identity = new SVGMatrix();
identity.rotate(myAngle);
var myPattern = context.createPattern(myImage, 'repeat');
myPattern.setTransform(identity);
context.fillStyle = myPattern;
```

More Text Metrics

In the previous iteration of the specification, there was nothing but a `width` property on the `TextMetrics` object returned by `context.measureText`. Text height, if you wanted it, had to be approximated. Now we have a host of measurement options.

The four most important additions define the bounding box for the text: `actualBoundingBoxLeft` and `actualBoundingBoxRight`, `actualBoundingBoxAscent`, and `actualBoundingBoxDescent`.

There are also values for the text baselines: `fontBoundingBoxAscent`, `fontBoundingBoxDescent`, `emHeightAscent`, `emHeightDescent`, `hangingBaseline`, `alphabeticBaseline`, and `ideographicBaseline`.

Resetting the Clipping Region

As we mentioned in the other canvas chapters, resetting the clipping region was a bit of a sore point in the specification, as it was the only part of the canvas context state that could not be reset on its own. Either you had to use `save` and `restore`, which acted upon all canvas state, or you reset the entire canvas state, but there was no way to reset solely the clipping region. With the addition of the `resetClip` method, we finally have this ability.

toBlob

The canvas specification has had a `toBlob` function for some time, though no browser has yet to implement it.

A blob is an object that represents immutable raw binary data. With respect to the canvas, the function of `toBlob` is similar to that of `toDataURL`. Instead of returning a string that describes an image, `toBlob` returns a file object that describes the canvas image.

Or it would, if it were implemented. This is too bad, as some applications passing around blob pointers ought to be more efficient than passing around (very large) strings representing Base64-encoded images.

Image Data

Image data methods now have three high-definition (HD) alternatives: `createImageDataHD`, `getImageDataHD`, and `putImageDataHD`. These methods work just like their non-HD counterparts, except these return image data that is sized to the backing store.

The backing store is the underlying pixel data that the browser uses to eventually draw to the canvas, which can have implications on some devices with high-definition screens. On devices such as the iPhone 4S, a 100-CSS-pixel-wide canvas is actually 200 "device" pixels wide, which is the width of the backing store. A 100-pixel-wide image drawn to the canvas will be upscaled and saved to the 200-pixel-wide backing store. This can be a pain if you want to manipulate that image data because `getImageData` scales it down an additional time to return image data that is 100 pixels wide, potentially losing data in the process.

The remedy for this is the creation of the HD alternatives for the image data methods. These return the pixel data from the backing store, instead of scaling it down to CSS-pixel canvas size.

Many consider this component of the web frustrating, as the backing store isn't particularly intuitive, and different implementations of canvas on high-definition devices can lead to some differences in rendering quality.

Others

A few new methods exist on the canvas itself that may be worth looking into once they are implemented by browsers:

▶ `canvas.supportsContext(contextString)` returns a Boolean value indicating whether or not the browser supports a specific kind of context.

▶ `canvas.setContext(context)` sets a canvas's rendering context to the given context.

▶ `canvas.transferControlToProxy()` returns a `CanvasProxy` object that can be used to transfer control of a canvas to another frame or to a web worker.

▶ `canvasProxy.setContext(context)` sets the context of a `CanvasProxy` to a given context. There's little published about these methods, but once implemented, they can be used to give web workers the ability to manipulate pixel data.

▶ `drawSystemFocusRing([path], element)` and `drawCustomFocusRing([path], element)` draw focus rings around the current default path or given `Path` object. Unlike most attributes and methods in this chapter, these methods have been in the specification for some time, but no browser has yet to implement them.

Hints from the Browsers

The specification isn't the only source for new canvas methods. It's a common occurrence in the world of HTML and JavaScript that browsers will implement some practical feature themselves before a specification body decides upon it, and other browsers adopt the feature long before it's ever standardized or set into a spec.

Canvas is no different, and if we want to get a glimpse of features that may make it into browsers before they make it into the specification, we can always peruse the canvas and context objects in browsers' debuggers or consoles.

Taking a look at the Firefox nightly build, we find these additional properties on the canvas context:

▶ `mozCurrentTransform`   ▶ `mozFillRule`

▶ `mozCurrentTransformInverse`   ▶ `mozImageSmoothingEnabled`

▶ `mozDash`   ▶ `mozTextStyle`

▶ `mozDashOffset`

Almost all of these are recently implemented attributes in the specification that will be unprefixed soon, though image smoothing has been in Firefox long before the specification had it. We also see that Mozilla has decided to add the ability to get the inverse transformation, which isn't in the specification, and it's also worth noting that `mozCurrentTransform` and `mozCurrentTransformInverse` return an array of six numbers instead of an `SVGMatrix` object, like the current specification demands.

On the canvas itself, there's a few interesting properties with the `moz-` prefix, most notably `mozOpaque`. This is a canvas attribute that coincides with the `moz-opaque` HTML attribute on the canvas, which lets the canvas know whether or not translucency will be a factor. If it isn't, Firefox is able to optimize rendering performance.

In Chrome, we notice that there are a lot of `set...` methods that aren't in the spec, but these are actually older deprecated methods, presumably from early implementations of canvas. The `drawImageFromRect` method in Chrome falls under the same category.

On the context in Chrome, there are two prefixed attributes: `webkitImageSmoothingEnabled` and `webkitBackingStorePixelRatio`. The first conforms to the specification's `imageSmoothingEnabled` attribute (though it was in Chrome before it was in the spec), and the second attribute describes the ratio between the canvas size and the backing store. The backing store is the underlying pixel data that the browser uses to eventually draw to the canvas, which can have some implications on devices with high-definition screens.

You'll also see `webkitGetImageDataHD` or just `getImageDataHD`, depending on the version, in webkit-based browsers. The HD methods were introduced in webkit before they were in the specification, and they're the only browsers to implement them so far.

3D (WebGL) Canvas

The HTML5 canvas API specifies a 2D canvas context, with a `getContext` method that allows for the possibilities of others. As of this writing, the only other prominent context available comes from the WebGL specification, which is maintained by the Khronos Group instead of the W3C/WHATWG, and is based on OpenGL ES 2.0, which the Khronos Group also maintains. When people talk about 3D Canvas, they are almost always talking about WebGL.

The WebGL specification, mailing list, and public Wiki can be found at http://www.khronos.org/webgl/.

> **NOTE**
>
> Khronos is a not-for-profit consortium backed by Intel, NVIDIA, AMD, and just about every other technology company with an interest in open, royalty-free graphics APIs. WebGL is backed by every major browser vendor except Microsoft.

WebGL is supported in some fashion in every desktop browser except Internet Explorer, where even Internet Explorer 10 has no support. What's more, blog posts from the Internet Explorer team make it seem like implementation is unlikely in the future.

Additionally, as of this writing, WebGL must be enabled manually in Opera and Safari. This may change rapidly, so have a look online for how to enable it, or if manual intervention is still needed.

WebGL support on mobile devices is spotty, though Firefox and Opera mobile both have some WebGL support on Android devices.

NOTE

Like most features in HTML5, WebGL is listed on caniuse.com showing a comprehensive table of up-to-date information on WebGL adoption: http://caniuse.com/#feat=webgl.

Although exposing the powerful OpenGL API to the Web is an exciting feat, the WebGL API is very involved, and requires a fair bit of knowledge of 3D mathematics to use for any nontrivial purpose. In fact, even a trivial example such as a textured sphere takes several hundred lines of code to achieve, and without the prior 3D vocabulary, would require quite a bit of explanation to understand. Giving appropriate coverage of WebGL assuming no prior knowledge would be a large task, and very likely there will be books in the future concerning only WebGL, as there are with OpenGL. In fact, many of the books published today with WebGL in the title concern themselves more with libraries built atop of WebGL and not with the bare API itself.

WebGL Libraries

Luckily for three-dimensional newcomers, programming in plain WebGL is bound to be uncommon, and the majority of 3D canvas users will not directly interact with the WebGL API. Instead, there are already a multitude of libraries that have sprung up with the common goal of making 3D development a far more gentle experience. These libraries introduce more intuitive concepts, such as scenes, cameras, and light sources, and often contain preset ways to create relatable effects, such as smoke, fire, and fog.

We don't cover any of these in detail, as this text does not aim to teach library-specific code, but we do offer a glimpse at the most popular WebGL library, `Three.js`, to show just how easy and possible 3D development can be.

Three.js

`Three.js` (https://github.com/mrdoob/three.js/) is a relatively lightweight WebGL library that allows newcomers to create 3D scenes intuitively and quickly.

Listing 8.1 contains a simple example of `Three.js` usage, creating a rotating cube that can be seen in Figure 8.1. Instead of understanding shaders, buffers, matrices, and vertexes, the `Three.js` demo lets us create a "scene," add a geometric object with some properties, and rotate it without even touching upon any complex math.

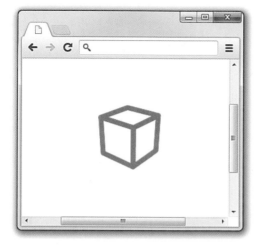

FIGURE 8.1   An animated cube created in just a few lines of code using `Three.js`.

LISTING 8.1   `threejs.html`—A Rotating Cube in `Three.js`

```
<!DOCTYPE html>
<head>
<script src="three.min.js"></script>

<script>
  // Three.js demo, from the example at: https://github.com/mrdoob/three.js
  var camera, scene, renderer;
  var geometry, material, mesh;

  window.addEventListener('load', function() {
    init();
    animate();
  }, false)

  function init() {
    camera = new THREE.PerspectiveCamera(75, 1, 1, 10000);
    camera.position.z = 1000;

    scene = new THREE.Scene();

    geometry = new THREE.CubeGeometry(200, 200, 200);
    material = new THREE.MeshBasicMaterial(
      { color: 0xff0000, wireframe: true, wireframeLinewidth: 8 });
```

```
    mesh = new THREE.Mesh(geometry, material);
    scene.add(mesh);

    renderer = new THREE.CanvasRenderer();
    renderer.setSize(500, 500);

    document.body.appendChild(renderer.domElement);
  }

  function animate() {
    // note: three.js includes requestAnimationFrame shim
    requestAnimationFrame(animate);

    mesh.rotation.x += 0.01;
    mesh.rotation.y += 0.02;

    renderer.render(scene, camera);
  }
</script>
</head>

<body>
  <!-- Empty to start, Three.js adds a canvas element to the body -->
</body>
```

This little demo gives a good approximation of just how easy it is to use `Three.js`, but it doesn't even scratch the surface of what's possible with the library. If you have any interest at all in 3D, we highly encourage you to have a look at all of the demos and associated code on the library repository site (http://mrdoob.github.com/three.js/).

Other Libraries and Resources
Several other libraries are less popular but worth mentioning, and no doubt many more will be created in the coming years. Some of the more popular WebGL libraries include the following:

▶ **PhiloGL**—https://github.com/senchalabs/philogl

▶ **GLGE**—https://github.com/supereggbert/GLGE

▶ **J3D**—https://github.com/drojdjou/J3D

▶ **SceneJS**—https://github.com/xeolabs/scenejs

As WebGL adoption increases, we can expect to see even more interest in the field of 3D libraries. It is always worthwhile to search online for newer libraries that may have arisen since publication of this text.

The Mozilla Developer Network maintains a page on useful WebGL resources, especially pertinent if you intend to develop without using a library: https://developer.mozilla.org/en-US/docs/WebGL.

The Chrome team maintains a page of "experiments" that showcase a good deal of what is possible in the browser with WebGL: http://www.chromeexperiments.com/webgl/.

Summary

The 2D Canvas API has already received a few major upgrades to its specification. No doubt more is to come as canvas gains in usage because the needs found in practice encourage both the WHATWG and browser vendors to implement features that eventually become widespread.

The 3D WebGL specification, although not yet supported on every major browser, is a very promising component of the Web. Powerful visualizations and games have already been created and we can expect to see more impressive works in the future.

CHAPTER 9

Geolocation API

In the last 50 years, two inventions have caused communication to change drastically, impacting almost every part of our society.

The first invention is the Internet. In ancient (pre-Internet) times, knowledge was a scarce resource, highly concentrated in the brains of experts and the pages of books. Most of the content in the world was not readily discoverable: You did not know, for instance, if your town had a knitting club, and it was not necessarily easy to find out. Simply finding potential vacation locations took enormous amounts of research, and many people would pay experts (travel agencies) just to be told what some of their options might be. In the pre-Internet era, diners had to brave restaurants without knowing the rest of the world's opinion of the place. In fact, even knowing that a restaurant existed at all could be difficult information to come about. In a lot of ways, the world before the Web was a rather opaque one.

Today, the power of the Web allows us to peruse and pursue any topic we might please. With a few clicks, we can discover facts about the sciences, culture, history, our cities and homes, and the world beyond. Other people's opinions, should we really want them, flow freely from fountains on the Internet. Thanks to powerful Internet search engines, encyclopedias, and forums, questions have answers like never before. The age of merely "wondering why" is over. Ask not for whom the bell tolls—you can look it up yourself.

The Internet began to open up the world, creating new communication channels, but there was one sore spot that remained unchanged. If you wanted to be contacted, you still had to stay put. New worlds of communication may have been opened with the Internet, but if you left your home, you dropped off the map. Once you began your road trip across the country, for instance, there was no way for someone to contact you to let you know you that you had forgotten your wallet.

The second great invention is the cell phone, which was in some ways more of a communication breakthrough than the Web. People became discoverable wherever they were. Plans no longer had to be finalized before leaving home, and people working or playing in the field became reachable. For the first time in human history, instead of the norm consisting of communication between two stationary endpoints manned by people, we have communication between two people. So spellbinding is this leap in communication that no teenager in the world has discovered that you do not have to answer your phone just because it rings.

Putting these two creations together has brought us the smartphone, one of the most incredible things we have in the world today. If you have a modern smartphone, odds are the device in your pocket is more powerful than the majority of the computers that have ever been owned. These devices provide instant portable access to the largest knowledge and communication infrastructure in the world. A rough approximation of the sum of human knowledge is literally carried along in our pockets. We can share, communicate, and learn from anywhere.

Now that we tend to carry massive information devices wherever we go, just where we are exactly happens to be more relevant to the websites we visit than ever before. The Geolocation application programming interface (API) represents more contextual breakthrough, extending our communication devices, mobile or not. It allows us to know more about and do more with our surroundings. This API enables Global Positioning System (GPS)—among other location techniques—in the browser, letting web pages do more with wherever we may be, so we can more easily see, share, and scratch the surface of the world that's right under our noses.

Although Geolocation is a very exciting technology to come to the browser, the API itself is rather small. The entirety of the data consists of obtaining a user's latitude and longitude, though the API can also offer speed, heading, and altitude when GPS is enabled. Although there aren't many attributes, the API is also incredibly simple, and if you have any reason to locate users, you should be using it.

Before we talk about the API itself, we cover a quick refresher on the latitude and longitude coordinate system, and then talk about the technical aspects of the different forms of location available. If you want to dive right in, feel free to skip these sections and turn straight to the "HTML5 Geolocation API" section.

Understanding Latitude and Longitude

The Geolocation API uses latitude and longitude to express locations. These two terms allow any point on Earth to be described by two angles, and in case you're unfamiliar with geographic coordinates, we detail them here. If you're confident in your understanding of latitude and longitude, feel free to skip this section.

The equator is an imaginary line that stretches from east to west through the "middle" of the Earth's sphere, halfway between the North and South Poles. Latitude is the angle north or south from the equator, so the equator acts as a reference line and is said to exist at zero degrees latitude. The North Pole and South Pole exist at 90 and −90 degrees latitude, respectively.

For longitude, we need a similar line that runs north to south (such lines are called meridians), but because there is no such thing as an east or west pole, we have no good reference point to use for a line. Because there is no natural reference, in the mid-1800s most countries settled on the common reference point of the Royal Observatory at Greenwich, in London. The line that runs north to south through this observatory is commonly called the *prime meridian*, and so the Royal Observatory in London rests at 0 degrees longitude.

Similarly to latitude, longitude is described with a positive angle when to the east of the prime meridian and a negative angle when to the west. In many places, instead of positive and negative, north and south or east and west are used to describe latitude and longitude, respectively. Because we intend to use these values computationally, the Geolocation API opts to use the positive and negative numbers.

Latitude only describes a degree on the top or bottom half of the Earth, so the largest values are 90 and −90 degrees, while longitude must go all the way around the Earth, making the largest values 180 and −180 degrees. This difference in total degrees is also apparent in maps, which are typically twice as wide (longitude) as they are tall (latitude).

Figure 9.1 shows the equator and prime meridian lines, giving an approximation of latitude and longitude values.

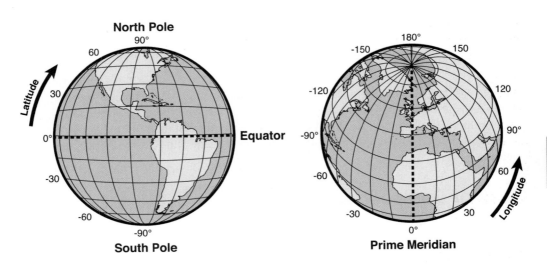

FIGURE 9.1 Latitude degrees relative to the equator, left, and longitude degrees relative to the prime meridian, right.

London is well north of the equator, located at about 51 degrees latitude. Because it houses the Royal Observatory that marks the prime meridian, it has a (roughly) zero-degree longitude.

Cape Town, for another example, is near the southern tip of Africa, well below the equator. Its location is said to be at –34 degrees latitude. It is located east of London at 18.4 degrees longitude.

The location where the equator and prime meridian meet gives us a latitude and longitude of zero. Figure 9.2 shows us where the two lines intersect on a map, somewhere off the coast of Africa. Because the prime meridian is arbitrary, the location at zero degrees latitude and longitude is just as arbitrary, and has no significance of its own.

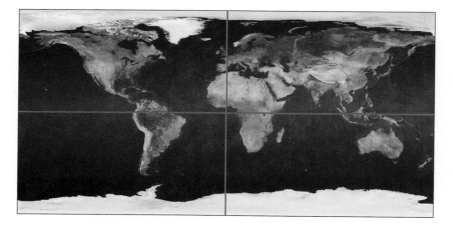

FIGURE 9.2   The equator and prime meridian, with their intersection pointing out the location at zero degrees latitude and longitude.

One degree of latitude or longitude is roughly 69 miles or 111 kilometers, so we can expect Geolocation results as well as services and APIs that use them to be in floating-point numbers. For instance, the front of New York's Empire State Building can be accurately described as located at 40.748076 degrees latitude and –73.984799 degrees longitude.

Types of Geolocation Data

Websites have sought user location data since the early days of the Web. Before the Geolocation API, we had only two realistic means of determining user location: IP addresses and asking the users themselves.

The Old Ways

Prior to Geolocation, there were two basic options for websites that wanted to obtain user location data.

IP Addresses

IP addresses are the original means of obtaining user location. Just as you cannot receive letters without giving out your (home) address, you cannot be served web pages without giving out an IP address, and so IP location has the advantage of always being available, even when the user has JavaScript disabled or is using a stone-age browser. Users can always browse through a proxy service in an attempt to spoof a location, which in Geolocation terms functions as a sort of virtual P.O. Box, but this is uncommon in typical Internet usage.

Unfortunately for website creators, just how well IP address location works varies intensely, and most common IP location is only accurate to the city level. In the smartphone age, IP addresses have become even less accurate, as mobile-phone IPs can be "located" in very different places than the actual users, sometimes several states away.

Further complicating matters, IP address location is typically processed server-side and almost always through a lookup service, most of which are not free. Nonetheless, it is still very popular where there is warranted utility or money to be made. Location-based advertising has been making heavy use of IP address Geolocation for years, and almost all large online advertising companies allow their clients the option of targeting ads locally, which usually means targeting through IP location.

User Entry

We have all come across websites that request our city or ZIP Code. Restaurant review sites, real-estate search engines, photo-sharing, or any site that intends to ship you a product will ask for some level of address detail.

Although this is considered an old way of locating users, manual entry is often a good option regardless of your use of Geolocation. Even if your app can take advantage of Geolocation, you should be careful to consider that your users might legitimately want to use the site at locations other than their own. An app that finds restaurants nearby, for instance, would be less useful if a user cannot also enter in a location that they might be traveling to soon, in order to look it up ahead of time.

On the other hand, manual entry can be considered bothersome by the user, and is no good if your user doesn't actually know where he or she is!

The HTML5 Way—New Methods for Geolocation

Geolocation offers us three new methods, presented next, from least accurate to most accurate. Although all three are used in Geolocation, the details of the methodology are hidden from both the user and the programmer. The Geolocation API simply always uses whatever methods are available. An exception is made for GPS because it drains battery life disproportionately to the others and, therefore, must be enabled via setting an optional attribute.

The relative accuracy differences between these three methods are discussed further and expressed visually in the API examples.

Cellular Networks

Cell phone networks are the broadest locator in the new Geolocation API. This method works by triangulating a user's position based on whatever towers might be nearby. Although this works rather quickly, the accuracy of the location provided can vary by several thousand meters, and not all devices (tablets, laptops, and desktops) have cellular capability.

Wi-Fi

Wi-Fi Geolocation is one of the most novel and astonishing location technologies, made possible only by the lengthy hustle of a few large companies.

Every Wi-Fi providing device has a unique identifier, called a MAC address, which is assigned to the hardware by its manufacturer. When a computer searches for Wi-Fi signals, it receives this address along with signal strength and the name (sometimes called SSID, service set identifier) of the access point.

Because this information is public and broadcasted by all Wi-Fi access points (both public and private), companies such as Google have sought to collect their locations. While Google's Street View cars were out taking pictures of vast numbers of roads, they were simultaneously mapping all the MAC addresses they could find to their coordinates in the world.

Google and Skyhook Wireless have both mapped MAC addresses like this and sell their location services to browsers such as Firefox and Safari, respectively. When using a browser that determines Geolocation with Wi-Fi, all nearby network MAC addresses and their associated signal strengths are sent to the browser (Chrome, Firefox, Safari, etc.), which then uses the Google Location Services or Skyhook database to determine where you might be relative to all the last known locations of Wi-Fi MAC addresses and their signal strengths.

In populated areas, this can be vastly more accurate than cellular triangulation, with meter accuracy measured between around 20 and 200.

GPS Coordinates

GPS is the flagship of Geolocation. It is extremely accurate and more informational than the other methods: Speed, heading, and altitude are available through the Geolocation API if you are connected with GPS.

On the other hand, GPS can take a long time to connect and drains the battery of mobile devices at a much faster rate. Because of this, requesting GPS is an optional attribute in the Geolocation API, defaulting to false. Some thought should be given to enabling it, as apps that merely need the vicinity of the user do not need the power or the potentially long wait time of a GPS signal.

HTML5 Geolocation API

The Geolocation API enables you to query the user for location data. If the user accepts the request, you can gather the user's location, either once or continuously as the user moves.

Geolocation Support

The Geolocation API enjoys wide support in all modern desktop and mobile browsers, though the browsers may go about Geolocation in different ways. For instance, some may be unable to locate via Wi-Fi.

Older browsers such as Internet Explorer 8 can enjoy some support by using a polyfill/ fallback library such as the popular Webshims Library (http://github.com/aFarkas/ webshim). Most polyfills make use of more antiquated IP-address only techniques of determining location, and their accuracy is generally incomparable to the Geolocation API.

Using Geolocation

Before we get into the details, let's take a peek at the minimum JavaScript needed to discover a user's location:

```
navigator.geolocation.getCurrentPosition(function(pos) {
  console.log("My latitude is " + pos.coords.latitude);
  console.log("My longitude is " + pos.coords.longitude);
  console.log("Accurate to " + pos.coords.accuracy + " meters");
});
```

This basic example produces the console output:

```
My latitude is 39.028094
My longitude is 125.775034
Accurate to 58 meters
```

And there we are. (Well, maybe not. That's North Korea.)

This tiny example encompasses the most common parts of the API. Three numbers may not seem like much, but they open up myriad use cases. Using latitude and longitude, we can find points of interest near our user, show his or her position on a map, develop turn-by-turn navigation, create a hyperlocal news site, make location-tagged posts in blogs and social websites, allow our user to generate his or her own paths or track his or her travel progress, and so on.

The API

The entire Geolocation API consists of just a few methods and their associated objects and properties.

As you saw in the "Using Geolocation" section, `navigator.geolocation` is where it all begins. From there, we have three functions:

▶ `getCurrentPosition(successCallback, [errorCallback, positionOptions])`

▶ `watchPosition(successCallback, [errorCallback, positionOptions])`

▶ `clearWatch(watchId)`

The `getCurrentPosition` and `watchPosition` methods asynchronously attempt to obtain the current location of the client's device. If successful, the first argument, `successCallback`, defines a function to be called. This function is called with a new `Position` object as its argument, which contains all the location data that could be obtained. The second and third arguments are optional.

Success and the `Position` Object

The argument passed to the success callback function is a JavaScript object with two attributes: `timestamp`, representing when the position was acquired, and `coords`, a nested object containing all the geographic information.

The `timestamp` is expressed in milliseconds since the Unix Epoch, which is the amount of time in milliseconds that has elapsed since midnight UTC, January 1, 1970. This is a very common way of representing time, and the JavaScript's built in `Date` object takes such a time stamp as an argument. If you'd prefer to work with JavaScript `Date` objects instead, you can simply convert the time stamp by providing it to the `Date` constructor:

```
var d = new Date(position.timestamp);
```

This `coords` JavaScript object is where the crux of the Geolocation API lies. It has seven numerical attributes of its own. Three of them are essential, and are always supplied:

- ▶ `latitude`
- ▶ `longitude`
- ▶ `accuracy`

The `latitude` and `longitude` attributes are the user's coordinates, expressed as either positive or negative degrees, and the `accuracy` attribute denotes the accuracy of these coordinates, expressed in meters. All three of these attributes were used in the previous example in the "Using Geolocation" section.

The four nonessential attributes in the `coords` object are supplied in only some browsers and devices and under only some circumstances, such as having an active GPS. They are as follows:

- ▶ `altitude`
- ▶ `altitudeAccuracy`
- ▶ `speed`
- ▶ `heading`

The `altitude` attribute specifies a height above the location in meters, and `altitudeAccuracy` expresses the accuracy of that measurement, also in meters. These values are `null` if the information cannot be supplied.

The `speed` attribute denotes the speed of the user (or user's device) and is specified in meters per second. This value is `null` if the information cannot be supplied or else it is a nonnegative number.

The `heading` attribute describes the direction of travel, if any, as a degree relative to true north. This means that a value of 0 means zero degrees, or a northward heading, and a value of 90 (degrees) means eastward, or a value of 135 (degrees) means a south-eastward heading. This value is `null` if the information cannot be supplied, but is `NaN` if the value can be supplied but there is currently no speed (therefore, the user is not "heading" in any particular direction).

Failure and the `PositionError` Object

The second argument to `getCurrentPosition` and `watchPosition` is an optional function to be called if the Geolocation request fails. This function is supplied with one argument, a `PositionError` object.

This object has two attributes: `code`, which is a number between one and three, and `message`, which is a human-readable description of each code. The possible codes and their meanings are as follows:

▶ **1**—Permission to use Geolocation was denied.

▶ **2**—The position of the device could not be determined.

▶ **3**—The Geolocation operation timed out.

The text messages from the `message` not only differ between browsers, they are not implemented in some of them (such as Firefox as of this writing). For instance, Chrome's `message` for a `code` of 1 is "User denied Geolocation" (with no period), while Internet Explorer's is "This site does not have permission to use the Geolocation API." (with a period). For consistency's sake, it is best to implement messages yourself using the codes.

> **NOTE**
>
> As of this writing, the error callback is not necessarily called if the user denies a request for Geolocation. For instance, in Firefox, three options exist: "Always share location," "Never share location," and "Not now." If the user elects to never share the location, the error callback function is called with a `code` of 1, but if the user selects "Not now," then the error function is simply not called.

6

Position Options

The third argument to `getCurrentPosition` and `watchPosition` is an optional JavaScript Object with three attributes:

▶ `enableHighAccuracy`—A Boolean value, defaults to `false` if not specified.

▶ `timeout`—A numerical value denoting the maximum length of time (in milliseconds) that is allowed to pass before `getCurrentPosition` or `watchPosition` call the error callback method instead of continuing the attempt to determine location. If not specified, the `timeout` value is `Infinity`.

▶ **maximumAge**—A numerical value indicating how long (in milliseconds) a cached location value is acceptable as a response. If the `maximumAge` is zero, the location functions immediately attempt to acquire a new user location. If the `maximumAge` is `Infinity`, the function always returns a cached location if one exists. The default value is zero.

Enabling high accuracy should not be done lightly. Many applications, such as those showing points of interest in a surrounding area, do not need to know precisely where the user is located. Setting `enableHighAccuracy` to true turns on the GPS (or other high-powered Geolocation providers) in devices that have the technology and allow them to be enabled, which often has a slower initial response than lower accuracy methods while also draining the battery life faster.

The attributes are all optional, so we may specify only the ones we need to change from the defaults. If all the defaults are acceptable, we can omit the third argument to `getCurrentPosition` and `watchPosition` altogether.

> **NOTE**
>
> Time spent obtaining user permission is not included in the time period covered by the `timeout` attribute, only real time attempting to determine location is counted.

Watching and Unwatching

The `getCurrentPosition` and `watchPosition` methods work nearly identically, except that `getCurrentPosition` only fires its success callback once. The `watchPosition` method, on the other hand, fires its success callback and then continuously monitors for position changes, firing the success callback again every time there is a change.

We might not want to watch for position changes indefinitely, so the `watchPosition` function works similarly to JavaScript's `setInterval`. It returns an identifier that you can use with a companion function, `clearWatch` (analogous to `clearInterval` in the case of `setInterval`) that takes the ID as an argument to stop the continuous monitoring of a particular `watchPosition` call. Typical usage might look like the following:

```
var myID = null;

// save the ID and start watching for location changes
function startWatching() {
  myID = navigator.geolocation.watchPosition(successCallback, errorCallback);
}
```

```
// Use a saved ID (if any) to stop watching for location changes
function stopWatching() {
  if (myID === null) return; // no watch started
  navigator.geolocation.clearWatch(myID);
}
```

Like with `setInterval`, it is common to use `watchPosition` and have no need for ever stopping. If you are enabling high accuracy, however, then you may want to stop watching if there comes a time when the app's Geolocation functionality is obviously not in use, so that you do not needlessly drain your users' batteries.

> **NOTE**
>
> Although `watchPosition` fires the success callback function on every position change, it only fires the error callback function once if something goes wrong.

Geolocation Reference

Because the Geolocation API isn't very large, we can construct a code snippet that mentions every single item in the API to use as a quick syntax reference. Listing 9.1 contains such a snippet. The code is only meant as a reference; it does not carry out any function, but you can use it as a starting template for writing your own Geolocation functions.

LISTING 9.1   A Reference Template for the Geolocation API

```
// A nonfunctioning example showing the location
// of every attribute in the API

// The function called if getCurrentPosition is successful
function successCallback(position) {
  // millisecond timestamp
  position.timestamp;

  // every attribute of position.coords is a number

  // The three reliable coords attributes
  position.coords.latitude;
  position.coords.longitude;
  position.coords.accuracy;

  // The four optional coords attributes
  position.coords.altitude;
  position.coords.altitudeAccuracy;
```

```
    position.coords.speed;
    position.coords.heading;
}

// A function that fires if something goes wrong
// The single argument is a JavaScript Object containing
// an error code (code) and a reason (message)
function errorCallback(positionError) {
    positionError.code;       // 1 to 3, inclusive
    positionError.message;    // error message string
}

// identical in syntax to navigator.geolocation.getCurrentPosition
// except watchPosition returns an id, and getCurrentPosition returns nothing
var myID = navigator.geolocation.watchPosition(
    // required first argument, a success function with one arg
    successCallback,
    // optional second argument, an error function with one arg
    errorCallback,
    // optional third argument, an Object of optional attributes
    // each attribute itself is also optional,
    // here are sample nondefault values:
    { enableHighAccuracy: true,    // true might enable GPS, default false
      timeout:    6000,            // 6 seconds, default Infinity
      maximumAge: 90000            // 90 seconds, default 0
    });

// stops watchPosition from continuously checking for location changes
// and firing the successCallback
navigator.geolocation.clearWatch(myID);
```

Geolocation in Action

Now that we have a grasp on the API, we are ready to see some practical examples.

Where Am I?

With the Geolocation API, we can make a simple web page that displays our current location on a map. Because creating a good map from scratch is a nontrivial exercise, we use the popular Google Maps API. This API conveniently allows us to bring up a map and place markers on that map at any latitude and longitude we please, so it makes a good fit for making use of the Geolocation data right away.

We'll author an HTML page, but for simplicity's sake it contains nothing but two script tags. The first tag is a link to the Google Maps API. The second tag contains a Geolocation request, a success function, and an error function.

We start with a call to `navigator.geolocation.getCurrentPosition`, but instead of just blindly calling the method, we should test to ensure the Geolocation API is supported in the user's browser:

```
// We should be accommodating to all users and always test for support
if (navigator.geolocation) {
  navigator.geolocation.getCurrentPosition(
    successCallback,
    errorCallback,
    // uncommenting this would enable GPS in GPS-capable devices
    //{ enableHighAccuracy: true }
  );
} else {
  document.write('HTML5 Geolocation is not supported in your browser!');
}
```

Before we can use this bit of code, we need to define the `successCallback` and `errorCallback` functions that it is referencing. We need our `successCallback` function to create a map and add it to the page. Then, we use the Geolocation data to center the map and place a marker at the precise location that the Geolocation API returned. Additionally, we use the `accuracy` attribute to create a radius around our marker, giving the user a visual for how accurate the data might be.

The `errorCallback` is smaller. We simply add a message to the page based on whichever error code was returned.

This makes for everything we need to display our own location and approximate accuracy on a map. The complete source for the demo is shown in Listing 9.2.

LISTING 9.2   `geo.html`—A Geolocation Example

```
<!--
Super Simple Geolocation
This is an HTML file, but to keep it small and flat
we don't declare a doctype, html, or body elements!
Instead we just have two script tags, and we'll
insert content into the DOM as we need it.
-->

<script type="text/javascript"
        src="http://maps.google.com/maps/api/js?sensor=false"></script>
<script type="text/javascript">

// A function that gets called if getCurrentPosition is successful
function successCallback(position) {
  // Create a div to use as the Google Map's container
  var myMap = document.createElement('div');
```

```
  myMap.style.width = '640px';
  myMap.style.height = '480px';
  document.body.appendChild(myMap);

  // The coordinates from our position argument are used to make
  // a LatLng object for interaction with the Google Maps API
  var myCoords = new google.maps.LatLng(
    position.coords.latitude,
    position.coords.longitude);

  // We create the map by specifying a Div and a set of options
  // Note that we center the map on our latitude and longitude
  var map = new google.maps.Map(
    myMap,
    { zoom: 15,
      center: myCoords,
      mapTypeId: google.maps.MapTypeId.ROADMAP
    });

  // Add marker to map at our coordinate
  var marker = new google.maps.Marker({
      position: myCoords,
      map: map
  });

  // Add circle describing accuracy radius
  var accuracyRadius = new google.maps.Circle({
    map: map,
    radius: position.coords.accuracy,
    fillColor: '#00AA00'
  });

  // Connect the circle's position to the marker's position
  accuracyRadius.bindTo('center', marker, 'position');
}


// A function that gets called if getCurrentPosition fails
function errorCallback(positionError) {
  // Not all browsers have positionError.message defined
  // So we'll make custom messages for each code
  var msg = {
    1: 'Permission to use Geolocation was denied!',
    2: 'The position of the device could not be determined!',
    3: 'The operation has timed out!'
  }
  document.write(msg[positionError.code]);
```

```
}

// We should be accommodating to all users and always test for support
if (navigator.geolocation) {
  navigator.geolocation.getCurrentPosition(
    successCallback,
    errorCallback
    // uncommenting this would enable GPS in GPS-capable devices:
    //, { enableHighAccuracy: true }
  );
} else {
  document.write('HTML5 Geolocation is not supported in your browser!');
}
</script>
```

Although the `successCallback` function isn't tiny, its contents are almost exclusively set up for the `Map` object. The entire interaction with Geolocation is solely the use of `position.coords.latitude` and `position.coords.longitude` for making the `LatLng` Google Maps API object, and `position.coords.accuracy` for defining the circle's radius.

The effect we see when we run this depends on what the Geolocation API is using to determine our position. A cell network ought to give us the largest radius, and we could expect to see output on a cell phone similar to Figure 9.3.

FIGURE 9.3   I am sitting in the Nashua River, give or take 2,000 meters.

As we covered in the "Types of Geolocation Data" section, Wi-Fi should give us a much more accurate picture, such as that shown in Figure 9.4.

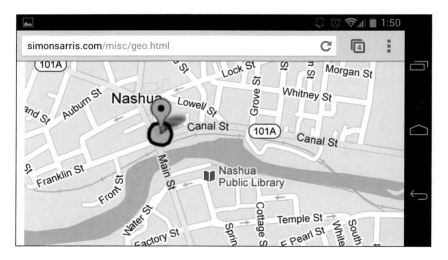

FIGURE 9.4   Wi-Fi data gives us a much better accuracy, 36 meters in this case.

Finally, if we uncomment the third argument to `getCurrentPosition`, GPS ought to give us the most accurate results, and we would see a much smaller circle, as shown in Figure 9.5.

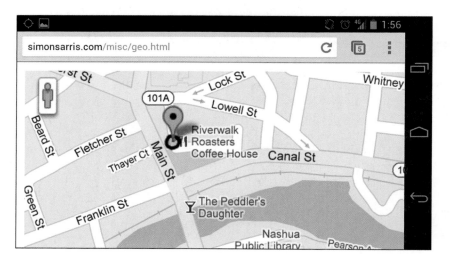

FIGURE 9.5   GPS positions me at the corner of the Riverwalk Roasters Coffee House, with an accuracy at last of 10 meters.

We can see that not all location methods are created equal. However, other than inferring from the accuracy value or deliberately turning off Wi-Fi, cell networks, or GPS, we have no way of determining which method was used to gather our location on any given callback from `getCurrentPosition` or `watchPosition`. Because of this, we must be careful when handling the data to reject any measurement that is too inaccurate for our uses.

A Trailblazing App

Next, let's see an example that demonstrates a more practical purpose. We'll locate ourselves on a map, and then continuously monitor our position, drawing a line connecting each new position that's been collected.

The result will be a web app that lets us see our progress on a map as we travel. Users could use this app to map out trails in the woods or other places where drawing a trail on a map is only feasible by actually being there, so we'll call it a trailblazing app.

The fundamentals of this app with respect to the Geolocation API don't change much. Instead of getting our position (and calling the `successCallback` function) once, we want to get it continuously. This means that we must change our Geolocation call from `getCurrentLocation` to `watchPosition`. We also absolutely need accurate positioning, so our third argument to `watchPosition` consists of an object with `enableHighAccuracy` set to `true`.

This time, we display some data alongside our map, so we create a div element for the map and another div to contain some information about our position that gets updated constantly. This informational div contains our starting location, our current location, how many times our location has been updated, and the accuracy of the last update. This information isn't critical, and if we were to display it in a production app, we might want to do it in a prettier fashion, but it gives the user enough information to know that the sample app is working, and just how well.

Listing 9.3 shows the DOM content needed for our app.

LISTING 9.3   DOM for Our Trailblazing App

```
<div id="myMap">
<!-- populated by Google Maps API -->
</div>
<!-- Some page information
     so we can be sure our app is working while we're using it -->
<div id="infoBox">
  <p> Starting Location: <span id="myStartLoc"></span> </p>
  <p> Current Location:  <span id="myCurrentLoc"></span> </p>
  <p> Locations Changed: <span id="myLocCount"></span> times.</p>
  <p> Last Accuracy:     <span id="myAccuracy"></span> meters.</p>
</div>
```

Because our `successCallback` function will be called constantly, there are a few pieces of state we need to be sure to remember. We want to know if it is the first time locating our user or not because map initialization and setting the starting location should only happen once, so we have a `firstTime` Boolean variable to do just that. We also want to keep an array of coordinates (myCoordList) that we add to each time we get a new location, and we want to save a reference to the map object (myGMap) and the Maps API Polyline object (myTrail) that we use to draw the path.

The process is fairly straightforward. First, we immediately throw away any coordinate data with an accuracy rating of more than 40 meters. Our GPS could lose signal for a moment, and this ensures that we don't insert a point from cellular triangulation into our trail, which may be extremely inaccurate and possibly located thousands of meters away.

If the data is accurate, we use our newest coordinates to make a Maps API LatLng object and save it into our array (myCoordList). If this is the first time, we initialize the map, place a starting marker, and start our Polyline object.

Finally, there are a few things we do every time a new position is found. We set the Polyline path to be equal to our updated points list, and update the rest of the informational DOM elements. The map automatically updates itself to reflect the latest Polyline.

This describes the mechanics of the web app. All that remains is some styling to make it look a little cleaner (though certainly not production worthy) and some simple error handling in the case of unsuccessful Geolocation, denied permission, or lack of support.

Listing 9.4 has the complete HTML page necessary for our app.

LISTING 9.4   trailBlaze.html—A Web App for Recording User Position as the User Moves

```
<!DOCTYPE html>
<html>
<head>
  <style>
    #myMap {
      border: 2px solid black;
      width: 640px;
      height: 480px;
    }

    #infoBox {
      border: 2px solid black;
      padding: 10px;
      margin: 10px;
    }

    p {
      font: 13px Monospace;
    }

    span {
      color: #0000CC;
    }
  </style>
```

```
</head>
<body>

<div id="myMap">
<!-- populated by Google Maps API -->
</div>
<!-- Some page information
     so we can be sure our app is working while we're using it -->
<div id="infoBox">
  <p> Starting Location: <span id="myStartLoc"></span> </p>
  <p> Current Location:  <span id="myCurrentLoc"></span> </p>
  <p> Locations Changed: <span id="myLocCount"></span> times.</p>
  <p> Last Accuracy:     <span id="myAccuracy"></span> meters.</p>
</div>

<script type="text/javascript"
        src="http://maps.google.com/maps/api/js?sensor=false"></script>
<script>

var first       = true, // set to false after the first location
    myCoordList = [],    // list of recorded locations
    myGMap      = null, // reference to our map
    myTrail     = null; // reference to the polyline that describes our trail
    // HTML elements:
    myMap         = document.getElementById('myMap'),
    myStartLoc    = document.getElementById('myStartLoc'),
    myCurrentLoc  = document.getElementById('myCurrentLoc'),
    myLocCount    = document.getElementById('myLocCount'),
    myAccuracy    = document.getElementById('myAccuracy');

// A function that gets called if getCurrentPosition is successful
function successCallback(position) {
  // If we accidentally lose GPS signal for a moment
  // we don't want a wild line sticking out in the middle of our trail
  // So we throw away any recording greater than 40 meters as junk.
  // We could probably make this value even smaller!
  if (position.coords.accuracy > 40) return;

  var myLat = position.coords.latitude,
      myLong = position.coords.longitude;

  // The coordinates from our position argument are used to make
  // a LatLng object for interaction with the Google Maps API
  var myCoords = new google.maps.LatLng(myLat, myLong);
  myCoordList.push(myCoords);
```

```
  // We have a lot of one-time stuff to do on the first Geolocation success
  if (first) {
    first = false;
    myStartLoc.innerHTML = myLat + ', ' + myLong;

    // The first time around, we initialize a map
    myGMap = new google.maps.Map(
      myMap,
      { zoom: 17,
        center: myCoords,
        mapTypeId: google.maps.MapTypeId.ROADMAP });

    // Add marker to map at our coordinate
    var marker = new google.maps.Marker({
        position: myCoords,
        map: myGMap });

    // Initialize a trail the first time
    myTrail = new google.maps.Polyline({
        strokeColor: "#FF0000",
        strokeOpacity: 1.0,
        strokeWeight: 2
      });
    myTrail.setMap(myGMap);
  }

  // Update our info box every time:
  myCurrentLoc.innerHTML = myLat + ', ' + myLong;
  myLocCount.innerHTML = myCoordList.length;
  myAccuracy.innerHTML = position.coords.accuracy;

  // Set the updated path of the trail (polyline) every time:
  myTrail.setPath(myCoordList);
}

// If watchPosition fails
function errorCallback(positionError) {
  var msg = {
    1: 'Permission to use Geolocation was denied!',
    2: 'The position of the device could not be determined!',
    3: 'The operation has timed out!'
  }
  // For conciseness only we're using an alert for errors
  // In a production app we should make something nicer and less jarring
  alert(msg[positionError.code]);
```

```
  }

  // We should be accommodating to all users and always test for support
  if (navigator.geolocation) {
    navigator.geolocation.watchPosition(
      successCallback,
      errorCallback,
      { enableHighAccuracy: true });
  } else {
    // For conciseness only we're using an alert for errors
    // In a production app we should make something nicer and less jarring
    alert('Sorry! The Geolocation API is not supported in your browser.')
  }

</script>

</body>
</html>
```

Loading the web page, we can walk around with a GPS-enabled device and watch as our path plays out on the map in real time. Because we only initialize the map on the first successful positioning, we might not see anything for a while. In a production app, we would want to fill the map div element with some informative note until it loads.

Once we've acquired GPS, we should expect the page to update regularly, about every second on most devices. Figure 9.6 shows what the app looks like after walking around for some time.

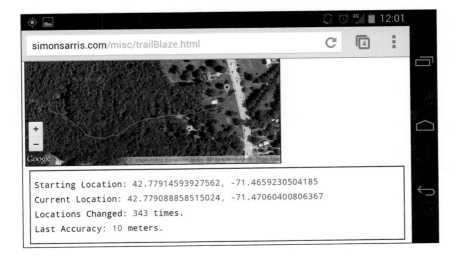

FIGURE 9.6 A screenshot of the `trailBlaze.html` page in action.

If we comment out the accuracy restriction and reload the page, we would see why it is so important. Instead of a relatively smooth, continuous path, we would find jarring lines interspersed in our trail, as minor blips in GPS may revert to cellular positioning. Figure 9.7 shows what the app looks like without an accuracy restriction.

FIGURE 9.7   Turning off the accuracy restriction, we occasionally receive cellular location data instead of GPS, confounding our path.

It wouldn't take much to turn this example into a full-fledged, useful website. We would want a way for users to save our maps, perhaps to load later or share with others. We could perhaps add a compass using the Geolocation's `heading` attribute that points in our current walking or driving direction. After that, all we need is more styling and presenting the map and data in a clean and appropriate fashion, and more production-worthy responses to errors.

NOTE

This web app and pages like it face some issues that native apps do not. Even with all the new tools and toys that HTML5 affords, we do not have a way to request or force the user's device to stay awake, or request that our web app run in the background. On most devices, sleeping or losing focus of the app means shutting down the GPS and therefore losing all of our utility. If we were to make this into a real web app, we would need to warn the user of such, perhaps suggesting that the user enable whatever option on his or her phone allows it to continue the longest without sleeping or deactivating the GPS.

Summary

The simplicity of the Geolocation API is one of its greatest assets, and thanks to the foot-work of Wi-Fi mapping companies, even non-GPS devices can enjoy a useful amount of accuracy. Locating users, especially the ones who do not know where they are themselves, has never been easier.

As with almost all of HTML5, the Geolocation API should be thought of as an optional extra. Unless your app explicitly rests on functionality only possible with the Geolocation API, you should allow your users the option of setting their own locations because they may not have Geolocation, may deny permission, or may simply want to use your app at another location.

CHAPTER 10

HTML5 Storage Options

Persistent local storage has long been a wish of web developers, and it has traditionally represented one of the big plusses for desktop or native applications over web applications. For much of the Web's history, there was no surefire way to store a large amount of data on the client, though many have tried to remedy this with various technologies. We begin this chapter with an overview of the older technologies, and continue on to the newer options available in the HTML5 era.

Older Storage Methods

The need in HTML for new specifications that allow native, persistent local storage existed because there was no browser-only solution that afforded more than a few kilobytes of space. We briefly cover the historical methods and their drawbacks.

Browser Cookies

Browser cookies have been around for quite some time and were first to be used for local storage. Cookies are typically used for authentication or tracking, and have serious drawbacks when used for storage. They must be included in every page request, a needless task with respect to mere storage, and they aren't particularly large, about 4KB.

There are also security concerns with the use of cookies in some situations, particularly over unencrypted Hypertext Transfer Protocol (HTTP) sessions over open Wi-Fi. Because browser cookies are passed around with each server request, they are susceptible to eavesdropping and cookie theft.

Flash Cookies

Adobe Flash allows programmers to create and store Local Shared Objects, commonly known as Flash cookies (or occasionally Flash Local Storage), which provide some serious benefits over cookies. These aren't cookies at all, though they sometimes fill similar roles, as they do not need to be continuously sent to and from the server.

Flash cookies are typically used for storing user preferences, saving game progress, or tracking users. They can store a fair bit more than cookies, about 100KB. Unlike regular cookies, Flash cookies take "cross-platform" to a whole new level: Flash cookies accessed or created in one browser are *accessible* in entirely different browsers. Some find this convenient when Flash is storing tool preferences or game data. Others find it unnerving, specifically when done with advertising data.

Flash, like many third-party plug-ins, comes with its own stability, privacy, and security concerns. Flash cookies in particular have given rise to privacy issues over the years because they can be used as more powerful cookies, acting as cookie backups and even restoring real cookies when they are deleted. Their power has also caused some ire as many users (understandably) do not want to be tracked.

userData

Microsoft created an alternative called the `userData` behavior that allowed small amounts of text data to be stored. This remained specific to Internet Explorer, which has since adopted more modern methods, starting with Internet Explorer 8.

The `userData` object allowed programmers to store up to 1MB of text data per domain. If supporting Internet Explorer 6 and 7 is necessary for your page (bless your soul), it may be worth looking into this as an alternative. There are a few polyfills out there that use this object as an Internet Explorer–specific fallback, such as `textStorage.js` (https://gist.github.com/1221115, note the comment below the file).

Along the Way

Various other plug-ins or shims filled the void along the way to local storage. The Google Gears browser extension, which could store unlimited amounts of data (with user permission), was popular for several years, but has since been superseded by HTML5, and is no longer bundled with Chrome or supported on modern browsers. Some individuals created libraries to pull together whatever options might be available on any given platform, but none of them allowed for the main wishes of many developers for a large amount of persistent storage using browser-only technologies.

As of about mid-2010, developers were able to get their hands on at least a few new options that work in every browser. Nowadays developers have several options (though not all of them are universally implemented), fulfilling different roles, and the rest of this chapter details the different application programming interfaces (APIs) now available.

Web Storage—`sessionStorage` **and** `localStorage`

Web Storage is an API that describes a very simple key-value pair store for persisting data on the client. The API isn't particularly powerful, but it fulfills a few roles well and its ease of use makes it a popular option. The Web Storage API is already widely supported, implemented in every major desktop browser and every major mobile browser.

With Web Storage, the specification recommends a limit of 5MB per origin (domain or subdomain), which far surpasses the older storage methods. Browsers are free to increase this limit, though some may use dialog boxes asking user permission if more storage is needed.

Web Storage is broken down into two similar parts with different goals, `sessionStorage` and `localStorage`.

> **NOTE**
>
> The Web Storage API specification can be found at http://www.w3.org/TR/webstorage/.

`sessionStorage`

The goal of session storage is to maintain somewhat ephemeral storage over the life of a single page session. This means that reloading or restoring the page does not clear the storage, but opening a new page (for instance, in a new tab) creates a new session. Page navigation within the same domain (for instance, creating session storage on example.com/page1 and navigating to example.com/page2) also maintains the session storage. For security reasons, session storage does not cross (sub-) domains.

More succinctly, session storage is storage accessible to any page from the same website opened in the same window.

> **NOTE**
>
> If you are on example.com and have some session storage set, and then navigate to w3.org, that session storage will be unavailable but not *gone*. If (in the same window and tab) you click the Back button or navigate from w3.org back to any page on example.com, you'll find that your session storage is safe and sound.

Limiting session storage to a single page has a few benefits that cookies alone do not handle well. For instance, shopping on a website with two tabs open may lead to actions on one of the pages to "leak" onto the other. Session storage allows scenarios where a designer wants to allow users to carry out multiple transactions in separate windows without having saved information in one affect the other.

Security itself is one of the most underrated benefits of session storage. No cookies have to be passed to and from servers. Nothing leaks from tab to tab. When the tab is closed, the storage is gone, but if it's closed accidentally (such as during a browser crash) and restored, it's still there for you should you need it.

`localStorage`

Local storage, unlike session storage, persists across all sessions on an entire origin, though like session storage, it is tied to just one origin.

This means that any local storage set on any page of Wikipedia is accessible on any other page of Wikipedia, even in different tabs and even if the page or browser is closed and reopened later. Cross-origin rules do draw the line at subdomains though, so local storage set on the English subdomain en.wikipedia.org will not be available or visible on the French subdomain fr.wikipedia.org.

> **NOTE**
>
> For a page to be considered the *same origin* as another page, the ports, protocols, and subdomains must all match. This means that local storage set on http://example.com will not be available on https://example.com because one is using HTTP and the other is using HTTPS (Hypertext Transfer Protocol Secure) as the protocol.

API

Local storage and session storage are implemented right on `window` as the `window.localStorage` and `window.sessionStorage` object. Although they differ slightly in function, they share the same API. We use `sessionStorage` in the API examples, but all code examples in this section work identically with `localStorage`.

The two most important methods on our storage objects are as follows:

- ▶ `setItem(key, value)`—Creates a new key-value pair (or overwrites an existing one) on the `sessionStorage` object

- ▶ `getItem(key)`—Gets a value for the given key, or `null` if there is no key

Usage is straightforward:

```
sessionStorage.setItem('super-power', 'flight');
sessionStorage.getItem('super-power'); // returns 'flight'
```

In fact, instead of using the methods, we can get and set right on the `sessionStorage` object as a shorthand:

```
sessionStorage['super-power'] = 'flight';
sessionStorage['super-power']; // returns 'flight'
```

Or mix both methods together. One slight difference: `getItem` returns `null` if there is no key, and using the shorthand returns `undefined`.

> **NOTE**
>
> As mentioned earlier in the chapter, the specification recommends that browsers only allow 5MB of storage per origin, and it's possible for `setItem` to throw a `QuotaExceededError` exception if this limit is reached.

Session storage has three more methods:

- ► `removeItem(key)`—Deletes a given key
- ► `clear()`—Deletes all session storage
- ► `key(position)`—Returns a key at the given position, or `null` if the given number is greater than or equal to the number of keys

Some usage examples (these can be tried right in the developer tools console):

```
sessionStorage['super-power'] = 'flight';
sessionStorage['cape'] = 'you bet';
sessionStorage['tights'] = 'for sure';
sessionStorage.removeItem('super-power');
console.log(sessionStorage['super-power']); // logs: undefined

var length = sessionStorage.length;
for (var i = 0; i < length; i++) {
  // logs: 'cape' and 'tights' keys, since 'super-power' has been removed
  console.log(sessionStorage.key(i));
}

sessionStorage.clear();
console.log(sessionStorage.length); // logs: 0
```

Storage Event

The specification also defines a storage event on `document` that fires whenever `localStorage` changes on any page except the current page. This event is useful when you have small pop-up windows that carry out functions that need to save and update the main window. The event's name is simply `'storage'`:

```
// Only fires when storage is modified in other tabs/windows!
document.addEventListener('storage', function(event) {
  // do something with
  // event.key, event.oldValue event.newValue
  // event.url, and event.storageArea
}, false);
```

10

It's a common point of confusion that this event does *not* fire on the page where `localStorage` is modified. So adding this event to three pages (A, B, and C) and modifying `localStorage` in tab A fires this event in tabs B and C.

The storage event contains additional information:

▶ `event.key`—The key that was modified

▶ `event.oldValue`—The old value of the key being modified, or `null` if it was a new key

▶ `event.newValue`—The new value of the key being modified

▶ `event.url`—The uniform resource locator (URL) of the page that changed the `localStorage`

▶ `event.storageArea`—A reference to the `Storage` object being modified

If `localStorage.clear()` is called, `key`, `oldValue`, and `newValue` will all be `null`.

Debugging Web Storage

It's easy enough to iterate through all of Web Storage, but some browsers also offer an additional visual inspector of local and session storage, which can come in handy if you want a live visualization of what's in storage without resorting to writing your own debug code or console commands.

Webkit-based browsers (Chrome and Safari) use the Webkit inspector panel for Web Storage, as shown in Figure 10.1. Opera has a similar panel, shown in Figure 10.2. These interfaces also allow you to edit or update records on the fly.

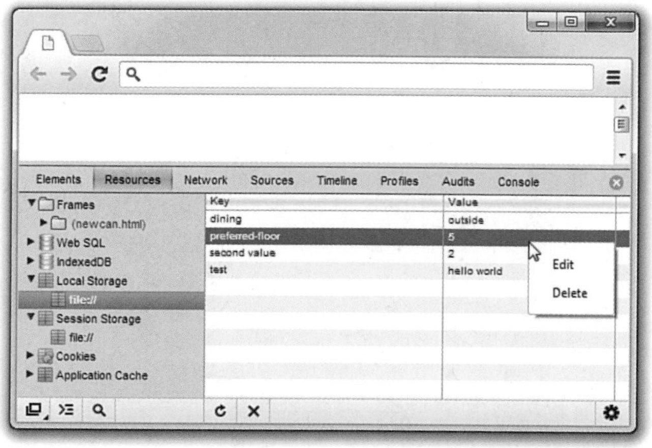

FIGURE 10.1   Web Storage debug screen in Chrome.

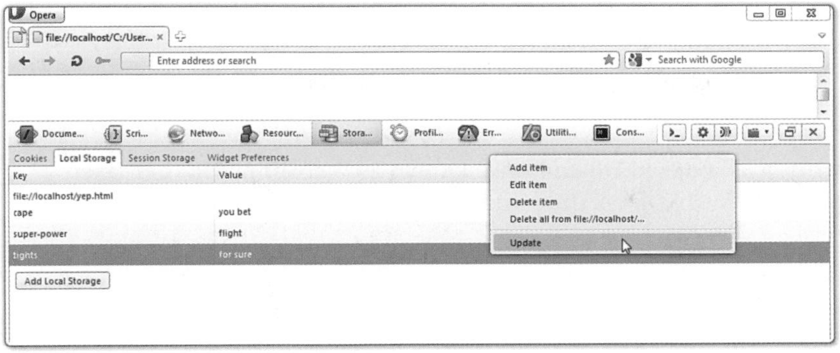

FIGURE 10.2   Web Storage debug screen in Opera.

WebSQL Database

WebSQL has a big subsection header in this chapter because it was previously considered a large up-and-coming part of HTML5. An API for local data storage using a SQL derivative (like SQLite) would be a powerful thing, and earlier HTML5 books have given promising notes and a few examples on the API.

Alas, WebSQL is no more, at least for the foreseeable future. The W3C has issued a de facto shutdown of this component, ceasing all work on the WebSQL Database specification. The specification page at http://www.w3.org/TR/webdatabase lists a very clear warning that can be seen in Figure 10.3.

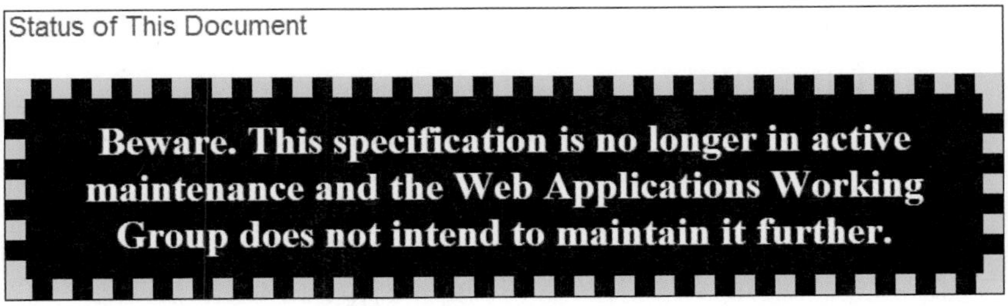

FIGURE 10.3   Official warning statement on the WebSQL Database page. Abandon all hope, ye who wished to use this API.

The specification gives a little more detail, noting that they reached an impasse as agreement could not be reached over implementation details with respect to the SQL back end. The Firefox team in particular refused to implement SQLite, suggesting that completely depending on the semantics and planning of a "somewhat quirky SQL implementation" would be bad for the Web.

10

The story doesn't end with WebSQL. The replacement for the WebSQL API is IndexedDB, the subject of our next section.

IndexedDB

IndexedDB, also written as Indexed DB and once known as WebSimpleDB, has taken over (from the deprecated WebSQL) as the standard queryable persistent local storage on the Web.

Unlike the Web Storage API, IndexedDB allows you to store very large amounts of data on the client (amount differs per browser) and comes with all the perks typically associated with databases, most notably efficient searching over values.

IndexedDB isn't well supported yet. Current support as of this writing is limited to Chrome, Firefox, and Internet Explorer 10 (and not Internet Explorer 9), but you can always check online for the latest support measures with sites such as caniuse.com (http://caniuse.com/#search=indexeddb).

Fortunately, although IndexedDB is not yet available on Opera, Safari, Android Browser, or iOS, WebSQL *is* available on those platforms, so there are a few polyfills that accommodate this difference by using WebSQL in the meantime on those platforms. The most popular polyfill as of this writing is the IndexedDBShim (https://github.com/axemclion/IndexedDBShim). As always, it is worth searching for newer or more popular polyfills before you commit to using one.

> **NOTE**
>
> The IndexedDB API specification can be found at http://www.w3.org/TR/IndexedDB/.

Getting Started with IndexedDB

The IndexedDB API describes a database as a collection of *object stores*, which are lists of records that contain key and associated values. This is in contrast to a relational database (like SQL and SQL variants), which contain a set of records that have common attributes typically represented by tables, rows, and columns. IndexedDB allows you to create indexes on object stores to efficiently search through large amounts of data.

IndexedDB records are typically updated via *transactions* of its asynchronous API. There is also a synchronous API for IndexedDB, but it is at risk of being removed from the specification due to lack of implementations, so we focus on the asynchronous API in the standard.

Many (especially those coming from relational databases) find object-oriented databases slightly counterintuitive, so this tutorial is broken up into several subsections. The last subsection is titled "Recap" and can be thought of as a quick reference. If you are reading through and get confused, it may be useful to skip to this section before continuing, as it provides an overview of all the objects and processes involved.

The IndexedDB object lives on the `window` as `window.indexedDB`, though for compatibility with new and experimental versions of IndexedDB, we may want to create a min-shim, in case browsers have implemented the feature but prefixed it:

```
// Combine with prefixed versions of indexedDB:
window.indexedDB = window.indexedDB || window.webkitIndexedDB ||
                   window.mozIndexedDB || window.msIndexedDB;

if (window.indexedDB === undefined) {
  // If true this browser still doesn't support indexedDB!
  // We should display something to our users, or use some kind of fallback
  // or find a shim that polyfills functionality with WebSQL
}
```

Of course, this won't be enough to use IndexedDB on browsers that have no implementation; you still need a proper shim for that, like the one mentioned at the start of this section.

> **NOTE**
>
> IndexedDB is also called IDB, and that abbreviation is used in many of the object names in the API, such as `IDBOpenDBRequest`, `IDBDatabase`, and so on.

Connecting to a Database

Creating a new database and opening it, or opening an existing database, is done with the same command:

```
var myRequest = indexedDB.open('myDatabase');
```

The `open` method is the entirety of interesting features on the `indexedDB` object itself. All IndexedDB functionality follows from this request and the returned `IDBOpenDBRequest` object.

Opening a database creates a new one if the name is not already taken. Like with Web Storage, IndexedDB databases are per-origin, so en.wikipedia.org and fr.wikipedia.org may each have a different database named `"myDatabase"`.

We often say we are opening a database, but really what we are doing is opening a *connection* to a database. Calling `indexedDB.open()` doesn't open or create a database right away; instead an object of type `IDBRequest` (specifically `IDBOpenDBRequest`) is returned with success and error values that we handle as events. The database is opened (and potentially created) only if the request is successful. One of the powerful features of databases (as opposed to simple Web Storage) is the ability to reliably read and write to them from many locations in code concurrently, and the framework of connections allows for an environment where we can expect operations to occur (or not) reliably.

> **NOTE**
>
> There's a second, optional argument to opening a connection: `indexedDB.open(name, version)`. The `version` must be a positive integer. We talk more about this versioning in the upcoming section, "Structuring (or Upgrading) the Database Schema."

Handling `IDBRequest` Events

To use our request, we typically attach two events, one for success and one for error handling. One of the two will be called automatically. Listing 10.1 shows the basic syntax.

LISTING 10.1   Opening a Database

```
var myRequest = indexedDB.open('myDatabase');
var myDB = null; // nothing yet, but will be an IDBDatabase object reference

// In both success and error events, event.target === myRequest
myRequest.onsuccess = function(event) {
  console.log('Success!');
  myDB = myRequest.result; // Save a reference to our database
};


myRequest.onerror = function(event) {
  console.log('Oh no!');
};
```

Errors are uncommon, save for a user denying database creation, but in production applications, we should always create appropriate error handlers wherever they can exist. In the coming examples, we omit error handling for the sake of code brevity.

The success callback gives us a reference to our database, but unlike the Web Storage API, we can't just start storing things willy-nilly. There are robust rules in place to enforce database correctness and speed. All reading and writing of data must occur inside of *transactions*. Before we get to those, we need to actually structure a database so we can store some information, and before we get to that, we cover closing and deleting our databases.

Closing and Deleting Databases

Deleting a database gives a glimpse at the event-oriented nature of the IndexedDB API. Like opening or creating a database, deleting a database is done with a call to `indexedDB.deleteDatabase(databaseName)` that returns an IDB request object.

Let's have a look at a small example of opening, closing, and deleting a database. This example intentionally runs into a blocking issue because we're going to try to delete a database before it's finished opening.

First, we call `indexedDB.open('myDatabase')` and attach an `onsuccess` event. This event fires after the database is finished opening, so we add a relevant console message. In the same `onsuccess` event, we also close the connection to the database immediately by calling `close()` on the `IDBDatabase` object generated in the function.

So once it's open, we close it. Simple enough, but right after we make the open request, we make a delete request. This is bad because the delete is going to be requested before the database has even finished its creation or opening. As a result, the delete request fires its `onblocked` event (that we define) to let us know that something is stopping immediate deletion of the database.

Importantly, the firing of the `onblocked` event does not mean that the database will not be deleted. It is not the same as an `onerror` event (the delete request has that, too, but we don't define it here). Once the database finishes opening, and we subsequently close it, the deletion request completes and its `onsuccess` function fires. Listing 10.2 has the complete code.

LISTING 10.2   Closing a Database, Slightly Out of Order

```
var myRequest = indexedDB.open('myDatabase');
var myDB = null; // nothing yet, but will be an IDBDatabase object reference

myRequest.onsuccess = function(event) {
  console.log('Database finished opening!');
  myDB = myRequest.result; // Save a reference to our database

  // We just finished opening, but we're going to close it right away:
  myDB.close();
};

// Delete the database. Note that since this code is not in
// the "myRequest.onsuccess" call, it occurs before code in that call
// This is (somewhat) bad, and initially database deletion will be blocked!
var deleteRequest = indexedDB.deleteDatabase('myDatabase');

deleteRequest.onsuccess = function(event) {
  console.log('Database deleted!');
}

deleteRequest.onblocked = function(event) {
  console.log('Delete blocked! Is a connection still open?');
}
```

Listing 10.2 would yield the following console output, in order:

```
Delete blocked! Is a connection still open?
Database finished opening!
Database deleted!
```

The first thing that fires is the `onblocked` event from the delete request, even before the database is opened, precisely *because* the database has not finished opening. Then some small amount of time later, the database opens successfully and the second console message is outputted. The connection is closed automatically once it is no longer in use (the end of the open request's `onsuccess` scope), so the `onsuccess` of the delete request could finally fire and output the third console message.

Structuring (or Upgrading) the Database Schema

Very broadly, there are two operations that programmers do to databases:

▶ Creating or modifying the structure of the database schema

▶ Modifying data inside of a database, reading and writing records

Modifying the database schema is a much rarer operation than modifying data inside of the database, but it must be done before we can store any data at all.

With the IndexedDB API, updating the structure of the database is called *upgrading* it, even if you're doing it for the first time. Otherwise, upgrading occurs when you open a database connection with a higher version than the existing version. The upgrading event only occurs if it's necessary, so the event is called `onupgradeneeded`.

When we open a connection to our database as we did in the first IndexedDB section, we implicitly gave the database a version argument of zero. Every database has a version, and when we use `indexedDB.open`, we can specify one as the second argument:

```
var myRequest = indexedDB.open('myDatabase', 1);
```

The version can be any nonnegative integer (specifically, it's an *unsigned long long* number).

When we create a database for the first time (version 0) or open with a larger version number than before, the `onupgradeneeded` fires, and in that event we can carry out our necessary database design tasks and even populate the database with some initial records. Before we take a look at that method, we need to take a look at how we can structure our IndexedDB databases.

IndexedDB uses object stores instead of tables (rows and columns) like SQL and other relational databases. Object stores are specified to use a *key path*, a *key generator*, or both. Specifying a key path means that only JavaScript objects can be stored in the object store, and the objects stored must contain a property with the key path as its name. Specifying a key generator means that any kind of value can be stored (JavaScript objects, numbers, strings, etc.) and the key is created automatically in an incrementing fashion.

We can create an object store that uses both, or neither, a key path or key generator. If neither is used, a separate key argument must be supplied whenever a value is supplied. The reasoning for using a specific combination of object store properties is scenario dependent, and our examples only concern themselves with using a key path or a key generator.

Object stores are often considered less intuitive than relational databases, so we begin with a (much) commented example of typical usage. In the `onupgradeneeded` event, we have a reference to our `IDBDatabase` object, and object stores are created with a call to `IDBDatabase.createObjectStore`. This method takes two arguments, a name and then an object with optional properties. The properties of this second argument allow us to create key path or key generator object stores, as we see in Listing 10.3.

LISTING 10.3 Creating Object Stores in the `onupgradeneeded` Event

```
// We are upgrading the existing (but empty) database from version 0 to 1:
var myRequest = indexedDB.open('myDatabase', 1);
var myDB = null; // nothing yet, but will be an IDBDatabase object reference

// If this event fires, it fires before onsuccess
myRequest.onupgradeneeded = function(event) {
  console.log('Commencing upgrade!');

  // We could also use event.target.result
  myDB = myRequest.result; // Save a reference to our database

  // Modify the database schema

  // Using a key store:
  var store1 = myDB.createObjectStore("myStore1", { keyPath: "ID" });

  // Create additional indexes for store1:
  store1.createIndex("lastLogin", "lastLogin", { unique: false });
  store1.createIndex("rank", "rank", { unique: true });

  // Using a key generator, allowing storage of primitives (like strings):
  var store2 = myDB.createObjectStore("myStore2", { autoIncrement: true });


  // Now that we've created a schema with two stores, we can add data.

  // For store1 (key path) the key is the ID,
  // so the "ID" property of the object is necessary:
  store1.add({ ID: "wvr2098", rank: 1, points: 92, lastLogin: "2013-01-01" });
  store1.add({ ID: "sas1031", rank: 2, points: 88, lastLogin: "2013-01-05" });

  // For store2 (key generator) the keys are set automatically:
  store2.add("Some data"); // Automatically gets a key of 1
  store2.add("More data"); // Automatically gets a key of 2
};
```

```
myRequest.onsuccess = function(event) {
  // Note that this event fires after onupgradeneeded, not before.
  console.log('Database finished opening (and upgrading)!');
};
```

Also note in Listing 10.3 the call to `createIndex`. Indexes can be created on object stores (that store JavaScript objects) to provide an easy way to look up values by properties other than the key. Indexes are covered a little later.

In Listing 10.3, we both created a database structure and added some starting data to the object stores, but data is not typically added or removed in the `onupgradeneeded` event. Instead, data operations are usually handled in separate transactions.

Transactions

Once our database is open, we use transactions to interact with the data in meaningful ways. Just like the event-oriented opening of a database connection, the purpose of these transactions is to give some security to the data. This allows for proper data recovery if something goes wrong and provides isolation when multiple connections are accessing the database concurrently.

Transactions have three typical modes:

▶ `readonly`—Used for accessing data

▶ `readwrite`—Used for accessing and writing data

▶ `versionchange`—Used to upgrade the database, also allows for read/write

Technically, we've already seen the `versionchange` transaction because one is automatically active inside of the `onupgradeneeded` event. Once our database is finished opening, we're free to create any of these transactions using the `transaction` method on the `IDBDatabase` object. The transaction method has two arguments, an array of the object stores we want to work on and the mode. For example:

```
var transaction = myDB.transaction(["myStore1"], "readwrite");
```

Like open requests, transactions return an `IDBTransaction` object that has callbacks, notably `onerror` and `oncomplete`. There's also `onabort`, which is called when the transaction is rolled back, either from an error or from explicitly calling `IDBTransaction.abort()`.

Transactions are meant to be short lived and are automatically completed once JavaScript returns to the event loop. Simply put, this means that once JavaScript is ready to process the next event (when all code in the event that a transaction is called is finished), the transaction is considered complete.

Inside of a transaction, we are able to access the requested object stores with `IDBTransaction.objectStore(storeName)`. This method returns an `IDBObjectStore` object with the following important methods, all of which return an `IDBRequest`:

- **add(value, [key])**—Adds a value at an optional key. This method throws an error if the key already exists in the store.

- **put(value, [key])**—Adds a value, potentially replacing (overwriting) an existing key.

- **delete(key)**—Deletes a given key.

- **get(key)**—Retrieves the data or object for a given key.

- **clear()**—Removes all records from the object store.

- **openCursor([range, direction])**—Returns an IDBRequest with a *cursor*, a special object that allows easier iteration over a store. This is discussed in detail in the "Cursors" section.

Additionally, there are several read-only attributes on the IDBObjectStore, mostly for convenience:

- **name**—The name of the object store

- **keyPath**—The key path, if one exists for this store

- **indexNames**—A list of string names of all indexes in this store

- **transaction**—A reference to the current transaction

- **autoIncrement**—Whether or not the auto-increment flag is set, describing whether or not this object store uses a key generator

Listing 10.4 gives an example of a readwrite transaction in action. Note how there are callbacks on both the IDBTransaction and the IDBRequest that is returned from calling add.

LISTING 10.4   Sample Transaction

```
var transaction = myDB.transaction(["myStore1, myStore2"], "readwrite");

// Do something when all the data is added to the database.
transaction.oncomplete = function(event) {
  console.log("transaction finished!");
};

transaction.onerror = function(event) {
  // Just like with opening, we should be handling errors here
};

var store1 = transaction.objectStore('myStore1');
var request1 = store1.add(
  { ID: "sei0028", rank: 4, points: 60, lastLogin: "2013-01-01" });
```

10

```
request1.onsuccess = function(event) {
 console.log('data successfully added to store1');
};
request1.onerror = function(event) {
  // And handling errors here too
};
```

Start to Finish

For a small but more complete example, we expand on the code in Listing 10.3 by adding a `readwrite` transaction that occurs after the database is opened and finished upgrading. Listing 10.5 illustrates all concepts covered so far: opening a database, upgrading it, adding data in the implicit `versionchange` transaction made during `onupgradeneeded`, and finishing with adding and accessing data in a second (`readwrite`) transaction. The code is heavily commented to aid those who prefer to learn by example.

LISTING 10.5   indexedDB.html—Complete IndexedDB Example

```
<!DOCTYPE html>
<body>
<script>
// Either we are creating a new database with version 1, or
// we are upgrading the existing (but empty) database from version 0 to 1:
var myRequest = indexedDB.open('myDatabase', 1);
var myDB = null; // nothing yet, but will be an IDBDatabase object reference

// If this event fires, it fires before onsuccess
myRequest.onupgradeneeded = function(event) {
  console.log('Commencing upgrade!');

  // We could also use event.target.result
  myDB = myRequest.result; // Save a reference to our database

  // Modify the database schema

  // Using a key store:
  var store1 = myDB.createObjectStore('myStore1', { keyPath: 'ID' });

  // Create additional indexes for store1:
  store1.createIndex('lastLogin', 'lastLogin', { unique: false });
  store1.createIndex('rank', 'rank', { unique: true });

  // Using a key generator, allowing storage of primitives (like strings):
  var store2 = myDB.createObjectStore('myStore2', { autoIncrement: true });
```

```javascript
  // Now that we've created a schema with two stores, we can add data.

  // For store1 (key path) the key is the ID,
  // so the 'ID' property of the object is necessary:
  store1.add({ ID: 'wvr2098', rank: 1, points: 92, lastLogin: '2013-01-01' });
  store1.add({ ID: 'sas1031', rank: 2, points: 88, lastLogin: '2013-01-05' });

  // For store2 (key generator) the keys are set automatically:
  store2.put('Some data'); // Automatically gets a key of 1
  store2.put('More data'); // Automatically gets a key of 2
};

// Note that this event fires after onupgradeneeded, not before.
myRequest.onsuccess = function(event) {
  console.log('Database finished opening (and upgrading)!');

  myDB = myRequest.result; // Save a reference to our database

  carryOutATransaction();
};



// In our example we only call this function after the database
// has completed opening, but we could call it any time,
// such as on a button press or form submission
function carryOutATransaction() {

  // A little safety:
  // if myDB is still null, then no database has been opened, so quit!
  if (myDB === null) return;

  // Create a new transaction. The first argument is an array of stores
  // The second argument is the type of operation we wish to carry out
  var transaction = myDB.transaction(['myStore1', 'myStore2'], 'readwrite');

  // Do something when all the data is added to the database.
  transaction.oncomplete = function(event) {
    console.log('Readwrite transaction finished!');
  };

  transaction.onerror = function(event) {
    // Just like with opening, we should be handling errors here too
  };
```

10

```
    var store1 = transaction.objectStore('myStore1');
    var store2 = transaction.objectStore('myStore2');

    // Some new data to add:
    var data = [
      { ID: 'mau0528', rank: 5, points: 12, lastLogin: '2013-03-08' },
      { ID: 'sei0028', rank: 4, points: 60, lastLogin: '2013-01-01' },
      { ID: 'gru3311', rank: 3, points: 78, lastLogin: '2013-02-05' }];

    for (var i = 0; i < data.length; i++) {
      var request = store1.add(data[i]);
      request.onsuccess = function(event) {
        console.log('Successfully added data');
      };
      request.onerror = function(event) {
        // Since we are using "add" and not "put",
        // this error might fire if the key already exists in the database
        console.log('Error in adding data');
      };
    }


    // Read some data at the end of our transaction:
    store1.get("sas1031").onsuccess = function(event) {
      console.log(event.currentTarget.result.points);
    }
    // Get the second key in store2
    store2.get(2).onsuccess = function(event) {
      console.log(event.currentTarget.result);
    }
  }
</script>
</body>
```

Running Listing 10.5 produces the following console output (in order):

```
Commencing upgrade!
Database finished opening (and upgrading)!
Successfully added data
Successfully added data
Successfully added data
88
More Data
Readwrite transaction finished!
```

We can explore the database from Listing 10.5 in some browser's developer tools. Figure 10.4 is a screen capture of the WebKit inspector in Google Chrome, showing the database after all transactions are completed, with two of the entries in myStore1 expanded to show detail.

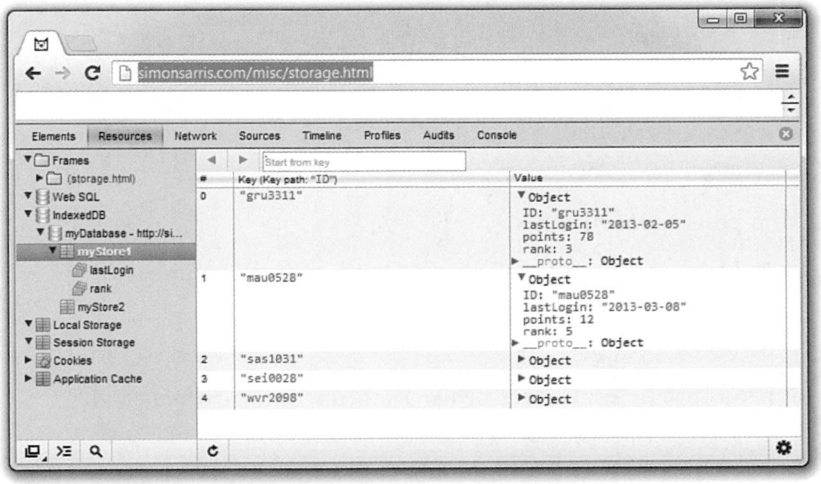

FIGURE 10.4   The resources pane of the WebKit inspector holds a good deal of information about IndexedDB databases, including indexes.

Cursors

Cursors are the iterators of IndexedDB. Requesting a cursor on an object store allows you to iterate over every key and perform operations on the associated values.

Listing 10.6 contains a simple example of a cursor used to output all IDs and their respective ranks.

LISTING 10.6   Using a Database Cursor

```
var transaction = myDB.transaction(['myStore1'], 'readwrite');
var store1 = transaction.objectStore('myStore1');
var cursorRequest = store1.openCursor();

cursorRequest.onsuccess = function(event) {
  var cursor = event.target.result;
  if (cursor) {
    console.log("ID " + cursor.key + " is ranked " + cursor.value.rank);
    cursor.continue();
  } else {
    console.log("Cursor complete");
  }
};
```

With the data from Listing 10.5 in the last section, using such a cursor would yield the following console output:

```
ID gru3311 is ranked 3
ID mau0528 is ranked 5
ID sas1031 is ranked 2
ID sei0028 is ranked 4
ID wvr2098 is ranked 1
Cursor complete
```

Note that it ordered the keys alphabetically.

The range and direction of cursors can also be specified with optional arguments:

```
var cursorRequest = store1.openCursor(keyRange, direction);
```

The range must be either a specific key, an `IDBKeyRange` object, or `null` (the default). `IDBKeyRange` objects are used to retrieve a specific range of keys, and are constructed by calling `IDBKeyRange` with one of four methods:

```
// Only consider the key 'mau0528'
var keyRange1 = IDBKeyRange.only('mau0528');
// Consider anything after 'mau0528' and 'mau0528' itself
var keyRange2 = IDBKeyRange.lowerBound('mau0528');
// Consider anything after 'mau0528' but not itself
var keyRange3 = IDBKeyRange.upperBound('mau0528', true);
//Match anything between "aaa0000" and "gaaa0000", including those two keys
var keyRange4 = IDBKeyRange.bound("aaa0000", "gaa0000", false, false);
```

The `true` and `false` arguments at the end are optional (default `false`) and describe whether or not the given key is included in the range. If no records match the range, the result of `openCursor` still fires an `onsuccess` event, but the `event.target.result` is `null`.

The cursor direction must be one of the four strings, `"next"`, `"nextunique"`, `"prev"`, or `"prevunique"`, describing the order of iteration. If one of the unique strings is chosen and multiple records exist with the same key, then only the first one is contained in the iteration.

Indexes

In Listing 10.5, we created a database schema that included some added indexes:

```
store1.createIndex("lastLogin", "lastLogin", { unique: false });
store1.createIndex("rank", "rank", { unique: true });
```

It's often convenient to look up items in a database by something other than the key, and indexes allow us to do this swiftly, without the need to construct a cursor and iterate.

With the database created in Listing 10.5, we can add another transaction that makes use of an index, shown in Listing 10.7.

LISTING 10.7   Database Transaction Using an Index

```
var transaction = myDB.transaction(['myStore1'], 'readwrite');
var store1 = transaction.objectStore('myStore1');
var indexRequest = store1.index("lastLogin");

indexRequest.get('2013-01-01').onsuccess = function(event) {
  // There are two records with a lastLogin of 2013-01-01,
  // ID sei0028 and ID wvr2098
  // The index will always return the one with the lowest value
  console.log(event.target.result.ID); // logs sei0028
}
```

As the comment in Listing 10.7 mentions, the `indexRequest.get` only returns the first record with the given index. If you want to return all of them, you can use `indexRequest.openCursor(IDBKeyRange.only("2013-01-01"))` instead to get an index-specific cursor and iterate over all records with the given `lastLogin`.

Using indexes is extremely fast compared with grabbing all of the objects (with a cursor or otherwise) and iterating over them yourself. Speed over arbitrary properties of a JavaScript object in the database (provided that property has an index created for it) is one of the primary benefits of using IndexedDB.

Hopefully, by now, the name IndexedDB makes sense as well!

Recap

There are a lot of objects and methods (and callbacks!) involved with IndexedDB, but chiefly the flow of operations can be reduced to a few points:

▶ Calling `indexedDB.open` returns an `IDBRequest` (specifically `IDBOpenDBRequest`) object.

▶ Requests use callbacks to notify success or failure. The `IDBOpenDBRequest` has `onblocked`, `onerror`, `onsuccess`, and `onupgradeneeded` callback functions. The `onupgradeneeded` function implicitly creates a `versionchange` transaction.

▶ Upgrading a database is the only way to modify its schema, and can only occur inside of `versionchange` transactions.

▶ The `event.target.result` of `IDBRequest` events contains a reference to the `IDBDatabase` object.

▶ `IDBDatabase.transaction` is used to create a new transaction of type `readonly`, `readwrite`, or `versionchange`. This method returns an `IDBTransaction` object.

10

▶ `IDBTransaction` objects have `onabort`, `oncomplete`, and `onerror` callbacks. They also have the method `IDBTransaction.objectStore(name)` that takes an object store name and returns an `IDBObjectStore` object.

▶ `IDBObjectStore` objects have many functions for modifying the database data, such as `add`, `put`, `delete`, `clear`, `get`, `openCursor`, and others for index interaction. These methods all return `IDBRequest` objects.

▶ The `IDBRequest` objects returned by most `IDBObjectStore` methods have their own `onsuccess` and `onerror` callbacks.

▶ The `event.target.result` in the `onsuccess` callback of an `IDBRequest` is usually the relevant data related to the operation, such as the object's key during an insertion or the object itself during a retrieval with the `get` method.

▶ Cursors are the iterators of IndexedDB and indexes allow you to use values other than the key to retrieve objects quickly.

Looking Further

Although this text covers the crucial points needed to use IndexedDB, it is not a comprehensive detailing of all possible configurations and operations. Reading the specification itself (http://www.w3.org/TR/IndexedDB) or perusing the Mozilla Developer Network documentation (https://developer.mozilla.org/en-US/docs/IndexedDB) will offer many more details, such as what kind of errors are available, and more detail on the nonessential (but extremely useful) components of IndexedDB, such as cursors and indexes.

Limitations, Storage, and Otherwise

With respect to storage limitations, there aren't any.

Well, not exactly, but the specification has yet to define any limit, so it varies per platform. Many browsers opt to ask permission once a certain size limit is reached. Firefox, for instance, asks user permission if a blob larger than 50MB is to be stored. Chrome, on the other hand, claims that *up to half of available disk space* may be available for temporary storage, and any given app may use up to 20% of that temporary storage space, and furthermore permission is not required.

IndexedDB has a few shortcomings that are worth mentioning:

▶ Usage of this API is at the whim of users. It's possible that the user requests a deletion of your database, and there's no recourse for this. This means that for many apps you will want to have some kind of backup of the database on the server. It's also possible that the user's settings disallow local storage at all, either explicitly by denying the creation of a database or implicitly by use of private browsing methods.

▶ There is no easy (or at least no built-in) way to back up or synchronize IndexedDB databases to a server. If you want this functionality, you have to build it yourself or wait for a library that accomplishes this task (see the next section for a few such libraries).

▶ There is no pattern searching like there is in SQL with the LIKE operator.

Finally, IndexedDB has been shaken up quite a bit in the past two years. While it's unlikely that the future will bring (more) incompatible changes, there have been quite a few differences between the API today and that of yesteryear, and there may be more to come. The only foreseeable change is that the synchronous API for IndexedDB, not discussed in this chapter (for this very reason), may be dropped from the specification altogether.

Libraries That Work with IndexedDB

There are already several popular libraries worth a mention that may make life easier for would-be IndexedDB users:

▶ PouchDB (http://pouchdb.com) is an API for JSON (JavaScript Object Notation) objects that easily syncs with JSON-based CouchDB databases.

▶ The generically named jQuery-IndexedDB (https://github.com/axemclion/jquery-indexeddb) aims to abstract the transactional syntax of IndexedDB into a jQuery-like setup with short, chainable commands.

▶ db.js (http://aaronpowell.github.com/db.js) is another wrapper that aims to make IndexedDB feel more like a more easily queryable API, also with method chaining.

There are doubtless more libraries on the Web, and it is always worth searching for newer or more popular libraries before making a framework choice.

FileSystem API for Local Read/Write Access

Instead of just text in a database, sometimes we want to store real binary data on a client's machine and not just JavaScript objects. There's a new FileSystem API that allows websites to read and write to real directories on a user's machine. This allows web apps to potentially share information with applications outside of the browser.

There are a multitude of use cases for such an API. The specification itself outlines many:

▶ Apps that need persistent uploading that could copy a directory to upload to the local sandbox and upload portions at a time

▶ Video games or other multimedia with large amounts of assets that could download a tarball or zipped collection of files of arbitrary (binary) types to expand and access locally

▶ Audio/Video/Photo editing using the local file system as a cache for speed

▶ Offline video viewing

▶ Offline web mail clients

Although this is a very powerful up-and-coming API, it is extremely new and not supported in a single browser except recent versions of Google Chrome. If this API sounds interesting, you should keep an eye on the caniuse.com page for this feature, http://caniuse.com/#search=filesy.

Because it is one of the least-supported features to be called HTML5, we don't cover it in depth, but we do provide a simple example to illustrate some common capabilities of the API.

> **NOTE**
>
> If more widely implemented, the FileSystem API would create additional use cases for the Drag and Drop API, discussed in Chapter 3, "Getting Started with HTML5: Semantic Tags, Forms, and Drag and Drop," and `<input type="file">` tags.

The file system visible from the FileSystem API is sandboxed as you'd reasonably expect. Even with this API, browsers still cannot read (or even peer at the structure of) your file system.

The specification does not say where this file system data resides, though it's a good guess that it will be found in the user's data directory (`AppData` in Windows or `/Library/Application Support` in OS X) for the given browser.

> **NOTE**
>
> The FileSystem API specification can be found at http://www.w3.org/TR/file-system-api/.

FileSystem API Example

To request file system access, we call the `requestFileSystem` method on the window:

```
window.requestFileSystem(type, size, success, [error])
```

It takes three required arguments and one optional argument:

- ▶ **type**—Whether the file storage should be persistent or not. Takes one of two constants, `window.TEMPORARY` or `window.PERSISTENT`, though these constants just evaluate to 0 and 1, respectively.

- ▶ **size**—The size in bytes requested for the file system.

- ▶ **success**—Success callback that has a `FileSystem` object as its argument.

- ▶ **error**—Optional error callback that fires in case of user or OS denial of file system access, called with a `FileError` object.

Creating and Writing to a File

Once we have our file system reference from the success callback of `requestFileSystem`, we have a few methods exposed. Chief among them is `getFile`:

```
FileSystem.getFile(path, [options], [success], [error])
```

The `path` must be a string filename. The `options` argument is an optional JavaScript object that can contain two properties, `create` and `exclusive`, set to `true` or `false`, and finally there are `success` and `error` (callback) events to be defined.

The `success` callback specified for `FileSystem.getFile` has one argument, the `FileSystem` object, and on `FileSystem.root` we have our first `DirectoryEntry` object, representing our root directory. From that directory, we can use the methods `getFile` and `getDirectory` to read (and build) our file structure.

The syntax for creating, traversing, and writing to files is somewhat similar to IndexedDB in that there are a large number of callbacks (mostly for success and error) to define.

The process of using `getFile` to open a file and write data to it is not particularly long or complex, though there are a lot of callbacks along the way that require some organizational foresight outside of simple examples. Listing 10.8 shows the complete process for creating a file named `newFile.txt` and writing some data to it. The code is heavily commented.

LISTING 10.8   Writing to a File with the FileSystem API

```
// take care of prefixes, right now it is only implemented in
// Chrome and only with a webkit prefix
window.requestFileSystem = window.requestFileSystem ||
                           window.webkitRequestFileSystem;

// 2*1024*1024 = 2MB of storage
window.requestFileSystem(window.TEMPORARY, 2*1024*1024, success, error);

function success(filesystem) {
  // The create option creates a file if it was not previously there
  // The only other option is "exclusive"
  // and when set to true will cause getFile to fail if the file already exists
  filesystem.root.getFile('newFile.txt', { create: true }, fileSuccess);

  function fileSuccess(fileEntry) {
    // Create a FileWriter object for our FileEntry (log.txt).
    fileEntry.createWriter(entrySuccess);

    function entrySuccess(fileWriter) {
```

```
    // The FileWriter object has a large number of callbacks not seen here
    // In addition to onwriteend there's also:
    // fileWriter.onerror, onabort, onprogress, onwrite, and onwritestart
    fileWriter.onwriteend = function(e) {
      console.log('Finished writing!');
    };

    // A Blob represents an object of immutable data
    var blob = new Blob(['Some text for our new file'], {type: 'text/plain'});

    fileWriter.write(blob);

   } // end entrySuccess
  } // end fileSuccess
} // end success

function error(event) {
  // outputs a number between 1 and 11 corresponding to a constant
  // You can find the constant names by looking at the FileError object
  // i.e., FileError.SECURITY_ERR (2), FileError.QUOTA_EXCEEDED_ERR (10)
  // These are considered likely to change in the future
  console.log(event.code);
}
```

As you can see, writing to a file at its most general consists of several nested success callbacks firing. In a production application, we would want to handle all error callbacks in a serious manner as well.

The FileSystem API may lead to great things in the future, but in the near term Chrome is the only browser offering an implementation, and it may take some time (and possibly large changes to the specification) before other browsers are on board.

Offline Pages and the Application Cache

Since the early days of HTML5, one of the most lauded features was the ability to run web apps offline. The Application Cache API (also called ApplicationCache, AppCache, or simply "the offline cache") is the feature that accomplishes this.

A web app's application cache is not just for offline apps, but it also serves the user in a general caching sense by offering faster page loads (cached resources tend to load faster) and reduced server load (upon refreshing or re-viewing, the only resources downloaded from the server are ones that have changed).

The application cache is supported in every modern browser, including Internet Explorer starting with Internet Explorer 10.

Using the Application Cache

We enable the application cache by setting the `manifest` attribute of the `<html>` tag to specify a cache manifest file:

```
<html manifest="myCache.appcache">
```

The `manifest` attribute is like the `src` attribute of many other HTML elements, it points to a file on the server using either a relative or absolute path.

A Simple Example

Inside of the manifest file, we need to provide a specific header, followed by a list of all files we'd like to cache. For example:

```
CACHE MANIFEST
# We can make comments with # signs
index.html
styles/main.css
styles/default.css
# we can list files by either relative or full paths:
http://example.com/images/myImage.png
javascript/loader.js
javascript/game.js
```

The first line, CACHE MANIFEST, is the required header. The previous example considers six files to be the contents of the cache.

What Changes with the Application Cache

Web pages with a cache manifest get a somewhat peculiar treatment when loaded subsequent times:

▶ If a previously accessed site with a cache is visited again, the browser loads directly from the locally stored files instead of the Web, typically speeding up page loading.

▶ *After* the resources have been loaded from the cache, the browser checks with the server to see if there is a newer cache manifest file. If there is no Internet connection or if the server is down, this step is not possible, but we've already got our offline page.

▶ If there is a newer manifest, the browser downloads it and its contents in the background and updates the cache accordingly. Importantly, this does not update the page accordingly, and a refresh is needed to see any updated cache content.

It may seem intuitive that updating a file (such as an image) listed in the manifest would be enough to trigger a manifest update, but this is not the case because the browser does not check every file in the manifest to see if a newer version exists. The only way for the browser to tell if there is a newer manifest is if the manifest file itself changes. Because of this, many developers put a date or version comment in the manifest file to change when they update files listed in the manifest. Typically, they may look like the following:

```
CACHE MANIFEST
# 2013-01-01 - V2
# (Rest of the manifest)
```

Cache Sections

The cache manifest file can have three sections, separated by three header keywords:

▶ CACHE—The default section of a manifest. Files listed under this header are cached after they're downloaded once.

▶ NETWORK—Files listed under this header explicitly require a connection to the server. Files in this section can use wildcards in their definitions.

▶ FALLBACK—Entries listed under this header specify fallback pages to use if a resource is not accessible. Each entry consists of two URLs, the first to check for accessibility, and the second to serve if the first is unavailable. Unlike the other sections, URLs specified here must be relative to the cache manifest file's location.

A More Complex Example

Using all the cache sections, we can make a more interesting manifest file:

```
CACHE MANIFEST
# 2013-01-01 - V2

# Since the CACHE header is the default, we don't have to write it
```

```
# But being explicit is nice
CACHE:
index.html
images/img1.png
images/img2.png
images/img3.png

# Use from network if available
NETWORK:
network.html

# Fallback content
FALLBACK:
# All noncached HTML pages will present fallback.html:
*.html fallback.html
# All noncached images will show a placeholder image:
images/*.png placeholder.png
```

The first comment is for us to change when we modify a file within the cache. For instance, if we make changes to `img1.png`, the cache will not know to fetch a new version from the server, so we must additionally update the cache manifest, typically by changing the date or version number in a comment.

Cache Status and the JavaScript API

The application cache comes with a small JavaScript API that rests on `window` as `window.applicationCache`. It has just one attribute, `applicationCache.status`, that returns a number corresponding to one of several constants:

- ▶ UNCACHED—0
- ▶ IDLE—1
- ▶ CHECKING—2
- ▶ DOWNLOADING—3
- ▶ UPDATEREADY—4
- ▶ OBSOLETE—5

Using these, we can determine if the application cache is, for instance, uncached:

```
if (applicationCache.status == applicationCache.UNCACHED) {
  // do something in the absence of a cache
}
```

10

There are also three methods on the `applicationCache`:

▶ `update()`—Attempts to update the cache on the client. If successful, the cache state goes to UPDATEREADY.

▶ `abort()`—Stops all progress of the cache download. This is only useful if you are tracking cache download progress and need to quit for some reason (such as the user clicking an Abort button to conserve bandwidth).

▶ `swapCache()`—If the cache state is UPDATEREADY, swaps in the new cache files.

Importantly, `update` and `swapCache` do not cause the page to reload or otherwise show the new resources to the client's already-rendered page. The user must reload before they see the new content, or you could reload the page for them with a call to `window.location.reload()`, though depending on the site you might want to ask the user first.

Finally, there are several handlers that can be attached to the `applicationCache`, should you need to know when specific events cache-related are occurring:

▶ `onchecking`—Fired when the cache is checking for an update.

▶ `onerror`—Fired on any assortment of errors, such as if the download failed or the cache file cannot be found.

▶ `onnoupdate`—Fired if the manifest file has been downloaded for the first time.

▶ `ondownloading`—Fired at the start of a cache download.

▶ `onprogress`—Fired after each individual resource in the cache has completed downloading.

▶ `onupdateready`—Fired when all resources have been newly downloaded, such as after `applicationCache.update()` is called. If those new resources are necessary, you could use this event to call `applicationCache.swapCache()` and then reload the page.

▶ `oncached`—Fired after the first time the manifest is finished caching.

▶ `onobsolete`—Fired if the manifest is not found, which ultimately deletes the cache.

Important Notes About the Application Cache

There are a few important gotchas with the application cache. Some were previously mentioned, but should not be missed, especially if troubleshooting the cache:

▶ The cache manifest must be served with the `text/cache-manifest` MIME-type, which may need additional server configuration. Additionally, it would be best for servers to set expire headers for files with the `appcache` extension to expire immediately, so that the cache file itself is not accidentally cached for any length of time.

▶ If there is a newer manifest file when a page is revisited, the updated content will be downloaded, but will not appear until the page is reloaded again.

▶ Specifying the manifest itself inside of the cache manifest is a very bad idea because caching the manifest would make it impossible to know if a new manifest is available.

▶ Relative URLs inside of the cache manifest are relative to the manifest file, *not* to the currently accessed page.

▶ Updating files listed in the cache manifest is not enough to update the manifest. The manifest file itself *must* be changed in order to trigger an update.

Summary

We covered several new storage options in this chapter, though they all fill different roles.

Web Storage provides a simple local storage mechanism that can be separated by session. IndexedDB has taken over the job from the now-deprecated WebSQL of storing and accessing large amounts of JavaScript data efficiently. The FileSystem API, while extremely new to the scene and only available on one browser, will eventually allow storage of arbitrary binary data on the client.

Finally, we took a look at the new Application Cache API, a specification that allows us to create offline web apps and pages more reliably than before.

10

CHAPTER 11

Messaging and Web Workers

JavaScript presents us with a more or less single-threaded scripting environment. If we have work for the browser to do, such as tabulating numbers or processing image data, we have to wait for all of it to complete before we can continue on to another task. In times past (and in most cases today), this is just fine. Even on sites with a large JavaScript payload, such as *The New York Times*, there usually isn't enough client-side JavaScript processing to necessitate concurrency.

As browsers take on a larger role as providers of powerful web applications, more work is expected to be done on client devices and the need for JavaScript to run concurrently in the background has become more desirable. Web workers (and their associated application programming interface [API]) afford us this ability.

Web workers live in a separate walled world from the normal web page and associated JavaScript, and we communicate back and forth with our workers using the Web Messaging API. This API has a more general function, to enable cross-document messaging, and we cover this before web workers.

The Web Messaging API and Cross-Document Messaging

Different tabs, windows, and iFrames all have their own *browsing contexts*, which are separate from each other. Mostly for security reasons, they are not allowed to communicate with each other. Most JavaScript novices first encounter this, often with accompanying frustration, when they find that iFrames are not allowed to communicate with their parent frames.

This simple divide has done us well for years, but often it would be a convenient fact if tabs or frames *could* communicate between each other. As long as we have careful rules in place, there aren't any insurmountable security issues, so the Web Messaging API was created to safely allow communication between these otherwise isolated browsing contexts of HTML documents.

All major mobile and desktop browsers support the Web Messaging API, including Internet Explorer 8+, though Internet Explorer's support is limited to sending messages in frames and iFrames, not across tabs or windows.

> **NOTE**
>
> The Web Messaging API is sometimes called the Messaging API, but the "Messaging API" is also the name of a different API that deals with accessing certain messaging functionality (such as phone text messages) in the browser. That API is not covered in this text.
>
> The Web Messaging API specification can be found at http://dev.w3.org/html5/postmsg/.

Sending and Receiving Messages

Sending messages to other windows is done with the `postMessage` method on the `window` object. It wouldn't make much sense to post a message to your own window, so to use this API you typically need a reference to another browsing context. You would get a reference to another window object from one of the following:

▶ A reference to an iFrame's window (`someFrame.contentWindow`)

▶ `window.frames`, which supplies a list of subframes of the current window

▶ A pop-up created with `window.open`

Once we have a window reference, we can call `postMessage` with two bits of information: our message and a target origin:

```
otherWindow.postMessage(message, targetOrigin);
```

The message is often a string, but as per the specification, it can be any kind of structured JavaScript object containing (almost) any sort of data.

The target origin is a string of an absolute uniform resource locator (URL) that must match the origin of the window that the message is being posted to. You may also send the message to any origin by using `"*"` or to only the same origin by using the string `"/"`.

> **NOTE**
>
> There's an optional third argument used for *channel messaging*, which is covered in the "Channel Messaging" section.

That's all we need to know to post a message:

```
var myFrame = document.getElementById('myFrame');
var msg = "Toto, I've got a feeling we're not in the parent frame anymore.";
myFrame.contentWindow.postMessage(msg, "/");
```

NOTE

If you want to create a system for broadcasting messages across multiple tabs or windows without needing a reference to them, you can use local storage (see Chapter 10, "HTML5 Storage Options") and its associated events instead.

Receiving Messages

To receive sent messages, we must listen for the message event on the messaged window. For example:

```
// in the iFrame that a message was posted to:
window.addEventListener('message', function(event) {
  // Do something with the message, event.data
  // Assuming the data is a string:
  document.write(event.data);
}, false);
```

The event argument is of type MessageEvent and contains three important attributes:

- ▶ data—The string or object sent as the message

- ▶ origin—The origin from which the message was posted, which is needed for security checking

- ▶ source—A reference to the source window of the message, which can be useful for return communication if expecting messages from multiple sources

A more typical message listener might look like this:

```
// in the iFrame that a message was posted to:
window.addEventListener('message', function(event) {
  // If the message is not from an intended domain, quit right away:
  if (event.origin === 'http://example.com') return;

  // Otherwise do something with event.data, and possibly send back a message:
  var msg = 'Parent frame, I think this is the beginning' +
          'of a beautiful friendship.';
  event.source.postMessage(msg, '/');

}, false);
```

With that, we have the basics of web messaging.

Channel Messaging

There's a relatively new (and so far, less supported) addition to web messaging that allows two browsing contexts to interact a little more directly, using a two-way pipe with ports at each end.

The purpose of these ports is to expose limited capabilities between frames. To make the utility of this clear, the specification offers an example: Suppose there is a site that embeds an address book in one iFrame and a game in a second iFrame. That gives us three distinct browsing contexts, perhaps with three different origins. For the address book iFrame to communicate with the game iFrame, it would have to go through the parent frame.

This scenario poses a problem. With what we know so far of messaging, the parent frame would have to act as a relay between the two iFrames, and so the address book would have to accept posts from the parent frame's domain (origin). But the address book doesn't want to accept posts from the parent frame's domain, which might be some arbitrary site. It only wants to accept posts from the game origin, which it knows and trusts.

Using channel messaging and ports, the game site and address book site iFrames can communicate with each other directly, with the parent frame merely acting as match-maker. In fact, the parent frame will have no knowledge of what is being transmitted between the two frames, and in the case of an address book iFrame sharing contacts with a game iFrame, the parent frame will not be able to peek at the contacts being passed.

Channels and Ports

Channel messaging involves the creation of a `MessageChannel` object that contains two ports as attributes, `port1` and `port2`, each of type `MessagePort`. `MessagePort` objects have three methods:

- ▶ `start`—Opens the port, starting communication
- ▶ `close`—Closes the port, disallowing any further messages
- ▶ `postMessage`—Used just like `window.postMessage`

On the pair of `MessagePort` objects is where we define our `message` event listeners.

Finally, there's a third optional argument to `window.postMessage` that is used for channel messaging:

```
someWindow.postMessage(message, targetOrigin [, transfer]);
```

The transfer argument is an array of objects that are sent over in the message and are literally transferred from one browsing context to another. This means that they are no longer usable in the browsing context that called `postMessage` (the sending side). This transfer is used to exchange ownership of ports between frames.

Channel Messaging Example

Let's take a look at a typical example based on a single parent page with two iFrames. In the first iFrame, we post a message to our parent frame (the only frame we know about), sending along one of the ports, and set up a listener on the other port to wait for a reply. Listing 11.1 has the code for our first frame.

LISTING 11.1   The First iFrame's JavaScript

```
// Based on an excellent example in Dev.Opera
// http://dev.opera.com/articles/view/window-postmessage-messagechannel/

window.addEventListener('DOMContentLoaded', function() {
  var mc = new MessageChannel();

  // Send a port to our parent document.
  var msg = 'First frame is ready!'
  window.parent.postMessage(msg,'http://a.example', [mc.port2]);

  // Set up our port event listener.
  mc.port1.addEventListener('message', function(event) {
    // Do something with the message we expect to receive back
    console.log(event.data);
  }, false);

  // Open the port
  mc.port1.start();
}, false);
```

Now that our parent frame has a message to look forward to (A ring from the kids! They finally called!), we set up a listener for the parent. Then, we have the parent frame post a message to the second iFrame, transferring the port that was given by the first iFrame.

Listing 11.2 contains the code for the parent frame.

LISTING 11.2   The Parent Frame's JavaScript

```
window.addEventListener('DOMContentLoaded', function() {
  var myFrame2 = document.getElementById('myFrame2').contentWindow;

  // Listen for the message from the first iFrame
  window.addEventListener('message', function(event){
    if( event.ports.length > 0 ){
      // transfer the port to the second iFrame
      var msg = 'The port on the first frame is open!';
      myFrame2.postMessage(msg, 'http://a.example', event.ports);
    }
  },false);
} ,false);
```

Note that the `MessageEvent` passed to the message listener has a `ports` attribute, which is a list of all transferred ports. In our case, we have just the one, and we pass it on to the second iFrame right away, so that they can start communicating between each other.

Lastly, we need to listen for this passed message on the second iFrame. Once we receive it, we are able to send messages from our second iFrame to the first iFrame without any more communication with the parent frame. Listing 11.3 has the JavaScript needed for the second iFrame.

LISTING 11.3   The Second iFrame's JavaScript

```
window.addEventListener('message', function(event) {
  // Now that we've received the message that came from the first iFrame
  // We can send messages back

  // The parent frame has no knowledge of this message
  var msg = 'Hello first iFrame, This is the second iFrame!';
  event.ports[0].postMessage(msg);
} ,false);
```

That's all there is to it. In the real world, we'd be passing more meaningful messages, but also checking origins, as we should only accept messages from domains that we are expecting to communicate with.

Security with Web Messages

The simplest way to ensure you're safe from receiving ill-sent messages is to not define any `message` event handlers. In other words, if you do not use the new Messaging API, you're still perfectly safe.

You should always check the `origin` attribute of any `MessageEvent` to ensure that it is coming from the expected domain. After checking the origin, you should also check to ensure that the incoming data is of the expected format. If you don't, and the message poster was attacked by some cross-site scripting flaw, it might be able to propagate the attack further.

Using the wildcard character (*) for a message's origin is generally bad practice, but especially so if the message contains some kind of sensitive (or nonpublic) data. If the origin is the wildcard, there's no way to guarantee that the message will only be delivered to its intended destination.

On the other hand, if you intend to accept messages from any domain at all, you should be wary that you may be opening yourself up to a denial of service attack, or similar event where a high volume of messages are posted to your page. To alleviate this concern, it would be wise to employ some kind of rate limiting, allowing only a contextually acceptable number of messages per minute.

Web Workers

If you've ever seen browser errors like those in Figure 11.1, you probably encountered buggy JavaScript, such as a script that contains an infinite loop. Sometimes, however, web pages simply have large amounts of data to crunch, and the time it takes to process this data causes a noticeable delay, perhaps irking the browser (and often the user). Web workers have the potential to alleviate these issues by introducing high-level multithreading to JavaScript.

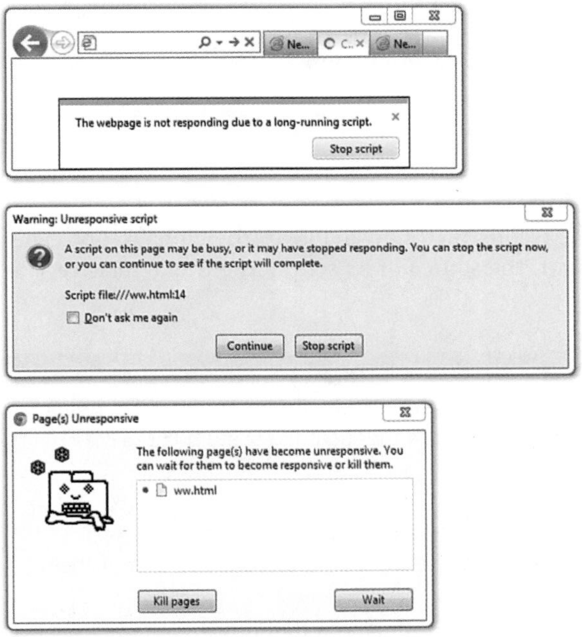

FIGURE 11.1   Unresponsive script errors in different browsers.

Web workers aren't supposed to be for everyone. They're considered a heavyweight solution to concurrency and background-processing problems. They're intended to be long-lived, and may have considerable startup costs in terms of time and memory. Adding web workers to your application isn't like turning on another lamp because you need more light; it's more like building a new power plant because you need more power.

Web workers are supported in every modern desktop browser, including Internet Explorer starting with Internet Explorer 10. Only iOS Safari has mobile support as of this writing, but it would be best to check online for an up-to-date compatibility table.

> **NOTE**
>
> The compatibility table site caniuse.com has a section for web workers at http://caniuse.com/#feat=webworkers.

We mentioned in the previous section that the Web Messaging API was created to facilitate communication between different browsing contexts. Web workers exist in their own browsing context, which necessitates the use of the Web Messaging API to access them, so the basics of the previous section are necessary for understanding how web workers communicate.

NOTE

Typical multithreaded applications deal with complex concurrency issues. Thankfully, web workers are a fairly high-level interface for threads, and it is hard to create real concurrency problems so long as you're moderately careful.

The web worker specification can be found at http://www.whatwg.org/specs/web-apps/ current-work/multipage/workers.html.

Getting Started with Web Workers

Web workers are created with the `Worker()` constructor, available in the global scope. The constructor has one (mandatory) argument, the source of its script, as either a relative, absolute, or `data:` URL.

NOTE

Running pages with web workers on locally might cause security errors on some browsers. Attempting to use web workers while serving a file from the local file system (`file:///`) in Google Chrome, for instance, will lead to this error:

`Uncaught Error: SecurityError: DOM Exception 18`

This is due to a design decision in Chrome. Some file access is disallowed because Chrome considers all files served from `file:///` to be from different origins, even if they are in the same folder.

When developing your web worker apps, you can start Chrome with the flag `--allow-file-access-from-files` to bypass this restriction. Because this loosens file access restrictions, it is not recommended that you use this flag except during development.

Starting a web worker is simple enough:

```
var muzhik = new Worker('workerScript.js');
```

If the argument file exists, then a new worker thread will be created.

To receive information from our worker, we need to define a `message` event listener on the `Worker` object:

```
muzhik.addEventListener('message', function(event) {
  console.log("The worker has sent the main page a message!");
}, false);
```

Before our worker's script runs, we need to start the worker, which doesn't happen auto-matically. This is typically done by sending the worker an empty message, giving it the go-ahead to begin running its JavaScript file.

```
muzhik.postMessage(''); // Send an empty message to start the worker
```

This kind of "starting" is only done if the worker runs code immediately without using a specific message event listener of its own. If the worker needed input from the page to begin meaningful work, which is more common, we would begin our interaction by sending that message instead.

Messages can be strings, but they can also be JSON (JavaScript Object Notation) objects, or any JavaScript construct that can be serialized. You cannot send nonserializable data, such as functions, to the workers.

The only other method on the `Worker` object is `terminate()`, used to stop the worker.

The previous chapter section, "The Web Messaging API and Cross-Document Messaging," showed the basics of creating and communicating by passing messages, and web workers are no different. Two contexts add `message` event handlers, in this case your page context and the worker context, and they use `postMessage` to pass data back and forth. The only difference with web workers is that our web worker operates as a windowless script instead of another frame. Let's take a closer look at web worker scripts.

The Web Worker JavaScript

When we created our web worker, we specified a file that was to contain the worker's script. The environment that this script runs in is different than a typical page. When running inside a worker script, there's no `window` object defined. Instead, workers have their own global scope with a few important attributes and functions.

The `self` attribute in a worker context is the equivalent of `window` in a normal browsing context, providing a reference to the global worker scope. This means that in the global scope of a worker, `self` is the default scope, and in the global scope `self` is equal to `this`.

The `location` attribute is an object that contains several properties detailing where the worker source file is located. Like `window.location`, this has (among others) `hostname`, `href`, `pathname`, `port`, and `protocol` string attributes.

The `close()` method stops all tasks and events on the web worker and prevents any new tasks from being queued, shutting down the worker. You can also terminate a worker from your main page by calling `workerName.terminate()`.

Listing 11.4 gives an example of what you might expect to find in a simple worker script.

LISTING 11.4   `workerScript.js`—Sample Web Worker Script

```
// Here in the global scope of the worker script
// We might have private worker state and functions
// These are inaccessible to the page that is calling the worker.
```

```
// (unless a script tag is added to that page referencing this file)
var somePrivateVar;

function somePrivateFunction() {
  // ...
}

// 'self' automatically exists in web worker contexts
// and references the web worker.
// Using 'this' or no prefix also works,
// so long as we're careful about which scope we're in!
self.addEventListener('message', function (event) {
  // use messages received from other contexts (like the main page)
  self.postMessage('Hello parent!');
}, false);
```

Typically, both the web worker script and the main page will have listeners to post one or more messages to each other. It's possible, however, for a web worker to have no message listeners. As we covered earlier, you can use a single empty `postMessage` to start the worker script, which lets its global scope execute, and this may involve sending one or more messages back after computing something that did not need the parent page's input. Such a worker could compute (large) random prime numbers without halting the web page, and send them back to the page when complete.

A Simple Example

Let's take a look at a little script that will compute Fibonacci numbers asynchronously, without halting the page. The Fibonacci series is an increasing number series where each number is computed by summing the previous two numbers, starting with 0 and 1. This series is typically used to illustrate recursion to aspiring programmers, but we are only using it because large Fibonacci numbers take a fair amount of time to compute, enough where computing the 50th number in the series might halt the page for several seconds.

Our page uses two web workers, named `muzhik1` and `muzhik2`, both sharing the same worker script.

The very first thing we do is send our first worker an empty message, just to note the console output later. After that initial message, the first worker is sent a number that is time consuming to compute, and then the second worker is sent a smaller number. As soon as a worker completes its job, it passes a message back, and any messages that our HTML page receives are output to the JavaScript console immediately.

Listing 11.5 has the HTML for our page.

LISTING 11.5   `worker.html`—The HTML Driving Two Web Workers

```html
<!DOCTYPE html>
<head>
  <title>Web Worker Test</title>
</head>
<body>

<script type="text/javascript">

var muzhik1 = new Worker('workerScript.js');
var muzhik2 = new Worker('workerScript.js');

muzhik1.addEventListener('message', function(event) {
  console.log(event.data); // log anything we get back
}, false);

muzhik2.addEventListener('message', function(event) {
  console.log(event.data); // log anything we get back
}, false);

// Send an empty message to start the worker
// (This is not necessary, as we'll see)
// NOTE: Some browsers do not accept completely empty messages
// (such as Firefox). You can substitute any non-number, such as 'blah'
muzhik1.postMessage();

muzhik1.postMessage(42);

muzhik2.postMessage(5);

</script>

</body>
```

In our worker code, the very first executable line of the code sends back a message ('Hello parent!') as soon as the individual web worker is started. Then we have a function, `fib()`, that only the web worker can use. Finally, we have a `message` event listener that checks incoming messages for numbers. If they are numbers, we compute the corresponding Fibonacci number and post a message back; otherwise, we post an error message back to our page.

Listing 11.6 contains our worker code.

LISTING 11.6   `workerScript.js`—The Web Worker Code

```js
// Notify the parent immediately that the web worker is running
self.postMessage('Hello parent!');

// In the Fibonacci series, each number is a sum of the previous two
// The first two numbers in the series are 0 and 1.
// 1 2 3 4 5 6 7 8  9th numbers are:
// 0 1 1 2 3 5 8 13 21, etc.
function fib(num) {
  if (num > 2) {
    return fib(num - 2) + fib(num - 1);
  } else {
    return num-1;
  }
}

// 'self' automatically exists in web worker contexts
// and references the web worker.
self.addEventListener('message', function (event) {
  // We are expecting a message that contains an integer
  if (isNaN(event.data)) {
    self.postMessage('We need a number!');
    return;
  }

  // Otherwise, let's compute it
  var computedNumber = fib(event.data);
  self.postMessage('The Fibonacci number is: ' + computedNumber);
}, false);
```

Our three sent messages:

```js
muzhik1.postMessage('');
muzhik1.postMessage(42);
muzhik2.postMessage(5);
```

yield five console statements from the main page (with line numbers added):

```
#1 - Hello parent!
#2 - We need a number!
#3 - Hello parent!
#4 - The Fibonacci number is: 3
#5 - The Fibonacci number is: 165580141
```

The first, empty message to `muzhik1` is sent, and statements #1 and #2 are a result. Because the worker was started by the empty message, it sent back its "hello." Afterward, the worker's `message` event listener fired, and it sent back the error message we defined because what it received was not a number.

Then our second message is posted to `muzhik1`, and the worker begins crunching away to compute the 42nd Fibonacci number. Nothing is output to the console yet.

Finally, the third message is posted, the only one to `muzhik2`. This message starts the second web worker and statement #3 appears. Shortly afterward, statement #4 appears as `muzhik2` completes its job before `muzhik1`, even though `muzhik1` started first. Then, after a good deal of deliberation, statement #5 appears in the console as `muzhik1` has finished its job.

The asynchronous work being done is obvious because one worker began first and finished last. Sometimes, this is a very desirable effect; other times, we must be careful to ensure that the data we send and receive is handled in the right order. If you re-create the preceding example and refresh the page several times, you can expect to see some of the messages displayed in a different order.

It's not observable in our example, but a more beneficial effect has taken place. While these two workers were crunching away, we would be able to keep interacting with our web page without the content and cursor freezing on us. That doesn't matter in our simple example, but in web pages where workers are dutifully carrying out image processing or other long-running tasks, it is a delightful plus to number-crunching scripts.

Shared Web Workers

Up until now, we've discussed only the new `Worker()` objects in JavaScript. These are referred to in the specification as *dedicated* workers, and there exists a second type, shared workers, that we create in the same way with the `SharedWorker()` constructor.

Shared workers are available to other pages with the same origin. A parent and several iFrames, for instance, can all send and post messages to the same web worker.

Shared workers are not as widely implemented as dedicated workers. Notably, Firefox, Internet Explorer 9 and 10, and Chrome for Android do not have shared worker support.

NOTE

The compatibility table site caniuse.com has a section for web workers at http://caniuse.com/#feat=sharedworkers.

Names
Shared workers are "named," and this is the largest difference between them and dedicated workers. This name allows any page with the same origin (such as a same-origin iFrame) to access a worker if it is already created.

This name is specified by the second argument to the shared worker constructor:
`SharedWorker(scriptURL, name)`. If no second argument is used, the name of the worker
is the empty string.

The following four constructors create only two shared workers. The `muzhik1` and `muzhik2`
vars will refer to the same worker that has the name `""` (the empty string). The `muzhik3`
and `muzhik4` also refer to the same worker, with the name `"myName"`:

```
// Four vars, only two workers!
var muzhik1 = new SharedWorker('shared.js');
var muzhik2 = new SharedWorker('shared.js');

var muzhik3 = new SharedWorker('shared.js', 'myName');
var muzhik4 = new SharedWorker('shared.js', 'myName');
```

These names allow you to easily access shared workers across browsing contexts. Shared
workers have an additional `name` attribute in their global scope, which references this
name, should you need to get it at runtime.

Shared Worker Example

Thankfully, shared worker construction is nearly identical to dedicated workers. Our
example illustrates that calling the `SharedWorker` constructor with the same name returns
the same worker, which can subsequently do work across multiple pages.

We use a parent page and an iFrame to reference the worker, with both pages asking the
worker to compute a Fibonacci number. Listing 11.7 contains the code for the parent
page.

LISTING 11.7   `shared.html`—Shared Workers Parent Page

```
<!DOCTYPE html>
<head>
  <title>Shared Workers</title>
</head>
<body>

<iframe id="frame" style="width:300px; height:120px" src="frame.html"></iframe>

<script type="text/javascript">

var muzhik = new SharedWorker('shared.js', 'Tolstoy');

// Instead of listening directly on the worker,
// we listen on the port attribute:
muzhik.port.addEventListener('message', function(event) {
  var p = document.createElement('p');
  p.innerText = event.data;
```

```
    document.body.appendChild(p);
  }, false);

muzhik.port.start();

// Send a message with a JSON object
// Describing the Fibonacci number we want computed
// And a name describing the page that is posting the message
muzhik.port.postMessage(
    { fib: 33,
      page: 'parent'
    });

</script>

</body>
```

Note how we must listen on the port attribute of the worker instead of the worker itself, and that we must call `port.start()`. Behind the scenes, dedicated workers use ports too, but they are started implicitly instead.

There is additionally a `port.close()` method, as an alternative to terminating the worker because any given page might want to no longer subscribe to that worker, but other pages might still want to use it.

Listing 11.8 contains the code for the iFrame nested in the parent page.

LISTING 11.8   `frame.html`—Shared Workers iFrame

```
<!DOCTYPE html>
<head>
  <title>Shared Worker Frame</title>
</head>
<body>

<script type="text/javascript">

var muzhik = new SharedWorker('shared.js', 'Tolstoy');

muzhik.port.addEventListener('message', function(event) {
  var p = document.createElement('p');
  p.innerText = event.data;
  document.body.appendChild(p);
}, false);

muzhik.port.start();
```

```
// Send a message with a JSON object describing the Fibonacci we want computed
// And a name describing the page that is posting the message
muzhik.port.postMessage(
  { fib: 5,
    page: 'iFrame'
  });

</script>

</body>
```

In both HTML pages, the SharedWorker constructor call is identical, meaning they both reference the named worker "Tolstoy". The second constructor to fire, therefore, does not create a new worker but simply references the shared worker that had been created previously. Both the parent page and the iFrame post a single message to the worker, a JSON object.

The shared worker script itself listens for incoming connections, and for each one it sends back a message totaling the connections so far. Then it adds a message event listener, to respond to any requests for Fibonacci computations.

Listing 11.9 contains the shared worker script.

LISTING 11.9   shared.js—The Shared Worker JavaScript

```
// The same Fibonacci function as the dedicated workers example
function fib(num) {
  if (num > 2) {
    return fib(num - 2) + fib(num - 1);
  } else {
    return num-1;
  }
}

var connections = 0;

self.addEventListener('connect', function (event) {
    var port = event.ports[0];

    connections++;
    port.postMessage('New connection. Total connections: ' + connections);

    port.addEventListener('message', function (event) {
      var data = event.data;
      var computed = fib(data.fib);
      port.postMessage('Hello ' + data.page);
      port.postMessage('The number you requested is: ' + computed);
```

```
    }, false);

    port.start();
}, false);
```

The result is straightforward: Two pages are able to access the same `SharedWorker` without ever communicating between each other. We know that the worker is the same one because the `connections` counter is incremented.

Figure 11.2 shows the visual output of our example. We can see that the iFrame was the first to connect because the iFrame script was parsed before the main page script. (If you want the pages to parse in the other order, you can set the iFrame source attribute at the very end of your main page script.)

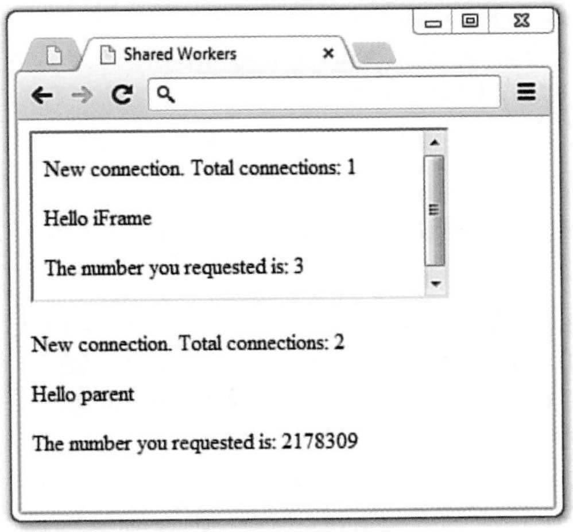

FIGURE 11.2   The results of our shared worker example.

Web Worker Considerations

There are several nuances to web workers that are worth mentioning. Web workers allow script importation for sharing utility code between many workers, and with a few considerations in mind, web workers can be nested, embedded, and debugged in some modern browsers.

Importing Scripts

The web worker scope has a previously unmentioned method in its global scope for importing scripts, `importScript()`. This method takes any number of strings representing JavaScript file sources and imports the JavaScript from that file into the worker's scope. Typical usage looks like:

```
self.importScripts('mathFunctions.js', 'searchFunctions.js');
```

This can be useful if multiple workers share common methods, especially if they need to mix and match functionality depending on the work they have to do.

Errors That Web Workers Encounter

Just as workers have a `message` event listener, they also have an `error` listener. Web worker–specific errors include syntax and network errors from `importScripts` or `postMessage`.

The event for these errors (confusingly, the type is `ErrorEvent`) contains` four additional attributes. They are `message` and `filename`, strings that convey an error message and give the location of the error, as well as `lineno` and `column`, which pinpoint the error in the file (unusually forgiving for a JavaScript error).

Nested Web Workers

Nothing in the specification prevents web workers from creating their own subordinate workers. These "nested" workers could be spawned to divide jobs among more threads recursively. Although this may be tempting for some applications, not all browsers currently support nested workers, most prominently Chrome, so it would be best to test such a scheme on all platforms if you intend to do it.

Embedding Workers

Instead of referencing separate scripts in the `Worker` constructor, you can "embed" web workers by referencing a `data:` URL.

`data:` URLs (or more accurately, uniform resource identifiers [URIs]) are strings that allow authors to embed small files into documents. These are typically seen in Cascading Style Sheets (CSS) to describe small images. You can use them to describe a JavaScript file for web workers, but although this is possible, it would be unorthodox.

Debugging Web Workers

Debugging web workers poses a challenge because their scripts are not loaded like typical page scripts, and do not appear in most JavaScript debuggers. Many developers create their own solutions to this problem, such as sending JSON messages with a flag to identify messages meant as debugging statements. For the short history of web workers, debugging has been regarded as a distasteful endeavor.

Luckily, Chrome now supports natively debugging web workers within the JavaScript inspector, and more browsers are sure to follow. In Chrome, when web worker debugging is enabled, a separate debugging context is created for each worker context, allowing for all of the expected tools, such as breakpoints and the console, to function on the scripts. Figure 11.3 shows the location of the web worker debugging option in the Chrome inspector.

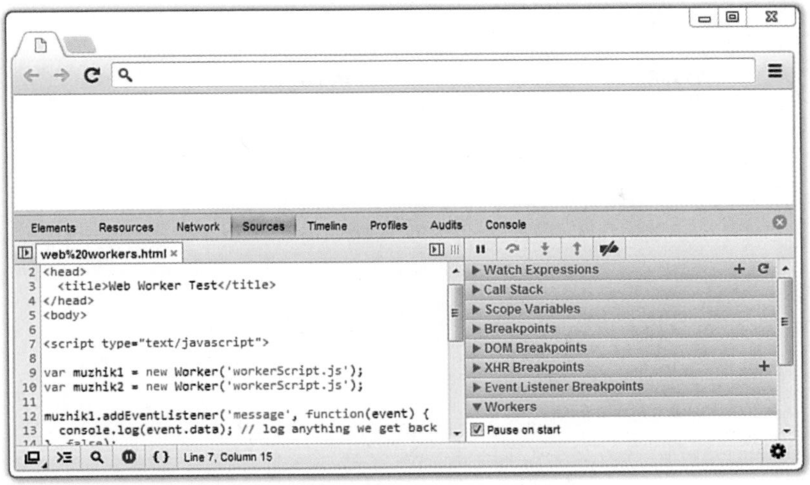

FIGURE 11.3   The Chrome inspector. The option to enable web worker debugging is near the bottom right of the panel.

Summary

The ability to communicate between separate browsing contexts, be they frames or workers, is a welcome addition to web applications. The security rules on interframe communication have been carefully relaxed to allow for relevant cross-document communication.

Thanks to web workers, programmers can safely run large processing tasks without fear of locking up the user's browser, and many with their sights set on large-scale apps may see a performance boost from the pseudo-multithreaded environment.

Due to their nature, the fallback options for these technologies need to be a little more custom than other components of HTML5. Luckily for users and developers, workers are already supported on every modern desktop browser, and cross-document messaging is supported on every browser and platform released in recent history, including Internet Explorer 8.

## CHAPTER 12

Network Communication: WebSockets and XMLHttpRequest Level 2

HTML5 largely concerns itself with enhancements to the client. At the same time, however, some technologies for client/server communication have come to fruition and implementation. Technically, neither of the technologies in this chapter are part of HTML5, but they both bring important new functionality to web browsers and already enjoy reasonably wide support.

WebSockets is a new technology for enabling full-duplex (simultaneous, two-way) communications between web pages and servers, and is the first subject of this chapter. The WebSocket protocol and application programming interface (API) allow for faster updating of live web pages, such as email web apps, and enable new possibilities (such as games built natively in the browser) for real-time interaction between pages and servers.

XMLHttpRequest is not a new technology, but it has recently gotten an upgrade and is the second subject of this chapter. This chapter details the new features of XMLHttpRequest Level 2, including binary file support (such as images), making requests across origins (domains), and progress event notifications.

Real-Time Communication with WebSockets

WebSockets refers to a new communications protocol and JavaScript API that enable two-way, interactive communication between a client browser and a server. This technology eliminates the need to use multiple Hypertext Transfer Protocol (HTTP) requests to communicate with a server; instead, you can simply send and receive event-driven reply messages without having to resort to polling techniques.

The WebSockets specification is considered very new, with the protocol undergoing several revisions (including important security fixes) in its short history. It was finally standardized in 2011, and most browsers are comfortable enough with the technology to support WebSockets without needing debug flags or name prefixes.

WebSockets is available on every modern desktop browser, including Internet Explorer starting with Internet Explorer 10. In the mobile sphere, WebSockets is supported by every major browser except the default Android browser (Chrome Mobile is supported). Also, unlike all other technologies in this text, WebSockets needs to be supported on both the browser and the server.

> **NOTE**
>
> The WebSockets API can be found at http://www.w3.org/TR/websockets/ or http://www.whatwg.org/specs/web-apps/current-work/multipage/network.html.
>
> If you want all the technical details, the WebSocket protocol specification can be found at http://tools.ietf.org/html/rfc6455.

Before WebSockets

Client/server communication has long been necessary for the web apps (such as mail clients) that may periodically or constantly receive new information from a server. Before WebSockets, once the page was completely loaded, there was no way for a web server to initiate sending new information for the client to use. Instead, two client-initiated methods have been used to afford this ability.

The first way to get updates from a server is called *polling*. This is the act of sending several HTTP requests from client to server, periodically, to check for updates. This works, and is used in a multitude of websites that might need to update a single page without reloading it, such as mail clients, chess apps, and stock tickers.

Polling is problematic because for some applications, such as real-time games, it does not act fast enough. Polling also leads to a good deal of overhead as the client does not know if there is actually anything for the server to send back, and in many cases a large percentage of requests turns out to have no useful response.

The utility of polling is obvious, but the end result is a back-and-forth messaging system where the client resembles a child on a car ride asking "Are we there yet?" for the duration of the page's existence. With polling, the server is only capable of responding affirmatively or negatively, but with the introduction of WebSockets, the server is able to say, "I'll tell you when we get there." (And unlike the metaphor, the client is certain to listen.)

Long-polling is the second common technique for receiving messages from a server. With long-polling, the client sends a request to the server and instead of replying right away, the server keeps the request open for a set period of time, until it has something useful to send, and may send its eventual reply back some time after the initial request was made. This is generally considered better than polling because it can make the responses more immediate (once data is available) and reduce some overhead because fewer polls could be made. However, the more frequently a client asks for information, for instance if the server is generating messages at a fast pace, the more long-polling begins to resemble polling and any advantage is lost.

Both of these methods use full-fledged HTTP requests, which contain nontrivial overhead of their own, considered unnecessary baggage for sending small messages between the server and the client. Polling methods are also not full-duplex, so messages cannot be sent and received simultaneously. Server-sent messages are all responses to client-sent messages, and this is generally unacceptable for applications that need large amounts of real-time updates.

Getting Started with WebSockets

WebSockets defines full-duplex communication over a single socket on the Web, and uses its own protocol instead of going over HTTP. This provides an enormous benefit to message sizes, response times, and, therefore, the general scalability of web apps that want to connect clients and servers.

The gains from WebSockets are dependent on your application, but various studies have shown latency reductions of 3:1 and drastic header payload reductions. Messages have the potential to be just a handful of bytes, instead of several kilobytes.

Creating a Connection

Creating a WebSocket connection in JavaScript uses the `WebSocket` constructor, which takes two arguments:

- ► `url`—The URL to connect to, which should be the server that will respond. This URL is prefixed with `ws:` or `wss:` as its protocol instead of `http:` or `https:`.

- ► `protocols`—A string or optional array of strings describing subprotocols to be used, if any. If omitted, the empty string is assumed as a default. If multiple protocols are given, the server selects one (or none) of the protocols based on its capabilities.

In practice, the constructor might look like one of the following:

```
var socket = new WebSocket('ws://example.com', 'xmpp');
var socket = new WebSocket('ws://example.com', ['someProtocol', 'soap']);
```

Once the connection is open, `socket.protocol` will be the subprotocol that the server decided upon, which may be any of the ones sent or else the empty string if no subprotocol was sent or supported.

> **NOTE**
>
> WebSocket subprotocols exist to fill niche specific needs. If you're not sure whether or not you need a subprotocol, you definitely don't need one!

WebSocket Attributes

Each `WebSocket` instance has a few attributes:

- ▶ `readyState`—A number representing the state of the connection, which will be one of the four ready state constants defined on the `WebSocket` object. The `readyState` will be a number between 0 and 3, corresponding to the states CONNECTING, OPEN, CLOSING, and CLOSED, respectively.

- ▶ `bufferedAmount`—The amount of data (in bytes) that has been queued to be sent to the server from this `WebSocket`. If this number is not zero, that means there is still data to send, and it would be a bad idea to close the connection.

- ▶ `protocol`—The subprotocol selected by the server, if any.

- ▶ `binaryType`—A string describing the type of data being transmitted. Either `"blob"` (the default) or `"arraybuffer"`.

- ▶ `url`—The URL of the `WebSocket`.

- ▶ `extensions`—There are currently no extensions defined for WebSockets, so as of this writing, extensions will only ever be an empty string.

WebSocket Events and Methods

WebSockets are event driven, and each `WebSocket` instance has four events:

- ▶ `open`—Called when the server responds to the WebSocket creation and the `readyState` changes to OPEN. Once this event has fired, your WebSocket is ready to send and receive data.

- ▶ `close`—Called when the `readyState` of the WebSocket changes to CLOSED. If an error occurs, the WebSocket is closed before any errors are fired.

- ▶ `message`—Called whenever the WebSocket receives a message from the server. The associated event type is `MessageEvent` and contains a `MessageEvent.data` attribute, with the message.

- ▶ `error`—Called if an error occurs, such as a security error or connection failure.

Once the `open` event has been called, we can send messages to our server. Sending messages is done with the WebSocket's `send` method:

```
socket.send('Hello server!');
```

Data can be sent as either a string, a binary blob, an `ArrayBuffer`, or an `ArrayBufferView`. Serializable JSON (JavaScript Object Notation) objects are acceptable, too.

When it is time to close the connection, we can call `socket.close()`, though we should always check that `socket.bufferedAmount` is zero before closing the connection, to be sure that there was no yet-to-be-sent data in queue.

The `socket.close()` method takes two optional arguments, a code as a number and a reason as a string. The numerical code must be a specific integer, though most of them are currently reserved and unused, with 1000 being the default value and meaning normal closure.

The `close` event fires with a special `CloseEvent` argument, which similarly contains `code` and `reason` attributes. If a server closes the connection, it provides a code, such as 1000 for normal closure or 1001 for the server "going away," either because of server failure or because the user is navigating off the page. Finally, there is a `CloseEvent.wasClean` attribute that indicates whether or not the connection was cleanly closed.

Limiting Sent Data

If you have a stream of constant updates to send the server, it may be a good idea to check the buffered amount to ensure that you are not just piling on to-be-sent data at a rate that is too fast for the server.

For example, you could send an update to the server every 50 milliseconds, unless there is still data queued, in which case you wait until the buffer is clear before sending the next update:

```
var socket = new WebSocket('ws://example.com');

socket.addEventListener('open', function(event) {
  setInterval(function() {
    if (socket.bufferedAmount === 0)
      socket.send( /* some update data */ );
  }, 50);
}, false);
```

This sort of rate limiting allows you to send updates at whatever speed the server can handle, without creating an ever-increasing buffer.

Errors

If an error occurs while attempting to connect, first the WebSocket's `error` event is fired with a generic error, and then the `close` event is fired, detailing the specific reason for closure.

There are a few other errors that may or may not need to be handled, depending on the application. Calling `socket.send()` before the `readyState` attribute is `CONNECTING` throws an `InvalidStateError`. Also, the WebSocket constructor can throw a `SecurityError` if the port is blocked, such as when establishing a `wss:` protocol connection on a server that is not set up to accept SSL connections.

A Complete WebSockets Example

WebSockets requires both client and server code to function, but we can still create a complete example without writing any server code. There are a handful of websites that supply "echo test" pages, which respond to any WebSocket messages received by relaying back the same message. Our test uses the site websocket.org, though several others can be found by searching the Web.

Listing 12.1 contains an HTML page that opens a WebSocket and listens to all four events. Upon opening the connection, it sends a message to the server and outputs the reply. The code isn't particularly interesting, but it illustrates just how easy it is to create the client end of a WebSockets app.

LISTING 12.1   `sockets.html`—WebSockets Sample Page

```
<!DOCTYPE html>

<body>
<!-- There are no visible HTML elements on this page,
     Everything happens in the developer console!
     If you wanted to write the messages to the HTML body
     You could use document.write instead of console.log -->

<script>
  var socket = new WebSocket('ws://echo.websocket.org');

  socket.addEventListener('open', function(event) {
    var msg = 'Hello server!';
    console.log('Connection open, sending message: ' + msg);

    // Once the connection is open, send a message to the server
    socket.send(msg);
  }, false);

  socket.addEventListener('close', function(event) {
    console.log('Connection closed.');
  }, false);

  socket.addEventListener('message', function(event) {
    console.log('Message received: ' + event.data + '');
```

```
    socket.close();
  }, false);

  socket.addEventListener('error', function(event) {
    console.log('Something went wrong!');
  }, false);

</script>

</body>
```

In the JavaScript console, we see the following messages:

```
Connection open, sending message: Hello server!
Message received: Hello server!
Connection closed.
```

Server-Side WebSockets

The server-side of WebSockets is very varied because implementations are platform dependent. This text concerns itself only with client-side development, and any given server WebSocket implementation is far too specific to cover.

Fortunately, WebSocket implementations already exist for most popular servers (nginx, Apache, IIS, etc.) either natively or as plug-ins. There are also several standalone WebSocket server projects in a multitude of languages, from C++ to Haskell.

Several websites maintain lists of WebSocket server implementations and tools, such as the Mozilla Developer Network (https://developer.mozilla.org/en-US/docs/WebSockets), Wikipedia (http://en.wikipedia.org/wiki/Comparison_of_WebSocket_implementations), and the Google-hosted site, HTML5Rocks (http://www.html5rocks.com/en/tutorials/websockets/basics/#toc-serversideimplementations). Of course, any plain web search may yield more up-to-date and popular options than the ones present in a compiled list.

New AJAX Capabilities with XMLHttpRequest Level 2

XMLHttpRequest (XHR) is a JavaScript API for sending HTTP requests to the server and receiving replies, giving developers the ability to communicate with a server and modify pages without reloading them. When people speak of Ajax (Asynchronous JavaScript and XML) development, XMLHttpRequest is the mechanism used.

> **NOTE**
>
> XMLHttpRequest is used in nearly every interactive web app, such as mail clients or chess websites, though on many apps (such as parts of Gmail), it is being replaced with WebSockets.

XMLHttpRequest has been around since 2000, becoming a de facto standard around 2004 and finally standardized by the World Wide Web Consortium (W3C) in 2006. Recently, in 2010, the XMLHttpRequest has received an API upgrade called XMLHttpRequest Level 2, or just XHR2. XHR2 increases functionality and eliminates the necessity of various work-arounds that are used to circumvent the prior limitations of XHR.

XHR2 is supported in every modern desktop and mobile browser, including Internet Explorer starting with Internet Explorer 10.

> **NOTE**
>
> In spite of Internet Explorer being the late adopter to XHR2, the original XMLHttpRequest was designed by Microsoft.

New Features in XHR2

From a development standpoint, making a request with XHR2 is superficially the same procedure. You still create a new `XMLHttpRequest`, use the `open` method to set the request type and URL, listen for desired events, and call `send` when you're ready. The changes all come as new features, most of which can be adopted into existing applications as incremental improvements.

Progress Events and Monitoring

Previously when we needed notification that an XMLHttpRequest was completed, we would listen for the `readystatechange` event. With the XHR2 additions, XMLHttpRequests can now opt to listen for several progress events instead, which takes a lot of the guess-work out of informing users (and your own code) of the request's status. The new events are as follows:

- ▶ `loadstart`—Fired when the request is sent

- ▶ `progress`—Fired while loading (sending or receiving) data

- ▶ `load`—Fired when the request has finished successfully

- ▶ `loadend`—Fired when the request has completed, regardless of success

- ▶ `abort`—Fired when the request has been aborted, either from calling `xhr.abort()` or user action such as navigating away from the page

- ▶ `error`—Fired when the request fails

- ▶ `timeout`—Fired when the (author-specified) timeout has passed before the request completes

In general, these events can completely replace the `readystatechange` event, though `readystatechange` will remain in the specification for backward compatibility.

Progress events have their own `ProgressEvent` type, which has additional attributes for the number of bytes transferred (`event.loaded`) and total number of bytes in the request (event.total). The total will not be available until a third attribute, event.lengthComputable is true. The lengthComputable is initially false and becomes true once the HTTP content header for the request is downloaded.

Listing 12.2 shows an example of the progress event itself.

LISTING 12.2   XHR Progress Event

```
var xhr = new XMLHttpRequest();
xhr.open('GET','hello.png');

xhr.addEventListener('progress', function(event) {
  if (event.lengthComputable) {
    var percentComplete = event.loaded / event.total;
    // Display the percent complete
  } else {
    // Unable to compute progress information since the total size is unknown
  }
}, false);

xhr.send();
```

The progress event is fired for every chunk of data, including the last chunk, and the XHR connection is closed before the final progress event is fired. Later examples in this chapter use the load event as the standard event when listening for completed requests.

Cross-Origin

In line with other HTML5 developments, XHR2 allows for cross-origin requests. This means that requests can be made to different domains, subdomains, and through different ports and protocols.

As with any client/server technology, both sides of the connection must support this new feature for it to work. If the server is not set up to allow for cross-origin requests, then the XMLHttpRequest will be denied.

> **NOTE**
>
> The website http://enable-cors.org details steps for enabling cross-origin resource sharing on various server platforms.
>
> Although Internet Explorer 8 and 9 do not support the new XHR2 features, they do sport the XDomainRequest object, which works similarly and allows cross-origin requests.

Cross-Origin Credentials

XMLHttpRequests have a new attribute, withCredentials, that specifies whether or not the user's credentials (SSL certificates, cookies, HTTP authentication) should be passed along with the cross-origin request. Setting the attribute to `true` will pass along the credentials:

```
var xhr = new XMLHttpRequest();
// Where example.com is a different domain than the current page
xhr.open('GET','http://example.com/someFile');
xhr.withCredentials = true;
xhr.addEventListener('load', function() {
  // Do something when the request has completed
});
xhr.send();
```

The `withCredentials` attribute is `false` by default.

Binary Data and Other Media Types

XHR objects have two new properties, `response` and `responseType`, which allow for proper requests of binary data.

Before a request is made, the `responseType` attribute can be set to `"text"`, `"blob"`, `"arraybuffer"`, `"json"`, `"document"`, or `""` (the empty string). The default is the empty string, which is identical to `"text"`. Other strings throw an error.

Once a request is successfully sent and returned, the `response` contains the appropriate data.

> **NOTE**
>
> Mismatches between the `responseType` and the file requested (for instance, a `responseType` of `"document"` and a text file) do not lead to errors, but the `response` will be `null` and the `xhr.status` code will be `0`.

Listing 12.3 contains an example using a blob `responseType` to fetch an image and create a `Blob` object. Then a `FileReader` is created to parse the blob and output the image to the document's body.

LISTING 12.3   `responseType` Example

```
var xhr = new XMLHttpRequest();
xhr.open('GET','hello.png');
xhr.responseType = 'blob';

xhr.addEventListener('load', function() {
  console.log(this.response);
  var blob = new Blob([this.response], {type: 'image/png'});

  var r = new FileReader();
  r.onload = function(e) {
```

```
    var img = new Image();
    img.src = r.result;
    document.body.appendChild(img);
  }
  r.readAsDataURL(blob);

}, false);


xhr.send();
```

> FileReader is part of the File API, covered in Chapter 13, "Microdata, Other Small Things, and Beyond HTML5."

In addition to fetching all the new forms of data, the xhr.send() has been overridden to accept sending Blob, Document, DOMString, FormData, and ArrayBuffer objects.

FormData

A new FormData object allows us to send key-value pairs to servers. Unlike sending JSON data, FormData can contain binary data.

FormData is created, then data is added using its data.append() method, which takes a key and value. For example:

```
var xhr = new XMLHttpRequest();
xhr.open('POST','/process');

var data = new FormData();
data.append('name','Maple');
data.append('age','1');
data.append('color','Black and Tan');


xhr.send(data);
```

The name FormData is not a coincidence. The FormData constructor can take a reference to an HTML form in its constructor to automatically populate key-value data. In a typical form submission handler, you could use the event.target for the reference needed:

```
var data = new FormData(event.target).
```

Timeouts

Requests can take a long time to complete for a multitude of reasons, such as poor network latency or an overloaded server. Longer requests can be disconcerting for the user, as he or she may think that something is broken (either with the app, server, or his or her own connection).

XMLHttpRequest now has a built-in request timeout, using a new `timeout` attribute and `timeout` event. The attribute allows developers to specify how long (in milliseconds) before they can opt to do something else, via the associated event.

Listing 12.4 gives an example of using a timeout to notify a user and remake the request.

LISTING 12.4 XHR Timeout

```
var xhr = new XMLHttpRequest();
xhr.open('GET', 'someText.txt');
xhr.timeout = 3000;

xhr.addEventListener('load', function(event) {
  // Do something with the response
});

xhr.addEventListener('timeout', function(event) {
  // Tell the user (perhaps with a soft pop-up) that the request is
  // taking a long time

  // Restart the request:
  event.target.open('GET', 'someText.txt');

  // Optionally, set a longer timeout to override the original:
  event.target.timeout = 6000;
  event.target.send();
}, false);

xhr.send();
```

NOTE

As of this writing, Chrome and Safari do not yet support XHR timeouts.

Summary

Client/server technologies are not the star of HTML5, in fact both technologies in this chapter are not technically part of HTML5 at all. But both WebSockets and XMLHttpRequest Level 2 offer important new functionality to web developers and are supported enough to already be of use.

CHAPTER 13

Microdata, Other Small Things, and Beyond HTML5

We began this book with the new HTML5 semantic tags, which allow a page's HTML content to be organized in meaningful, structured ways. This final chapter introduces a small but powerful application programming interface (API) that brings much more semantic utility to HTML.

Semantic information is information with annotations or signifiers. Microdata is a specification in HTML5 that can be used to nest semantics within existing web content, allowing authors to create any kind of arbitrary annotation. Programs (especially search engines and web crawlers) can search for these annotations and extract this data, making use of the Microdata marked-up content to provide more meaningful results.

After Microdata, we quickly cover new specifications and browser features that were not given a full mention in this book. Finally, we briefly consider the future of the Web.

Microdata

Semantic web is a buzzword that has faded in and out of the press ever since people got tired of hearing *Web 2.0*. The term was coined in 2001 by Tim-Berners Lee, the inventor of the Web, and has been swept up in a flurry of misuse since its inception.

Berners-Lee intended the term *semantic web* to mean a web with more structured content. In 2001, he wrote of websites that would not just provide information, but provide it in such a way that programs could pick up on it, and programmers could design for it. Most of the Web is written for humans to read, not computers to manipulate automatically, and Berners-Lee wanted to ensure that both human-readable and machine content are possible and common on the Web.

Many web pages contain data—such as movie times, restaurant locations, business hours, and so on—that would be very useful to search engines and other programs that sift through data. Since 2001, search engines have gotten much better at inferring all of this information, but it would be even better if we as content authors could be more explicit, and *point out* data to the software peeking at our pages. The semantic web is a web where authors have mechanisms of creating such structured data.

In 2006, Berners-Lee stated (one imagines with some frustration) that his "simple idea" had gone largely unrealized. Pleasantly, seven years later, we can begin to see the fruits of a semantic web brought on by a combination of ever-more-powerful inference and structured semantic data. Google hasn't changed much visually since 2001, and Bing might be considered "merely derivative" on a good day, but with a close look at modern search results, we can see web semantics in action.

Figure 13.1 shows Google and Bing searches for a recipe and movie showtimes, respectively. In both examples, review information is inserted directly into the page. Google shows the total cooking time and calorie count when available, and Bing shows movie length and genres. Part of this information is inference, but the other part is the semantic web in action, specifically Microdata.

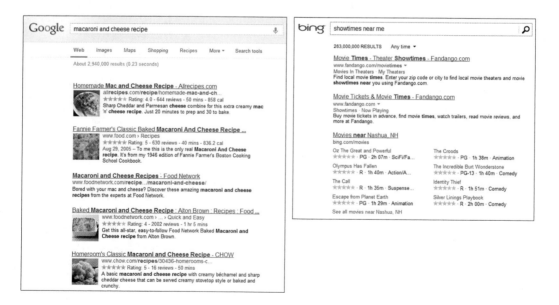

FIGURE 13.1   Search results from Google and Bing pulling a combination of semantic and inferred data from search results.

HTML5 marks the largest leap toward a truly semantic web. This is clear with the new semantic elements, such as `<article>` and `<section>`, which are used to define meaning instead of looks. Microdata allows authors to go beyond a few constrained tags, and create the equivalent of `<people>`, `<doctors-office>`, `<calorie-count>`, `<recommended-dose>`, and so on. Microdata doesn't use separate HTML tags; instead, it has its own specification that doesn't conflict with the existing DOM or backward compatibility.

> **NOTE**
>
> You can read Tim Berners-Lee's complete vision for the semantic web in the original 2001 *Scientific American* article online at http://www.scientificamerican.com/article.cfm?id=the-semantic-web.

Getting Started with Microdata

Microdata is added to existing web page content in the form of HTML tag attributes. Depending on your content, you may need to add `<span>` or `<div>` tags to specify some content. Otherwise, the DOM and Cascading Style Sheets (CSS) remain unchanged.

The examples in this section are related to the way search engines today use Microdata, but this is not to suggest that search engines are the only utilizers of Microdata, just the most common so far.

> **NOTE**
>
> Historically, there have been three formats for such structured data: Microdata, Microformats, and RDFa to name a few. At this point, most search engines have converged on HTML5's Microdata as the standard, though many sites still support the other two.
>
> If you're interested in exploring these further, Microformats information can be found at http://microformats.org, and the W3C maintains a primer on RDFa at http://www.w3.org/TR/xhtml-rdfa-primer.

Microdata Syntax and Schema.org

Microdata lets you annotate content with a vocabulary, but that vocabulary needs to come from somewhere. The most widely supported (and promoted) vocabulary is maintained on the website schema.org. This site was born in 2011 out of collaboration between Microsoft, Google, and Yahoo! so that search engines and other "big-data" users could converge on a single vocabulary for annotating data. Their effort was a success, and schema.org is widely considered the most-recommended vocabulary for Microdata.

> **NOTE**
>
> There are other, older schema sites such as data-vocabulary.org, which use a vocabulary that is still widely supported. You'll notice if you go to the data-vocabulary.org home page, however, that it contains a short explanation of why you should use schema.org instead!

Now let's take a look at how to use a Microdata vocabulary. Listing 13.1 contains a simple snippet of HTML describing a person.

LISTING 13.1   HTML Snippet

```
<div>
  Hello, I'm Simon Sarris, a Software Developer living at
  5 HTML Road Nashua, NH.
  My homepage is <a href="http://www.simonsarris.com">simonsarris.com</a>.
</div>
```

Listing 13.2 contains the same HTML snippet, marked up with Microdata.

LISTING 13.2   HTML Snippet with Microdata

```
<div itemscope itemtype="http://schema.org/Person">
  Hello, I'm <span itemprop="name">Simon Sarris</span>,
  a <span itemprop="jobTitle">Software Developer</span> living at
  <div itemprop="address" itemscope itemtype="http://schema.org/PostalAddress">
    <span itemprop="streetAddress">5 HTML Road</span>
    <span itemprop="addressLocality">Nashua</span>,
    <span itemprop="addressRegion">NH</span>.
  </div> <!-- end of PostalAddress item scope -->
  My homepage is <a href="http://www.simonsarris.com" itemprop="url">
  simonsarris.com</a>.
</div> <!-- end of Person item scope -->
```

The Microdata-marked-up code is decidedly less pretty to look at, but users see the exact same thing on a page. Looking closely at the marked-up content, we see three new HMTL attributes.

The `itemscope` attribute specifies a new Microdata item. It is accompanied by an `itemtype`, in this case a Person, and by setting the value we declare that we'll be using the vocabulary from schema.org/Person. Web crawlers and other programs that are familiar with schema.org will be able pick up on our Microdata content.

Inside our Person `itemscope` div, we have several new `<span>` tags that each point out a property of our person, marked with `itemprop` attributes. In the middle of our Person item, we have a nested Address item, denoted by another `itemscope` with its own `itemtype`.

With all these attributes, web crawlers and other programs reading this page can definitively "know" several things:

▶ There is a Person described on this page named Simon Sarris. According to schema.org/Person, a Person can be anyone alive, dead, undead, or fictional.

▶ That person has a website, simonsarris.com.

▶ That person had an address, which may or may not be his or her home.

Programs do not know several other facts that a reader may merely assume, such as whether Simon is still alive (I am), and Simon's gender. Very smart programs may attempt to infer these, but with Microdata we could be much more specific if we were so inclined, and the schema.org/Person vocabulary is fairly comprehensive. There are several more `itemprop` properties that may come in handy, such as `birthDate`, `deathDate`, `gender`, `homeLocation` (as opposed to `address`), `awards`, `alumniOf`, `siblings`, and so on.

These may seem a tad creepy when describing any given person, but consider the applications for encyclopedic sites such as Wikipedia. Google already uses information from encyclopedias, such as the information shown on Gandhi in Figure 13.2.

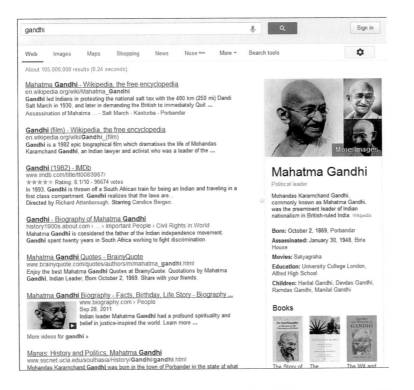

FIGURE 13.2   A Google search result for "Gandhi," showing several "properties" of the person in the sidebar, with relevant links to additional information.

Microdata items can be nested, as we saw with the Address inside of the Person, and all `itemprop` properties expect a certain *type*. For instance, a Person's `address` is expected to be another Microdata item, of type `PostalAddress` (http://schema.org/PostalAddress). Their `siblings` should be other Person items. The majority of properties simply require text or a number.

The schema.org website contains information on every supported type. For instance, the page http://schema.org/Person contains all of the possible Microdata properties for a Person, with descriptions and expected types. Most pages on schema.org also contain a practical example or two after the property descriptions.

> **NOTE**
>
> You can browse the entire schema hierarchy at http://schema.org/docs/full.html.

Nonvisible Microdata

In general, you should never display one set of content to a user and another set to programs such as search engines. Doing so can be taken as dishonesty or an attempt to "game" a search engine, and search engines may punish your content for it.

However, sometimes we need to format our Microdata values differently than the values presented on the page. For instance, schema.org types of CreativeWork (http://schema.org/CreativeWork) have a `datePublished` property, and this property has an expected type of "date". Dates can be presented to users in a multitude of ways, but typically programs would prefer if they followed a canonical pattern. Specifically, the date required is a string that conforms to the standard ISO 8601 (http://en.wikipedia.org/wiki/ISO_8601). These dates are in the format "YYYY-MM-DD", "YYYY-MM", and so on.

You may want to write dates in a more human-readable format, and to accommodate both humans and Microdata, the proper way to write a date is with an added `<meta>` tag, before or after the content, specifying both `itemprop` and `content` attributes:

```
<meta itemprop="datePublished" content="2013-06-21" />June 21, 2013
```

For another example, when marking up reviews, we must do more than just mark the score. Users may assume that an author saying "I rate this movie a 6" means a score of 6 out of 10, but Microdata can make no such assumption. After all, Zagat rates restaurants using a 1 to 30 scale, and many film critics rate movies out of zero to 4 stars. To remedy this, the Rating schema has `bestRating` and `worstRating` properties that can be inserted via `<meta>` tags:

```
<div itemprop="rating" itemscope itemtype="http://schema.org/Rating">
   Rating: <span itemprop="ratingValue">6</span>
   <meta itemprop="bestRating" content="10" />
</div>
```

If no `bestRating` or `worstRating` are specified, the values 5 and 1 are assumed, respectively.

A Microdata Recipe Example

Let's take a look at an example that we can immediately parse with a search engine. We start with a recipe, mark it up with Microdata, and then use a tool published by Google to visualize the result.

Marking Up a Recipe

For brevity's sake, we won't use a real recipe, just snippets of a fictional cookie recipe. We also won't include the purely presentational divs, spans, and headers you might expect to see in normal HTML.

Listing 13.3 has the gist of our fictional recipe.

LISTING 13.3   Recipe Skeleton

```
<div>
    Kookie Brittle
    By Walter V.R., May 8, 2013
    <img src="cookiephoto.jpg" />

    Kookie Brittle are cookies that you break with your hands into pieces.

    Prep Time: 15 minutes
    Cook time: 25 minutes
    Yield: 5 dozen

    Nutrition facts:
    240 calories, 9 grams fat

    Ingredients:
    1 cup butter
    1 cup sugar
    2 cups flour
    6 ounces chocolate chips
    ...

    Instructions:
        Preheat the oven to 375 Degrees
        Cream Butter and beat in sugar until fluffy
        ...

    140 comments:
    From Janel, May 5 -- thank you, great recipe!
    ...
</div>
```

Listing 13.4 has the same recipe, marked up with Microdata.

LISTING 13.4   Recipe Marked Up with Microdata

```
<div itemscope itemtype="http://schema.org/Recipe">
 <span itemprop="name">Kookie Brittle</span>
 By <span itemprop="author">Walter V.R.,</span>
 <meta itemprop="datePublished" content="2013-06-21">June 21, 2013
 <img itemprop="image" src="cookiephoto.jpg" />

 <span itemprop="description">
   Kookie Brittle are cookies that you break with your hands into pieces.
 </span>

 Prep Time: <meta itemprop="prepTime" content="PT15M">15 minutes
 Cook time: <meta itemprop="cookTime" content="PT25M">25 minutes
 Yield: <span itemprop="recipeYield">5 dozen</span>

 <div itemprop="nutrition"
    itemscope itemtype="http://schema.org/NutritionInformation">
    Nutrition facts:
    <span itemprop="calories">240 calories</span>,
    <span itemprop="fatContent">9 grams fat</span>
 </div>

 Ingredients:
 * <span itemprop="ingredients">1 cup butter</span>
 * <span itemprop="ingredients">1 cup sugar</span>
 * <span itemprop="ingredients">2 cups flour</span>
 * <span itemprop="ingredients">6 ounces chocolate chips</span>
 ...

 Instructions:
 <span itemprop="recipeInstructions">
   Preheat the oven to 375 Degrees
   Cream Butter and beat in sugar until fluffy
   ...
 </span>

</div>
```

We have a Microdata item of type NutritionInformation, which is a nested type, and
`<meta>` tags are needed for dates and times. Otherwise, the markup is very straightforward.

Visualizing the Recipe in Search Results

For visualizing Microdata, Google offers a "structured data testing tool," which can be found at www.google.com/webmasters/tools/richsnippets.

The tool lets us test the appearance of our own Microdata. Using our marked-up recipe, we can see a preview of what it might look like in search results. Figure 13.3 shows our recipe in the data testing tool.

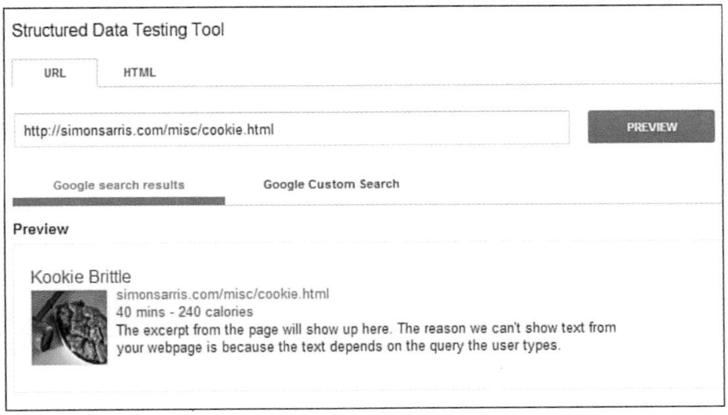

```
Structured Data Testing Tool

  [ URL ]    HTML

  http://simonsarris.com/misc/cookie.html                          [ PREVIEW ]

  Google search results       Google Custom Search
  ─────────────────────

  Preview

  Kookie Brittle
            simonsarris.com/misc/cookie.html
            40 mins - 240 calories
            The excerpt from the page will show up here. The reason we can't show text from
            your webpage is because the text depends on the query the user types.
```

FIGURE 13.3   The Kookie Brittle recipe as it might be rendered in Google Search results.

Google's tool also contains various examples that would appear in search results. For any page, the tool gives a list of all extracted fields in the Microdata, giving warnings where appropriate.

> **NOTE**
>
> Bing has a similar tool (https://ssl.bing.com/webmaster/diagnostics/markup/validator), but you need to sign up for their webmaster services to utilize it.

New Browser Features Not Covered in This Text

HTML5 and the future of the Web are home to a host of smaller or less-implemented APIs that could not fill their own chapters, but still deserve a mention. This section lists several such APIs, as well as other components not mentioned in this text.

Honorable Mention: The File API

The File API (not to be confused with the vastly less-supported FileSystem API) gives developers the ability to represent file objects within JavaScript and access their data. This API is not covered in depth in this text, but it is an exciting enough API that it deserves a quick rundown.

The File API gives us four new objects:

- `File`—Represents a file, allowing us to read basic file information. Has the properties `lastModifiedDate`, `name`, `size`, and `type`.

- `FileList`—Represents an array of files, to be used with `<input type="file">`.

- `Blob`—Represents raw binary data.

- `FileReader`—Provides methods to read `File` and `Blob` objects, using an event-driven model to obtain the results.

The File API is supported on all modern browsers, including Internet Explorer starting with Internet Explorer 10. The specification can be found at http://www.w3.org/TR/FileAPI/.

File Inputs, `FileList`s, and `File`s

Using an `<input type="file">` on a supported browser renders a Choose File button, allowing for a selection of files. Once chosen, we can get the `FileList` and `File` objects:

```
// assuming <input type="file" id="myFileInput">
var fileInput = document.getElementById('myFileInput');
var fileList = fileInput.files;
var individualFile = fileInput.files[0];
```

In a practical setting, we'd usually listen to the `change` event:

```
// assuming <input type="file" id="myFileInput">
var fileInput = document.getElementById('myFileInput');
fileInput.addEventListener("change", function(event) {
  var fileList = this.files;
  // do something with the file list
}, false);
```

FileReader

Once you have a reference to a `File` or `Blob` object, you can read its contents using a `FileReader`. `FileReader` has several methods for asynchronously loading a file:

- `readAsBinaryString(BlobOrFile)`

- `readAsText(BlobOrFile)`

- `readAsDataURL(BlobOrFile)`

- `readAsArrayBuffer(BlobOrFile)`

`FileReader`s are event driven, and you must listen to the load event to get the file data. If the file is loaded successfully, `event.result` will contain the file data.

There is a lot of potential utility in the File API, and with the final inclusion of Internet Explorer it may see serious use in the near future. For a short practical example using `Blob` objects and `FileReader`, see Chapter 12, "Network Communication: WebSockets and XMLHttpRequest Level 2," under the "New AJAX Capabilities with XMLHttpRequest Level 2" section (Listing 12.3).

Other New Browser Features

Most of these features fill smaller, specific needs, and some enjoy little to no support. (A big notable exception is the first one.) We quickly mention them, and if a particular feature interests you, it's a good idea to look up current compatibility. Most of the features mentioned here are on compatibility sites such as caniuse.com, which also provides resource links to specifications and tutorials for most features.

All the APIs and specifications in this section are World Wide Web Consortium (W3C)–proposed recommendations or drafts, unless stated otherwise.

CSS3

CSS3 is the name of a multitude of newer specification documents (called "modules") that extend the capabilities of CSS in meaningful ways. Much of CSS3 is widely supported and immediately useful, and web designers would benefit from learning its new bag of tricks today. There's a large amount of new possibilities with CSS3, and it's the subject of many books already published. If you're a web designer, familiarizing yourself with these new possibilities is essential.

CSS3 feature support varies wildly per browser, and so it comes with its own host of development issues. The compatibility website caniuse.com has an entire section for CSS, where you can see all of the new CSS3 features and their associated level of support: http://caniuse.com/#cats=CSS.

> **NOTE**
> You can read about the several CSS3 module specifications at the W3C site: www.w3.org/Style/CSS/specs.

FileSystem API

The FileSystem API is an official W3C working draft that's been around for more than a year, though as of this writing it is supported only in Google Chrome.

The API allows for reading and writing files and directories to a sandboxed section of a user's file system. There are a host of uses for such an API: Video games or applications with lots of downloadable assets, offline web-mail, and web-based photo editors could all benefit from manipulation of a local directory structure.

> **NOTE**
> The FileSystem API specification can be found at www.w3.org/TR/file-system-api.

13

Web Audio API

The Web Audio API is a specification developed by Google for creating your own audio on the Web. This includes synthesizing, mixing, and other processing of audio that is essential for musical applications and complex games.

Like with the FileSystem API, only Chrome currently supports this specification.

> **NOTE**
>
> The Web Audio API specification can be found at www.w3.org/TR/webaudio.

Media Capture and Streams APIs

This up-and-coming set of APIs allows the browser to request local media, such as microphone and webcam streams. This is an essential step toward allowing real-time communication and recording in the browser.

The Media Capture APIs are already partially supported in Chrome, Firefox, and Opera, and several technology previews exist using these APIs.

> **NOTE**
>
> The Media Capture and Streams API specifications can be found at www.w3.org/TR/mediacapture-streams.

WebRTC

WebRTC (Web Real-Time Communication) is a project and associated API that aims to allow browser-to-browser applications for voice calling, video chat, and other P2P applications. WebRTC is a W3C draft and the project portion is run by Google. Google maintains an associated site with a good deal of information on the current status of the project at webrtc.org, including some very exciting proof-of-concept demos.

So far, the WebRTC capabilities are available in Chrome and the nightly (beta) version of Firefox.

> **NOTE**
>
> For more information on the current status of WebRTC, be sure to check out http://webrtc.org. The WebRTC specification itself can be found at www.w3.org/TR/webrtc.

Web Notifications

Web Notifications is an API for displaying unobtrusive notifications to users, typically envisioned as being displayed "outside" of the browser context. Because browser platforms vary in their displays and operating systems, the specification does not make any demands as to how the notifications are displayed. On desktop machines, the notifications might typically appear on the operating system's status bar, or the corner of a desktop. On mobile devices, notifications might be present in the area typical for the OS.

So far, only Chrome and Firefox 22 support web notifications. Notably, Google is already using this API for Gmail desktop notifications.

> **NOTE**
>
> The Web Notifications specification can be found at www.w3.org/TR/notifications.

Page Visibility

Page Visibility is a relatively new specification that allows developers to determine the current visibility state of a page.

Specifically, this simple API does two things: It adds a `hidden` attribute to the Document and adds a `visibilitychange` event. A page is considered hidden if the browser is minimized, the page is in a background tab, or the operating system lock screen is on.

If `document.hidden` is true, developers may be able to make runtime decisions to improve user experiences, such as pausing a browser game or animation if the browser gets minimized, or stopping some functionality that might otherwise consume battery power.

This tiny API is fairly well supported on desktop browsers, with the notable exception of Safari. Internet Explorer supports Page Visibility starting with Internet Explorer 10. All common mobile browsers except iOS Safari and the default Android browser support Page Visibility.

> **NOTE**
>
> The Page Visibility specification can be found at www.w3.org/TR/page-visibility.

Full Screen and Pointer Lock

The Full Screen API is a simple specification for allowing content (such as video or an HTML canvas element) to take up the entire screen.

The API contains two read-only attributes and two methods.

The `requestFullScreen()` method is called on an element, such as `someCanvas.requestFullScreen()`. The document then has `document.exitFullScreen()`. There are also the attributes `document.fullscreenEnabled`, which is `true` or `false` depending on the full-screen status, and `document.fullScreenElement`, a reference to the current element taking up the screen, or else `null`.

Note that most current implementations use prefixes for this API, such as `webkitRequestFullScreen`. This API is supported for most modern browsers with the appropriate prefix (and Opera unprefixed), but is not yet supported in any version of Internet Explorer.

Pointer Lock is a related API that allows developers to access raw mouse data and remove the cursor from the screen. This is similarly supported, and can be useful in full-screen web games.

> **NOTE**
>
> The Full Screen and Pointer Lock specifications can be found at www.w3.org/TR/fullscreen and www.w3.org/TR/pointerlock, respectively.

Device Orientation Events

Several new smaller specifications are targeted toward mobile devices in an effort to bring web apps up to speed with native apps. Device Orientation events are one such effort, giving an API for detecting device motion and orientation while in the browser.

The primary new event listeners in this API are `deviceorientation` and `devicemotion`, and the associated events contain information about orientation, rotation, acceleration, and so on.

This API is understandably not well supported on desktop browsers (only Chrome bothers), but enjoys near universal mobile support.

> **NOTE**
>
> The Device Orientation events specification can be found at www.w3.org/TR/orientation-event.

Navigation Timing

Navigation Timing is a new API to help developers understand and measure performance, and is accessed through the `window.performance` object. The Navigation Timing API is available on Internet Explorer 9 and 10, Firefox, and Chrome, but not Safari, Opera, or most mobile browsers.

> **NOTE**
>
> The Navigation Timing specification can be found at www.w3.org/TR/navigation-timing.

The Future

HTML5 had its first public working draft released in 2008. It was received as a novelty at the time, a specification in near-constant flux.

After years of debates, edits, and serious adoption efforts by every browser vendor, almost all of HTML5 is ready for the mainstream, and many components are already in use by some of the highest traffic sites in the world. HTML5 itself was declared complete in December of 2012.

There was a big leap in time and breadth from HTML 4.1 to HTML5, and this is largely considered a mistake in the history of the Web. Browser vendors and standards committees from here on out intend for new advances to be far more incremental than dramatic in nature. Along this line, there is unlikely to be an HTML6. The Web Hypertext Application Technology Working Group (WHATWG) and W3C have suggested that future HTML development will simply be called "HTML" development.

The Future of Web Development

Beyond HTML's upgrades, we can expect to see further development by browser vendors, standards committees, and others in the field of web development languages. ECMAScript 5, the standard behind JavaScript implementations, has recently given several minor feature upgrades to the language. ECMAScript Harmony (or ECMAScript 6, or ES6) promises to add even more language features such as Maps, Sets, and use of the `const` and `let` declarations. The ES6 changes are exciting, but it has yet to have any concrete timeline and adoption could take some time.

JavaScript language development itself aside, some other interesting recent and future initiatives are detailed here.

CoffeeScript
CoffeeScript is a relatively new way to write JavaScript, using a less-verbose, more-functional "wrapper" language. CoffeeScript is intended to enhance the readability of JavaScript, and is run by producing (far-less-pretty) JavaScript for the browser to process. This syntactic simplification comes at the expense of potentially debugging in two languages, the written CoffeeScript and the transcompiled JavaScript that the browser runs. CoffeeScript remains a popular choice, especially among programmers and communities that favor brief languages such as Ruby.

Dart
Dart is a new web programming language developed by Google. Dart is intended to address shortcomings of JavaScript, while making it easier to program large-scale projects. Dart features classes, interfaces, generics, and optional typing, making for a web development experience more akin to Java than JavaScript. Dart code can be compiled into JavaScript, or run on a browser that has an embedded Dart virtual machine, which would typically support faster execution.

Google employees have publicly stated that the goal of Dart is to ultimately replace JavaScript as the go-to web development language, but it's uncertain if other browser vendors will adopt the language at all.

asm.js
Another tactic for writing large applications in JavaScript is being taken by the asm.js project, spearheaded by Mozilla. The goal of asm.js is to provide a subset of JavaScript that can be targeted by other compilers and run efficiently in a number of existing browsers. As asm.js is a subset of ECMAScript 5/JavaScript, it is backward compatible on existing browsers that do not efficiently handle the idioms used in the library.

Summary

This chapter primarily covered Microdata, the Swiss army knife of the semantic web. Implementing such semantics can only help your site, especially if you're concerned about appearance in search results. This chapter then touched upon several smaller topics not covered elsewhere in this text.

HTML5 has added a lot to the Web's power in recent history. Regardless of the changes over the years, at its heart HTML5 remains a combination of new semantics, new features, and new ways to do old tasks, but with less code and zero plug-ins.

This brings us to the end of the book. Making things is one of the most important pursuits in life, and we have a truly blessed profession that lets us flex our creative and logical muscles alongside each other. I hope this text has helped expand what you can do with the Web.

Be good to your users.

Index

Numbers

3D canvas. *See* WebGL canvas
45-degree rotations (canvas), 148
1990s rich media content, 69

A

AAC audio format, 78
abort event, 360
abort() method, 330
add() method, 315
addColorStop() method, 200
aligning canvas text, 197-198
altitude attribute, 284
animations, 210
    cancelAnimationFrame() method, 212
    canvas interactivity app example
        canvas state, tracking, 218-219
        <canvas> tag, 216
        complete code, 225-230
        doDown, doMove, and doUp events,
          221-222
        finished example, 231
        input coordinates, retrieving, 222-223
        JavaScript functionality, adding, 217
        mouse and touch events, 220-222
        shape constructor with prototype
          methods, creating, 217-218
        shapes, drawing, 223-224
    frames per second, 212-213
    requestAnimationFrame() method
        browser support, 211-212
        implementing, 210-211
        syntax, 212
    timing, 213-214
APIs (Application Programming Interfaces)
    Application Cache, 326-327
        cache files, swapping, 330
        cache sections, 328
        current state, checking, 329

        download, stopping, 330
        enabling, 327
        events, handling, 330
        example, 327-329
        file updates, 328
        manifest files, 327
        specification website, 327
        support, 326
        troubleshooting, 330-331
        updating, 330
    canvas. *See* canvas
    Device Orientation events, 378
    File, 373-375
        file inputs, 374
        loading files, 374
        objects, 374
        specification website, 374
        support, 374
    FileSystem, 323, 375
        file system access, 324
        specification website, 324
        support, 324
        writing to files, 325-326
    Full Screen, 100, 377-378
    Geolocation, 278
        altitude, 284
        coordinate information, 284
        coords object, 284-285
        current location on map, displaying,
          288-293
        direction of travel, 285
        latitude and longitude, 278-280
        methods, 283-284
        position changes, 285-287
        PositionError object, 285
        reference, 287-288
        request failure, 285
        support, 283
        syntax, 283
        timestamp object, 284
        trailblazing app, 293-298
        user location data, gathering, 280-282
        user speed, 285

B

Boilerplate templates, 23

 tag, 25
browsers
  canvas
    hints, 270-271
    support, 104-105
  compatibility
    application cache, 326
    audio formats, 78
    CSS3, 375
    Device Orientation events, 378
    drag and drop, 67
    feature detection, 18-19
    File API, 374
    FileSystem API, 324
    Geolocation API, 283
    IndexedDB, 309
    Media Capture APIs, 376
    Navigation Timing API, 378
    Page Visibility API, 377
    requestAnimationFrame() method, 211-212
    shared workers, 345
    tables, 18-19
    video formats, 73
    Web Audio API, 376
    Web Messaging API, 334
    Web Notifications, 377
    web workers, 339
    WebGL canvas, 272
    WebRTC, 376
    WebSockets, 354
    XHR2, 360
  cookies, 301
  development tools, 16-17
  Google. See Google
  Internet Explorer
    canvas support, 105
    drag and drop compatibility, 67
  media
    control appearance, 88
    fallback options, 81-82
    support, 81-82
  Mosaic, 8
  new features
    CSS3, 375
    Device Orientation events, 378
    File API, 373-375

    FileSystem API, 375
    Full Screen API, 377-378
    Navigation Timing, 378
    page visibility, 377
    Pointer Lock API, 378
    Web Audio API, 376
    web notifications, 377
    WebRTC, 376
  performance profilers, 244-245
  plug-ins
    future, 14
    origins, 10
bufferedAmount attribute, 356

C

caching
  canvas context attributes, 248-250
  images, 251
  text, 252
Cailliau, Robert, 8
cancelAnimationFrame() method, 212
canPlayType() method
  <audio> tag, 79
  <video> tag, 74
canvas
  advantages, 109
  animations, 210
    cancelAnimationFrame() method, 212
    frames per second, 212-213
    requestAnimationFrame() method, 210-212
    timing, 213-214
  applications, 103
  attributes, sizing, 115-116
  browser support, 104
    Internet Explorer, 105
    testing, 105
  <canvas> tag
    content, 112
    syntax, 111
  clearing, 151-152
  clipping region, 189
    nonrectangular areas, clearing, 191-192
    overview, 189
    resetting, 269

How can we make this index more useful? Email us at indexes@samspublishing.com

J

J3D library, 274
JavaScript
  animations, 210
    cancelAnimationFrame() method, 212
    frames per second, 212-213
    requestAnimationFrame() method, 210-212
    timing, 213-214
  application cache, 329
  asm.js project, 379
  benchmarking, 240-244
    Benchmark.js, 240-242
    jsPerf.com, 242-244
  canvas attributes, 115-116
  canvas interactivity app example
    CanvasState constructor, 218-219
    complete code, 225-230
    input coordinates, retrieving, 222-223
    mouse and touch events, 220-222
    Shape constructor, 217-218
    shapes, drawing, 223-224
  canvas transformations, tracking, 152-154
  channel messaging example
    first iFrame, 337
    parent frame, 337-338
    second iFrame, 338
  Chrome console tutorial, 3
  console, 17
  Geolocation API minimum, 283
  HTML5 Media Project, 82
  media API, 90-91
    attributes, 90
    currentTime attribute, 92-93
    custom controls, creating, 95
    events, 90
    methods, 90
    playbackRate attribute, 93
    readyState attribute, 92
    sequential playlists, creating, 94-95
    W3C demonstration page, 91
  MediaElement.js library, 82
  performance optimization
    loops, 245-246
    math, 246-247
    scope, 246

  shared worker script, 348-349
  web worker example, 341-342
  WebSocket connections, creating, 355-356
jQuery-IndexedDB library, 323
jsPerf.com, 242-244

K

kappa, 134
<kegen> tag, 53
key() method, 305
keyPath attribute, 315
Khronos, 271

L

latitude and longitude, 278-280
latitude attribute, 284
libraries
  Benchmark.js, 240-242
  db.js, 323
  feature detection, 19
  HTML5 Media Project, 82, 96
  IndexedDB supported, 323
  jQuery-IndexedDB, 323
  MediaElement.js, 82
  polyfill, 18
  PouchDB, 323
  WebGL, 272-274
    GLGE, 274
    J3D, 274
    PhiloGL, 274
    SceneJS, 274
    Three.js, 272-274
  Webshims, 22-23
line styles (canvas), 125-127
  corners, 126
  ending points, 125-126
  mitering ratio, 127
  width, 125-126
linear gradients, 173-175
  creating, 173
  entire canvas example, 173-174
  small shapes example, 175

How can we make this index more useful? Email us at indexes@samspublishing.com

N

O

S

save() method (canvas)
  performance, 250-251
  state, 140-141, 200
  troubleshooting, 236-237
Scalable Vector Graphics (SVG), 104
scale() method, 143, 202
scaling
  canvas, 143
  images, 252
SceneJS library, 274
scope (canvas performance), 246
<script> tag, 25
search input (forms), 47
<section> tag, 32
security
  canvas images, 171-173
    CORS, 172
    drawImage() method with image from different domain, 171
    information leakage, 171-172
    local file access without restrictions, 172-173
    origin-clean flag, 171
  web messaging, 338
self attribute, 341
self-closing tags syntax, 25
semantic tags, 31-33
  <article>, 32
  <aside>, 33
  <bdi>, 37
  <command>, 35
  <details>, 35-36
  <figcaption>, 36
  <figure>, 36
  <header> and footer>, 32
  <hgroup>, 33
  <mark>, 36-37
  <menu>, 35
  <nav>, 32
  <ruby>/<rt>/<rp>, 37
  <section>, 32
  <summary>, 35-36
  <time>, 37

semantic web, 16
  Berners-Lee vision, 366-367
  microdata, 367
    cookie recipe example, 371-372
    CreativeWork types, 370
    dates, 370
    nesting, 369
    nonvisible, 370
    person description example, 368-369
    reviews, 370
    schema hierarchy, 370
    types supported website, 370
    visualizing, 373
    vocabulary, 367
  search engine results, 366
send() method, 357
sending messages, 334-335
servers
  long-polling, 355
  polling, 354-355
server-side WebSockets, 359
session storage, 303
sessionStorage attribute, 303
setItem() method, 304
setTransform() method, 151, 202, 268
shadowBlur attribute, 182, 200
shadowColor attribute, 182, 200
shadowOffsetX attribute, 182, 200
shadowOffsetY attribute, 182, 200
shadows, 182
  attributes, 182, 200
  clipping region problems, 183
  performance, 253
    blur, 254
    faking, 254
    precomputing, 254
  transformation effects on offsets, 182-183
  zoom scale effects, 184
shared workers, 345
  constructor, 345
  example, 346-349
    JavaScript code, 348-349
    nested iFrame, 347-348
    output, 349
    parent page, 346-347
  names, 345-346
  support, 345

How can we make this index more useful? Email us at indexes@samspublishing.com

syntax
    new features, 25
    stylistic
        case, 27
        quotations, 28
        tag closures, 28-29

T

tags
    <audio>, 79-80
        attributes, 85-90
        canPlayType() method, 79
    backward compatibility, 22
        HTML5 Boilerplate templates, 23
        Webshims library, 22-23
    <blink>, 30
    <body>, 25

, 25
    <canvas>
        content, 112
        fallback content, 112-113
        fillRect() method, 115
        syntax, 111
    case, 25, 27
    closing tags syntax, 25
    closures, 28-29
    <datalist>, 51-52
    document outlines, 33-35
    <embed>, 101
    <form>, 50
    <head>, 25
    <html>, 25
    <iframe>, 29
    <img />, 25
    <keygen>, 53
    <link>, 25
    <meta>, 24
    <output>, 52
    quotations, 25
    <script>, 25
    semantic, 31-33
        <article>, 32
        <aside>, 33
        <bdi>, 37
        <command>, 35
        <details>, 35-36

        document outlines, 33-35
        <figcaption>, 36
        <figure>, 36
        <header> and footer>, 32
        <hgroup>, 33
        <mark>, 36-37
        <menu>, 35
        <nav>, 32
        <ruby>/<rt>/<rp>, 37
        <section>, 32
        <summary>, 35-36
        <time>, 37
    <video>, 75-77
        audio shared attributes, 85-90
        canPlayType() method, 74
        controls attribute, 76
        source element type attribute,
           specifying, 77
        syntax, 75
        video-only attributes, 82-85
    visual, 37-40
        <meter>, 38-39
        <progress>, 39-40
telephone numbers (forms), 47
templates, 23
terminate() method, 341
testing
    audio formats, 78-79
    canvas support, 105
    hit
        approximation, 258
        circular, 258
        pixel-perfect, 259-260
        rectangular, 258
    video formats, 74-75
text, 192
    accessibility problems, 192
    alignment, 197-198
    along paths, drawing, 267
    alphabetic baseline, 194
    attributes, 202-203
    baselines, 197, 269
    bounding box, 269
    caching, 252
    drawing, 194-195
    fonts, 195-196
    future metrics, 269
    Greeking, 253
    kerning problems, 193-194

How can we make this index more useful? Email us at indexes@samspublishing.com

Chrome JavaScript console tutorial, 3
cross-origin resource sharing, 361
CSS3, 375
db.js, 323
Device Orientation events specification, 378
File API specification, 374
FileSystem API specification, 324, 375
Full Screen API specification, 378
GLGE, 274
Google structured data testing tool, 373
HTML4 versus HTML5, 30
HTML5
    Boilerplate templates, 23
    Media Project library, 82, 96
IndexedDB
    resources, 322
    specification, 308
IndexedDBShim, 308
ISO 8601, 370
J3D, 274
jQuery-IndexedDB, 323
linter, 27
Media Capture APIs specifications, 376
MediaElement.js library, 82, 95
microdata
    CreativeWork types, 370
    schema hierarchy, 370
    types supported, 370
microformats, 367
Miro Video Converter, 81
Mozilla validator, 26
Navigation Timing specification, 378
obsolete features, 30
Page Visibility specification, 377
PhiloGL library, 274
Playr, 99
Pointer Lock specifications, 378
polyfill libraries, 18
PouchDB, 323
SceneJS, 274
server-side WebSockets, 359
shared worker compatibility, 345
source code listings downloads, 3
Streams API specification, 376
Three.js repository, 274
Video.js, 95
VLC media player, 81

W3C (World Wide Web Consortium)
    JavaScript media API demonstration, 91
    validator, 26
Web
    Audio API, 101, 376
    Messaging API specification, 334
    Notifications specification, 377
    Storage API, 303
web worker specification, 340
WebGL canvas, 271
    resources, 275
    support, 272
WebRTC, 98, 376
Webshims library, 23
WebSockets, 354
WebSQL specification, 307
WebSockets, 354
    attributes, 356
    connections, creating, 355-356
    errors, 357-358
    events, 356-357
    sample page, 358-359
    sent data, limiting, 357
    server-side, 359
    specification, 354
    support, 354
WebSQL, 307
WebVTT, 98-100
WHATWG (Web Hypertext Application
    Technology Working Group), HTML5, 11
    creating, 11
    specifications, 12
whitespace characters (attributes), 25
width
    canvas text, 194-195
    line styles, 125-126
width attribute
    canvas, 115-116
    <video> tag, 83
Wi-Fi geolocation, 282, 291
winding number rule. See nonzero winding
    number rule
withCredentials attribute, 362
Worker() method, 340
World Wide Web Consortium. See W3C
WorldWideWeb project, 8

X–Z

Essential Resources for
HTML5 Programmers and Developers
informit.com/html5

UNLEASHED

Unleashed takes you beyond the basics, providing an exhaustive, technically sophisticated reference for professionals who need to exploit a technology to its fullest potential. It's the best resource for practical advice from the experts, and the most in-depth coverage of the latest technologies.

informit.com/unleashed

Android Programming Unleashed
ISBN-13: 9780672336287

Windows Phone 8 Unleashed
ISBN-13: 9780672336898

informit.com/sams

Windows 8 Apps with HTML5 and JavaScript Unleashed
ISBN-13: 9780672336058

Your purchase of *HTML5 Unleashed* includes access to a free online edition for 45 days through the **Safari Books Online** subscription service. Nearly every Sams book is available online through **Safari Books Online**, along with thousands of books and videos from publishers such as Addison-Wesley Professional, Cisco Press, Exam Cram, IBM Press, O'Reilly Media, Prentice Hall, Que, and VMware Press.

Safari Books Online is a digital library providing searchable, on-demand access to thousands of technology, digital media, and professional development books and videos from leading publishers. With one monthly or yearly subscription price, you get unlimited access to learning tools and information on topics including mobile app and software development, tips and tricks on using your favorite gadgets, networking, project management, graphic design, and much more.

Activate your FREE Online Edition at
informit.com/safarifree

STEP 1: Enter the coupon code: ENVLPEH.

STEP 2: New Safari users, complete the brief registration form. Safari subscribers, just log in.

If you have difficulty registering on Safari or accessing the online edition, please e-mail customer-service@safaribooksonline.com